W9-AJS-143
Houghton Mifflin Harcourt
Texas
GO Math!
Volume 1
COLORADO
Trinidad
Raton
Las Vegas
Clovis
Roswell
Hobbs
Carlsbad
Midland
Odessa
Abilene
San Angelo
TEXAS
DAVIS MTS.
STOCKTON PLATEAU
EDWARDS PLATEAU
Emory Pk. 7835 ft.
Austin
San Antonio
Houston
Waco
Irving
Fort Worth
Dallas
Emporia
Wichita
Tulsa
McAlester
Ardmore
Joplin
MATAGORDA
Corpus Christi
Nuevo Laredo
Laredo
PADRE ISLAND
EXICO

Printed in the U.S.A.

ISBN 978-0-544-06155-2

8 9 10 11 12 0877 22 21 20 19 18 17 16

4500587543 B C D E F G

Cover Image Credits: (boots) ©pidjoe/Getty Images; (cow) ©Dmitry Bruskov/Shutterstock; (cactus) ©Radius Images/Getty Images; (boat) ©Richard Cummins/Getty Images.

Dear Students and Families,

Welcome to **Texas Go Math!**, Grade 2! In this exciting mathematics program, there are hands-on activities to do and real-world problems to solve. Best of all, you will write your ideas and answers right in your book. In **Texas Go Math!**, writing and drawing on the pages helps you think deeply about what you are learning, and you will really understand math!

By the way, all of the pages in your **Texas Go Math!** book are made using recycled paper. We wanted you to know that you can Go Green with **Texas Go Math!**

Sincerely,

The Authors

Made in the United States
Printed on 100% recycled paper

Authors

Juli K. Dixon, Ph.D.
Professor, Mathematics Education
University of Central Florida
Orlando, Florida

Edward B. Burger, Ph.D.
President
Southwestern University
Georgetown, Texas

Matthew R. Larson, Ph.D.
K-12 Curriculum Specialist for Mathematics
Lincoln Public Schools
Lincoln, Nebraska

Martha E. Sandoval-Martinez
Math Instructor
El Camino College
Torrance, California

Consultant

Valerie Johse
Math Consultant
Texas Council for Economic Education
Houston, Texas

Volume 1

Unit 1 • Number and Operations: Place Value, Fraction Concepts, and Addition

Module 1 Place Value

Module 2 Size of Numbers

Look for these:

H.O.T. Problems
Higher Order Thinking
Multi-Step Problems

Homework and TEKS Practice in every lesson.

DIGITAL RESOURCES
Go online for the Interactive Student Edition with Math on the Spot Videos. Use *i*Tools, the Multimedia *e*Glossary, and more.

Look for these:

H.O.T. Problems
Higher Order Thinking
Multi-Step Problems

GO DIGITAL Resources

DIGITAL RESOURCES
Go online for the Interactive Student Edition with Math on the Spot Videos. Use *i*Tools, the Multimedia *e*Glossary, and more.

Module 7 More 2-Digit Addition

Volume 1

Unit 2 • Number and Operations: Computation, Money, and Equal Groups

Module 8 2-Digit Subtraction

Module 9 More 2-Digit Subtraction

Look for these:

H.O.T. Problems
Higher Order Thinking
Multi-Step Problems

Homework and Practice

Homework and TEKS Practice in every lesson.

Module 10 3-Digit Addition and Subtraction

Module 11 Money

Module 12 Multiplication and Division Concepts

Look for these:

H.O.T. Problems
Higher Order Thinking
Multi-Step Problems

DIGITAL RESOURCES
Go online for the Interactive Student Edition with Math on the Spot Videos. Use *i*Tools, the Multimedia *e*Glossary, and more.

Volume 2

Unit 3 • Algebraic Reasoning

Module 13 Patterns and Strategies

Volume 2

Unit 4 • Geometry and Measurement

Module 14 Plane Figures

Look for these:

H.O.T. Problems
Higher Order Thinking
Multi-Step Problems

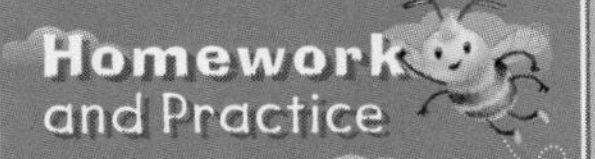

Homework and TEKS Practice in every lesson.

Module 15 Solid Figures

Module 16 Length

Module 17 More Measurement

Module 18 Time

Look for these:

H.O.T. Problems
Higher Order Thinking
Multi-Step Problems

DIGITAL RESOURCES
Go online for the Interactive Student Edition with Math on the Spot Videos. Use *i*Tools, the Multimedia *e*Glossary, and more.

Volume 2

Unit 5 • Data Analysis

Module 19 Data

Look for these:

H.O.T. Problems
Higher Order Thinking
Multi-Step Problems

Homework and TEKS Practice in every lesson.

Volume 2

Unit 6 • Personal Financial Literacy

Module 20 Concepts in Finance

Look for these:

H.O.T. Problems
Higher Order Thinking
Multi-Step Problems

GO DIGITAL Resources

DIGITAL RESOURCES
Go online for the Interactive Student Edition with Math on the Spot Videos. Use *i*Tools, the Multimedia *e*Glossary, and more.

Unit 1 Number and Operations: Place Value, Fraction Concepts, and Addition

Show What You Know

Check your understanding of important skills.

Name ______________________

Identify Numbers to 30

Write the number that tells how many.

1. 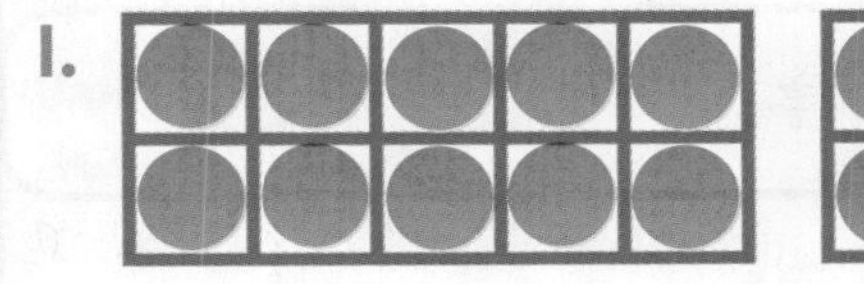

______

Count by Ones to 100

Use the hundred chart.

2. Count from 36 to 47. Which of the numbers below will you say? Circle them.

42 31 48 39 37

1	2	3	4	5	6	7	8	9	10
11	12	13	14	15	16	17	18	19	20
21	22	23	24	25	26	27	28	29	30
31	32	33	34	35	36	37	38	39	40
41	42	43	44	45	46	47	48	49	50
51	52	53	54	55	56	57	58	59	60
61	62	63	64	65	66	67	68	69	70
71	72	73	74	75	76	77	78	79	80
81	82	83	84	85	86	87	88	89	90
91	92	93	94	95	96	97	98	99	100

Explore Tens

Write how many tens. Write the number.

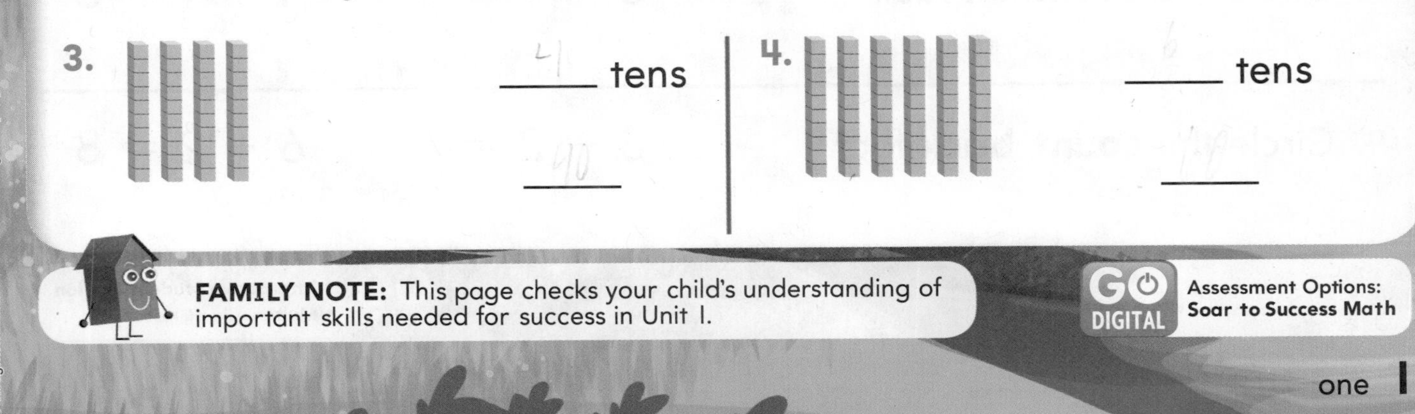

3. ______ tens

______

4. ______ tens

______

FAMILY NOTE: This page checks your child's understanding of important skills needed for success in Unit 1.

GO DIGITAL Assessment Options: Soar to Success Math

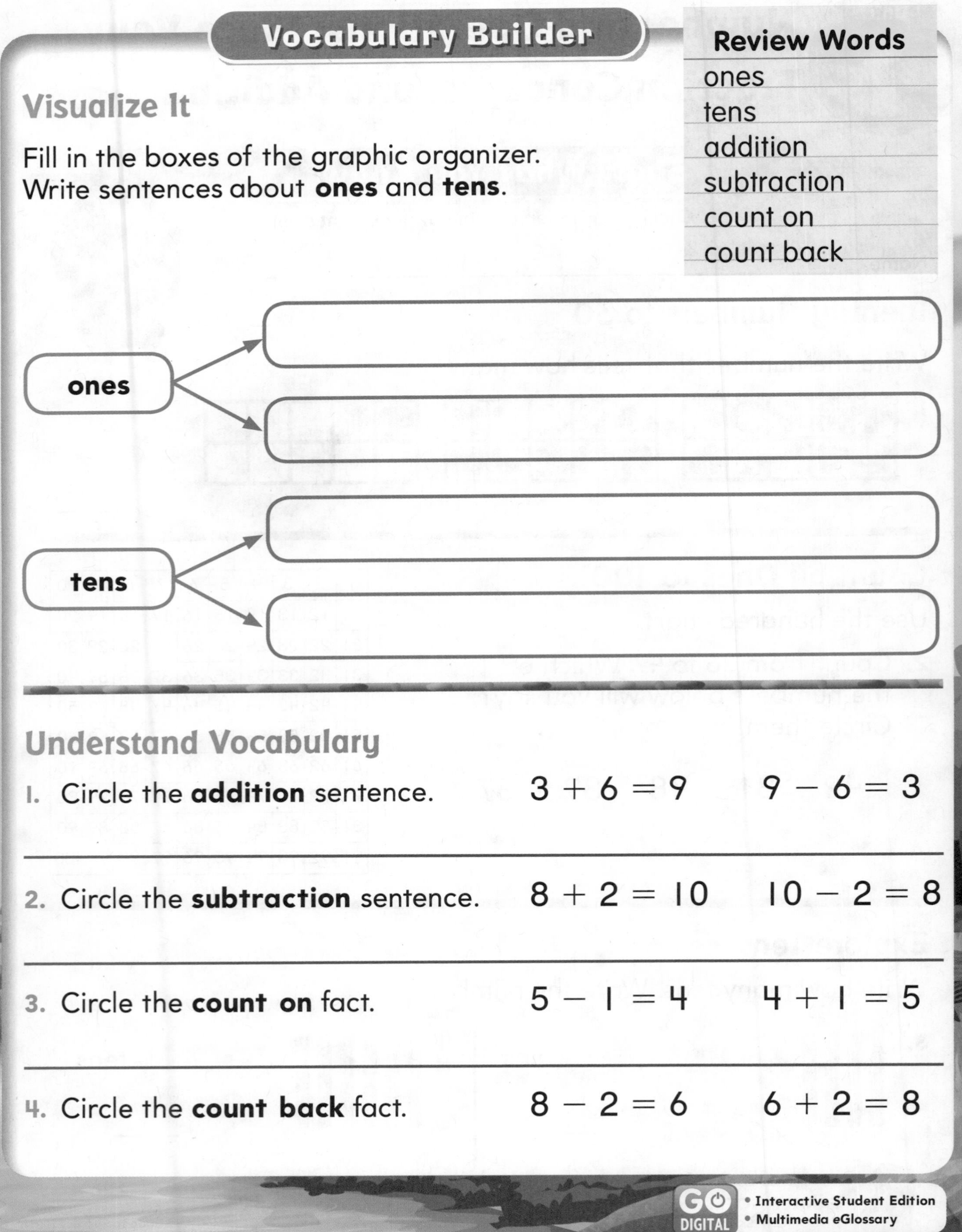

Vocabulary Builder

Visualize It

Fill in the boxes of the graphic organizer.
Write sentences about **ones** and **tens**.

Review Words
ones
tens
addition
subtraction
count on
count back

Understand Vocabulary

1. Circle the **addition** sentence. $3 + 6 = 9$ $9 - 6 = 3$

2. Circle the **subtraction** sentence. $8 + 2 = 10$ $10 - 2 = 8$

3. Circle the **count on** fact. $5 - 1 = 4$ $4 + 1 = 5$

4. Circle the **count back** fact. $8 - 2 = 6$ $6 + 2 = 8$

GO DIGITAL
- Interactive Student Edition
- Multimedia eGlossary

Vocabulary Reader

"Finding Ten"

written by Mike Mason

This Take-Home Book belongs to

____

Reading and Writing Math

This take-home book will help you review tens and ones.

MATHEMATICAL PROCESSES 2.1.A, 2.1.E

Keri will make things for a craft fair.
Keri has a list of things she needs to get for her crafts.
Can you read her list?

Keri needs 12 stickers for her project.
The stickers are sold in sets of ten or one at a time.
Circle the stickers you think Keri will buy.

Keri needs 24 buttons. The buttons are sold in sets of ten or as single buttons. Circle the buttons you think Keri will buy.

Next, Keri needs 33 beads. Beads are sold in sets of ten, or as single beads. Circle the beads you think Keri will buy.

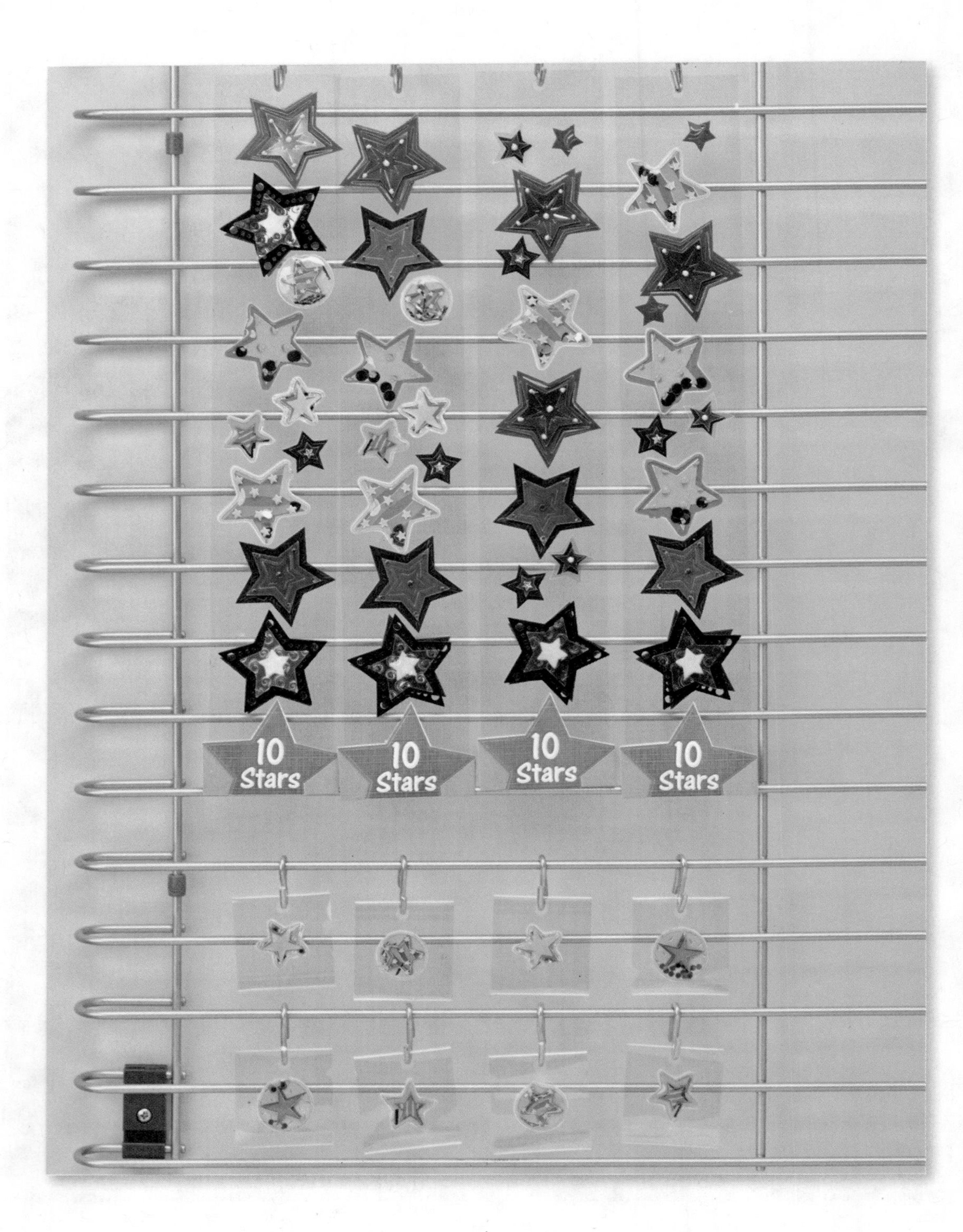

Keri needs 16 stars. Stars are sold in sets of ten, or as single stars.
Circle the stars you think Keri will buy.

Keri needs 18 clothespins.
Which clothespins will she buy?
Circle them.

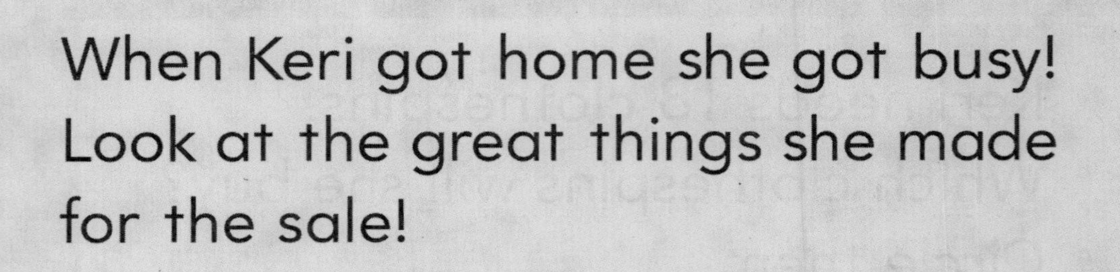

When Keri got home she got busy!
Look at the great things she made
for the sale!

Name ______________________________

Write about the Math

Write Math Look at the picture. Draw and write your own story about buying buttons. Use tens and ones in your story.

Vocabulary Review
- tens
- ones

10 Buttons 10 Buttons 10 Buttons

____

____

____

____

____

____

Place Value of 2-Digit Numbers

Use the picture to answer the questions.

1. How many sets of 10 beads are there?

   ________ sets of 10 beads

2. How many single beads are there?

   ________ beads

3. How many beads are there in all?

   ________ beads

4. How many beads would you get if you buy 2 sets of 10 beads and 3 single beads?

   ________ beads

5. How many beads would you get if you buy 4 sets of 10 beads and 5 single beads?

   ________ beads

Write a riddle about a 2-digit number.
Have a classmate solve your riddle.

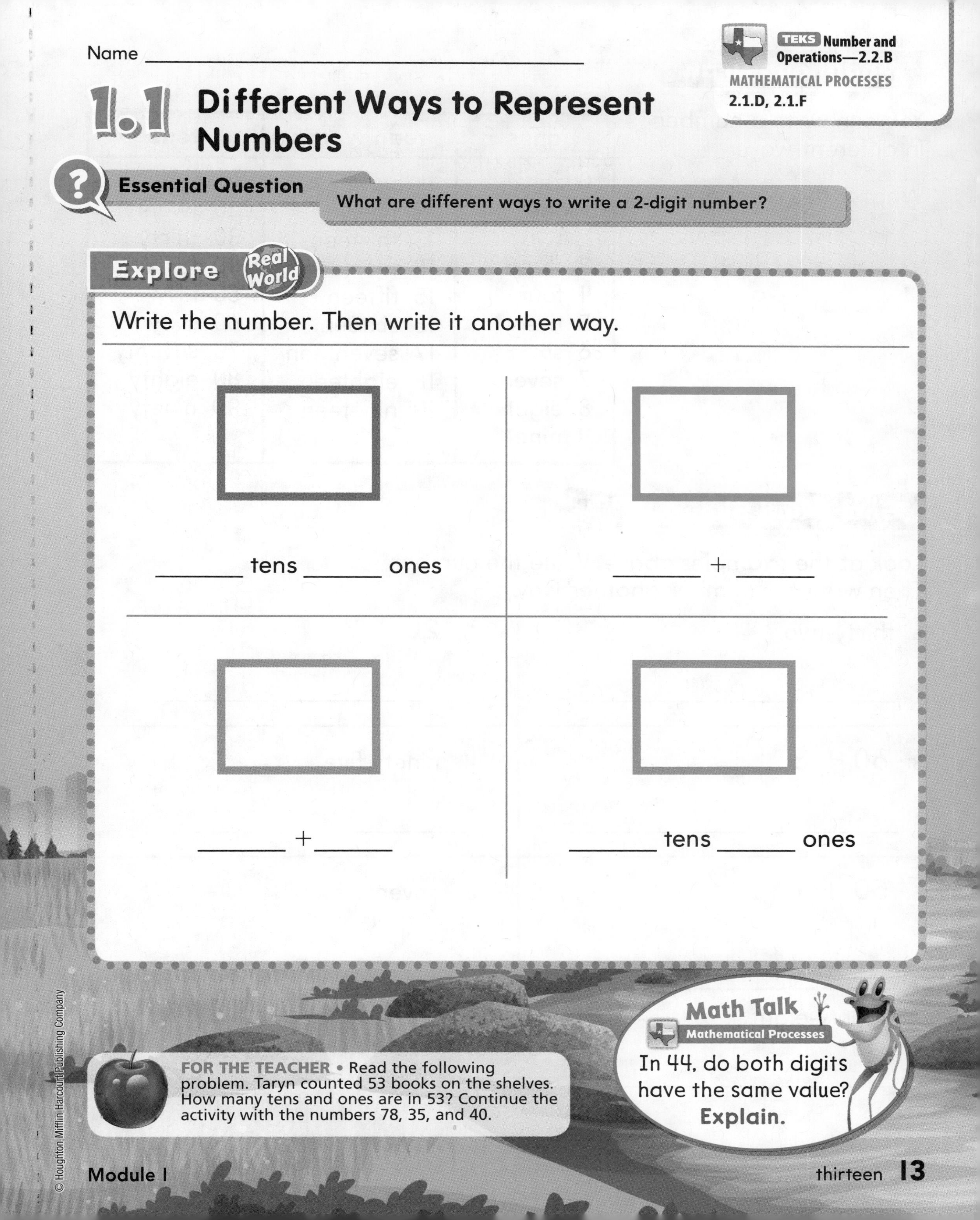

Name ______________________

TEKS Number and Operations—2.2.B
MATHEMATICAL PROCESSES 2.1.D, 2.1.F

1.1 Different Ways to Represent Numbers

Essential Question What are different ways to write a 2-digit number?

Explore Real World

Write the number. Then write it another way.

[ ]

______ tens ______ ones

[ ]

______ + ______

[ ]

______ + ______

[ ]

______ tens ______ ones

FOR THE TEACHER • Read the following problem. Taryn counted 53 books on the shelves. How many tens and ones are in 53? Continue the activity with the numbers 78, 35, and 40.

Math Talk Mathematical Processes

In 44, do both digits have the same value? **Explain.**

Model and Draw

You can write a number in different ways.

What is this number?

fifty-nine

50 + 9

______

ones	teen words	tens
0 zero	11 eleven	10 ten
1 one	12 twelve	20 twenty
2 two	13 thirteen	30 thirty
3 three	14 fourteen	40 forty
4 four	15 fifteen	50 fifty
5 five	16 sixteen	60 sixty
6 six	17 seventeen	70 seventy
7 seven	18 eighteen	80 eighty
8 eight	19 nineteen	90 ninety
9 nine		

Share and Show

Look at the examples above. Write the number.
Then write the number another way.

1. thirty-two

______

2. 20 + 7

______

3. 60 + 3

______

4. ninety-five

______

5. 50 + 1

______

6. seventy-six

______

7. twenty-eight

______

8. 80 + 0

______

Name ___________________

Problem Solving

Write the number another way.

9. 20 + 4

____

10. 37

____

11. eighty-five

____

12. 54

____

13. twelve

____

14. 90 + 9

____

15. 62

____

16. forty-one

____

Circle the answer for each riddle.

17. **H.O.T.** A number has the digit 4 in the ones place and the digit 7 in the tens place. Which of these is another way to write this number?

40 + 7

70 + 4

4 + 7

18. **H.O.T.** **Multi-Step** A number has a digit less than 6 in the tens place and a digit greater than 6 in the ones place. Which of these could be the number?

eighty-four

sixty-six

fifty-seven

Daily Assessment Task

Choose the correct answer.

19. **Connect** Marty's team shirt has the number 19 on it. Which is another way to write 19?

○ 1 + 9

○ ninety

○ 10 + 9

20. **Representations** There are fifty-seven balloons at the party. Which is another way to write fifty-seven?

○ seventy-five

○ 50 + 7

○ 75

21. Craig lives at 62 Kent Avenue. Which is another way to write 62?

○ 20 + 6

○ sixty-two

○ 6 + 2

22. **TEXAS Test Prep** Which is another way to write 42?

○ 40 + 2

○ twenty-four

○ 4 + 2

TAKE HOME ACTIVITY • Write 20 + 6 on a sheet of paper. Have your child write the 2-digit number. Repeat for 4 tens 9 ones.

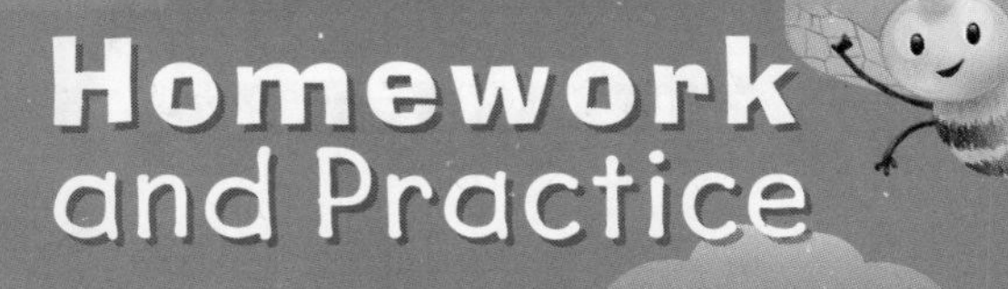

TEKS Number and Operations—2.2.B
MATHEMATICAL PROCESSES 2.1.D, 2.1.F

Name ______________________

1.1 Different Ways to Represent Numbers

Write the number another way.

1. 38 ______________

2. eighty-nine ______________

3. $30 + 7$ ______________

4. 26 ______________

5. fifteen ______________

6. $60 + 2$ ______________

Problem Solving

Circle the answer for each riddle.

7. Lee has a favorite number. The number has the digit 3 in the ones place and the digit 9 in the tens place. Which of these is another way to write this number?

○ $30 + 9$ ○ $90 + 3$ ○ $3 + 9$

8. **Multi-Step** Rita's locker code is a number that has a digit less than 3 in the tens place. It also has a digit greater than 7 in the ones place. Which of these could be the number?

○ thirty-seven ○ eighty-two ○ twenty-eight

Lesson Check

TEXAS Test Prep

Choose the correct answer.

9. Beth lives at 79 Main Street. Which is another way to write 79?

○ 90 + 7

○ seventy-nine

○ 7 + 9

10. There are 48 muffins in a large basket. Which is another way to write 48?

○ eighty-four

○ 40 + 8

○ 84

11. Sue has eighty-seven buttons. Which is another way to write eighty-seven?

○ 80 + 7

○ seventy-eight

○ 8 + 7

12. **Multi-Step** Dan's number has a digit greater than 5 in the ones place and a digit less than 5 in the tens place. Which could be the number on Dan's shirt?

○ 5 + 5 ○ forty-six ○ 70 + 3

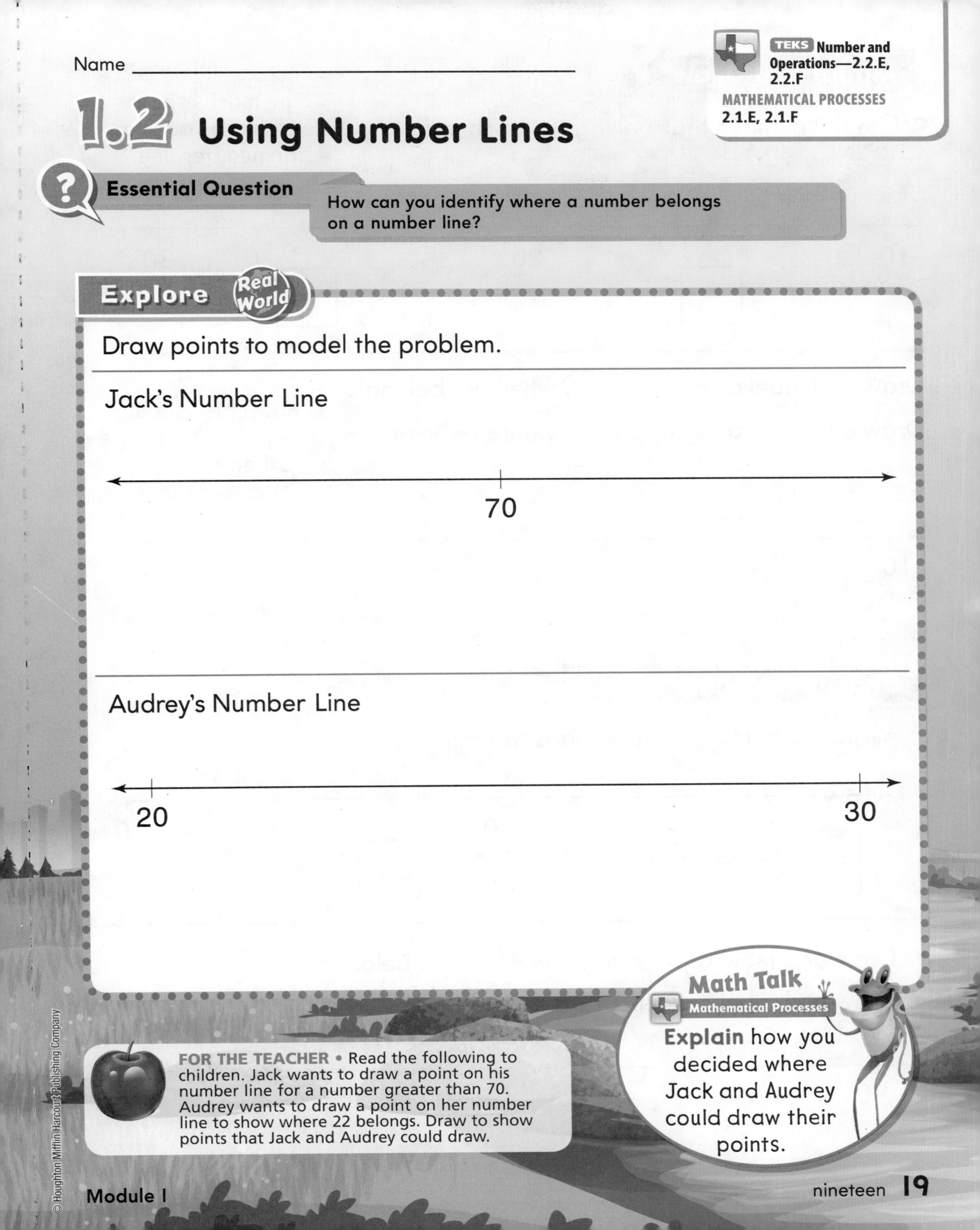

Name ______________________________

TEKS Number and Operations—2.2.E, 2.2.F
MATHEMATICAL PROCESSES 2.1.E, 2.1.F

1.2 Using Number Lines

Essential Question How can you identify where a number belongs on a number line?

Explore Real World

Draw points to model the problem.

Jack's Number Line

Audrey's Number Line

Math Talk Mathematical Processes
Explain how you decided where Jack and Audrey could draw their points.

FOR THE TEACHER • Read the following to children. Jack wants to draw a point on his number line for a number greater than 70. Audrey wants to draw a point on her number line to show where 22 belongs. Draw to show points that Jack and Audrey could draw.

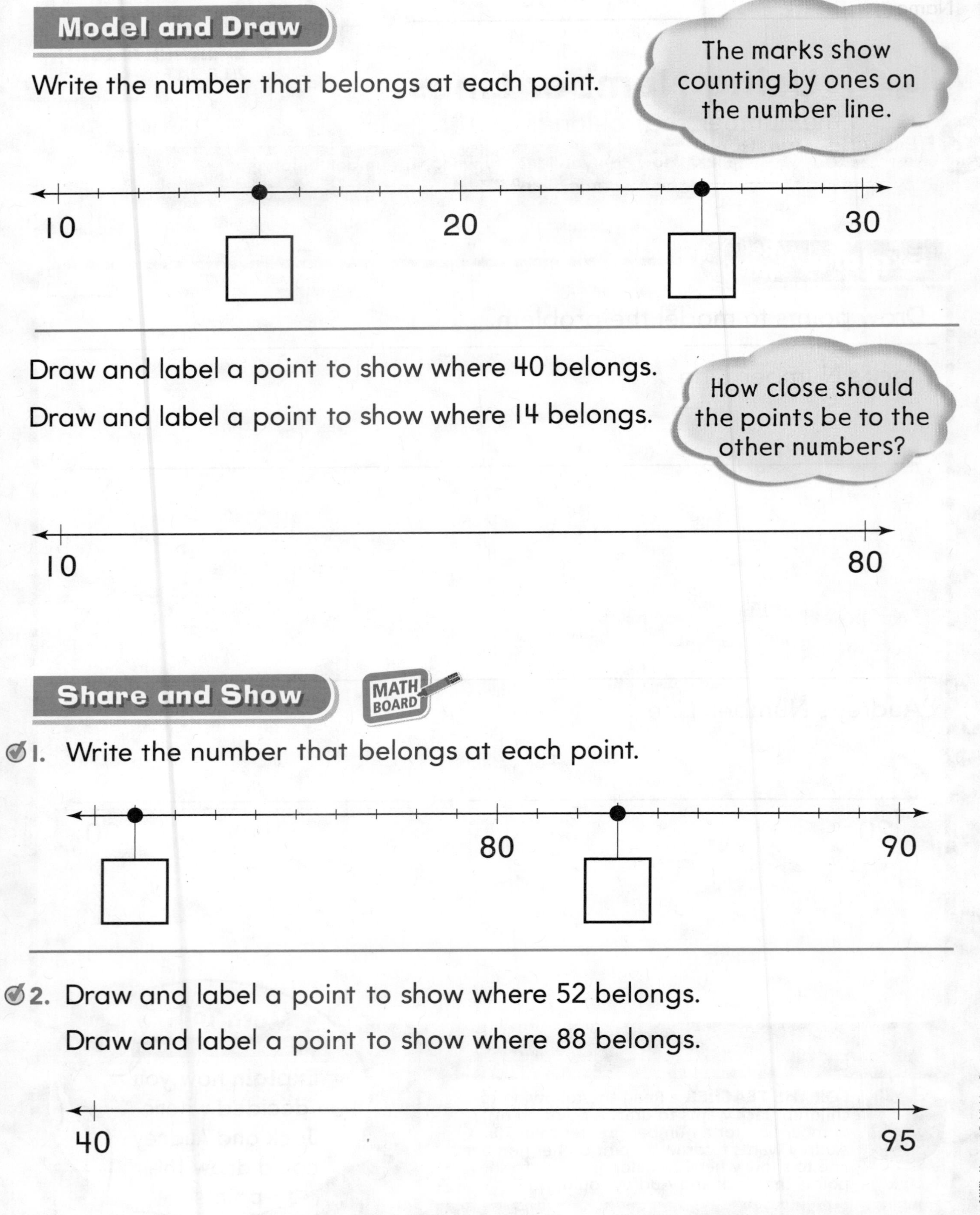

Model and Draw

Write the number that belongs at each point.

Draw and label a point to show where 40 belongs.

Draw and label a point to show where 14 belongs.

Share and Show

1. Write the number that belongs at each point.

2. Draw and label a point to show where 52 belongs.

   Draw and label a point to show where 88 belongs.

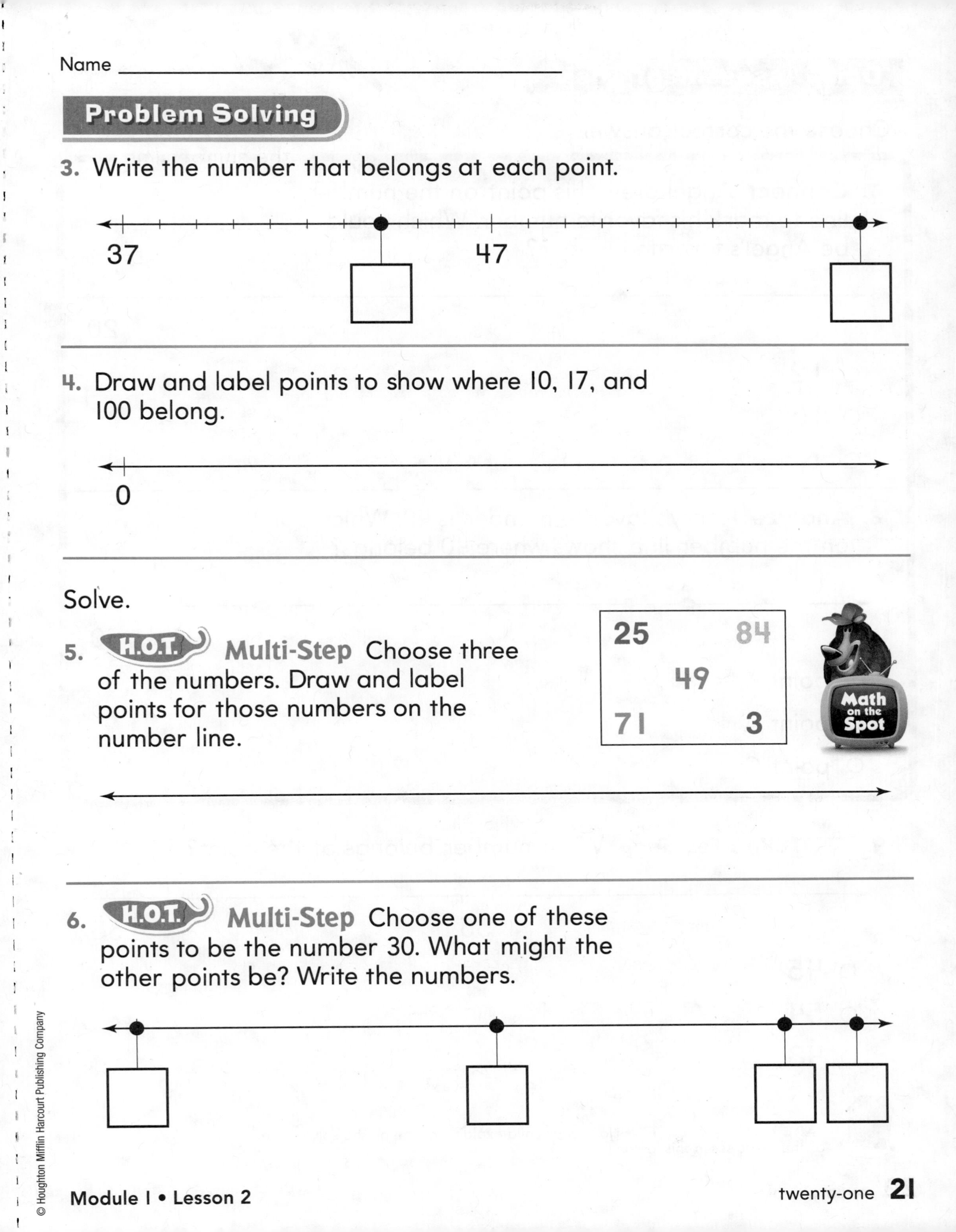

Name ____________________

Problem Solving

3. Write the number that belongs at each point.

4. Draw and label points to show where 10, 17, and 100 belong.

Solve.

5. H.O.T. **Multi-Step** Choose three of the numbers. Draw and label points for those numbers on the number line.

6. H.O.T. **Multi-Step** Choose one of these points to be the number 30. What might the other points be? Write the numbers.

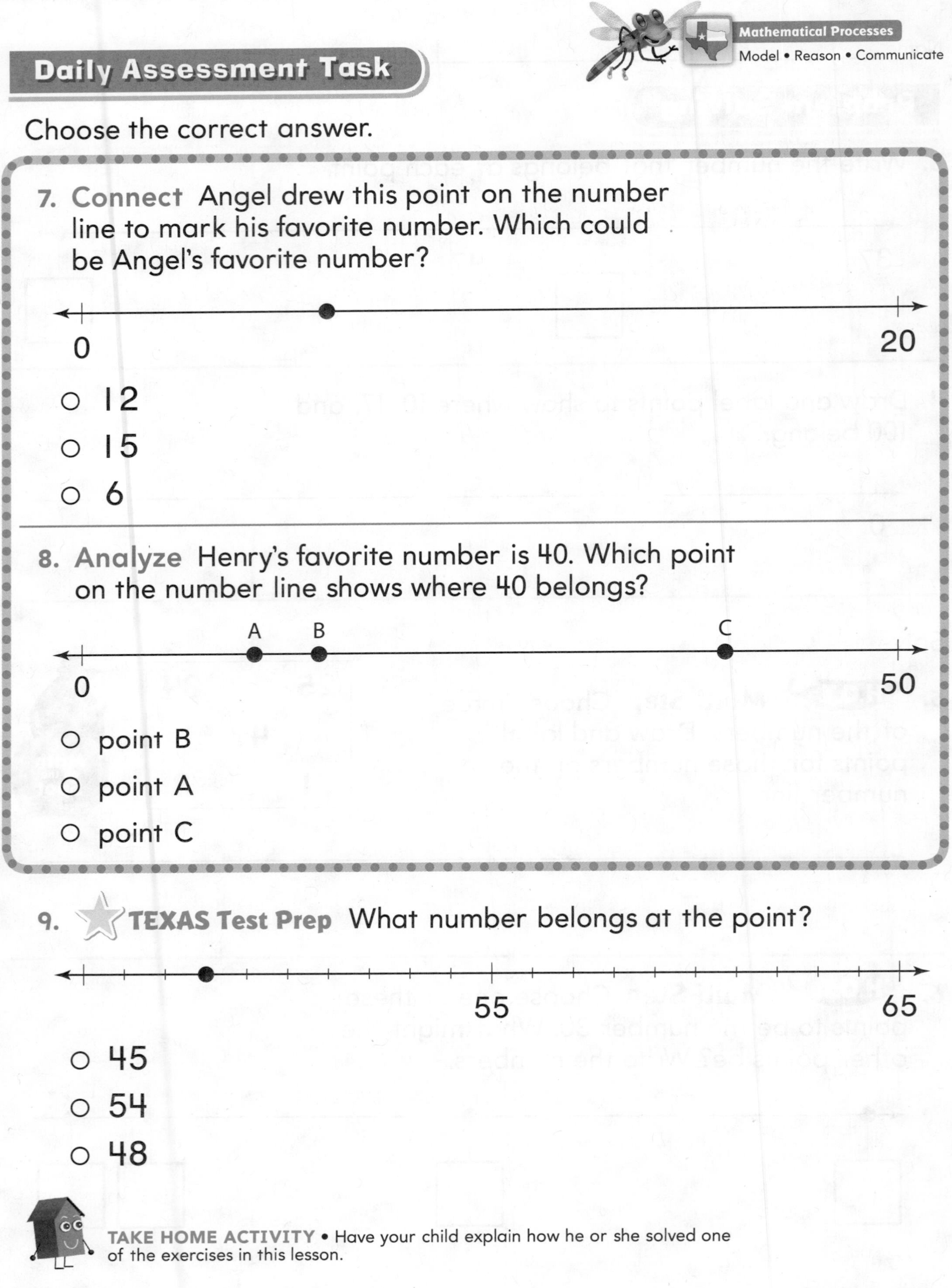

Daily Assessment Task

Choose the correct answer.

7. **Connect** Angel drew this point on the number line to mark his favorite number. Which could be Angel's favorite number?

- ○ 12
- ○ 15
- ○ 6

8. **Analyze** Henry's favorite number is 40. Which point on the number line shows where 40 belongs?

- ○ point B
- ○ point A
- ○ point C

9. **TEXAS Test Prep** What number belongs at the point?

- ○ 45
- ○ 54
- ○ 48

TAKE HOME ACTIVITY • Have your child explain how he or she solved one of the exercises in this lesson.

TEKS Number and Operations—2.2.E, 2.2.F
MATHEMATICAL PROCESSES 2.1.E, 2.1.F

Name ____________________

1.2 Using Number Lines

1. Write the number that belongs at each point.

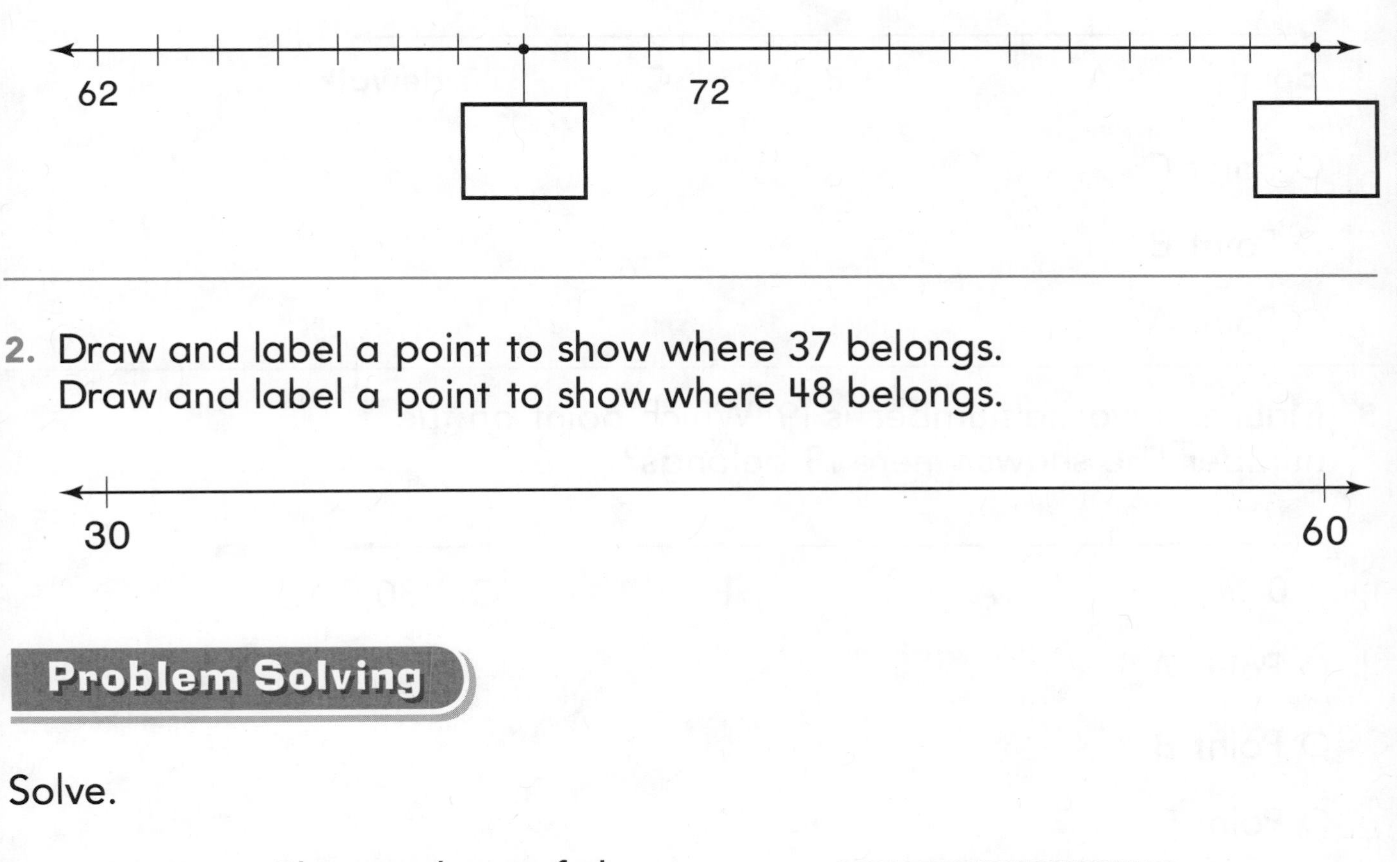

2. Draw and label a point to show where 37 belongs.
Draw and label a point to show where 48 belongs.

Problem Solving

Solve.

3. **Multi-Step** Choose three of the numbers. Draw and label points for those numbers on the number line.

15 39 59 61 7

Lesson Check

TEXAS Test Prep

Choose the correct answer.

4. It is 10 steps from the front door of Jake's house to the sidewalk. Jake walks 7 steps from the door to his bike. Which point could show where Jake's bike is?

door A B C sidewalk

○ Point C

○ Point B

○ Point A

5. Maura's favorite number is 19. Which point on the number line shows where 19 belongs?

0 A B C 30

○ Point A

○ Point B

○ Point C

6. Look at the points for the numbers 0, 20, and 100. What number might the missing point be?

0 20 □ 100

○ 60

○ 80

○ 90

Name ____________________

TEKS Number and Operations—2.2.A
MATHEMATICAL PROCESSES 2.1.F

1.3 Explore 3-Digit Numbers

Essential Question How do you write a 3-digit number for a group of tens?

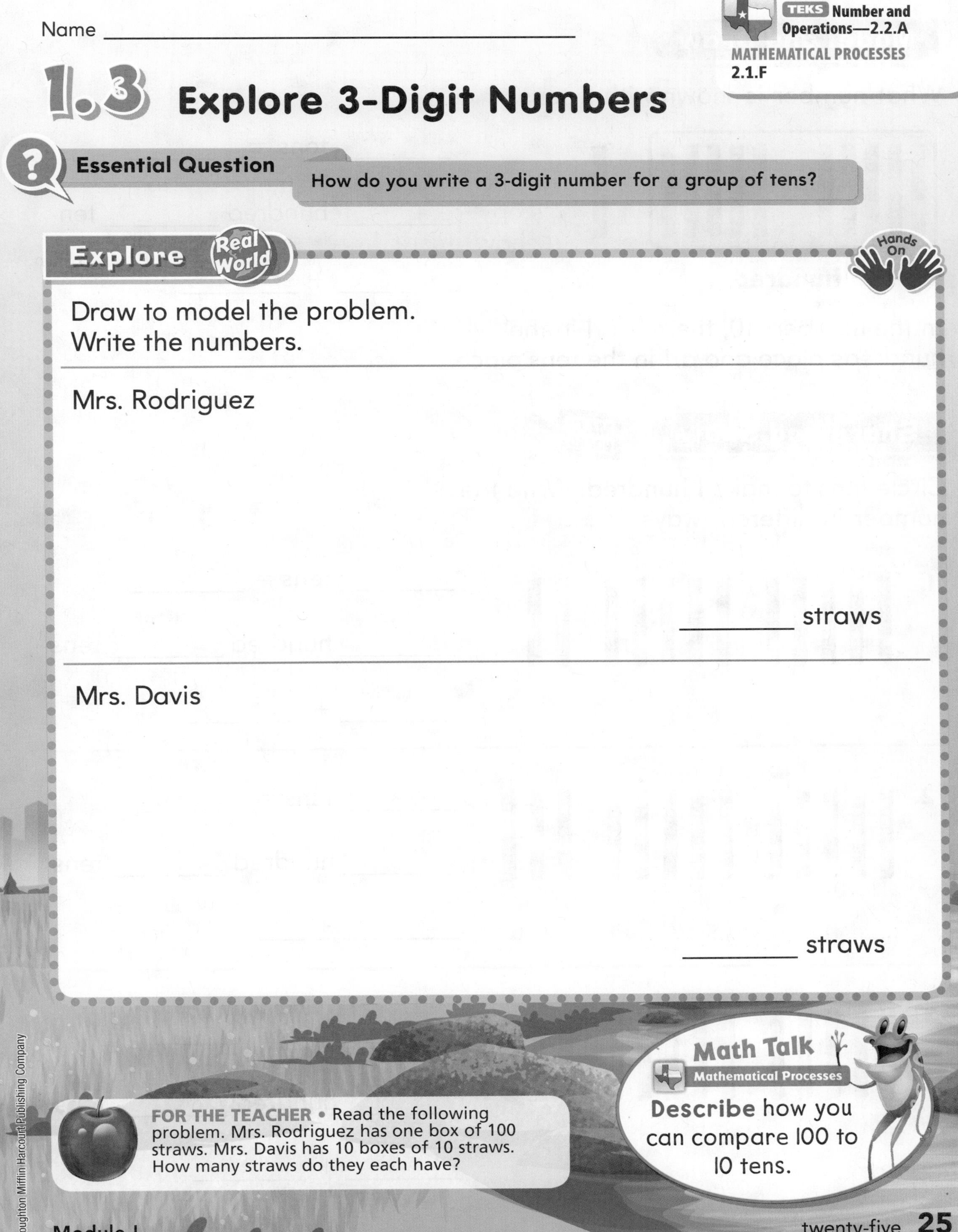

Explore Real World

Hands On

Draw to model the problem.
Write the numbers.

Mrs. Rodriguez

________ straws

Mrs. Davis

________ straws

FOR THE TEACHER • Read the following problem. Mrs. Rodriguez has one box of 100 straws. Mrs. Davis has 10 boxes of 10 straws. How many straws do they each have?

Math Talk Mathematical Processes

Describe how you can compare 100 to 10 tens.

Model and Draw

What number is shown with 11 tens?

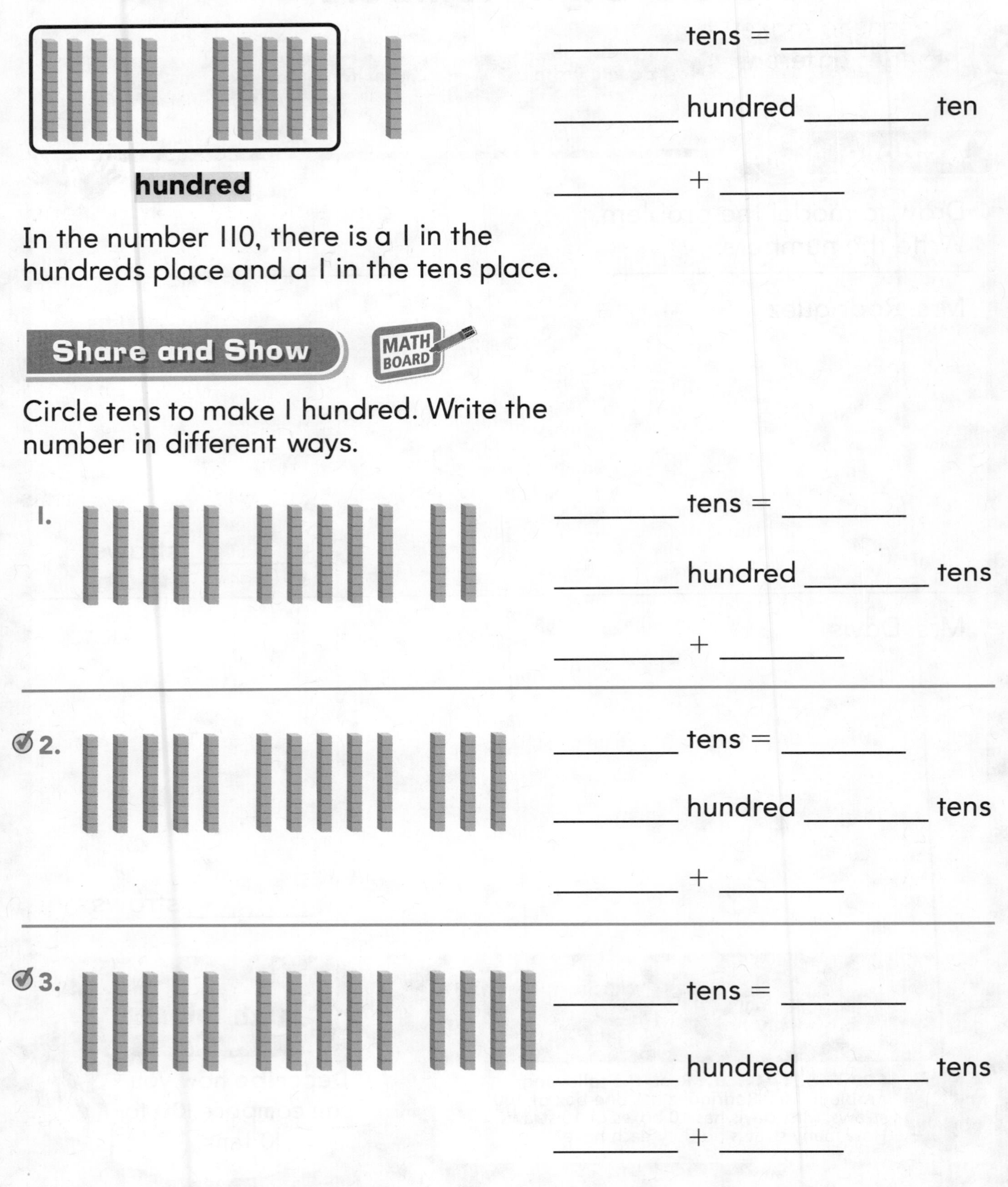

_____ tens = _____

_____ hundred _____ ten

_____ + _____

In the number 110, there is a 1 in the hundreds place and a 1 in the tens place.

Share and Show

MATH BOARD

Circle tens to make 1 hundred. Write the number in different ways.

1\.

_____ tens = _____

_____ hundred _____ tens

_____ + _____

2\.

_____ tens = _____

_____ hundred _____ tens

_____ + _____

3\.

_____ tens = _____

_____ hundred _____ tens

_____ + _____

Name ______________________________

Problem Solving

Circle tens to make 1 hundred. Write the number in different ways.

4. ________ tens = ________

________ hundred ________ tens

________ + ________

5. ________ tens = ________

________ hundreds ________ tens

________ + ________

Solve. Write or draw to explain.

6. H.O.T. Kendra has 120 stickers. 10 stickers fill a page. How many pages can she fill?

Math on the Spot

________ pages

7. H.O.T. **Multi-Step** Ed has 150 marbles. How many bags of 10 marbles does he need to get so that he will have 200 marbles in all?

________ bags of 10 marbles

Mathematical Processes
Model • Reason • Communicate

Daily Assessment Task

Choose the correct answer.

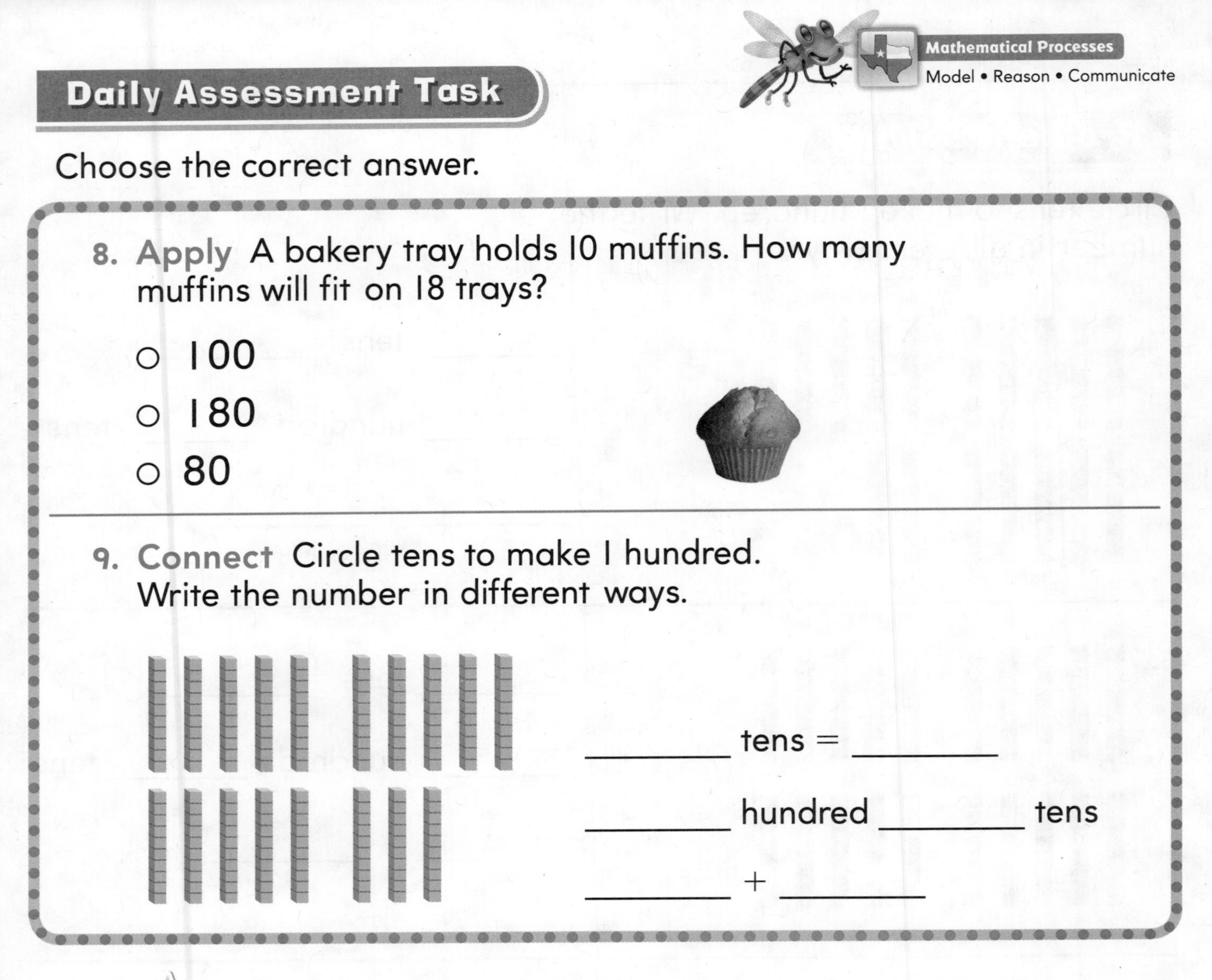

8. **Apply** A bakery tray holds 10 muffins. How many muffins will fit on 18 trays?

○ 100
○ 180
○ 80

9. **Connect** Circle tens to make 1 hundred. Write the number in different ways.

_____ tens = _____

_____ hundred _____ tens

_____ + _____

10. **TEXAS Test Prep** Which has the same value as 17 tens?

○ 17 hundreds
○ 1 ten 7 ones
○ 1 hundred 7 tens

TAKE HOME ACTIVITY • Have your child draw 110 Xs by drawing 11 groups of 10 Xs.

TEKS Number and Operations—2.2.A
MATHEMATICAL PROCESSES 2.1.F

Name ______________________

1.3 Explore 3-Digit Numbers

Circle tens to make 1 hundred. Write the number in different ways.

1. ____ tens = ____

____ hundred ____ tens

____ + ____

2. ____ tens = ____

____ hundred ____ tens

____ + ____

Problem Solving

Solve. Write or draw to explain.

3. Kate has 110 bows. 10 bows fit in a bag. How many bags can she fill?

____ bags

4. **Multi-Step** Dan has 140 markers. How many more boxes of 10 markers does he need to get so that he will have 180 markers in all?

____ boxes of markers

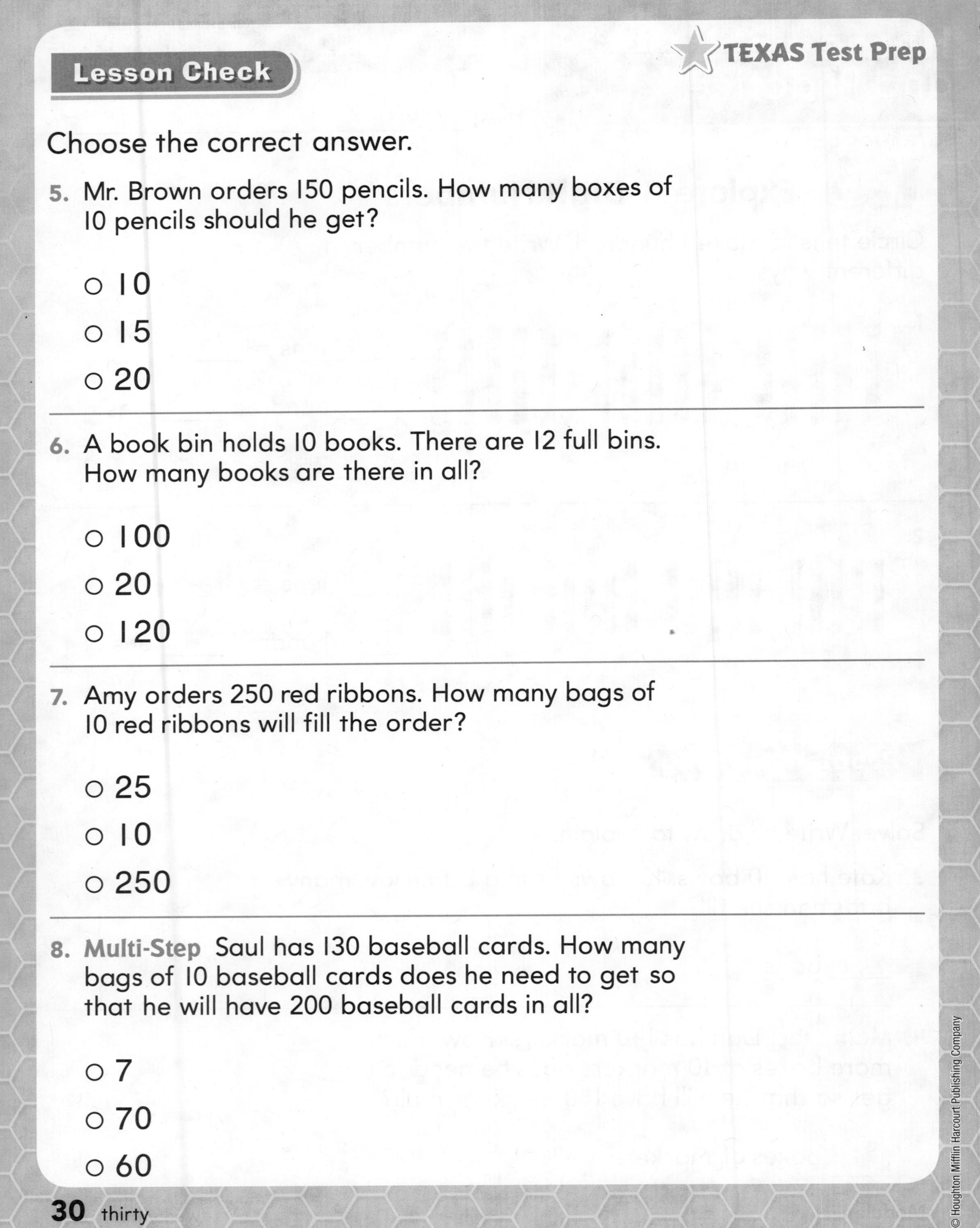

Lesson Check

TEXAS Test Prep

Choose the correct answer.

5. Mr. Brown orders 150 pencils. How many boxes of 10 pencils should he get?

   ○ 10
   ○ 15
   ○ 20

6. A book bin holds 10 books. There are 12 full bins. How many books are there in all?

   ○ 100
   ○ 20
   ○ 120

7. Amy orders 250 red ribbons. How many bags of 10 red ribbons will fill the order?

   ○ 25
   ○ 10
   ○ 250

8. **Multi-Step** Saul has 130 baseball cards. How many bags of 10 baseball cards does he need to get so that he will have 200 baseball cards in all?

   ○ 7
   ○ 70
   ○ 60

Name ______________________________

TEKS Number and Operations—2.2.A
MATHEMATICAL PROCESSES 2.1.C, 2.1.D, 2.1.G

1.4 HANDS ON

Model 3-Digit Numbers

Essential Question How do you show a 3-digit number using blocks?

Explore Real World

Hands On

Use [tens block]. Draw to show what you did.

FOR THE TEACHER • Read the following problem. Jack has 12 tens blocks. How many hundreds and tens does Jack have? Have children show Jack's blocks and then draw quick pictures. Then have children circle 10 tens and solve the problem.

Math Talk
Mathematical Processes
If Jack had 14 tens, how many hundreds and tens would he have? **Explain.**

Model and Draw

In the number 348, the 3 is in the hundreds place, the 4 is in the tens place, and the 8 is in the ones place.

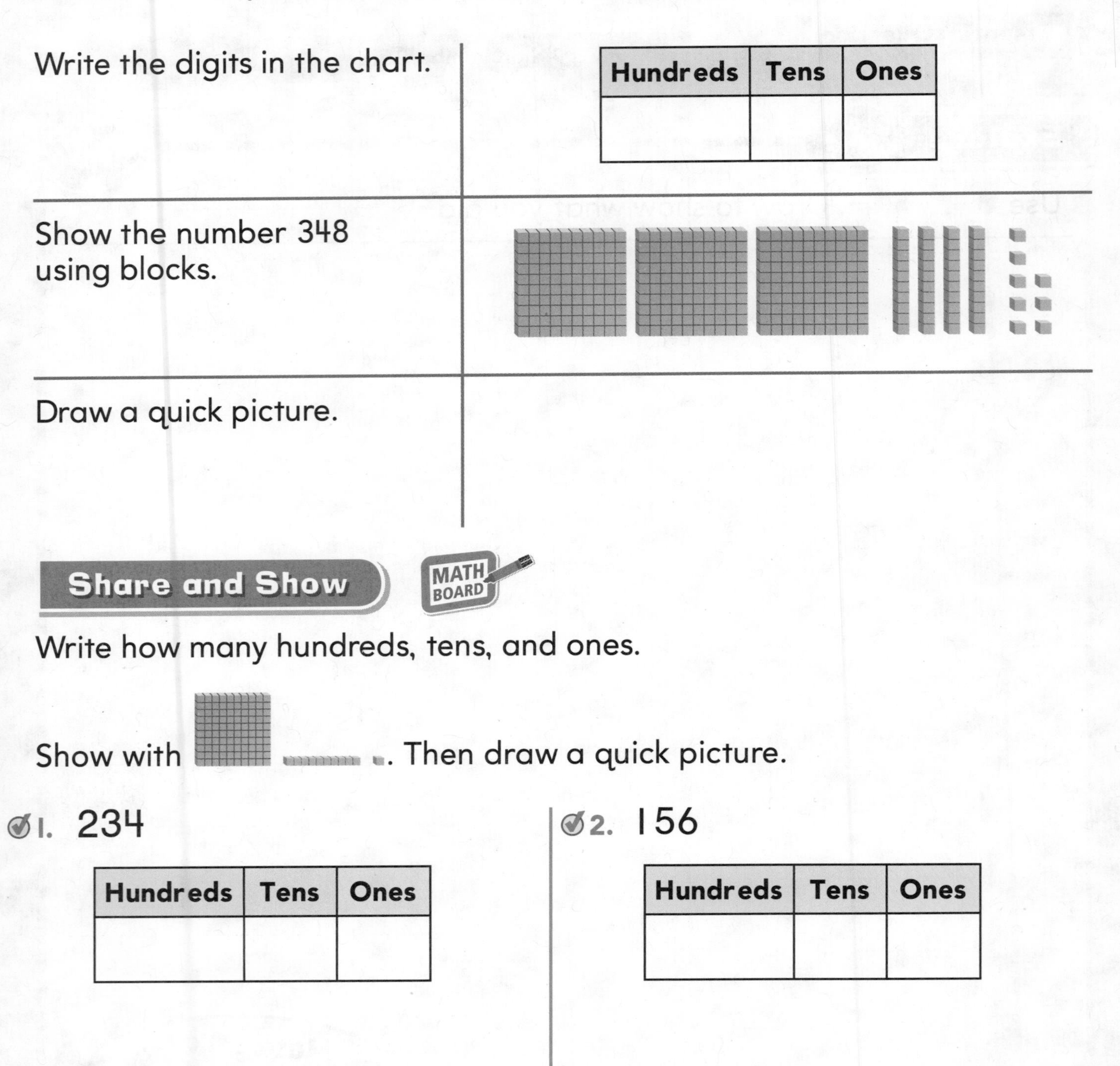

Write the digits in the chart.

Hundreds	Tens	Ones

Show the number 348 using blocks.

Draw a quick picture.

Share and Show

MATH BOARD

Write how many hundreds, tens, and ones.

Show with ▦ ▬ ▪. Then draw a quick picture.

✓1. 234

Hundreds	Tens	Ones

✓2. 156

Hundreds	Tens	Ones

Name ____________________

Problem Solving

Write how many hundreds, tens, and ones.

Show with [hundreds block] [tens block] [ones block]. Then draw a quick picture.

3. 125

Hundreds	Tens	Ones

4. 312

Hundreds	Tens	Ones

Solve.

5. H.O.T. How are the numbers 342 and 324 alike? How are they different?

____

____

____

____

6. H.O.T. **Multi-Step** I have 10 hundreds blocks, 5 ones blocks, and 8 tens blocks. I use all my blocks to model two 3-digit numbers. What could my two numbers be?

________ and ________

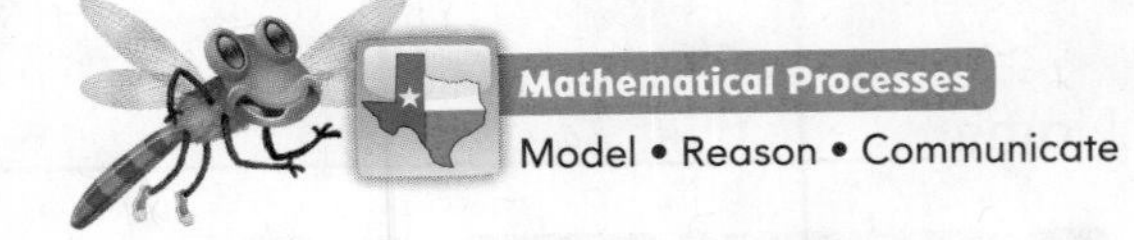

Daily Assessment Task

Choose the correct answer.

7. **Analyze** Mr. Martin's cookie order includes 6 boxes of 100 cookies. Which could be the number of cookies in his order?

   ○ 461 cookies

   ○ 336 cookies

   ○ 697 cookies

---

8. **Connect** Elmo delivers 7 boxes of 10 cookies, 3 boxes of 100 cookies, and 4 single cookies. How many cookies does Elmo deliver?

   ○ 347

   ○ 734

   ○ 374

9. **TEXAS Test Prep** What number is shown with these blocks?

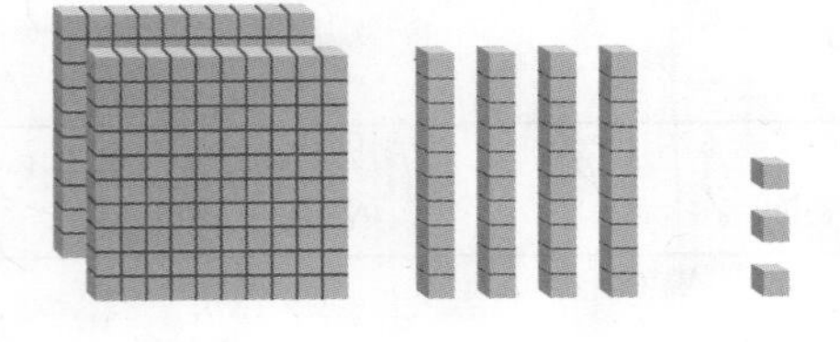

   ○ 342

   ○ 243

   ○ 432

TAKE HOME ACTIVITY • Write the number 438. Have your child tell you the values of the digits in the number 438.

Name ______________________

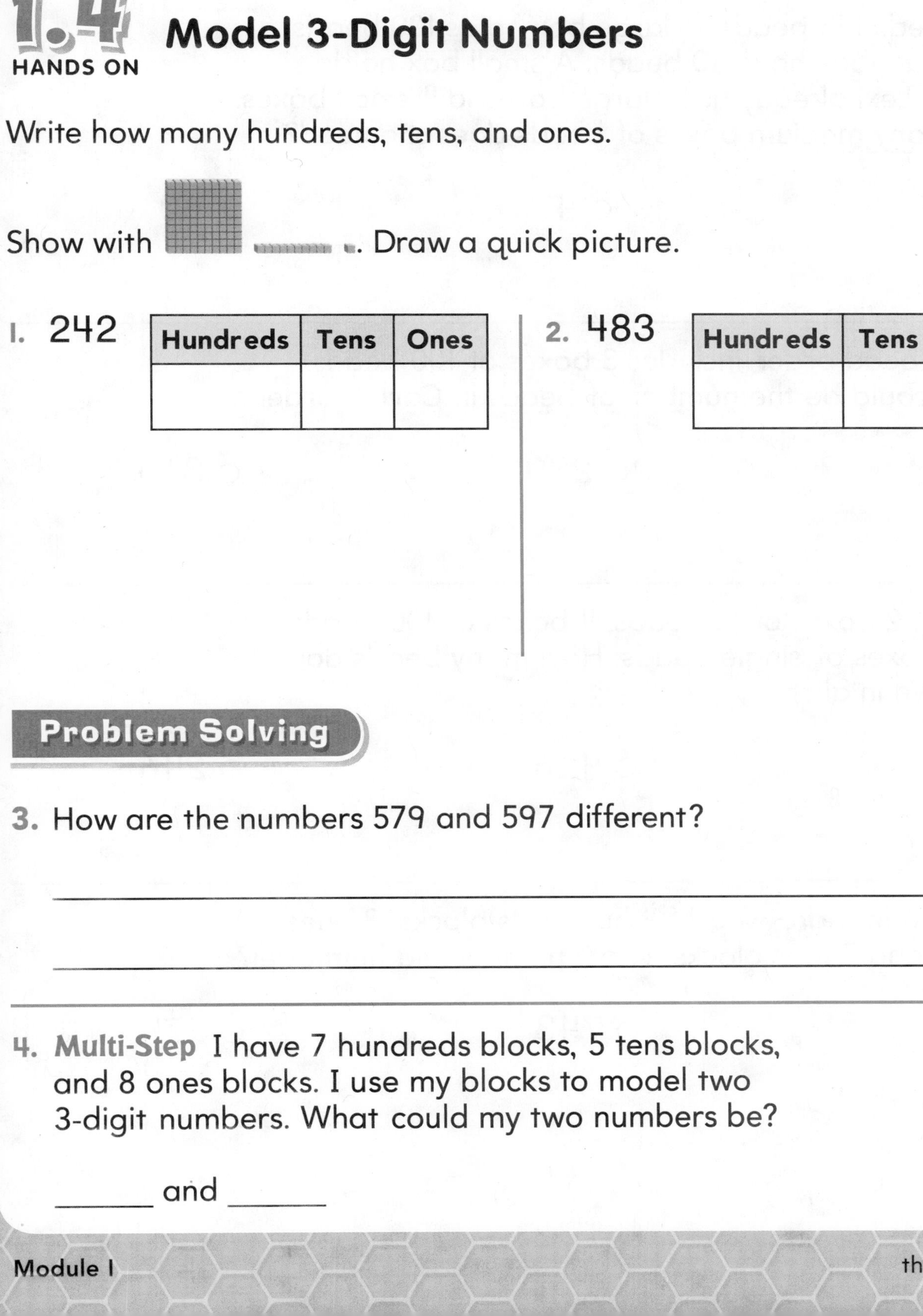

1.4 HANDS ON Model 3-Digit Numbers

Write how many hundreds, tens, and ones.

Show with [hundreds block] [tens block] [ones block]. Draw a quick picture.

1. 242

Hundreds	Tens	Ones

2. 483

Hundreds	Tens	Ones

Problem Solving

3. How are the numbers 579 and 597 different?

____

____

4. **Multi-Step** I have 7 hundreds blocks, 5 tens blocks, and 8 ones blocks. I use my blocks to model two 3-digit numbers. What could my two numbers be?

______ and ______

Lesson Check

TEXAS Test Prep

Choose the correct answer.

5. Lexi needs 144 beads. A large box holds 100 beads. A medium box holds 10 beads. A small box holds 1 bead. Lexi already has 1 large box and 4 small boxes. How many medium boxes of beads does she need?

○ 104 ○ 4 ○ 40

6. Carla's bead order includes 3 boxes of 100 beads. Which could be the number of beads in Carla's order?

○ 263 ○ 230 ○ 314

7. Tess has 2 boxes of 10 beads, 4 boxes of 100 beads, and 6 boxes of single beads. How many beads does Tess have in all?

○ 642 ○ 426 ○ 246

8. Dave made a drawing of 4 hundreds blocks, 3 ones blocks, and 7 tens blocks. What number did he model?

○ 473 ○ 743 ○ 374

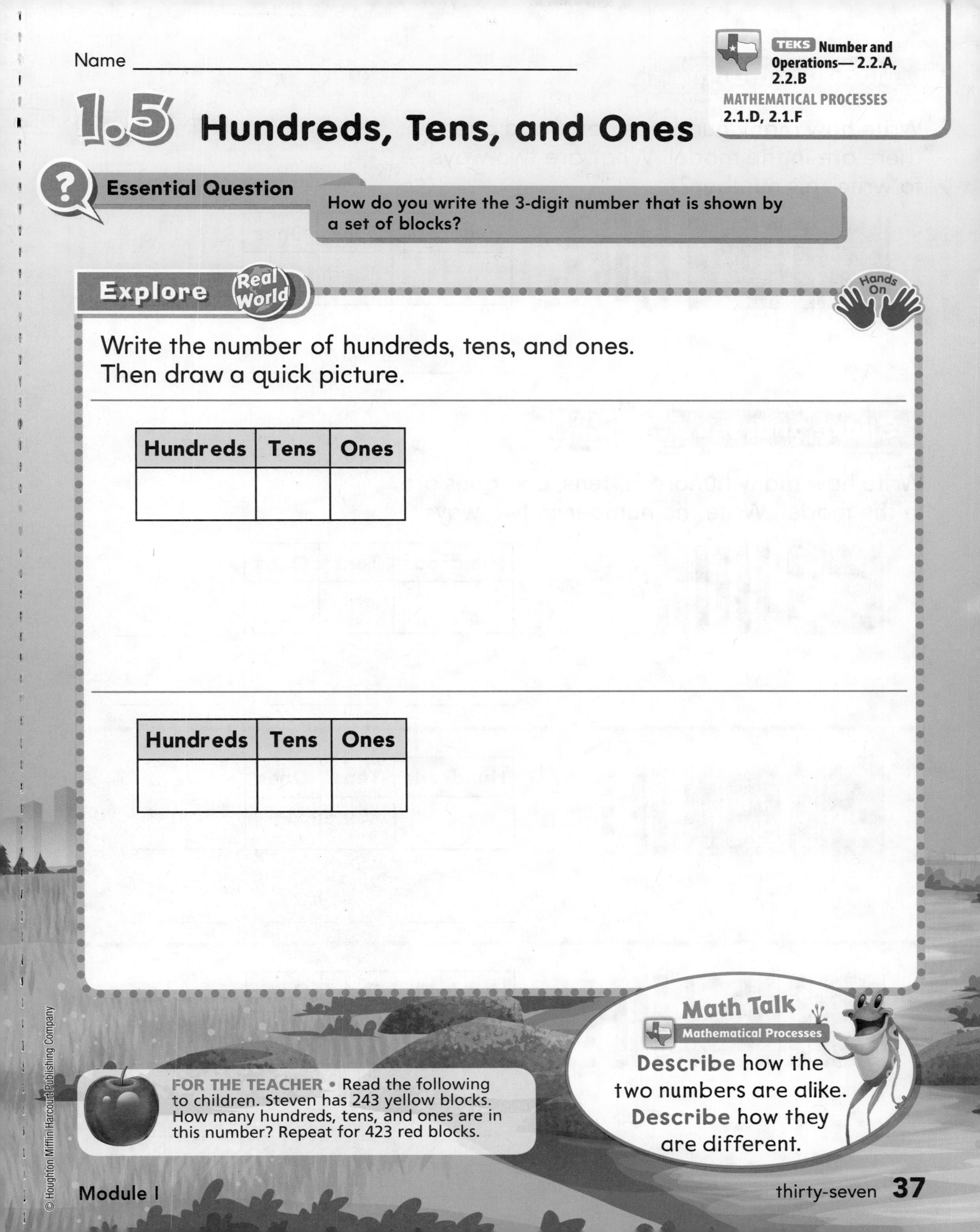

Name ______________________________

TEKS Number and Operations— 2.2.A, 2.2.B
MATHEMATICAL PROCESSES 2.1.D, 2.1.F

1.5 Hundreds, Tens, and Ones

Essential Question How do you write the 3-digit number that is shown by a set of blocks?

Explore Real World

Hands On

Write the number of hundreds, tens, and ones. Then draw a quick picture.

Hundreds	Tens	Ones

Hundreds	Tens	Ones

FOR THE TEACHER • Read the following to children. Steven has 243 yellow blocks. How many hundreds, tens, and ones are in this number? Repeat for 423 red blocks.

Math Talk Mathematical Processes

Describe how the two numbers are alike. **Describe** how they are different.

Model and Draw

Write how many hundreds, tens, and ones there are in the model. What are two ways to write this number?

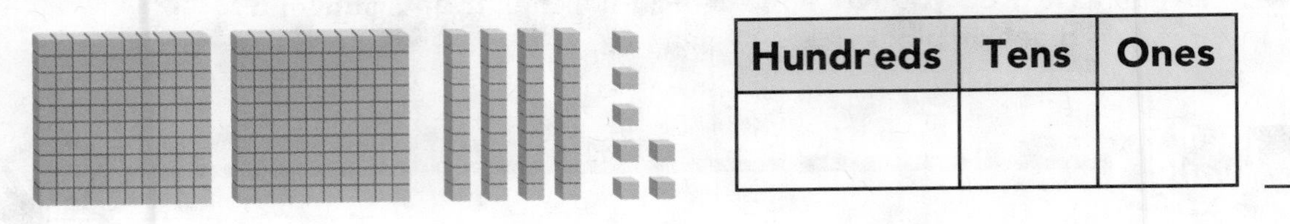

Hundreds	Tens	Ones

______

______ + ______ + ______

Share and Show

Write how many hundreds, tens, and ones are in the model. Write the number in two ways.

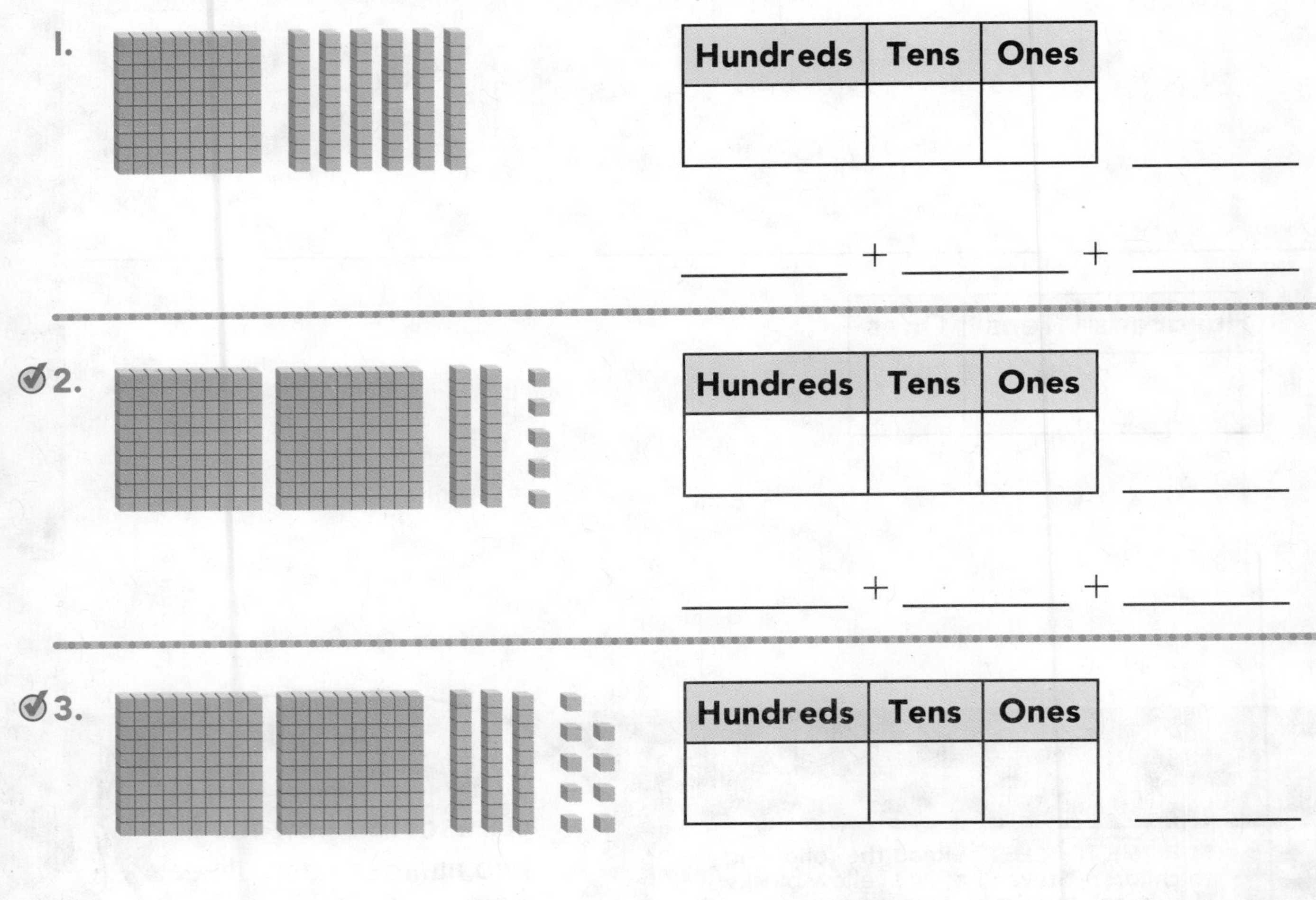

1.

Hundreds	Tens	Ones

______

______ + ______ + ______

✓2.

Hundreds	Tens	Ones

______

______ + ______ + ______

✓3.

Hundreds	Tens	Ones

______

______ + ______ + ______

Name ______________________________

Problem Solving

Write how many hundreds, tens, and ones are in the model. Write the number in two ways.

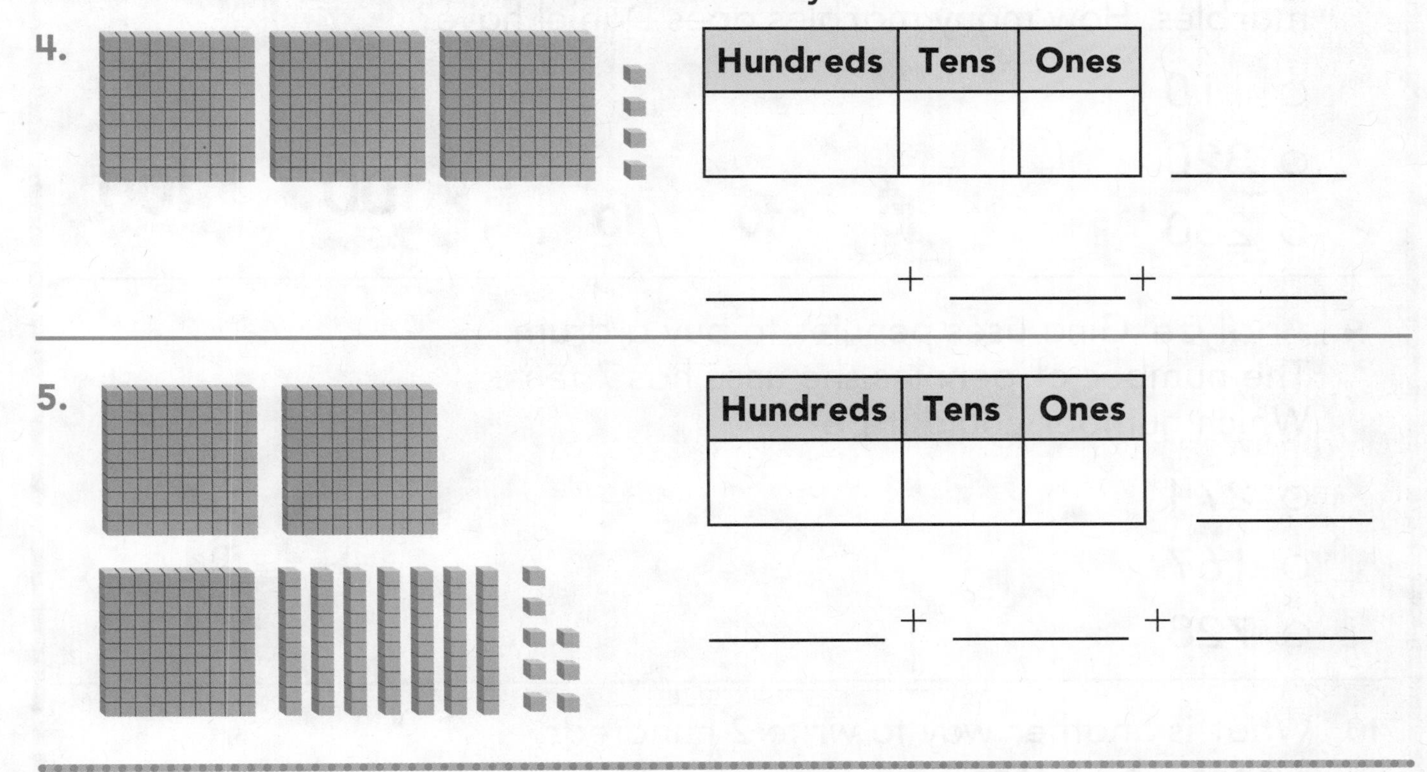

4.

Hundreds	Tens	Ones

______

______ + ______ + ______

5.

Hundreds	Tens	Ones

______

______ + ______ + ______

Solve. Write or draw to explain.

6. H.O.T. A model for my number has 4 ones blocks, 5 tens blocks, and 7 hundreds blocks. What number am I?

______

7. H.O.T. **Multi-Step** The hundreds digit of my number is greater than the tens digit. The ones digit is less than the tens digit. What could my number be? Write it in two ways.

______ + ______ + ______

______

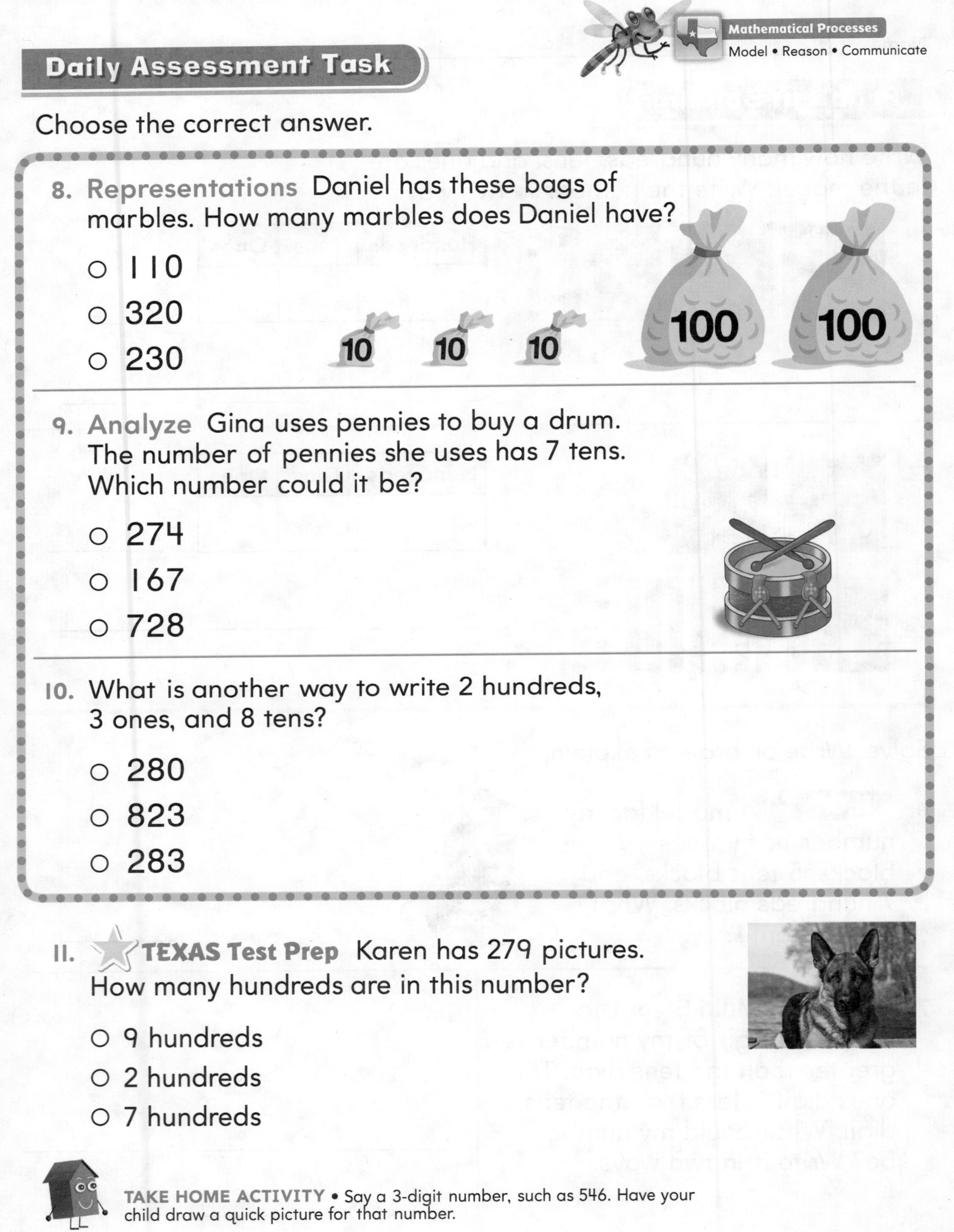

Mathematical Processes
Model • Reason • Communicate

Daily Assessment Task

Choose the correct answer.

8. **Representations** Daniel has these bags of marbles. How many marbles does Daniel have?

- ○ 110
- ○ 320
- ○ 230

9. **Analyze** Gina uses pennies to buy a drum. The number of pennies she uses has 7 tens. Which number could it be?

- ○ 274
- ○ 167
- ○ 728

10. What is another way to write 2 hundreds, 3 ones, and 8 tens?

- ○ 280
- ○ 823
- ○ 283

11. **TEXAS Test Prep** Karen has 279 pictures. How many hundreds are in this number?

- ○ 9 hundreds
- ○ 2 hundreds
- ○ 7 hundreds

TAKE HOME ACTIVITY • Say a 3-digit number, such as 546. Have your child draw a quick picture for that number.

TEKS Number and Operations—2.2.A, 2.2.B
MATHEMATICAL PROCESSES 2.1.D, 2.1.F

Name ________________

1.5 Hundreds, Tens, and Ones

Write how many hundreds, tens, and ones are in the model. Write the number in two ways.

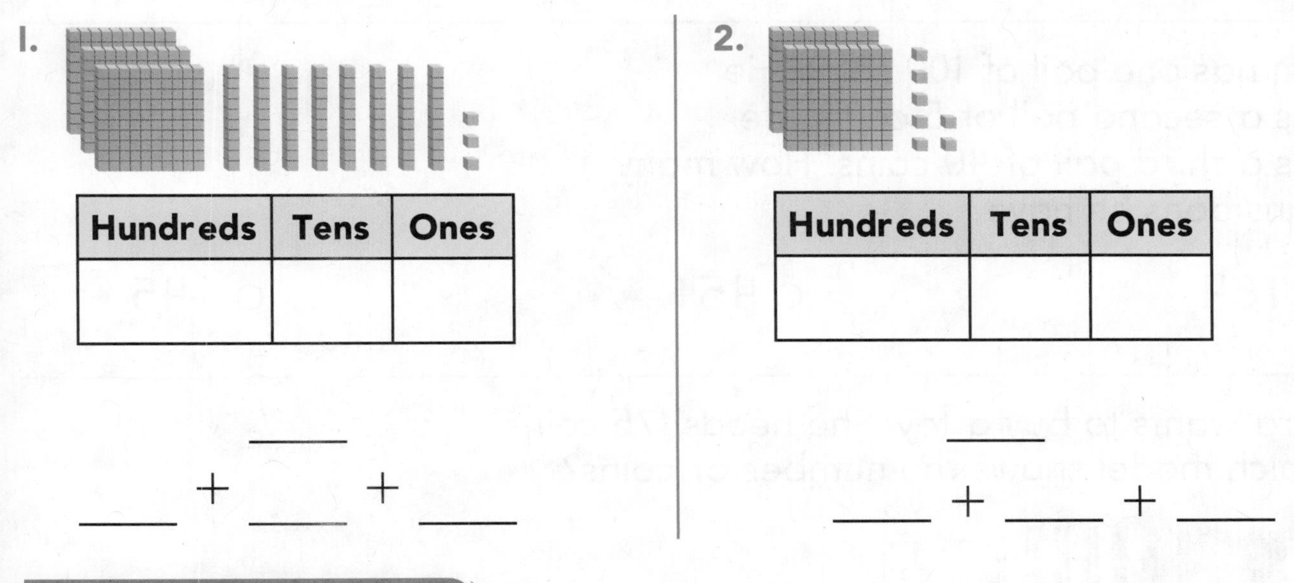

1.

Hundreds	Tens	Ones

____

____ + ____ + ____

2.

Hundreds	Tens	Ones

____

____ + ____ + ____

Problem Solving

Solve. Write or draw to explain

3. A model for my number has 6 ones blocks, 2 tens blocks, and 8 hundreds blocks. What number am I?

____

4. **Multi-Step** The hundreds digit of my number is less than the tens digit. The ones digit is greater than the tens digit. What could my number be?

____ + ____ + ____

____

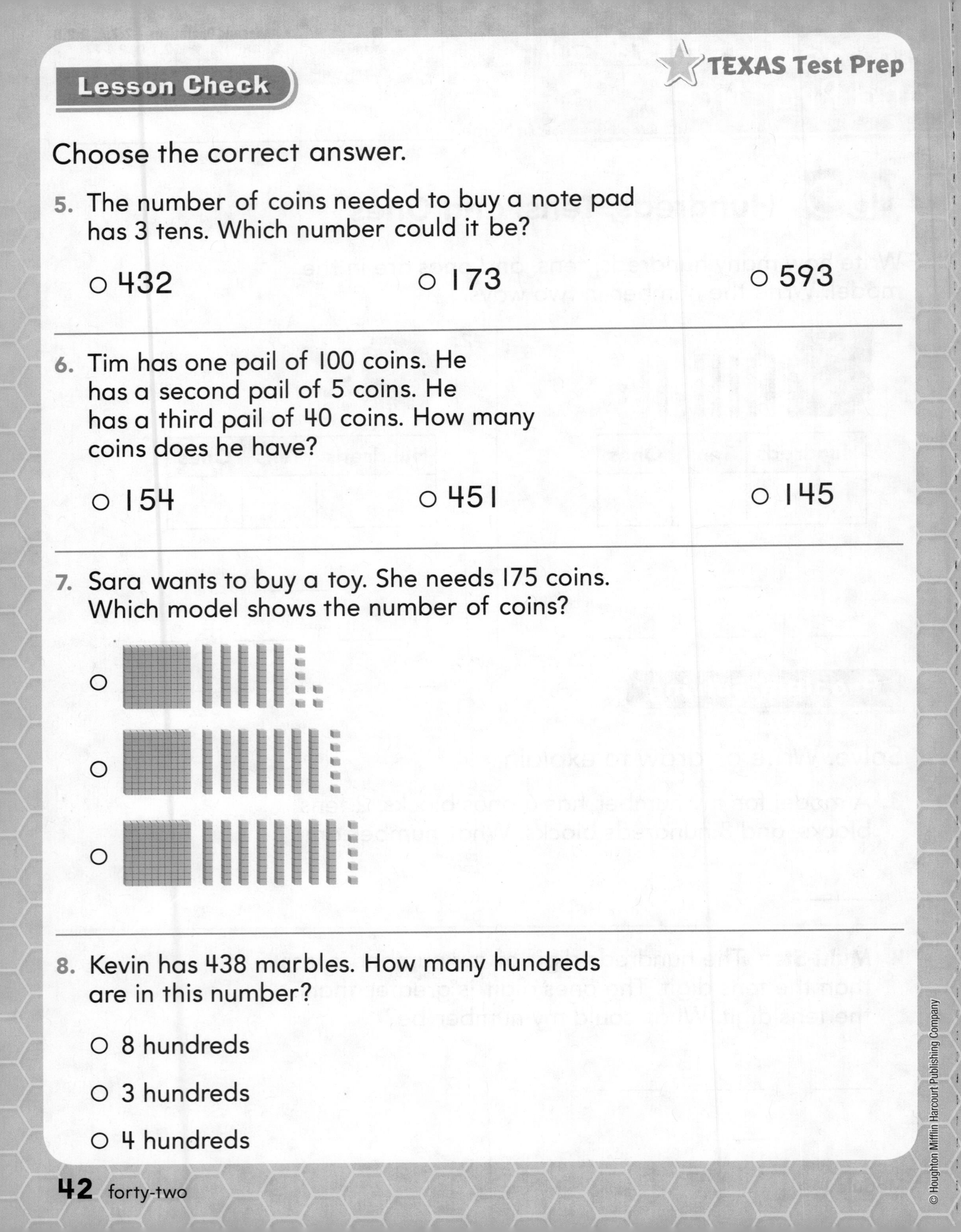

Lesson Check

TEXAS Test Prep

Choose the correct answer.

5. The number of coins needed to buy a note pad has 3 tens. Which number could it be?

○ 432 ○ 173 ○ 593

6. Tim has one pail of 100 coins. He has a second pail of 5 coins. He has a third pail of 40 coins. How many coins does he have?

○ 154 ○ 451 ○ 145

7. Sara wants to buy a toy. She needs 175 coins. Which model shows the number of coins?

○
○
○

8. Kevin has 438 marbles. How many hundreds are in this number?

○ 8 hundreds

○ 3 hundreds

○ 4 hundreds

Name ___________________________

1.6 Word Form for Numbers

Essential Question How do you write 3-digit numbers using words?

Explore

Write numbers to complete the chart. Then find and circle the word form of these numbers below.

	12	13		15	16	17	18	19	20
21	22	23	24	25	26	27	28		30
31	32	33	34		36	37	38	39	40
41	42	43	44	45		47	48	49	50
51		53	54	55	56	57	58	59	60

forty-one
eleven
fifty-three

ninety-two
thirty-five
twenty-nine

fourteen
forty-six
fifty-two

Math Talk Mathematical Processes

Describe how to use words to write the number with a 5 in the tens place and a 7 in the ones place.

FOR THE TEACHER • Read the following problem. Chelsea finds this page in her book of math puzzles. How can Chelsea complete the page?

Model and Draw

You can use words to write 3-digit numbers. First, look at the hundreds digit. Then, look at the tens digit and ones digit together.

245 → two hundred forty-five

713 → seven hundred thirteen

Share and Show

Write the number using words.

1. 506

____

2. 189

____

3. 328

____

Write the number.

4. four hundred fifteen _______

5. two hundred ninety-one _______

6. six hundred three _______

7. eight hundred forty-seven _______

Name ____________________

Problem Solving

Write the number.

8. six hundred forty-three

______

9. nine hundred twelve

______

Write the number using words.

10. 632

____

11. 568

____

12. 321

____

13. H.O.T. Alma counts two hundred sixty-eight leaves. Which is another way to write this number? Circle your answer.

Math on the Spot

2 + 6 + 8

200 + 60 + 8

2 + 60 + 8

14. H.O.T. **Multi-Step** My 3-digit number has a 4 in the hundreds place. It has a greater digit in the tens place than in the ones place. The sum of the digits is 6.

What is my number? ______

Write the number using words. ______________________________

Daily Assessment Task

Choose the correct answer.

15. Denzel has two hundred thirty-two crayons. Which number shows how many crayons Denzel has?

○ 223

○ 322

○ 232

16. **Representations** Together, Denzel and his brother have 593 crayons. Which is another way to write 593?

○ three hundred ninety-five

○ five hundred ninety-three

○ nine hundred fifty-three

17. **Analyze** Katie and her sister have six hundred twelve crayons. Which shows this number?

○ 126

○ 620

○ 612

18. **TEXAS Test Prep** There are five hundred thirty-seven chairs at the school. Which shows this number?

○ 507

○ 537

○ 357

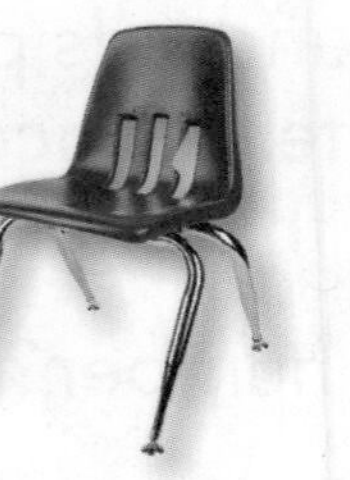

TAKE HOME ACTIVITY • Ask your child to write the number 940 using words.

Homework and Practice

TEKS Number and Operations—2.2.B
MATHEMATICAL PROCESSES 2.1.D, 2.1.E

Name ______________________

1.6 Word Form for Numbers

Write the number using words.

1. 292 ______________________

2. 467 ______________________

3. 668 ______________________

Write the number.

4. five hundred thirteen ______________

5. eight hundred twenty-four ______________

6. two hundred fifty-nine ______________

7. three hundred forty-six ______________

Problem Solving

Solve.

8. Adam counts one hundred ninety-six plants. Which is another way to write this number?

○ 1 + 9 + 6　○ 100 + 90 + 6　○ 1 + 90 + 6

Lesson Check

TEXAS Test Prep

Choose the correct answer.

9. Lindsey has one hundred twenty-three markers. Which number shows how many markers Lindsey has?

○ 321 ○ 123 ○ 213

---

10. Together, Lindsey and her friend have 295 markers. Which is another way to write 295?

○ five hundred ninety-two

○ two hundred fifty-nine

○ two hundred ninety-five

---

11. Tim and his brother collect bottle caps for a school project. So far, they have five hundred nineteen bottle caps. Which is another way to write the number?

○ 591 ○ 159 ○ 519

---

12. There are a great many desks at the school. The number has a 3 in the hundreds place. It has the same digit in the tens place. The sum of those two digits is in the ones place. How many desks are at the school?

○ 336 ○ 363 ○ 360

Name ________________________________

TEKS Number and Operations—2.2.A
MATHEMATICAL PROCESSES 2.1.C, 2.1.D

1.7 HANDS ON Different Ways to Show Numbers

Essential Question How can you use blocks or quick pictures to show the value of a number in different ways?

Explore Real World

Hands On

Draw quick pictures to solve.
Write how many tens and ones.

_______ tens _______ ones

_______ tens _______ ones

FOR THE TEACHER • Read this problem to children. Mrs. Peabody has 35 books on a cart to take to classrooms. She can use boxes that each hold 10 books and she can also place single books on the cart. What are two different ways she can put the books on the cart?

Math Talk Mathematical Processes

Describe how you found different ways to show 35 books.

Model and Draw

Here are two ways to show 148.

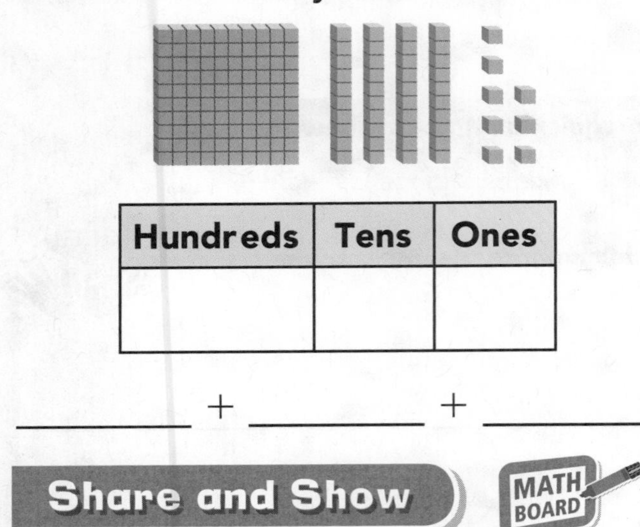

Hundreds	Tens	Ones

_____ + _____ + _____

Hundreds	Tens	Ones

_____ + _____ + _____

Share and Show

MATH BOARD

Write how many hundreds, tens, and ones are shown. Then use blocks. Draw and write another way to show the number.

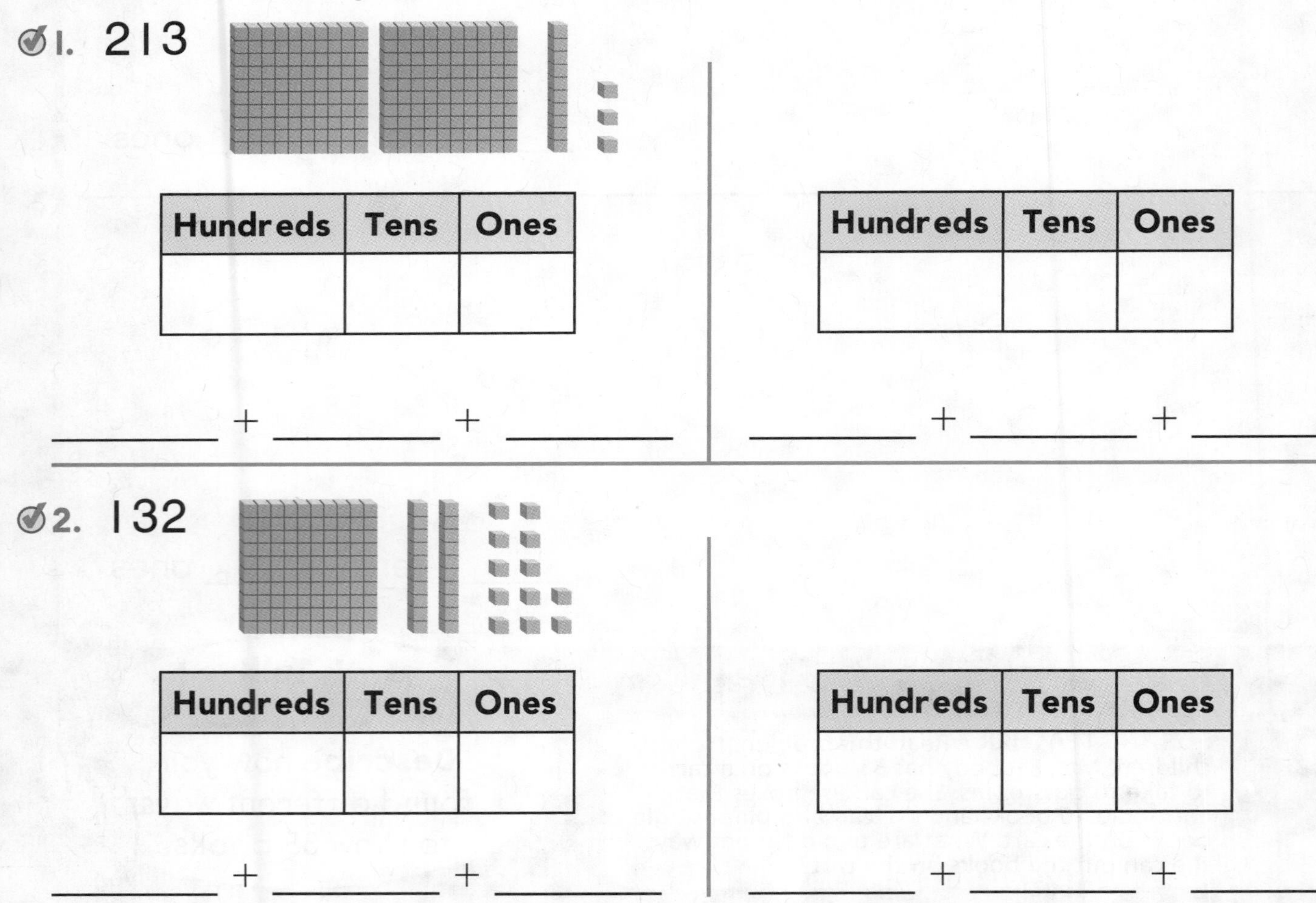

1. 213

Hundreds	Tens	Ones

_____ + _____ + _____

Hundreds	Tens	Ones

_____ + _____ + _____

2. 132

Hundreds	Tens	Ones

_____ + _____ + _____

Hundreds	Tens	Ones

_____ + _____ + _____

Name ______________________________

Problem Solving

Write how many hundreds, tens, and ones are shown. Then use blocks. Draw and write another way to show the number.

3. 144

Hundreds	Tens	Ones

_______ + _______ + _______

Hundreds	Tens	Ones

_______ + _______ + _______

Marbles are sold in boxes, in bags, or as single marbles. Each box has 10 bags of marbles in it. Each bag has 10 marbles in it.

4. H.O.T. Draw pictures to show two ways to buy 324 marbles.

Math on the Spot

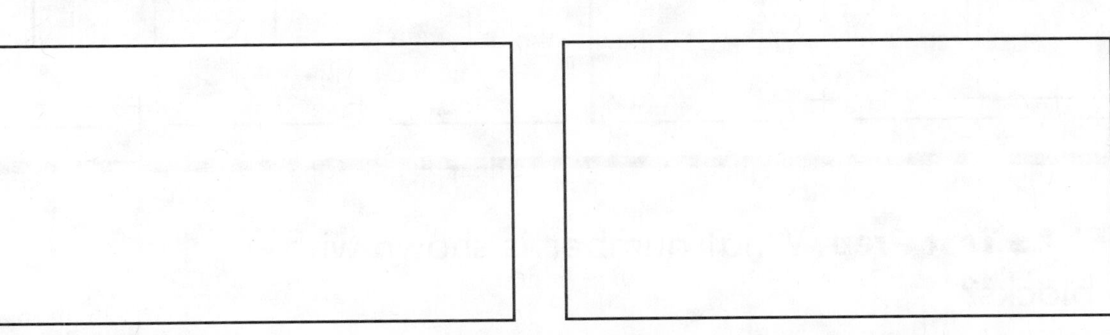

5. H.O.T. **Multi-Step** There is only one box of marbles in the store. There are many bags of marbles and single marbles. Draw a picture to show a way to buy 312 marbles.

Mathematical Processes
Model • Reason • Communicate

Daily Assessment Task

Choose the correct answer.

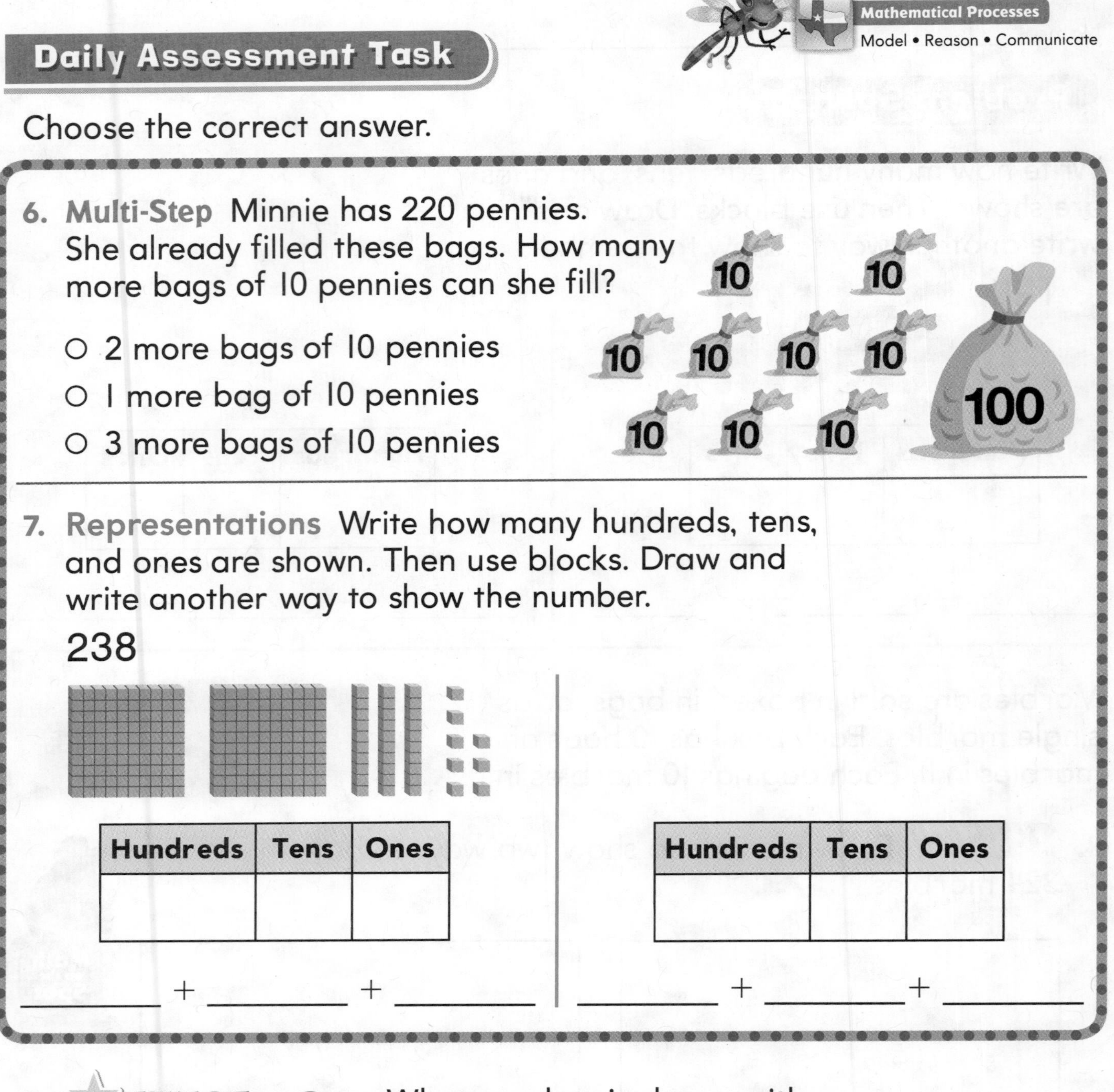

6. **Multi-Step** Minnie has 220 pennies. She already filled these bags. How many more bags of 10 pennies can she fill?

   ○ 2 more bags of 10 pennies
   ○ 1 more bag of 10 pennies
   ○ 3 more bags of 10 pennies

7. **Representations** Write how many hundreds, tens, and ones are shown. Then use blocks. Draw and write another way to show the number.

   238

Hundreds	Tens	Ones

_______ + _______ + _______

Hundreds	Tens	Ones

_______ + _______ + _______

8. **TEXAS Test Prep** What number is shown with these blocks?

   ○ 317
   ○ 342
   ○ 327

TAKE HOME ACTIVITY • Write the number 156. Have your child draw quick pictures to show this number two ways.

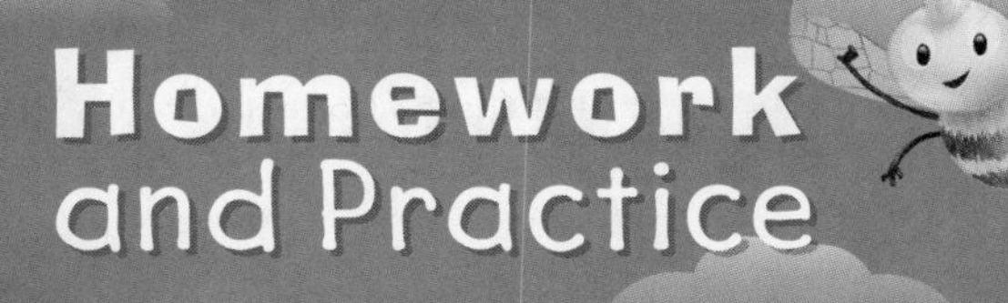

Name ______________________

1.7 HANDS ON Different Ways to Show Numbers

Write how many hundreds, tens, and ones are shown.
Write another way to show the number.

1. 162

Hundreds	Tens	Ones

_______ + _______ + _______

Hundreds	Tens	Ones

_______ + _______ + _______

Problem Solving

Solve.

2. **Multi-Step** Paper plates are shipped in boxes. Each box has 10 bags of plates. Each bag has 10 plates. Draw quick pictures to show how many boxes and bags of paper plates are needed for 180 paper plates.

Lesson Check

Choose the correct answer.

3. What number is shown with these blocks?

   ○ 463

   ○ 634

   ○ 436

---

4. Ted wants to buy a paperback book for 270 coins. He has 7 bags of 10 coins. How many more bags of 10 coins does he need?

   ○ 20 bags of 10 coins

   ○ 2 bags of 10 coins

   ○ 10 bags of 10 coins

---

5. There are 280 people at the soccer game. Which is a way to show 280?

   ○ 2 hundreds 18 ones

   ○ 2 hundreds 7 tens 10 ones

   ○ 8 hundreds 2 tens

Name ______________________

Module 1 Assessment

Concepts and Skills

Write the number. TEKS 2.2.B

1. six hundred forty-seven

______

2. nine hundred twenty-one

______

Write the number using words.

3. 562 ______________________

4. Draw and label points to show where 25 and 61 belong. TEKS 2.2.E

20 ———————————————— 80

5. Write how many hundreds, tens, and ones are shown. Then use blocks. Draw and write another way to show the number. TEKS 2.2.A

123

Hundreds	Tens	Ones

______ + ______ + ______

Hundreds	Tens	Ones

______ + ______ + ______

Fill in the bubble for the correct answer choice.

TEXAS Test Prep

6. There are four hundred twelve pennies in a jar. Which shows this number? TEKS 2.2.B

- ○ 400
- ○ 420
- ○ 412

7. There are 10 crackers on each plate. There are 16 plates in all. How many crackers are there? TEKS 2.2.A

- ○ 160
- ○ 116
- ○ 206

8. Ben draws a point on the number line. Which number belongs at the point? TEKS 2.2.F

60 80

- ○ 67
- ○ 65
- ○ 70

9. Tammy has 237 marbles. Which is another way to show this number? TEKS 2.2.B

- ○ 200 + 70 + 3
- ○ 200 + 30 + 7
- ○ 700 + 30 + 2

Name ____________________________

TEKS Number and Operations—2.2.B, 2.2.A
MATHEMATICAL PROCESSES 2.1.D

2.1 Different Forms of Numbers

Essential Question What are three ways to write a 3-digit number?

Explore Real World

Write the number. Use digits to write how many hundreds, tens, and ones.

[ ] ____ hundreds ____ tens ____ ones

[ ] ____ hundreds ____ tens ____ ones

[ ] ____ hundreds ____ tens ____ ones

FOR THE TEACHER • Read the following: Evan has 426 marbles. How many hundreds, tens, and ones are in 426? Continue the activity for 204 and 341.

Math Talk Mathematical Processes

How many hundreds are in 368? **Explain.**

Model and Draw

You can use a quick picture to show a number.
You can write a number in different ways.

five hundred thirty-six

____ hundreds ____ tens ____ ones

______ + ______ + ______

______

Share and Show

MATH BOARD

Read the number and draw a quick picture.
Then write the number in different ways.

1. four hundred seven

____ hundreds ____ tens ____ ones

______ + ______ + ______

______

2. three hundred twenty-five

____ hundreds ____ tens ____ ones

______ + ______ + ______

______

3. two hundred fifty-three

____ hundreds ____ tens ____ ones

______ + ______ + ______

______

Name ___________________________________

Problem Solving

Read the number and draw a quick picture.
Then write the number in different ways.

4. one hundred seventy-two

_____ hundreds _____ tens _____ ones

________ + ________ + ________

____

5. three hundred forty-six

_____ hundreds _____ tens _____ ones

________ + ________ + ________

____

Solve.

6. H.O.T. **Multi-Step** Ellen used these blocks to show 452. What is wrong? Cross out blocks and draw quick pictures for missing blocks.

7. H.O.T. Think of a 3-digit number with a zero in the ones place. Use words to write that number.

____

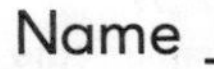

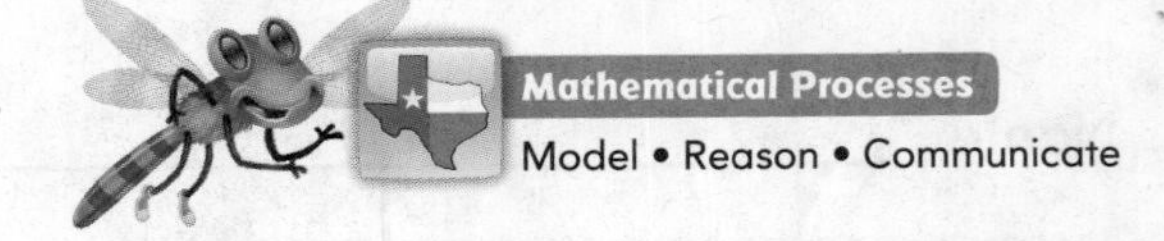

Daily Assessment Task

Choose the correct answer.

8. **Reasoning** Tony's card shows 4 hundreds 7 ones. Which of the following has the same value?

○ 500 + 80 + 1

○ 407

○ seven hundred forty

9. Owen's number has the digit 5 in the tens place. Which of the following could be his number?

○ 500

○ three hundred five

○ 754

10. **Representations** Julia's card shows the number 630. Which of the following is another way to write this number?

○ 600 + 3

○ six hundred thirty

○ 60 + 3

11. **TEXAS Test Prep** Gianna writes 845 on the board. Which is another way to write 845?

○ 800 + 40 + 5

○ 800 + 4 + 5

○ 80 + 40 + 5

TAKE HOME ACTIVITY • Ask your child to show the number 315 in three different ways.

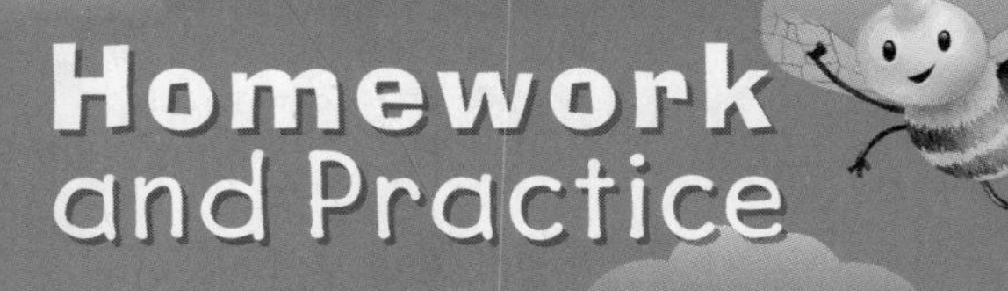

Name ______________________

2.1 Different Forms of Numbers

Read the number and draw a quick picture.
Then write the number in different ways.

1. 209

____ hundreds ____ tens ____ ones

____ + ____ + ____

____

2. 463

____ hundreds ____ tens ____ ones

____ + ____ + ____

____

Problem Solving

Solve.

3. **Multi-Step** Stan used these blocks to show 378. What is wrong? Cross out blocks and draw quick pictures for the missing blocks.

Lesson Check

TEXAS Test Prep

Choose the correct answer.

4. Which is another way to write 722?

   ○ $700 + 20 + 2$

   ○ $70 + 20 + 2$

   ○ $700 + 2 + 2$

5. Which number has 3 tens?

   ○ three hundred six

   ○ 439

   ○ 300

6. Hal wrote a number that has 6 hundreds and 2 ones. Which is another way to write this number?

   ○ 602

   ○ two hundred six

   ○ $300 + 60 + 2$

Name ______________________________

TEKS Number and Operations—2.2.D
MATHEMATICAL PROCESSES 2.1.D, 2.1.G

2.2 Compare Numbers

ALGEBRA

Essential Question How do you compare 3-digit numbers?

Explore Real World

Hands On

Draw quick pictures to solve the problems. Then complete the sentences.

More ______________ were at the zoo.

Fewer ______________ were at the park.

FOR THE TEACHER • Read the following problem and have children draw quick pictures to compare the numbers. There were 82 butterflies and 86 birds at the zoo. Were there more butterflies or more birds? Repeat for the following problem: There were 47 water fountains at the park and 92 benches at the park. Were there fewer benches or fewer water fountains?

Math Talk Mathematical Processes

Explain how you compared the numbers in the first problem.

Model and Draw

Use place value to **compare** numbers. Start by looking at the digits in the greatest place value position first.

$>$ is greater than
$<$ is less than
$=$ is equal to

Hundreds	Tens	Ones
4	8	3
5	7	0

4 hundreds $<$ 5 hundreds

483 ◯ 570

Hundreds	Tens	Ones
3	5	2
3	4	6

The hundreds are equal.

5 tens $>$ 4 tens

352 ◯ 346

Share and Show

Compare the numbers. Write ***is greater than***, ***is less than***, or ***is equal to.*** Write $>$, $<$, or $=$.

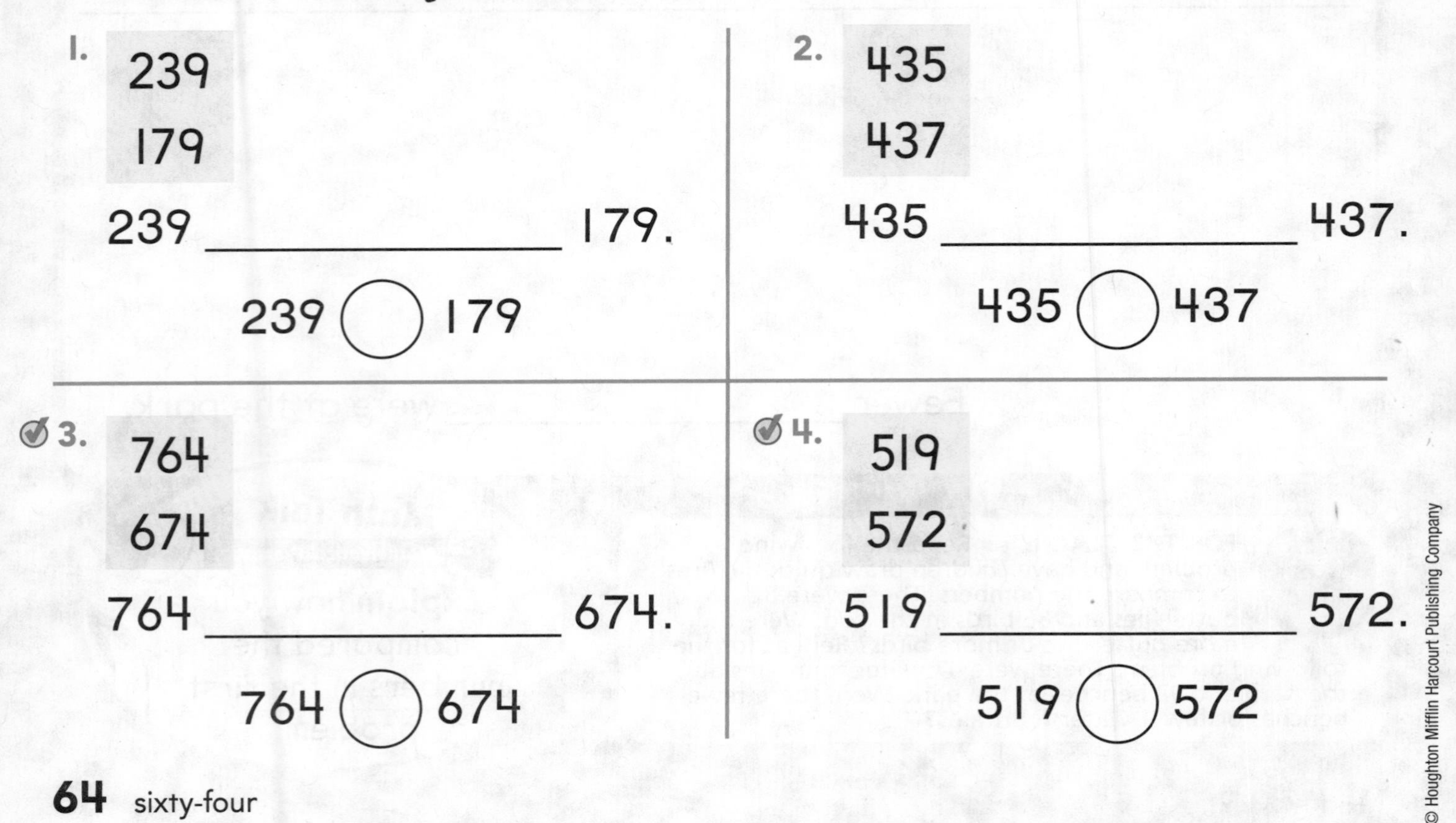

1. 239
   179

   239 ____________ 179.

   239 ◯ 179

2. 435
   437

   435 ____________ 437.

   435 ◯ 437

3. 764
   674

   764 ____________ 674.

   764 ◯ 674

4. 519
   572

   519 ____________ 572.

   519 ◯ 572

Name ____________________

Problem Solving

Compare the numbers. Write ***is greater than***, ***is less than***, or ***is equal to***. Write $>$, $<$, or $=$.

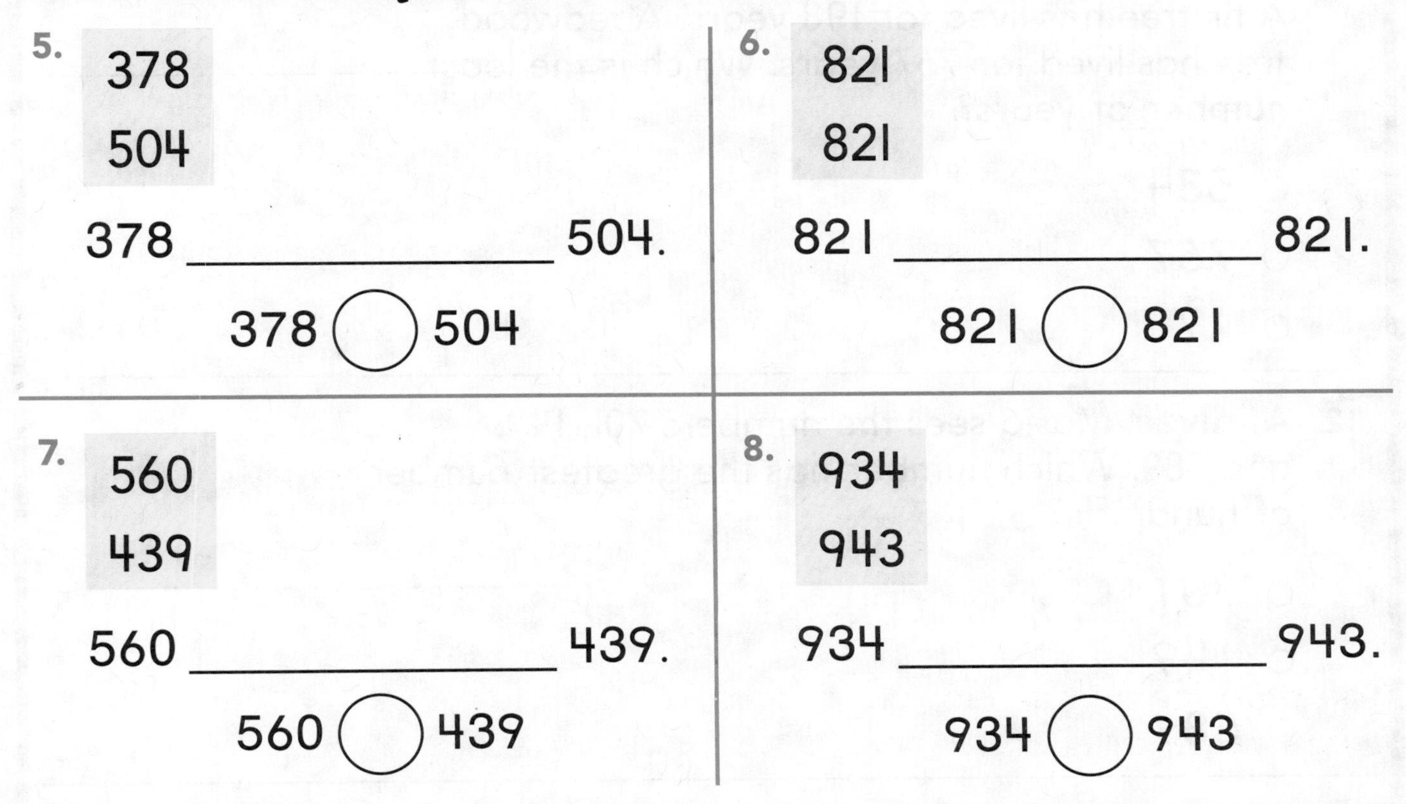

5. 378 504

378 ______________ 504.

378 ◯ 504

6. 821 821

821 ______________ 821.

821 ◯ 821

7. 560 439

560 ______________ 439.

560 ◯ 439

8. 934 943

934 ______________ 943.

934 ◯ 943

Solve. Write or draw to explain.

9. **H.O.T.** Mrs. York has 300 red stickers, 50 blue stickers, and 8 green stickers. Mr. Reed has 372 stickers. Who has more stickers?

____

10. **H.O.T.** **Multi-Step** Use the digits on these cards to make two 3-digit numbers. Use each card only once. Compare the numbers.

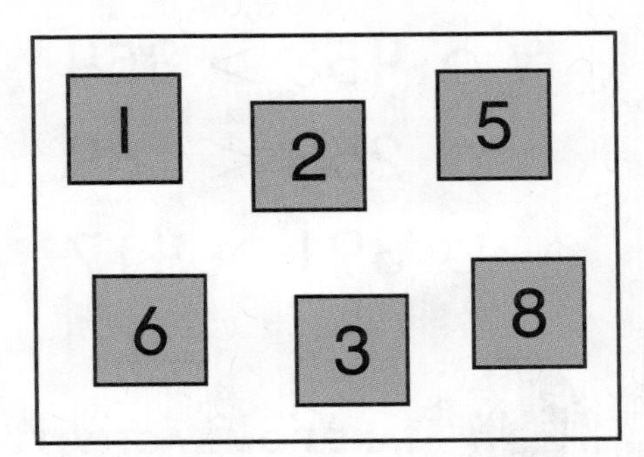

__________ ◯ __________

Daily Assessment Task

Choose the correct answer.

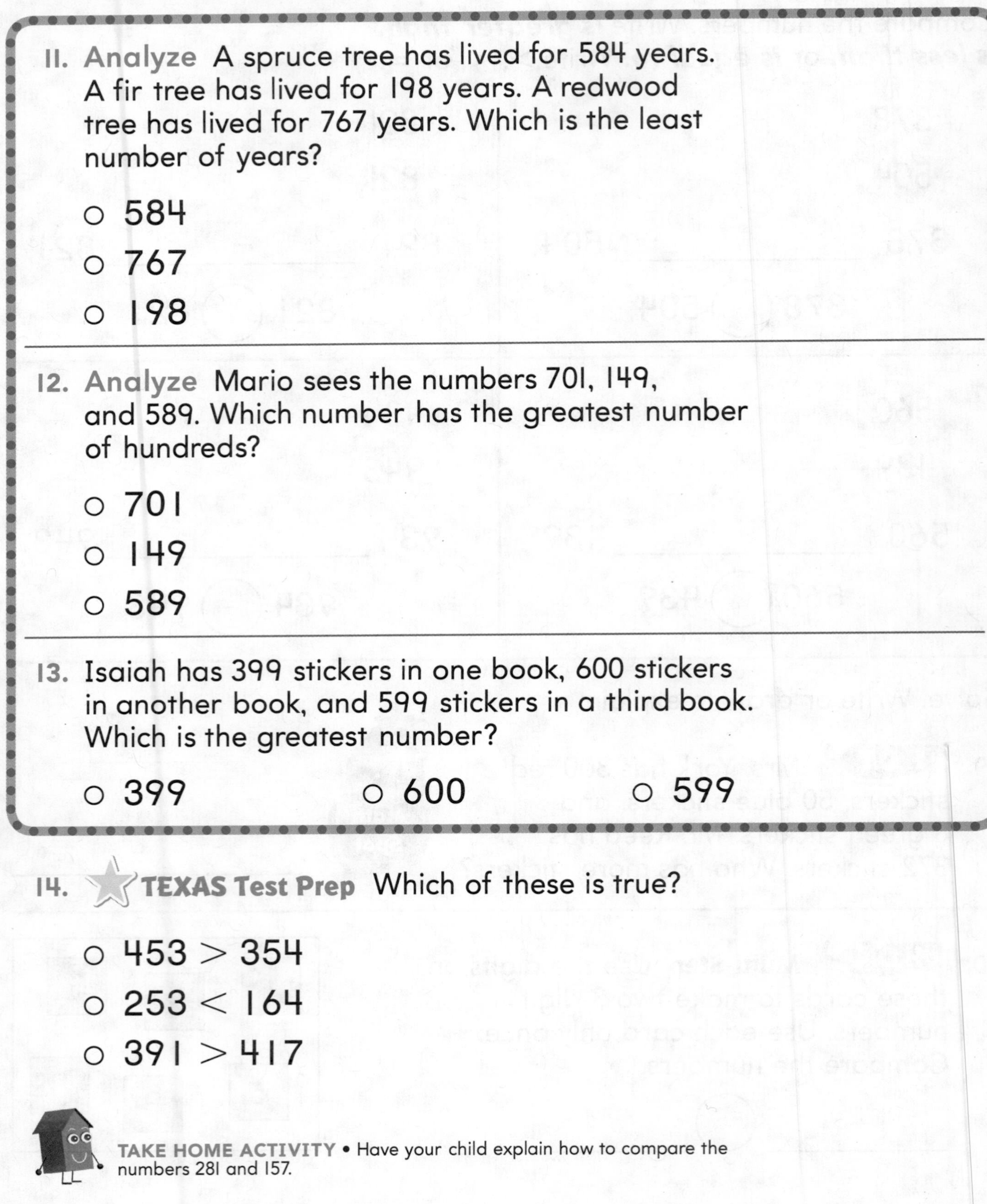

11. **Analyze** A spruce tree has lived for 584 years. A fir tree has lived for 198 years. A redwood tree has lived for 767 years. Which is the least number of years?

   ○ 584
   ○ 767
   ○ 198

12. **Analyze** Mario sees the numbers 701, 149, and 589. Which number has the greatest number of hundreds?

   ○ 701
   ○ 149
   ○ 589

13. Isaiah has 399 stickers in one book, 600 stickers in another book, and 599 stickers in a third book. Which is the greatest number?

   ○ 399 ○ 600 ○ 599

14. **TEXAS Test Prep** Which of these is true?

   ○ $453 > 354$
   ○ $253 < 164$
   ○ $391 > 417$

TAKE HOME ACTIVITY • Have your child explain how to compare the numbers 281 and 157.

TEKS Number and Operations—2.2.D
MATHEMATICAL PROCESSES 2.1.D, 2.1.G

Name ____________________

2.2 Compare Numbers

ALGEBRA

Compare the numbers. Write *is greater than*, *is less than*, or *is equal to*. Write >, <, or =.

1.

Hundreds	Tens	Ones
4	3	9
2	7	9

439 ____________ 279

439 ◯ 279

2.

Hundreds	Tens	Ones
6	6	4
6	8	2

664 ____________ 682

664 ◯ 682

Problem Solving

Solve. Write or draw to explain.

3. **Multi-Step** Beth has some number cards. Use the digits on the cards to make two 3-digit numbers. Use each card only once. Compare the numbers.

1	2	4
5	7	9

____________ ◯ ____________

Lesson Check

TEXAS Test Prep

Choose the correct answer.

4. Which number has the greatest number of hundreds?

- ○ 941
- ○ 107
- ○ 859

5. Which of these is true?

- ○ $853 > 874$
- ○ $335 < 173$
- ○ $547 = 547$

6. Which is the greatest number?

- ○ 678
- ○ 206
- ○ 728

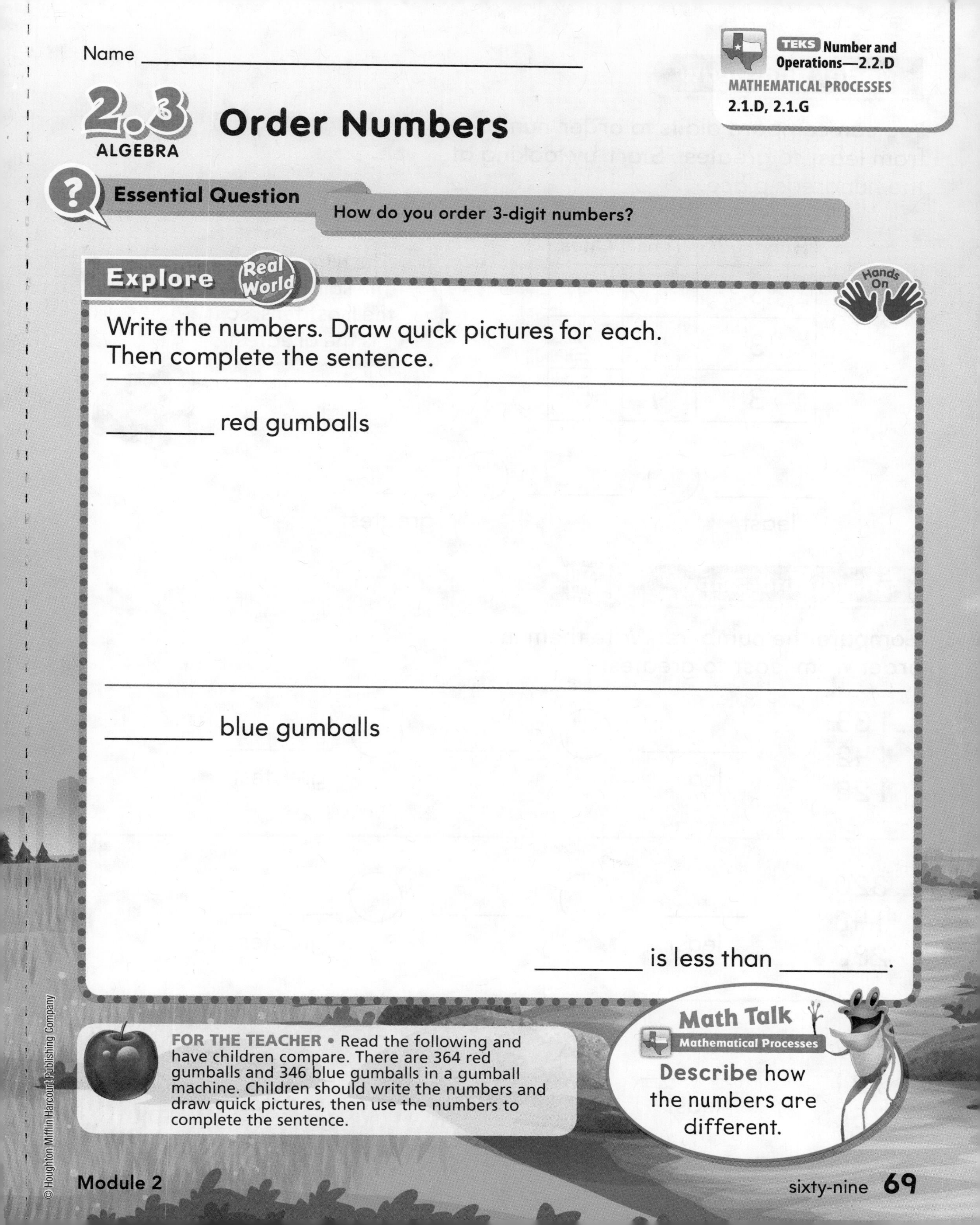

Name ____________________

TEKS Number and Operations—2.2.D
MATHEMATICAL PROCESSES
2.1.D, 2.1.G

2.3 ALGEBRA

Order Numbers

Essential Question How do you order 3-digit numbers?

Explore Real World

Hands On

Write the numbers. Draw quick pictures for each. Then complete the sentence.

_______ red gumballs

_______ blue gumballs

_______ is less than _______.

FOR THE TEACHER • Read the following and have children compare. There are 364 red gumballs and 346 blue gumballs in a gumball machine. Children should write the numbers and draw quick pictures, then use the numbers to complete the sentence.

Math Talk Mathematical Processes

Describe how the numbers are different.

Model and Draw

You can compare digits to order numbers from least to greatest. Start by looking at the hundreds place.

Hundreds	Tens	Ones
3	4	9
3	4	2
3	9	5

The hundreds are the same. 395 has the most tens, so it is the greatest.

_____ ◯ _____ ◯ _____
least greatest

Share and Show

MATH BOARD

Compare the numbers. Write them in order from least to greatest.

1. 133
142
125

_____ ◯ _____ ◯ _____
least greatest

2. 320
148
230

_____ ◯ _____ ◯ _____
least greatest

3. 599
901
755

_____ ◯ _____ ◯ _____
least greatest

Name ________________________________

Problem Solving

Compare the numbers. Write them in order from least to greatest.

4. 212
222
202

_______ ◯ _______ ◯ _______
least   greatest

5. 325
501
215

_______ ◯ _______ ◯ _______
least   greatest

6. 418
148
481

_______ ◯ _______ ◯ _______
least   greatest

Solve. Write or draw to explain.

7. **H.O.T.** **Multi-Step** Mr. Damon has three boxes of paper with 153 sheets, 214 sheets, and 180 sheets. Write the numbers in order from greatest to least. Remember to write comparison symbols.

_______ ◯ _______ ◯ _______
greatest   least

8. **H.O.T.** Nisha wrote these numbers in order from least to greatest. She spills some water on her paper. Write the missing number.

$335 < \square < 350$

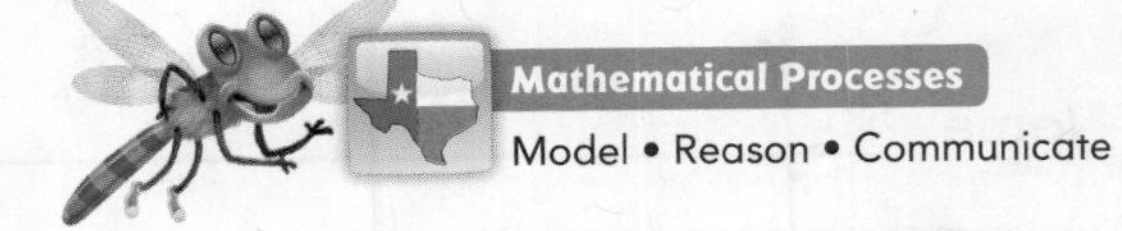

Daily Assessment Task

Choose the correct answer.

9. There are 3 bags with 453 peanuts, 721 peanuts, and 598 peanuts. Which is the greatest number?
   - ○ 453
   - ○ 721
   - ○ 598

10. **Representations** Sam writes 631, 321, and 621 on a piece of paper. Which of these numbers is the greatest?
   - ○ 631
   - ○ 321
   - ○ 621

11. **Multi-Step** John writes the following numbers on a piece of paper. Which of these numbers is the least?
   - ○ four hundred twenty-six
   - ○ $200 + 30 + 9$
   - ○ 371

12. **TEXAS Test Prep** Which of these is true?
   - ○ $161 < 149 < 152$
   - ○ $161 < 152 < 149$
   - ○ $149 < 152 < 161$

TAKE HOME ACTIVITY • Ask your child to show how he or she solved an exercise in the lesson.

Name ______________________

2.3 ALGEBRA Order Numbers

Compare the numbers. Write them in order from least to greatest.

1. 513 523 503

_____ ◯ _____ ◯ _____
least greatest

2. 227 701 147

_____ ◯ _____ ◯ _____
least greatest

3. 656 566 665

_____ ◯ _____ ◯ _____
least greatest

Problem Solving

Solve. Write or draw to explain.

4. **Multi-Step** Curtis has three boxes of wrapping paper with 135 rolls, 250 rolls, and 160 rolls. Write the numbers in order from greatest to least. Remember to write comparison symbols.

_____ ◯ _____ ◯ _____
greatest least

Lesson Check

TEXAS Test Prep

Choose the correct answer.

5. Which of these numbers is the greatest?

○ 136

○ 113

○ 163

6. Which of these numbers is the least?

○ four hundred twenty-six

○ $400 + 20 + 4$

○ 472

7. Jasper, Harold, and Bella are bunnies at a zoo. Jasper eats 103 carrots. Harold eats 158 carrots. Bella eats 124 carrots. Which bunny eats the most carrots?

○ Jasper

○ Harold

○ Bella

8. Karen scores 512 points. Josh scores 491 points. Emily scores 611 points. Which of these is true?

○ $611 < 491 < 512$

○ $611 < 512 < 491$

○ $491 < 512 < 611$

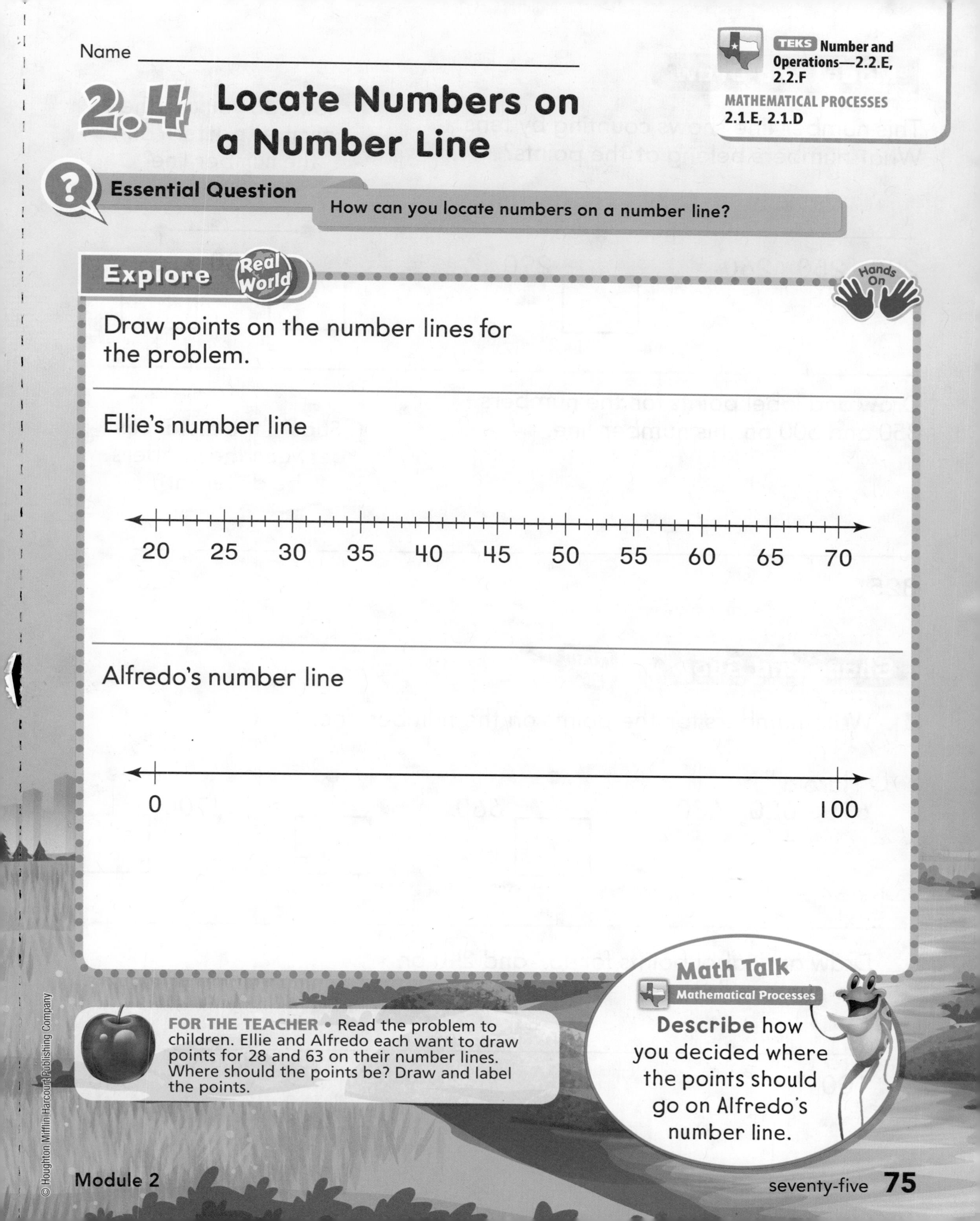

Name ______________________________

2.4 Locate Numbers on a Number Line

Essential Question How can you locate numbers on a number line?

Explore Real World

Hands On

Draw points on the number lines for the problem.

Ellie's number line

Alfredo's number line

FOR THE TEACHER • Read the problem to children. Ellie and Alfredo each want to draw points for 28 and 63 on their number lines. Where should the points be? Draw and label the points.

Math Talk Mathematical Processes

Describe how you decided where the points should go on Alfredo's number line.

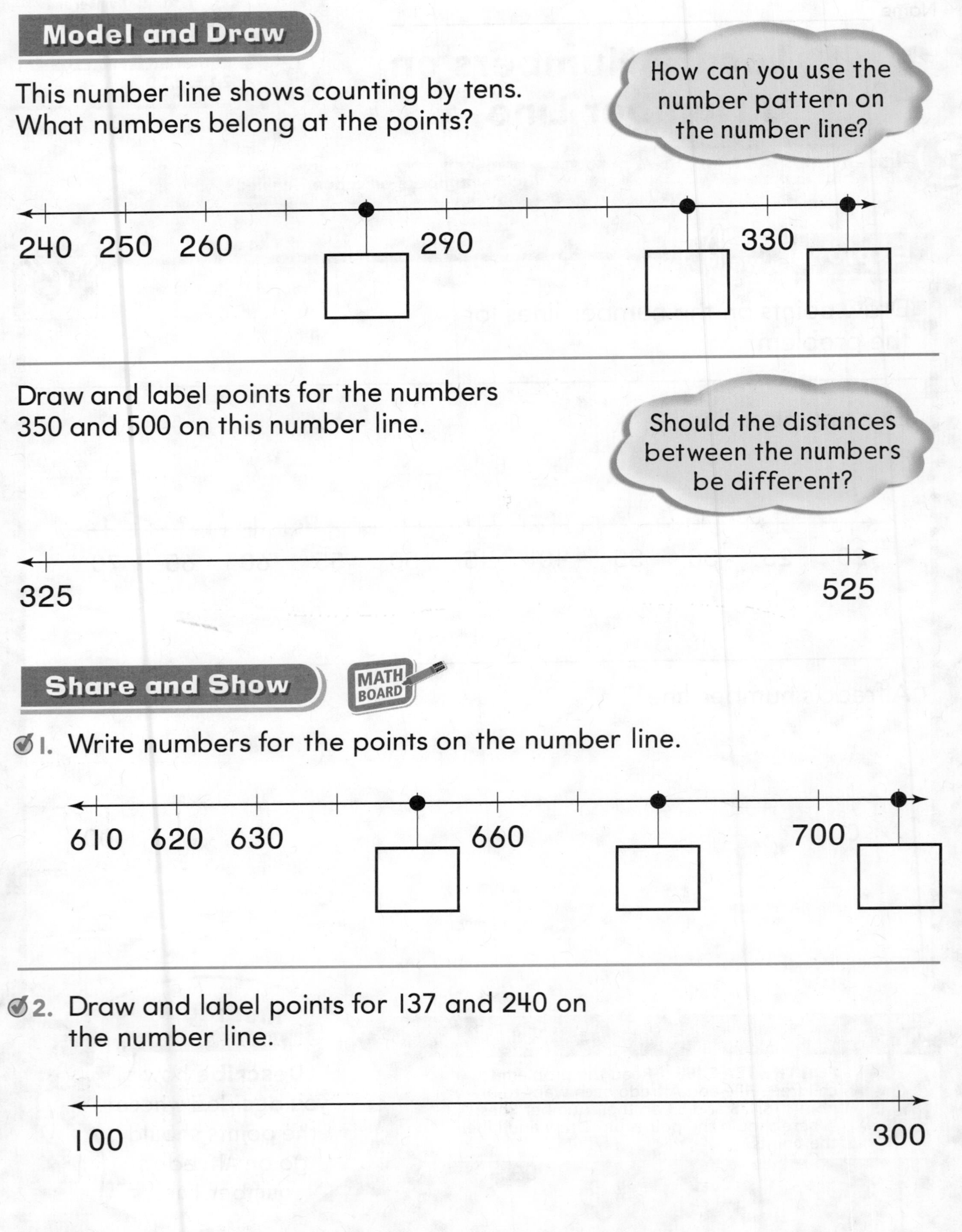

Model and Draw

This number line shows counting by tens. What numbers belong at the points?

How can you use the number pattern on the number line?

240 250 260 ☐ 290 ☐ 330 ☐

Draw and label points for the numbers 350 and 500 on this number line.

Should the distances between the numbers be different?

325 525

Share and Show

MATH BOARD

1. Write numbers for the points on the number line.

610 620 630 ☐ 660 ☐ 700 ☐

2. Draw and label points for 137 and 240 on the number line.

100 300

Name ______________________________

Problem Solving

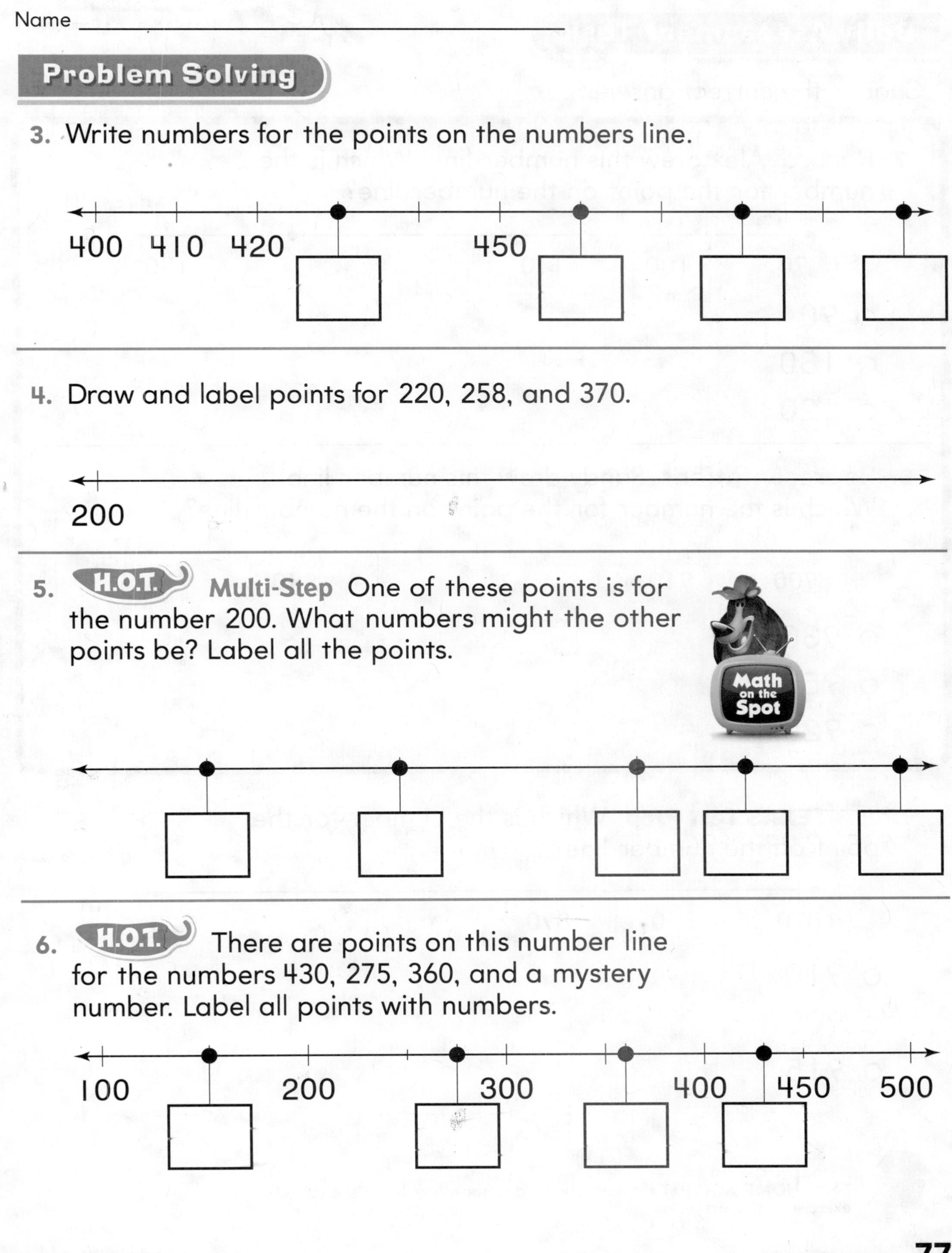

3. Write numbers for the points on the numbers line.

4. Draw and label points for 220, 258, and 370.

5. H.O.T. **Multi-Step** One of these points is for the number 200. What numbers might the other points be? Label all the points.

6. H.O.T. There are points on this number line for the numbers 430, 275, 360, and a mystery number. Label all points with numbers.

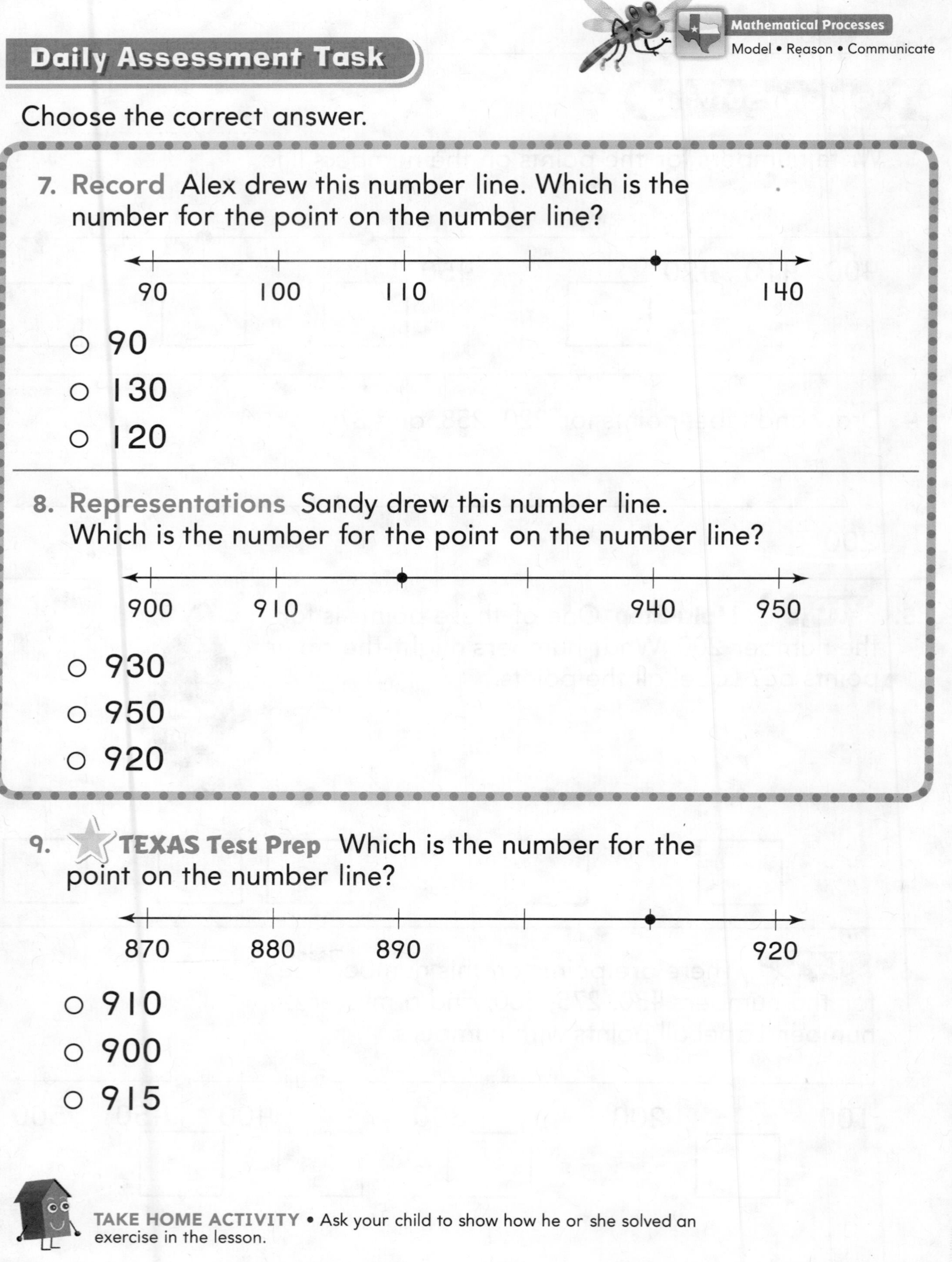

Mathematical Processes

Model • Reason • Communicate

Daily Assessment Task

Choose the correct answer.

7. **Record** Alex drew this number line. Which is the number for the point on the number line?

○ 90

○ 130

○ 120

8. **Representations** Sandy drew this number line. Which is the number for the point on the number line?

○ 930

○ 950

○ 920

9. **TEXAS Test Prep** Which is the number for the point on the number line?

○ 910

○ 900

○ 915

TAKE HOME ACTIVITY • Ask your child to show how he or she solved an exercise in the lesson.

Homework and Practice

TEKS Number and Operations—2.2.E, 2.2.F
MATHEMATICAL PROCESSES 2.1.D, 2.1.E

Name ____________________

2.4 Locate Numbers on a Number Line

1. Write numbers for the points on the number line.

200 210 220 230 [ ] 250 [ ] [ ] [ ]

2. Draw and label points for 310, 348, and 420.

300 430

Problem Solving

Solve.

3. **Multi-Step** There are points on this number line for the numbers 525, 560, and a mystery number. Label all points with numbers.

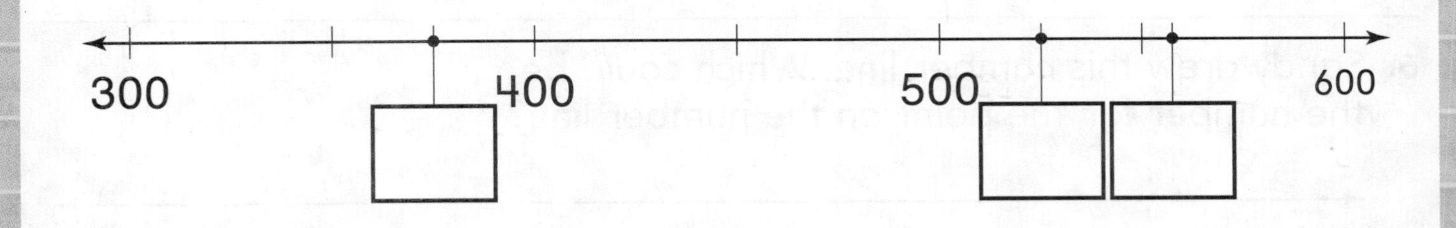

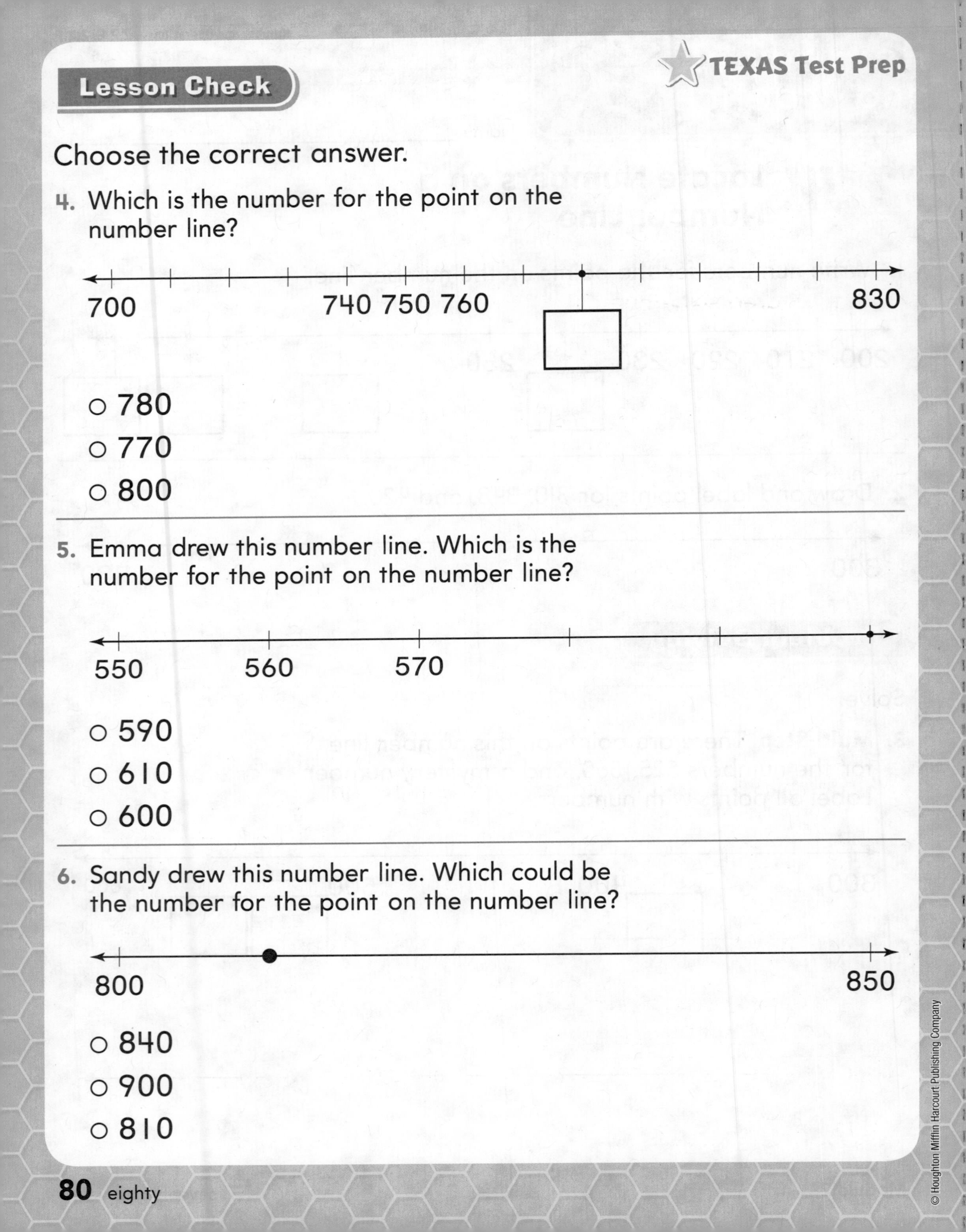

Lesson Check

TEXAS Test Prep

Choose the correct answer.

4. Which is the number for the point on the number line?

○ 780
○ 770
○ 800

5. Emma drew this number line. Which is the number for the point on the number line?

○ 590
○ 610
○ 600

6. Sandy drew this number line. Which could be the number for the point on the number line?

○ 840
○ 900
○ 810

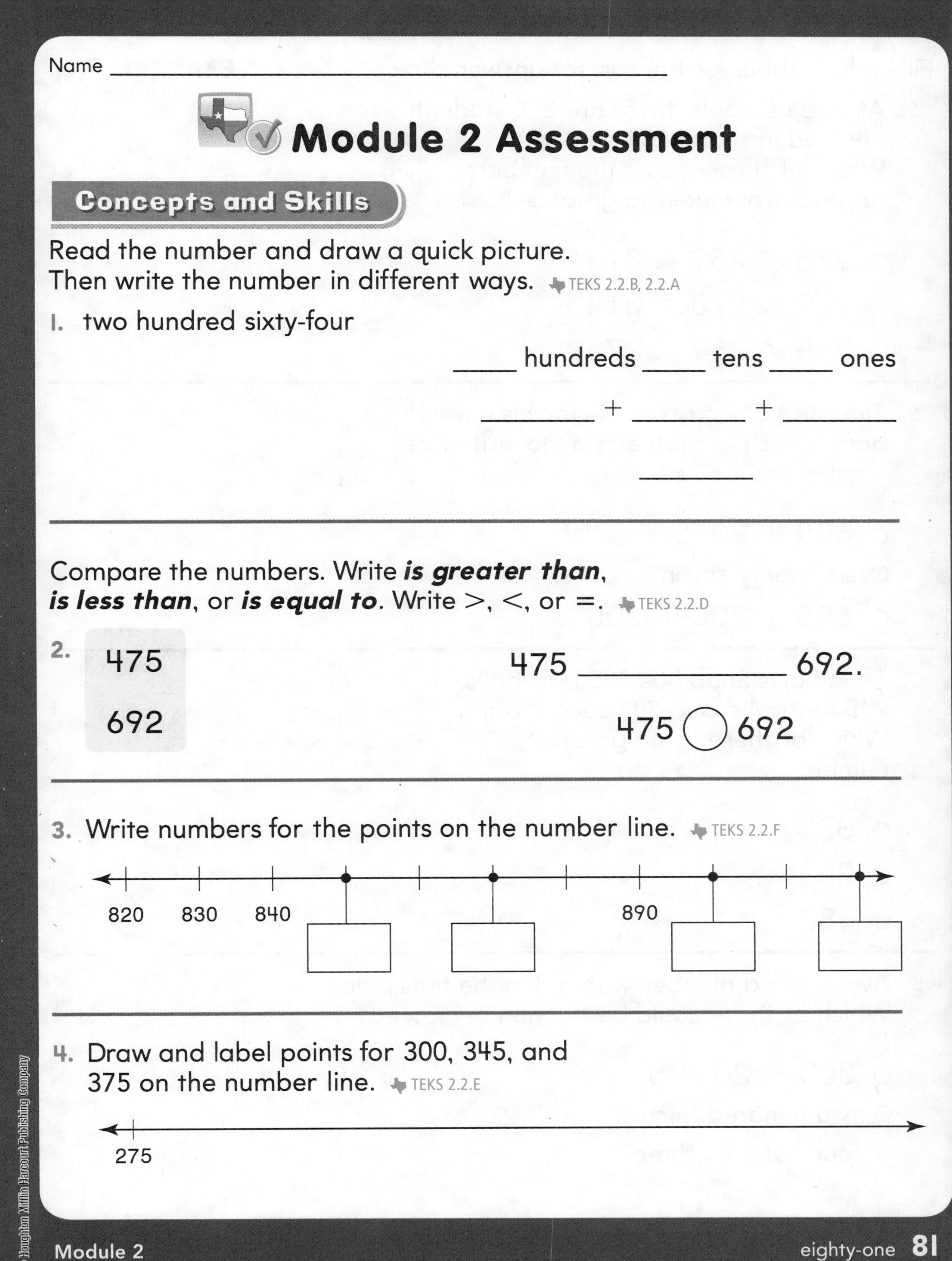
Name ______________________________

Module 2 Assessment

Concepts and Skills

Read the number and draw a quick picture.
Then write the number in different ways. TEKS 2.2.B, 2.2.A

1. two hundred sixty-four

____ hundreds ____ tens ____ ones

________ + ________ + ________

____

Compare the numbers. Write ***is greater than***, ***is less than***, or ***is equal to***. Write >, <, or =. TEKS 2.2.D

2. 475

692

475 ____________ 692.

475 ◯ 692

3. Write numbers for the points on the number line. TEKS 2.2.F

4. Draw and label points for 300, 345, and 375 on the number line. TEKS 2.2.E

Fill in the bubble for the correct answer choice.

5. At three schools, there are 278 students, 314 students, and 259 students. Which of these shows the numbers ordered from least to greatest? TEKS 2.2.D

- ○ $278 < 259 < 314$
- ○ $259 < 278 < 314$
- ○ $314 < 259 < 278$

---

6. Jim used 627 craft sticks for his model boat. Which is another way to write this number? TEKS 2.2.B

- ○ $600 + 20 + 7$
- ○ six twenty-seven
- ○ $600 + 200 + 700$

---

7. The Sports Shop has 325 baseballs, 245 footballs, and 387 soccer balls. Which of these is the greatest number? TEKS 2.2.D

- ○ 325
- ○ 245
- ○ 387

---

8. Ava wrote a number with a 3 in the tens place. Which of these could be the number? TEKS 2.2.B

- ○ $300 + 20 + 5$
- ○ two hundred thirty
- ○ four hundred three

Name ______________________

TEKS Number and Operations—2.2.A
MATHEMATICAL PROCESSES 2.1.D, 2.1.E, 2.1.G

3.1 HANDS ON

Model 4-Digit Numbers

Essential Question How can you show and write 4-digit numbers?

Explore Real World

Hands On

Use blocks. Draw to show your models.
Write the numbers.

Aaron

______

Tasha

______

FOR THE TEACHER • Read the following problem. Aaron models a number with 4 hundreds, 3 tens, and 7 ones. Tasha models a different number that uses the same three digits.

Math Talk Mathematical Processes

What is the value of the digit 4 in each number you wrote? **Explain.**

Model and Draw

There are 10 hundreds in 1 **thousand**.

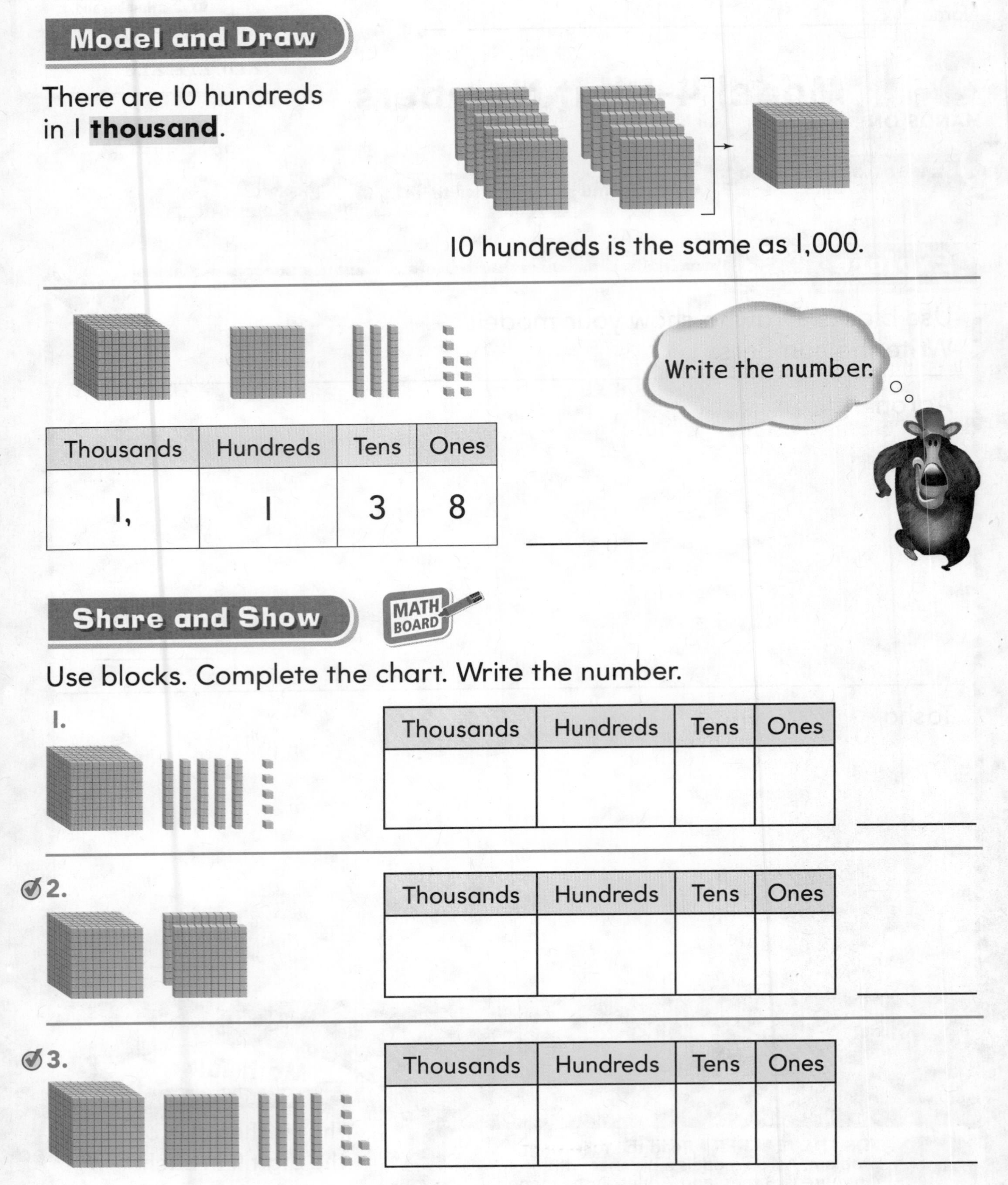

10 hundreds is the same as 1,000.

Thousands	Hundreds	Tens	Ones
1,	1	3	8

______

Share and Show

Use blocks. Complete the chart. Write the number.

1.

Thousands	Hundreds	Tens	Ones

______

2.

Thousands	Hundreds	Tens	Ones

______

3.

Thousands	Hundreds	Tens	Ones

______

Name ______________________________

Problem Solving

Use blocks. Complete the chart. Write the number.

4.

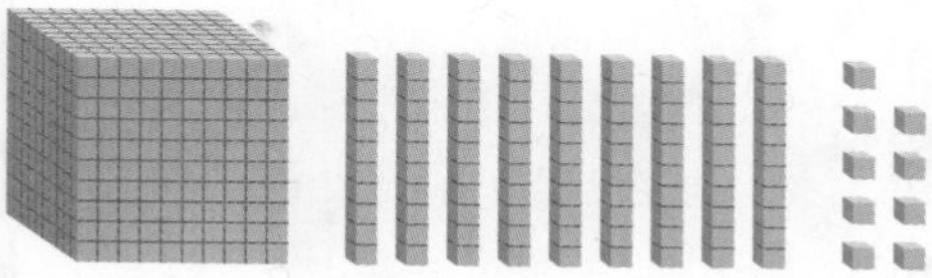

Thousands	Hundreds	Tens	Ones

______

5.

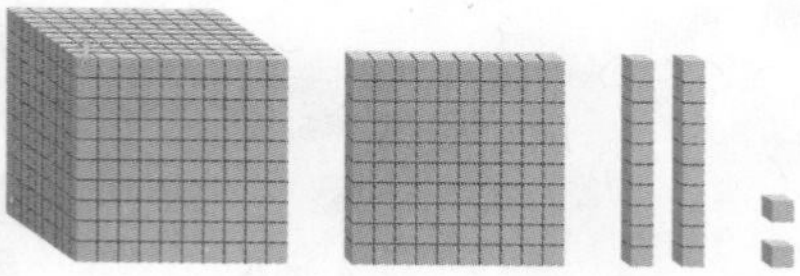

Thousands	Hundreds	Tens	Ones

______

Write a number to match the clues. Use blocks if you need to.

6. H.O.T. My 4-digit number has fewer than 2 thousands. It has no hundreds, tens, or ones. What is my number?

______

7. H.O.T. **Multi-Step** My number has 1 hundred and 1 thousand. It has double the number of tens as ones. What could my number be?

______

8. H.O.T. Cathy wants to model the number 1,100 using only hundreds blocks. How many does she need?

______ hundreds blocks

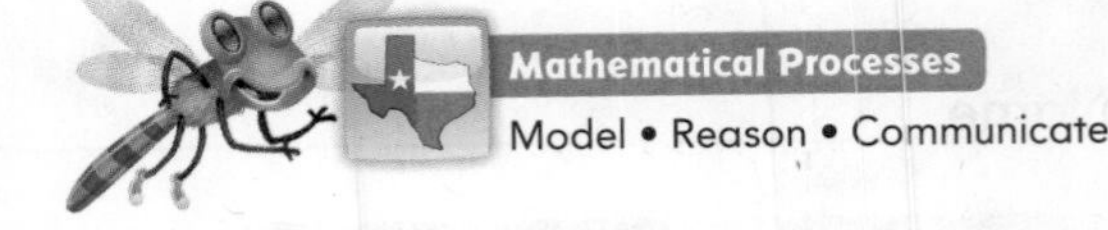

Daily Assessment Task

Choose the correct answer.

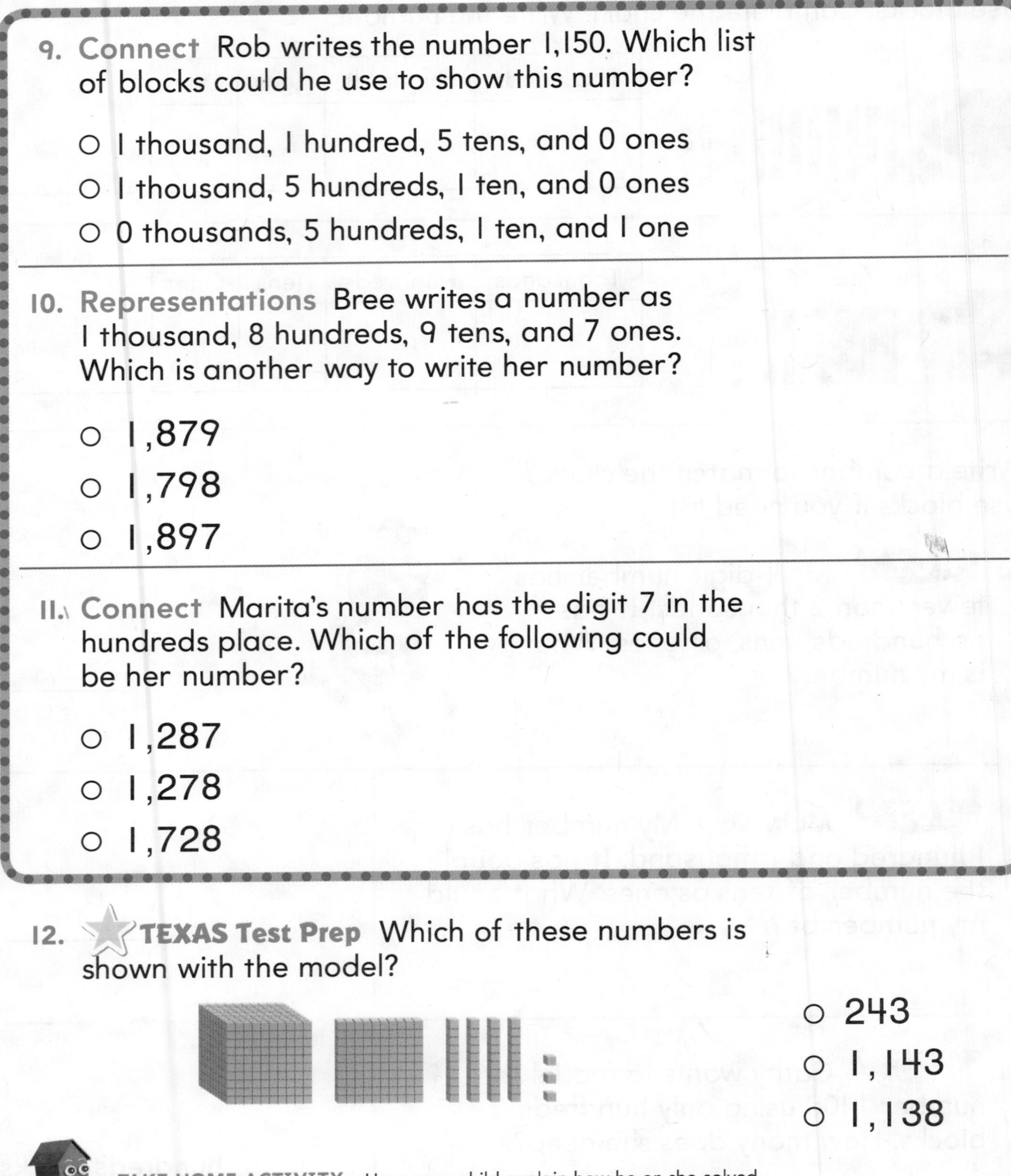

9. **Connect** Rob writes the number 1,150. Which list of blocks could he use to show this number?

○ 1 thousand, 1 hundred, 5 tens, and 0 ones
○ 1 thousand, 5 hundreds, 1 ten, and 0 ones
○ 0 thousands, 5 hundreds, 1 ten, and 1 one

10. **Representations** Bree writes a number as 1 thousand, 8 hundreds, 9 tens, and 7 ones. Which is another way to write her number?

○ 1,879
○ 1,798
○ 1,897

11. **Connect** Marita's number has the digit 7 in the hundreds place. Which of the following could be her number?

○ 1,287
○ 1,278
○ 1,728

12. **TEXAS Test Prep** Which of these numbers is shown with the model?

○ 243
○ 1,143
○ 1,138

TAKE HOME ACTIVITY • Have your child explain how he or she solved one of the exercises in this lesson.

Name ______________________________

3.2 Different Forms of 4-Digit Numbers

TEKS Number and Operations—2.2.B
MATHEMATICAL PROCESSES 2.1.D, 2.1.E

Essential Question What are three ways to write a 4-digit number?

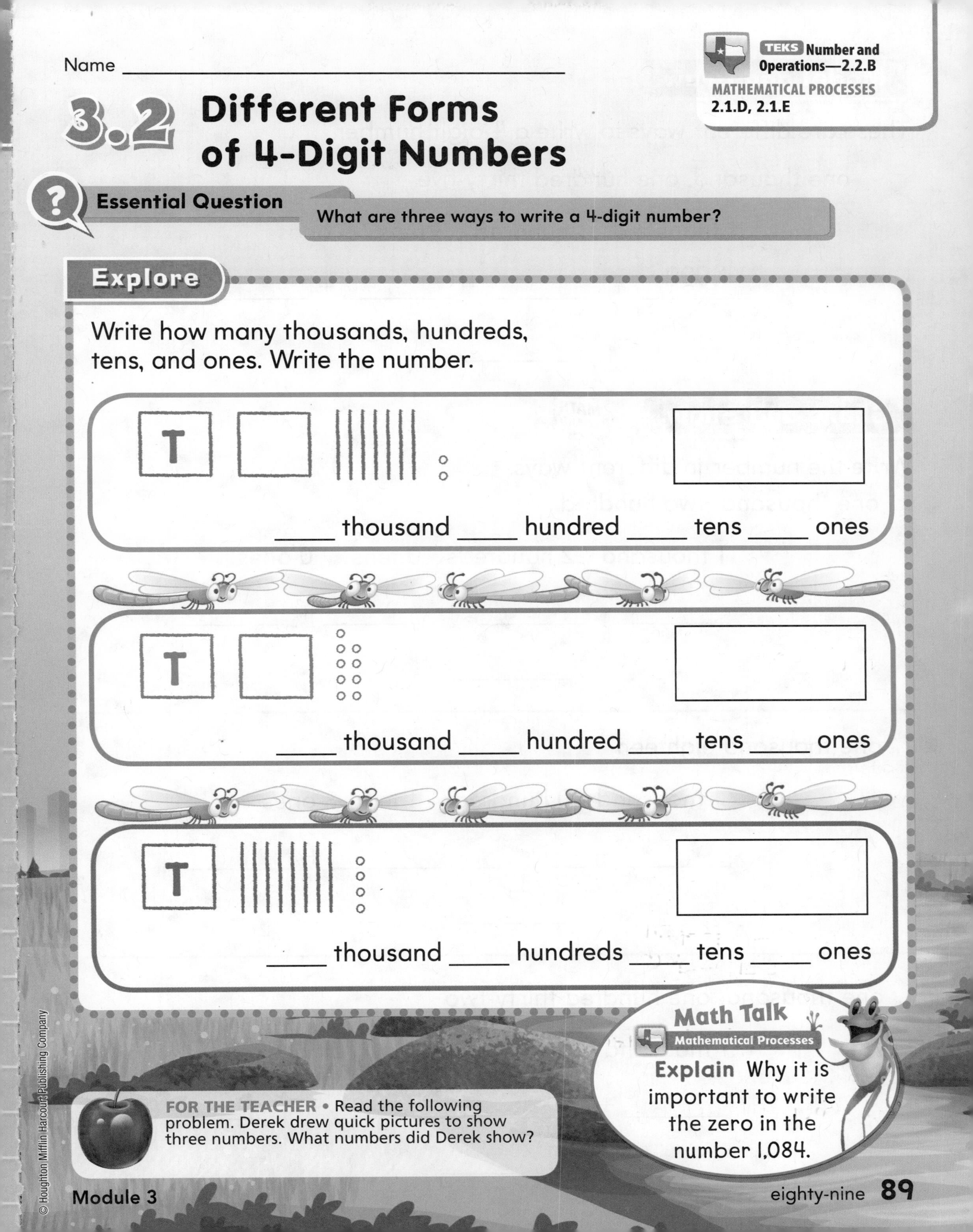

Explore

Write how many thousands, hundreds, tens, and ones. Write the number.

____ thousand ____ hundred ____ tens ____ ones

____ thousand ____ hundred ____ tens ____ ones

____ thousand ____ hundreds ____ tens ____ ones

Math Talk Mathematical Processes

Explain Why it is important to write the zero in the number 1,084.

FOR THE TEACHER • Read the following problem. Derek drew quick pictures to show three numbers. What numbers did Derek show?

Model and Draw

These are different ways to write a 4-digit number.

one thousand, one hundred thirty-five

I thousand   I hundred   3 tens   5 ones

1,000 + ______ + ______ + ______

______

Share and Show

MATH BOARD

Write the number in different ways.

1. one thousand, two hundred

I thousand   2 hundreds   0 tens   0 ones

______ + ______ + ______ + ______

______

2. one thousand eighteen

I thousand   0 hundreds   I ten   8 ones

______ + ______ + ______ + ______

______

3. one thousand, one hundred thirty-two

I thousand   I hundred   3 tens   2 ones

______ + ______ + ______ + ______

______

Name ____________________

Problem Solving

Write the number in different ways.

4. one thousand, one hundred seventy

I thousand I hundred 7 tens 0 ones

______ + ______ + ______ + ______

______

5. one thousand, one hundred eight

I thousand I hundred 0 tens 8 ones

______ + ______ + ______ + ______

______

6. H.O.T. Terry wrote to show a number. Draw quick pictures to show Terry's number. Write the number.

Math on the Spot

100 + 9 + 1,000 + 50

______

7. H.O.T. **Multi-Step** Manny writes a 4-digit number.

- The number has I thousand.
- The hundreds digit is less than the thousands digit.
- The sum of the tens and ones digits is I0.

What number could Manny write? ______

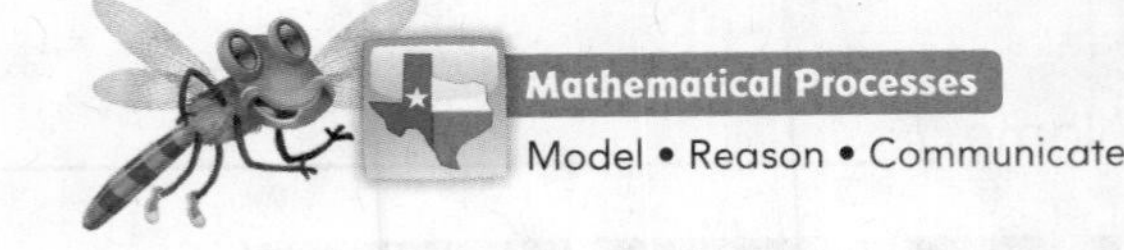

Daily Assessment Task

Choose the correct answer.

8. **Representations** Kimmie writes this number. Which is another way to write this number?

I thousand, I hundred, 3 tens, and 2 ones

○ 1,122
○ 232
○ 1,132

---

9. **Multi-Step** Byron writes this number. Which is another way to write the number?

one thousand, forty-two

○ 1,000 + 40 + 2
○ 1,000 + 400 + 20
○ 100 + 40 + 2

10. **TEXAS Test Prep** At the Holland Corn Festival, 1,150 ears of corn were cooked for the corn eating contest. Which is another way to write 1,150?

○ 1,000 + 100 + 50
○ 100 + 100 + 50
○ 1,000 + 10 + 5

TAKE HOME ACTIVITY • Have your child explain how he or she solved one of the exercises in this lesson.

TEKS Number and Operations—2.2.B
MATHEMATICAL PROCESSES 2.1.D, 2.1.E

Name ____________________

3.2 Different Forms of 4-Digit Numbers

Write the number in different ways.

1. one thousand, seventy-three

   1 thousand 0 hundreds 7 tens 3 ones

   ______ + ______ + ______ + ______

   ______

2. one thousand, one hundred, sixty-eight

   1 thousand 1 hundred 6 tens 8 ones

   ______ + ______ + ______ + ______

   ______

Problem Solving

Solve.

3. Wendy wrote to show a number. Draw quick pictures to show Wendy's number. Write the number.

   100 + 4 + 1,000 + 30

   ______

Lesson Check

TEXAS Test Prep

Choose the correct answer.

4. Bart wrote to show a number. Which is another way to write Bart's number?

   I thousand, 0 hundreds, 8 tens, and I one

   ○ 181
   ○ 811
   ○ 1,081

---

5. Lee Ann wrote to show a number. Which is another way Lee Ann could write the number?

   one thousand, fifty-six

   ○ $1,000 + 50 + 6$
   ○ $1,000 + 500 + 6$
   ○ $100 + 50 + 6$

---

6. Sam is making a quick picture for 1,159. He draws 9 ones, 5 tens, and I thousand. How many hundreds will he draw?

   ○ 1
   ○ 17
   ○ 7

Name ______________________________

TEKS Number and Operations—2.2.A

MATHEMATICAL PROCESSES 2.1.C, 2.1.D, 2.1.E

3.3 HANDS ON Build Numbers in Different Ways

Essential Question How can you show 4-digit numbers in different ways?

Explore Real World

Hands On

Draw quick pictures to solve. Write how many hundreds, tens, and ones.

________ hundreds ________ tens ________ ones

________ hundreds ________ tens ________ ones

FOR THE TEACHER • Read this problem to children. Mrs. Walters wants to buy exactly 275 oranges for a community project. She can buy oranges in boxes of 100, bags of 10, and as single oranges. What are two different ways she can buy the oranges?

Math Talk Mathematical Processes

Describe another way to show the number.

Model and Draw

Here are two different ways that show the same number.

_____ thousands + _____ hundreds + _____ tens + _____ ones

_____ thousands + _____ hundreds + _____ tens + _____ ones

The number is ____________.

Share and Show

MATH BOARD

Use blocks to show the same number a different way. Draw a quick picture of your model. Write the numbers.

1.

_____ thousands + _____ hundreds + _____ tens + _____ ones

_____ thousands + _____ hundreds + _____ tens + _____ ones

The number is ____________.

2.

_____ thousands + _____ hundreds + _____ tens + _____ ones

_____ thousands + _____ hundreds + _____ tens + _____ ones

The number is ____________.

Name ______________________________

Problem Solving

Use blocks to show the same number in two other ways.
Draw quick pictures. Write the number.

3.

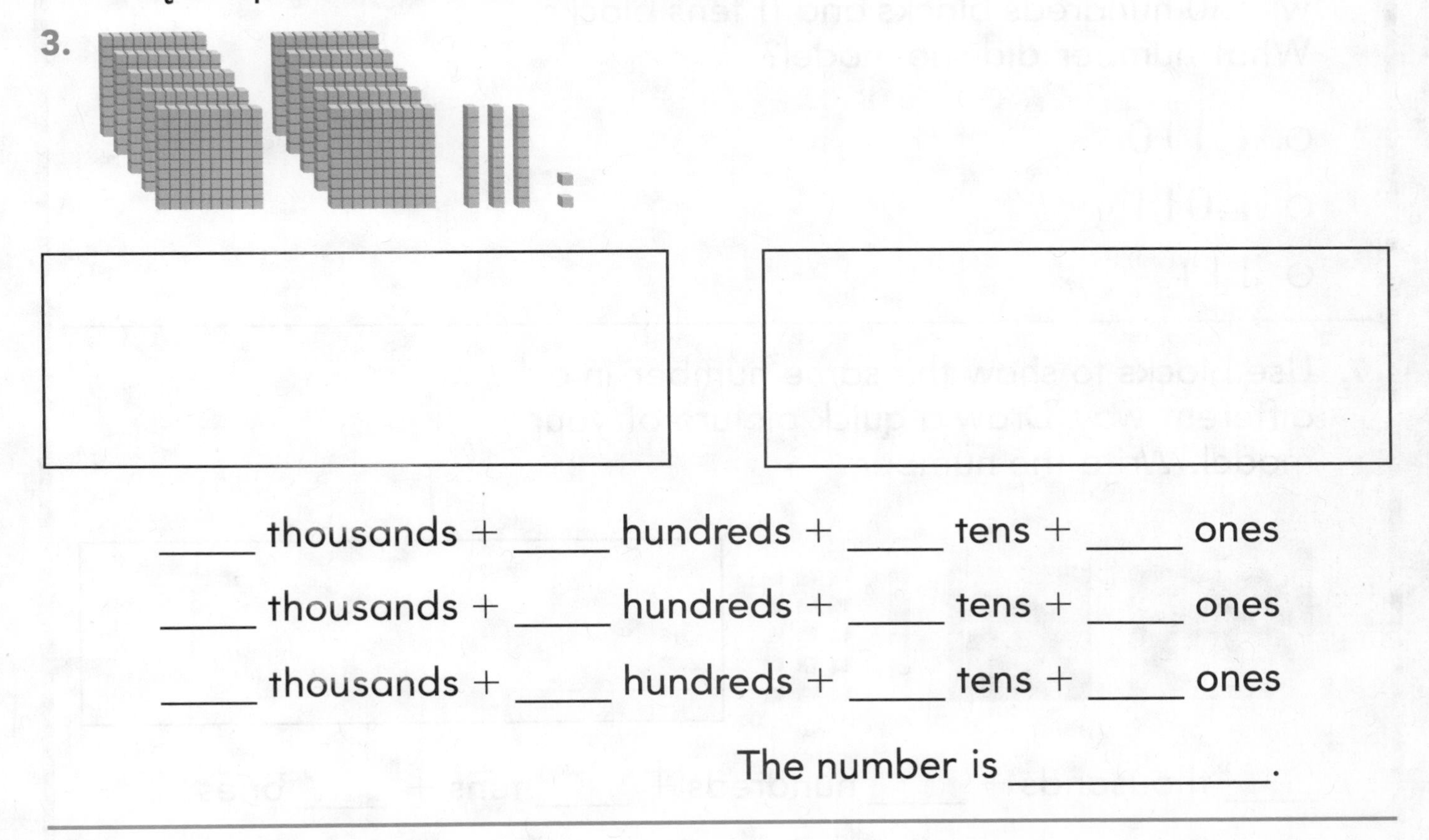

____ thousands + ____ hundreds + ____ tens + ____ ones

____ thousands + ____ hundreds + ____ tens + ____ ones

____ thousands + ____ hundreds + ____ tens + ____ ones

The number is ____________.

Solve. Write or draw to explain.

4. H.O.T. I have 10 hundreds blocks, 10 tens blocks, and 10 ones blocks. I use all my blocks to make a number. What is my number?

____

5. H.O.T. **Multi-Step** I have 9 hundreds blocks, 3 tens blocks, and 4 ones blocks. I get 5 more tens blocks and 2 more hundreds blocks. I use all my blocks to make a number. What is my number?

____

Choose the correct answer.

6. **Representations** Wendy modeled a number with 10 hundreds blocks and 11 tens blocks. What number did she model?

- ○ 1,110
- ○ 1,011
- ○ 111

---

7. Use blocks to show the same number in a different way. Draw a quick picture of your model. Write the number.

____ thousands + ____ hundreds + ____ tens + ____ ones

____ thousands + ____ hundreds + ____ tens + ____ ones

The number is __________.

8. **TEXAS Test Prep** Which shows the same number?

- ○ 1,063
- ○ 1,163
- ○ 1,073

TAKE HOME ACTIVITY • Have your child explain how he or she solved one of the exercises in this lesson.

Name ______________________________

TEKS Number and Operations—2.2.D
MATHEMATICAL PROCESSES 2.1.D, 2.1.F

3.4 Compare and Order Numbers

ALGEBRA

Essential Question How can you compare and order numbers up to 1,200?

Explore Real World

Hands On

Draw quick pictures to model the problem.
Then solve.

Friday	Saturday	Sunday
______	______	______

The least number of people went to the fair on ______________.

The greatest number of people went to the fair on ______________.

FOR THE TEACHER • Read the problem. On Friday, 823 people went to the fair. On Saturday, 831 people went to the fair. On Sunday, 649 people went to the fair. On which day were the least number of people at the fair? On which day were the greatest number of people at the fair?

Math Talk Mathematical Processes

Explain how you compared to find the least and greatest numbers.

Model and Draw

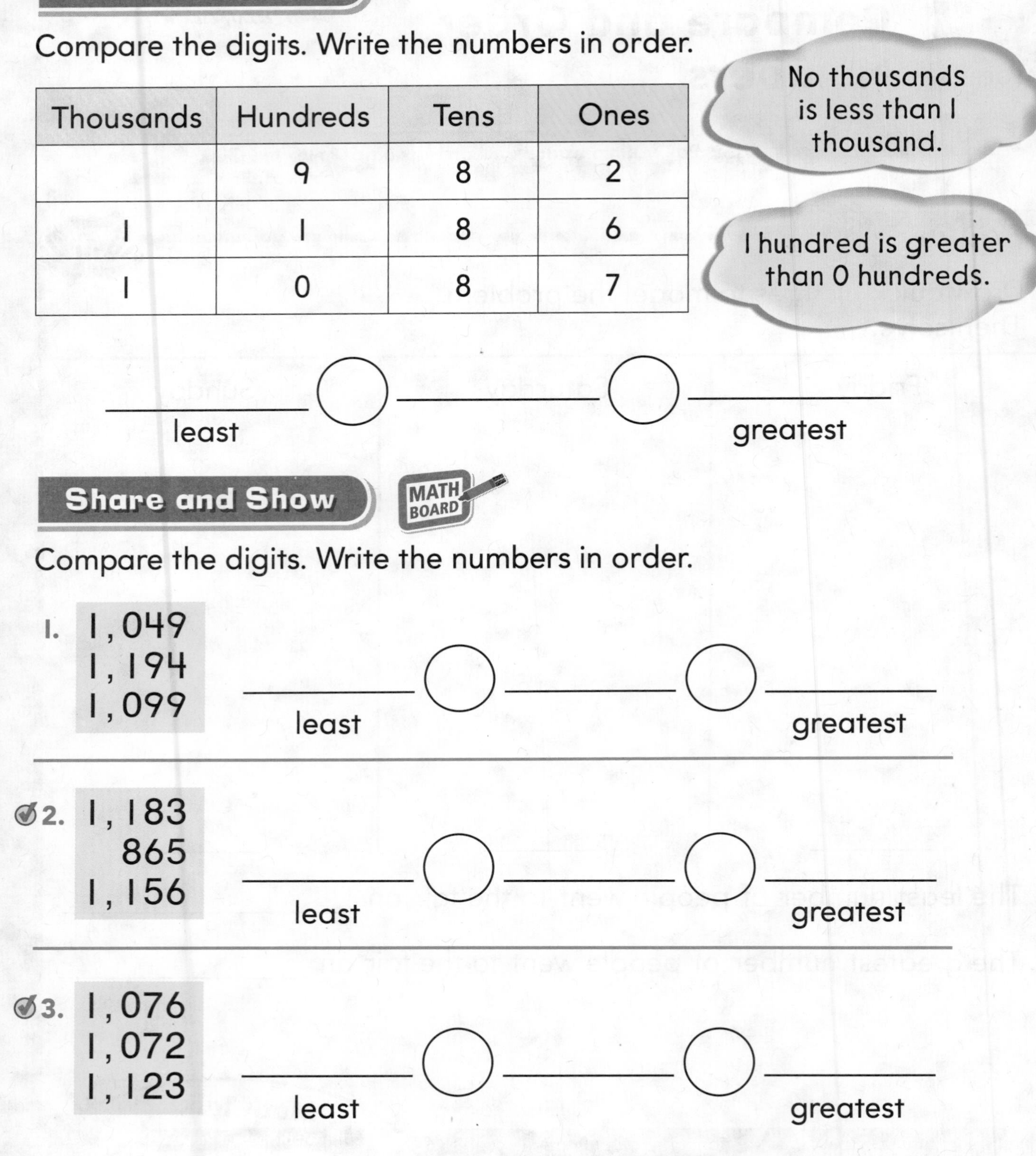

Compare the digits. Write the numbers in order.

Thousands	Hundreds	Tens	Ones
	9	8	2
1	1	8	6
1	0	8	7

_______ ◯ _______ ◯ _______
least   greatest

Share and Show

Compare the digits. Write the numbers in order.

1. 1,049 1,194 1,099

_______ ◯ _______ ◯ _______
least   greatest

2. 1,183 865 1,156

_______ ◯ _______ ◯ _______
least   greatest

3. 1,076 1,072 1,123

_______ ◯ _______ ◯ _______
least   greatest

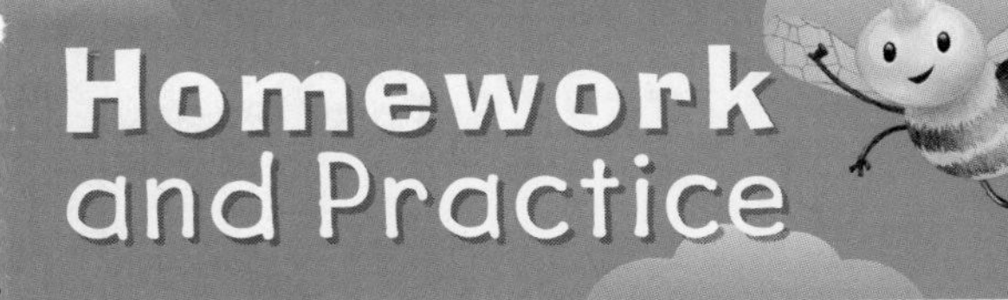

TEKS Number and Operations—2.2.D
MATHEMATICAL PROCESSES 2.1.D, 2.1.F

Name ______________________

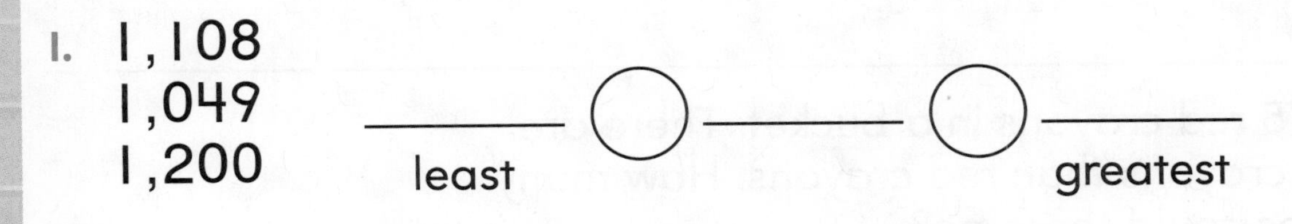

Compare and Order Numbers

Compare the digits. Write the numbers in order.

1. 1,108
   1,049
   1,200

   ________ ◯ ________ ◯ ________
   least   greatest

Use the numbers in the box to complete the sentences.

960
1,186
1,074

2. 1,061 is less than ________.

3. 1,000 is greater than ________.

4. ________ is greater than 1,000.

Problem Solving

Solve the problem.

5. **Multi-Step** The number of stickers Robert has is less than 1,145 but greater than 1,100.

   How many stickers might he have? ________

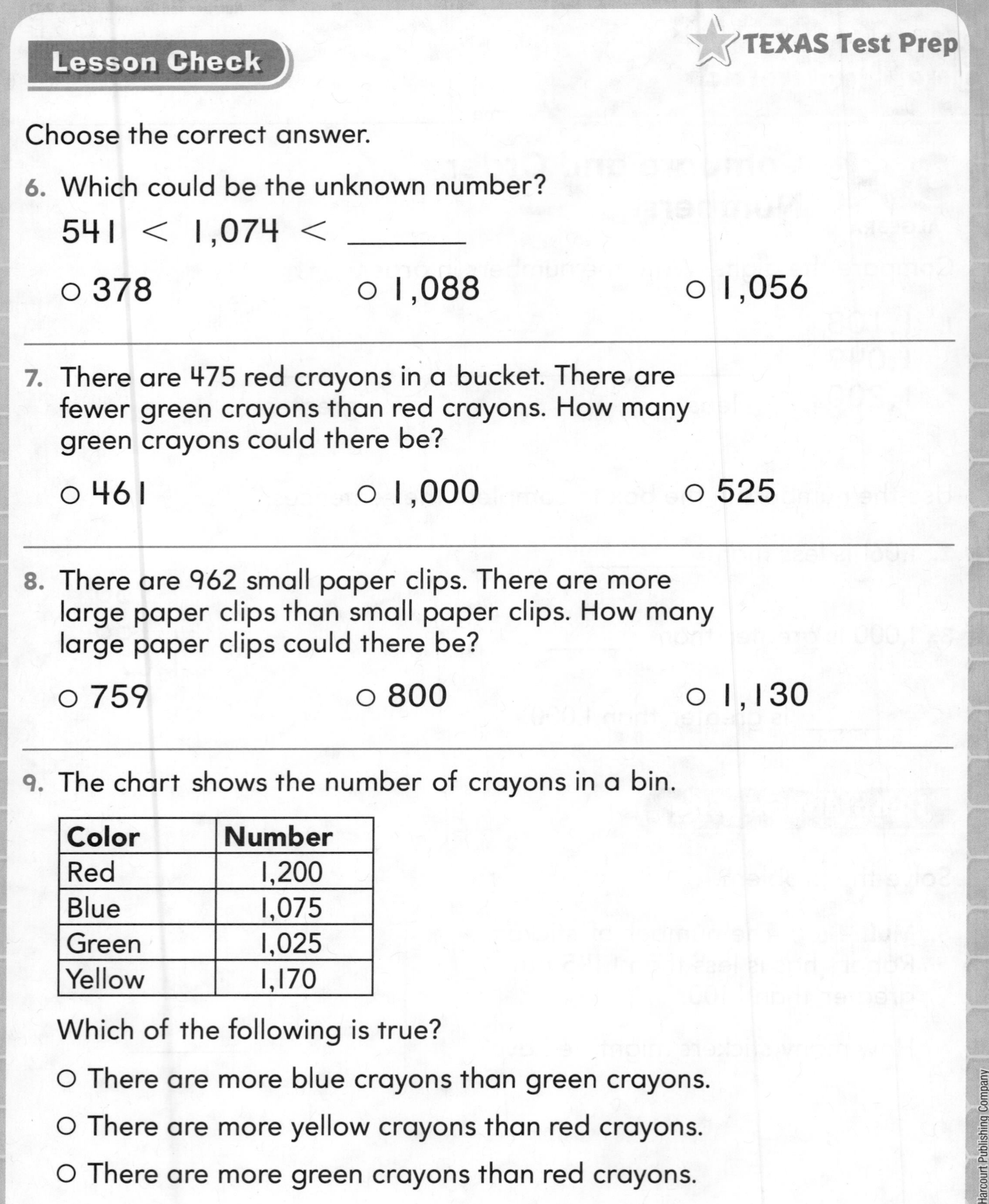

Lesson Check

TEXAS Test Prep

Choose the correct answer.

6. Which could be the unknown number?

$541 < 1{,}074 <$ ______

○ 378 ○ 1,088 ○ 1,056

7. There are 475 red crayons in a bucket. There are fewer green crayons than red crayons. How many green crayons could there be?

○ 461 ○ 1,000 ○ 525

8. There are 962 small paper clips. There are more large paper clips than small paper clips. How many large paper clips could there be?

○ 759 ○ 800 ○ 1,130

9. The chart shows the number of crayons in a bin.

Color	Number
Red	1,200
Blue	1,075
Green	1,025
Yellow	1,170

Which of the following is true?

○ There are more blue crayons than green crayons.

○ There are more yellow crayons than red crayons.

○ There are more green crayons than red crayons.

Name ____________________

TEKS Number and Operations—2.2.C
Also 2.2.D

MATHEMATICAL PROCESSES
2.1.C, 2.1.E, 2.1.F

3.5 Use Place Value to Name Numbers

Essential Question How can you name a number that is greater than or less than a given number?

Explore Real World

Hands On

Write the numbers. Draw quick pictures to show the problem.

Evan's pennies ________

Gina's pennies ________

Evan's dimes ________

Gina's dimes ________

________ counts more pennies.

________ counts more dimes.

Math Talk Mathematical Processes
Which of the four numbers is greatest? **Explain.**

FOR THE TEACHER • Read the following problem. Evan and Gina count coins the class collected. Evan counts 758 pennies and 1,197 dimes. Gina counts 1,003 pennies and 1,194 dimes. Who counts more pennies? Who counts more dimes?

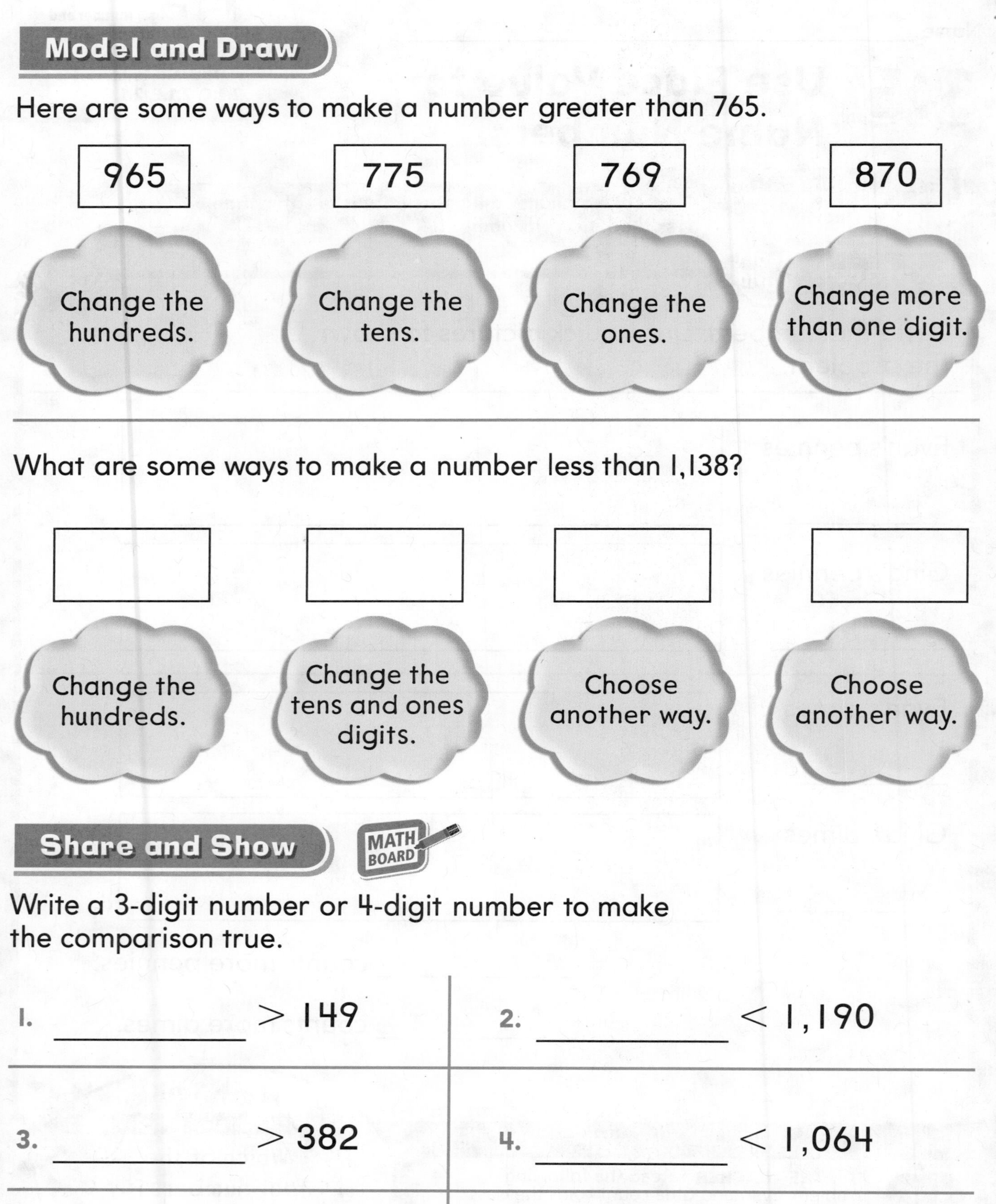

Model and Draw

Here are some ways to make a number greater than 765.

965	775	769	870
Change the hundreds.	Change the tens.	Change the ones.	Change more than one digit.

What are some ways to make a number less than 1,138?

Change the hundreds.	Change the tens and ones digits.	Choose another way.	Choose another way.

Share and Show

MATH BOARD

Write a 3-digit number or 4-digit number to make the comparison true.

1. ______ > 149

2. ______ $< 1,190$

3. ______ > 382

4. ______ $< 1,064$

5. ______ $< 1,111$

6. ______ > 575

Name ______________________

Problem Solving

Write a 3-digit number or 4-digit number to make the comparison true.

7. ____________ $<$ 1,183

8. ____________ $>$ 809

9. 1,065 $>$ ____________

10. 721 $<$ ____________

Solve. Write or draw to explain.

11. **H.O.T.** Kyla uses the digits 4, 0, 1, and 9 to make a number less than 1,158. What is a number Kyla could make?

____

12. **H.O.T.** There are 1,156 fiction books and 934 nonfiction books at the store. Are there more fiction books or more nonfiction books at the store?

more ________________ books

13. **H.O.T.** **Multi-Step** My book has fewer than 1,200 pages. It has more pages than Marco's book. Marco's book has more than 950 pages. How many pages could our books have?

________ ◯ ________

pages in Marco's book | pages in my book

Mathematical Processes

Model • Reason • Communicate

Daily Assessment Task

Choose the correct answer.

14. **Analyze** Zack has more than 900 seashells but fewer than 1,100 seashells. Which of the following could be the number of seashells he has?

○ 1,006

○ 899

○ 600

15. Mrs. Tyler has more than 1,005 beads. How many beads could she have?

○ 586

○ 1,010

○ 1,003

16. **Reasoning** Mrs. Simon has a greater number of red beads than green beads. She has 342 green beads. How many red beads could she have?

________ red beads

17. **TEXAS Test Prep** Which of the following numbers will make the comparison true?

________ > 1,128

○ 1,119

○ 921

○ 1,182

Name ______________________________

Module 3 Assessment

Vocabulary

Use a word from the box to complete the sentence.

hundred
ten
thousand

1. 10 hundreds is the same as 1 ______________. (p. 84)

Concepts and Skills

Complete the chart. Write the number. TEKS 2.2.A

2.

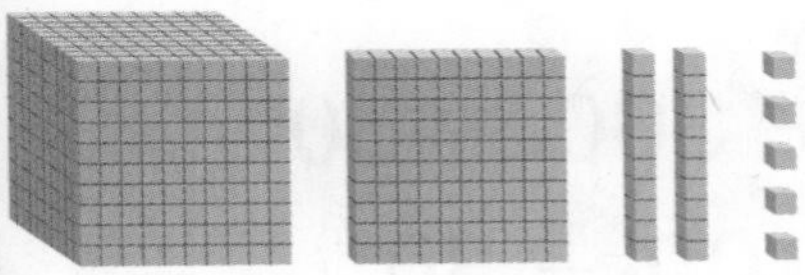

Thousands	Hundreds	Tens	Ones

____

3. Write a 4-digit number to make the comparison true. TEKS 2.2.C

__________ < 1,156

4. Use blocks to show the same number a different way. Draw a quick picture of your model. Write the number. TEKS 2.2.A

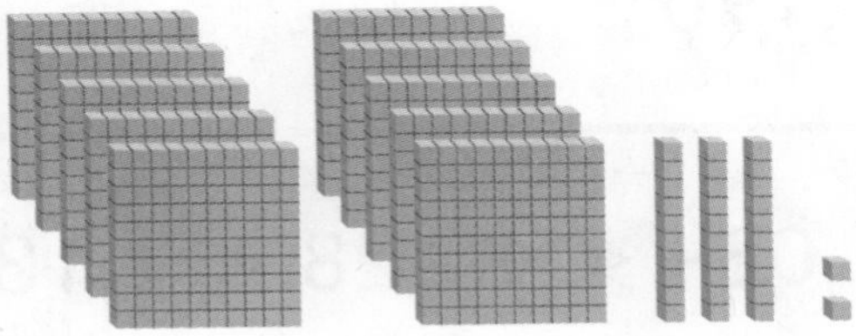

_____ thousands + _____ hundreds + _____ tens + _____ ones

_____ thousands + _____ hundreds + _____ tens + _____ ones

The number is ____________.

Fill in the bubble for the correct answer choice.

TEXAS Test Prep

5. The number of students in Lee's school is less than 1,164. Which could be the number of students in Lee's school? TEKS 2.2.D

   - ○ 1,164
   - ○ 1,181
   - ○ 995

6. Craig's class collects one thousand one hundred thirty nickels for a class project. Which is another way to write this number? TEKS 2.2.B

   - ○ 1,000 + 300 + 30
   - ○ 100 + 100 + 30
   - ○ 1,000 + 100 + 30

7. Pam thinks of a number. She writes the value of its digits. What is the number? TEKS 2.2.B

   1,000 + 100 + 90 + 9

   - ○ 1,099
   - ○ 1,199
   - ○ 1,190

8. Kevin wants to put the numbers 1,128, 1,084, and 1,134 in order from least to greatest. Which is true? TEKS 2.2.D

   - ○ 1,084 < 1,128 < 1,134
   - ○ 1,134 < 1,084 < 1,128
   - ○ 1,084 < 1,134 < 1,128

Name ______________________________

TEKS Number and Operations—2.3.A
MATHEMATICAL PROCESSES 2.1.F

4.1 Equal Parts

Essential Question What are halves, fourths, and eighths of a whole?

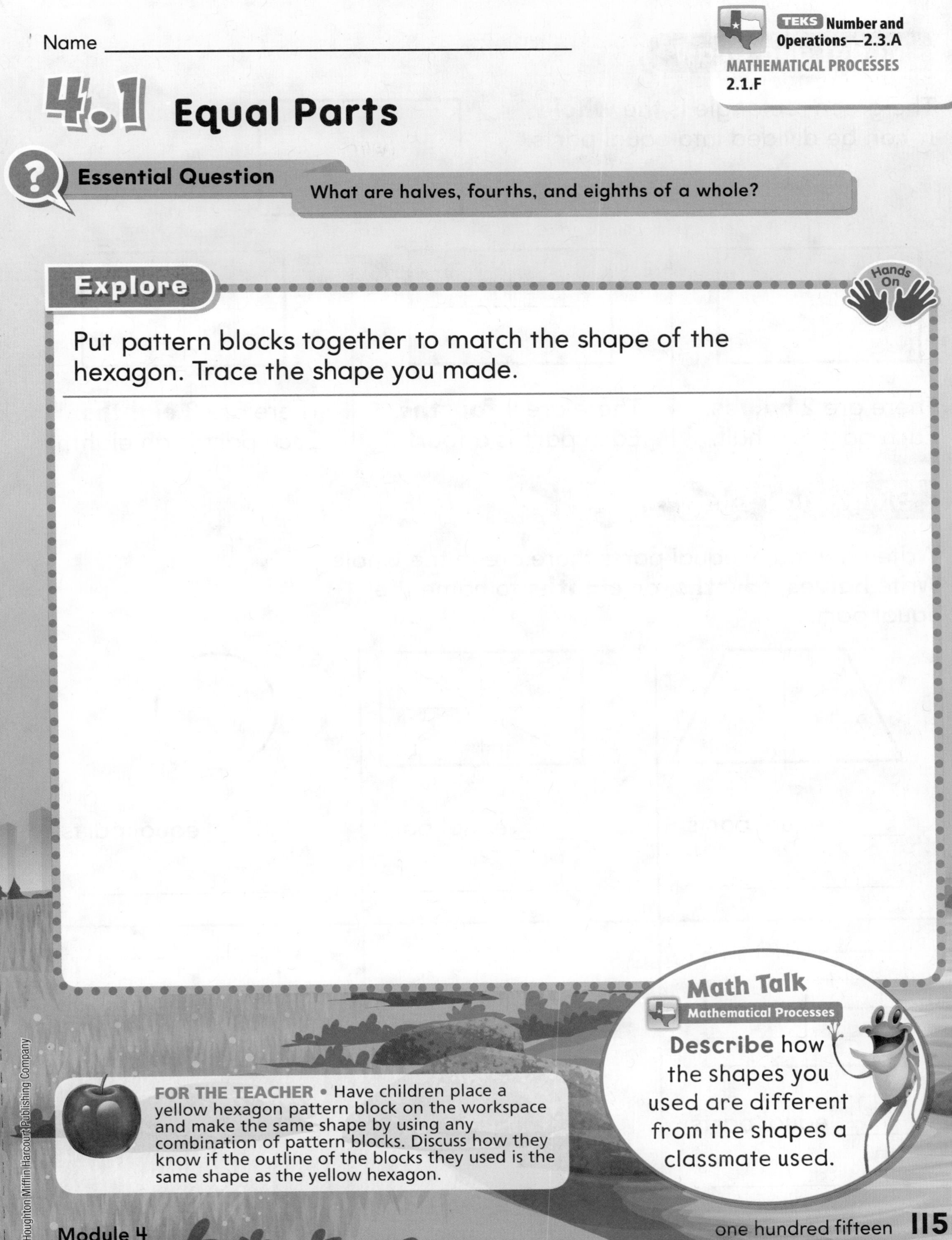

Explore

Put pattern blocks together to match the shape of the hexagon. Trace the shape you made.

Math Talk
Mathematical Processes

Describe how the shapes you used are different from the shapes a classmate used.

FOR THE TEACHER • Have children place a yellow hexagon pattern block on the workspace and make the same shape by using any combination of pattern blocks. Discuss how they know if the outline of the blocks they used is the same shape as the yellow hexagon.

Model and Draw

The green rectangle is the **whole**.
It can be divided into equal parts.

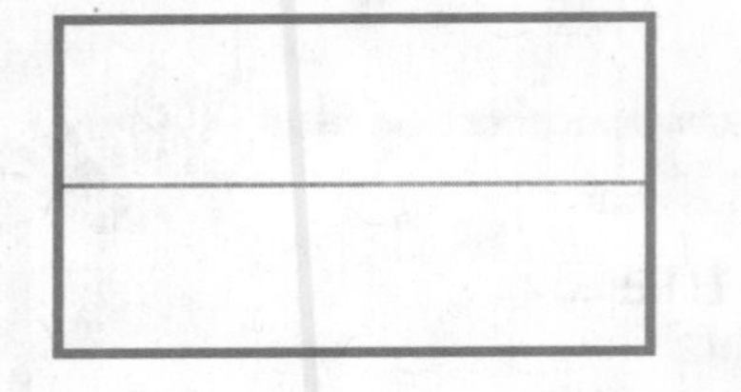

There are 2 **halves**.
Each part is a half.

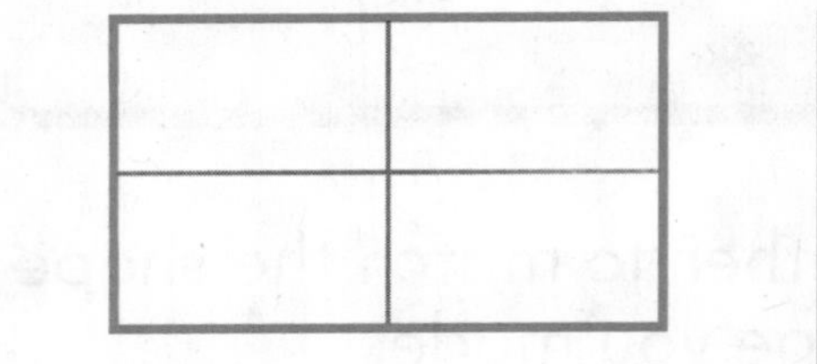

There are 4 **fourths**.
Each part is a fourth.

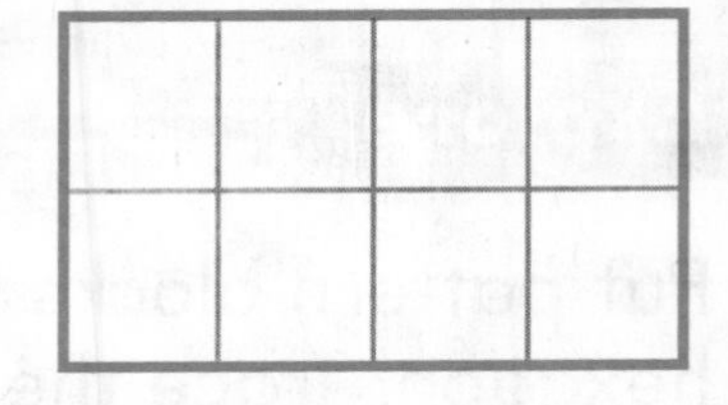

There are 8 **eighths**.
Each part is an eighth.

Share and Show

Write how many equal parts there are in the whole.
Write **halves**, **fourths**, or **eighths** to name the equal parts.

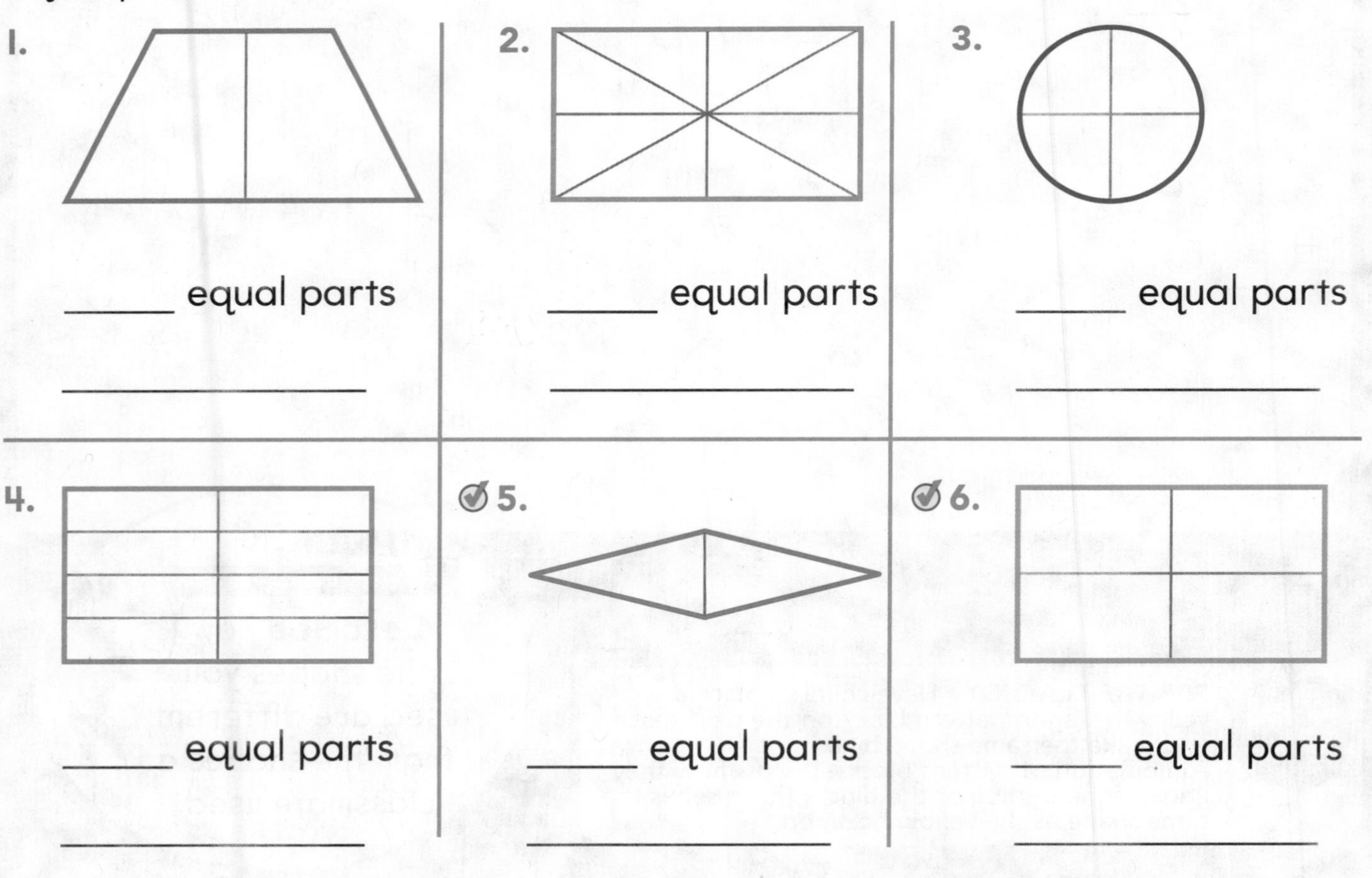

1. ______ equal parts

____

2. ______ equal parts

____

3. ______ equal parts

____

4. ______ equal parts

____

5. ______ equal parts

____

6. ______ equal parts

____

Name ______________________________

Problem Solving

Write how many equal parts there are in the whole. Write **halves**, **fourths**, or **eighths** to name the equal parts.

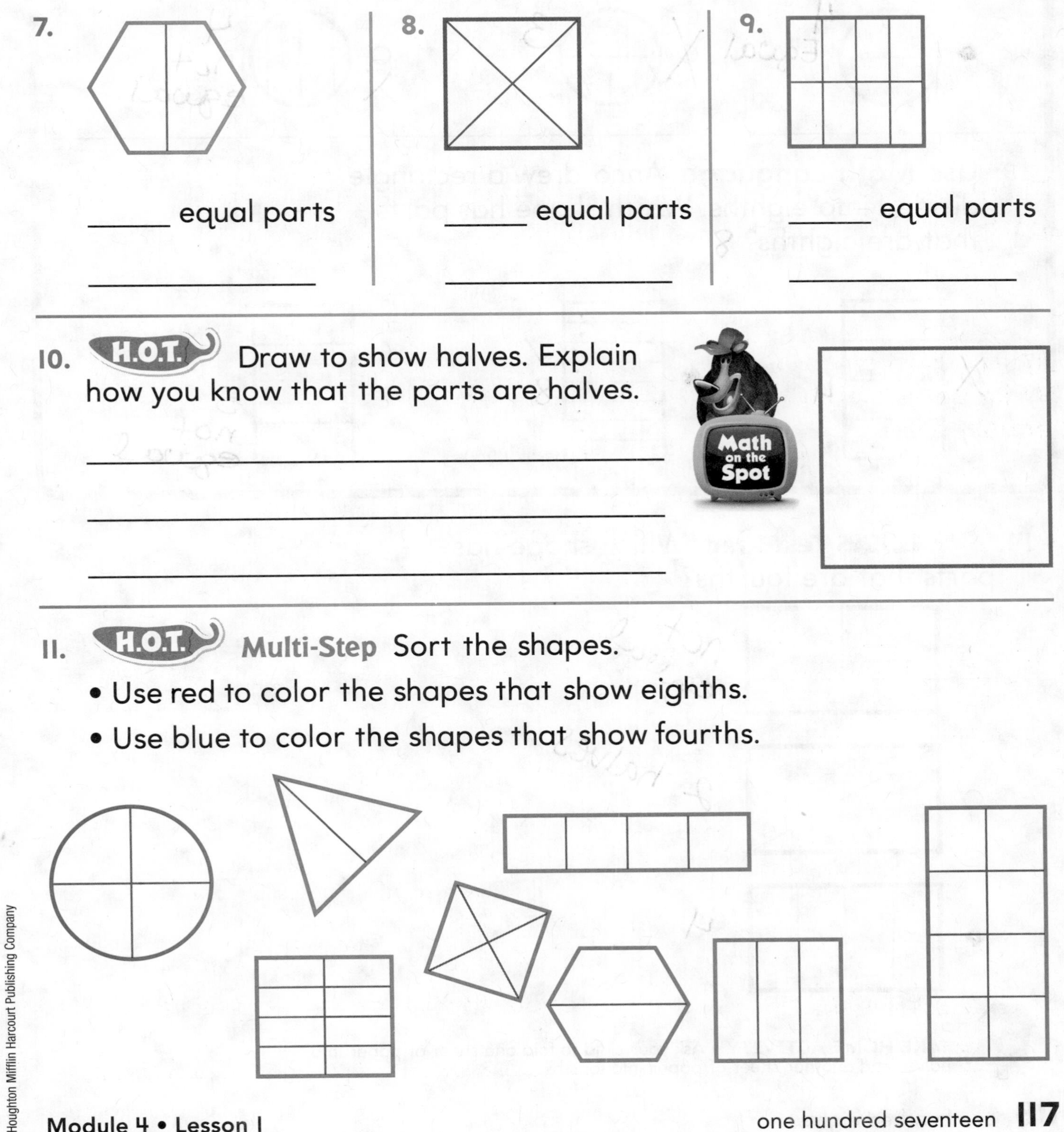

7. _____ equal parts

____

8. _____ equal parts

____

9. _____ equal parts

____

10. H.O.T. Draw to show halves. Explain how you know that the parts are halves.

____

____

____

11. H.O.T. **Multi-Step** Sort the shapes.

- Use red to color the shapes that show eighths.
- Use blue to color the shapes that show fourths.

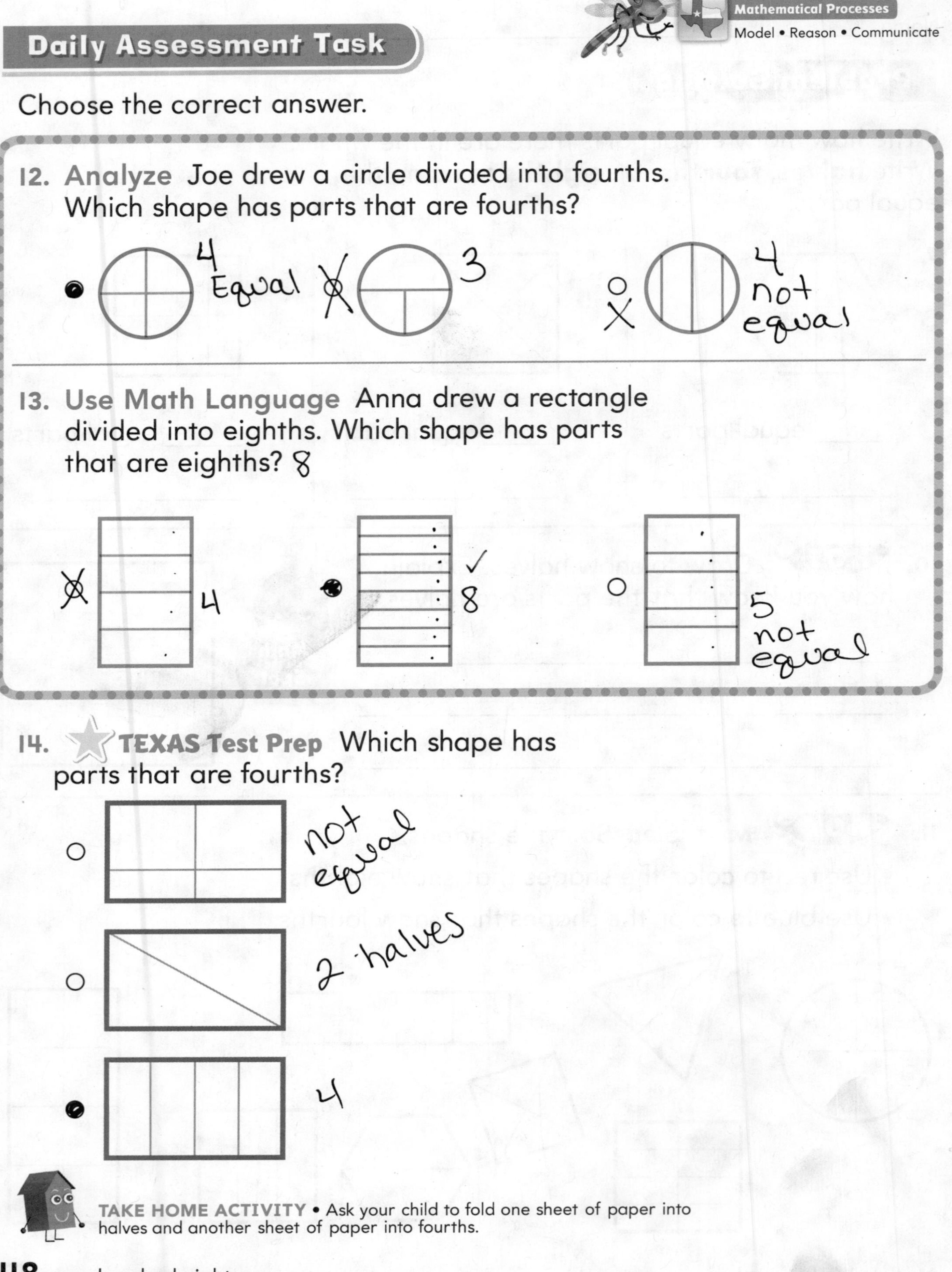

Daily Assessment Task

Mathematical Processes
Model • Reason • Communicate

Choose the correct answer.

12. **Analyze** Joe drew a circle divided into fourths. Which shape has parts that are fourths?

13. **Use Math Language** Anna drew a rectangle divided into eighths. Which shape has parts that are eighths?

14. **TEXAS Test Prep** Which shape has parts that are fourths?

TAKE HOME ACTIVITY • Ask your child to fold one sheet of paper into halves and another sheet of paper into fourths.

Name ______________________________

TEKS Number and Operations—2.3.A, 2.3.C, *Also* 2.3.D
MATHEMATICAL PROCESSES 2.1.E, 2.1.G

4.2 Show Equal Parts of a Whole

Essential Question

How do you know if a shape shows halves, fourths, or eighths?

Explore

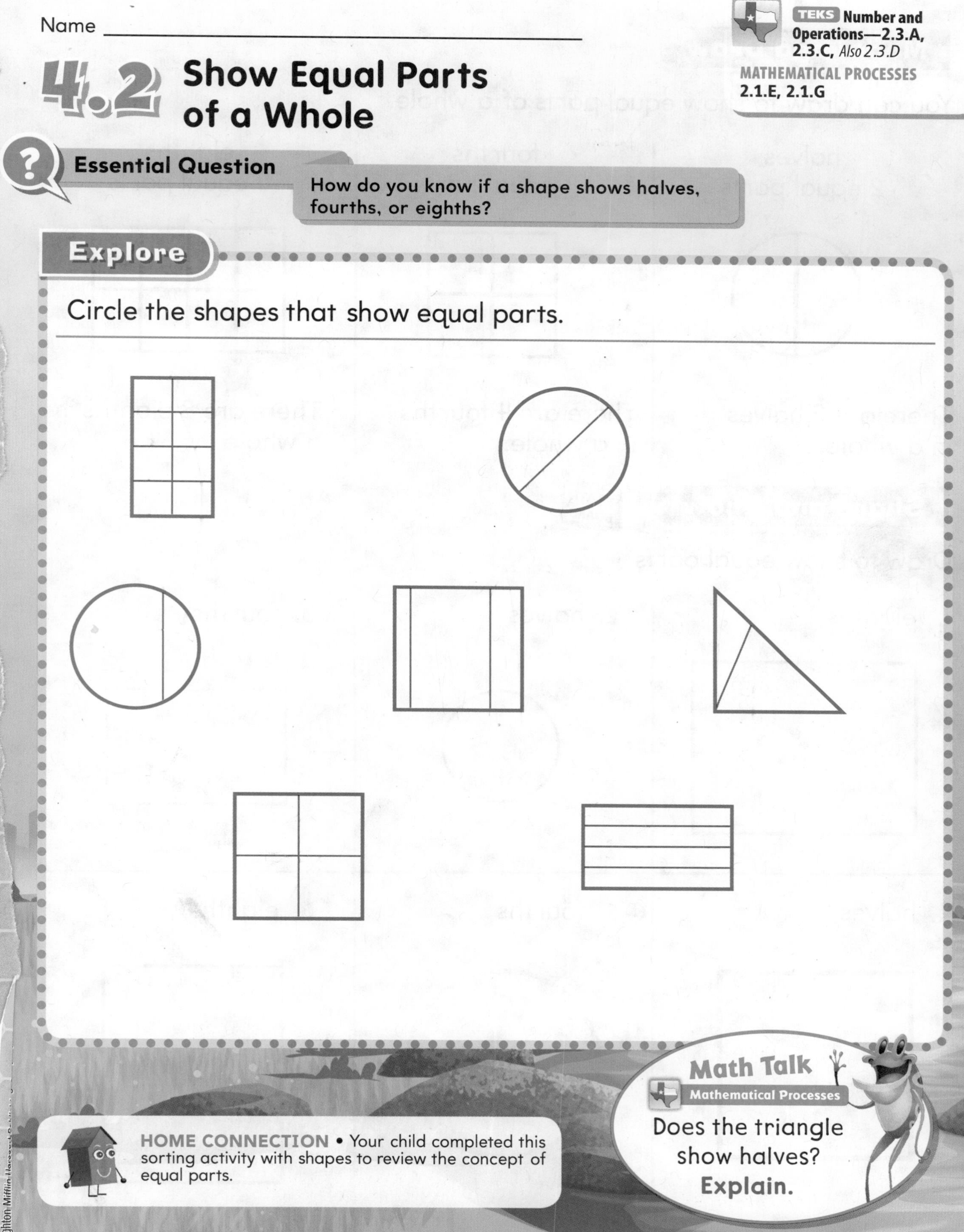

Circle the shapes that show equal parts.

HOME CONNECTION • Your child completed this sorting activity with shapes to review the concept of equal parts.

Math Talk
Mathematical Processes

Does the triangle show halves? **Explain.**

Model and Draw

You can draw to show equal parts of a whole.

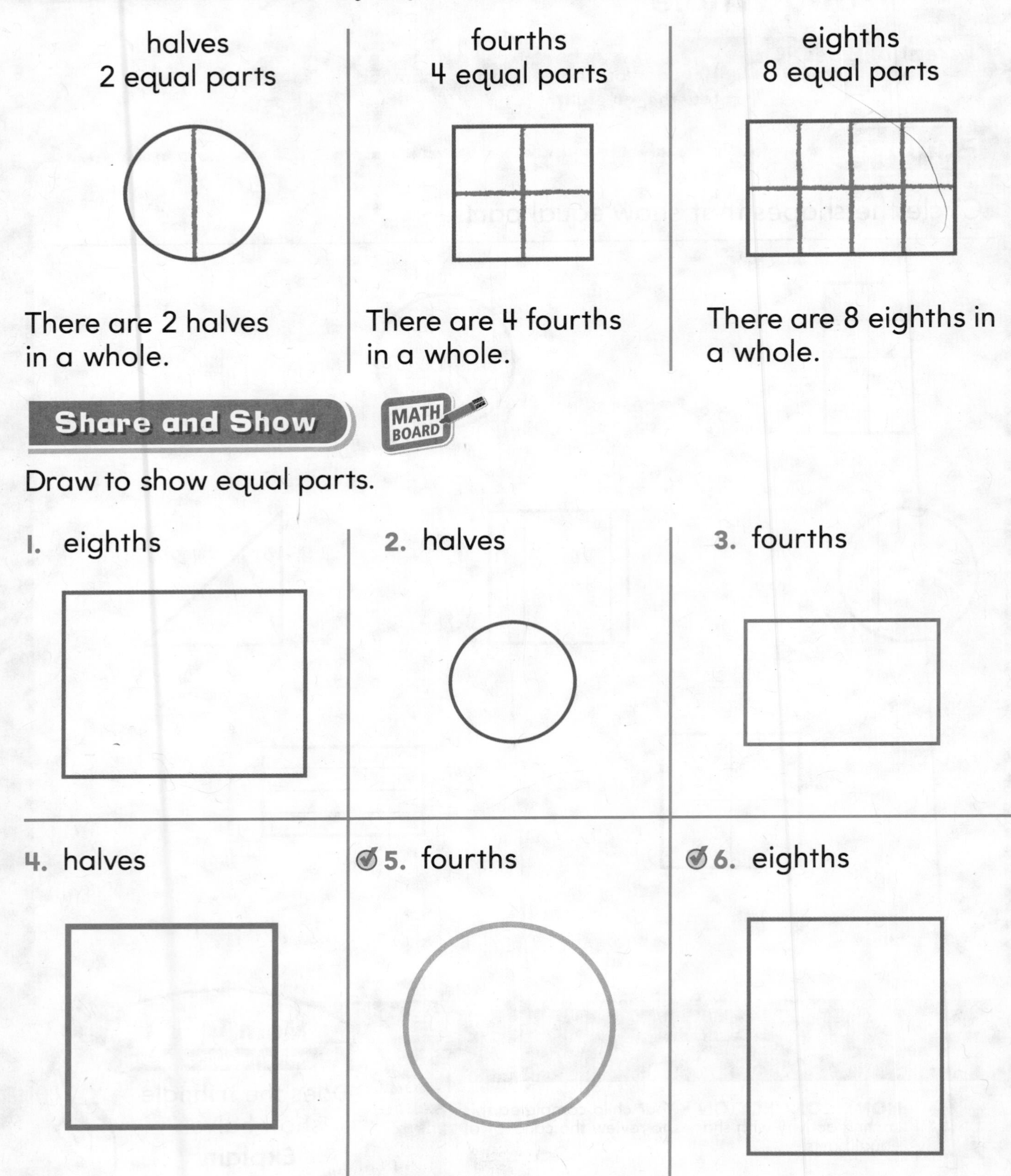

halves
2 equal parts

There are 2 halves in a whole.

fourths
4 equal parts

There are 4 fourths in a whole.

eighths
8 equal parts

There are 8 eighths in a whole.

Share and Show

MATH BOARD

Draw to show equal parts.

1. eighths

2. halves

3. fourths

4. halves

✓5. fourths

✓6. eighths

Name ___________________________________

TEKS Number and Operations—2.3.B
MATHEMATICAL PROCESSES
2.1.F

4.3 Describe Equal Parts

Essential Question How are equal parts different for same-size wholes when there are different numbers of parts?

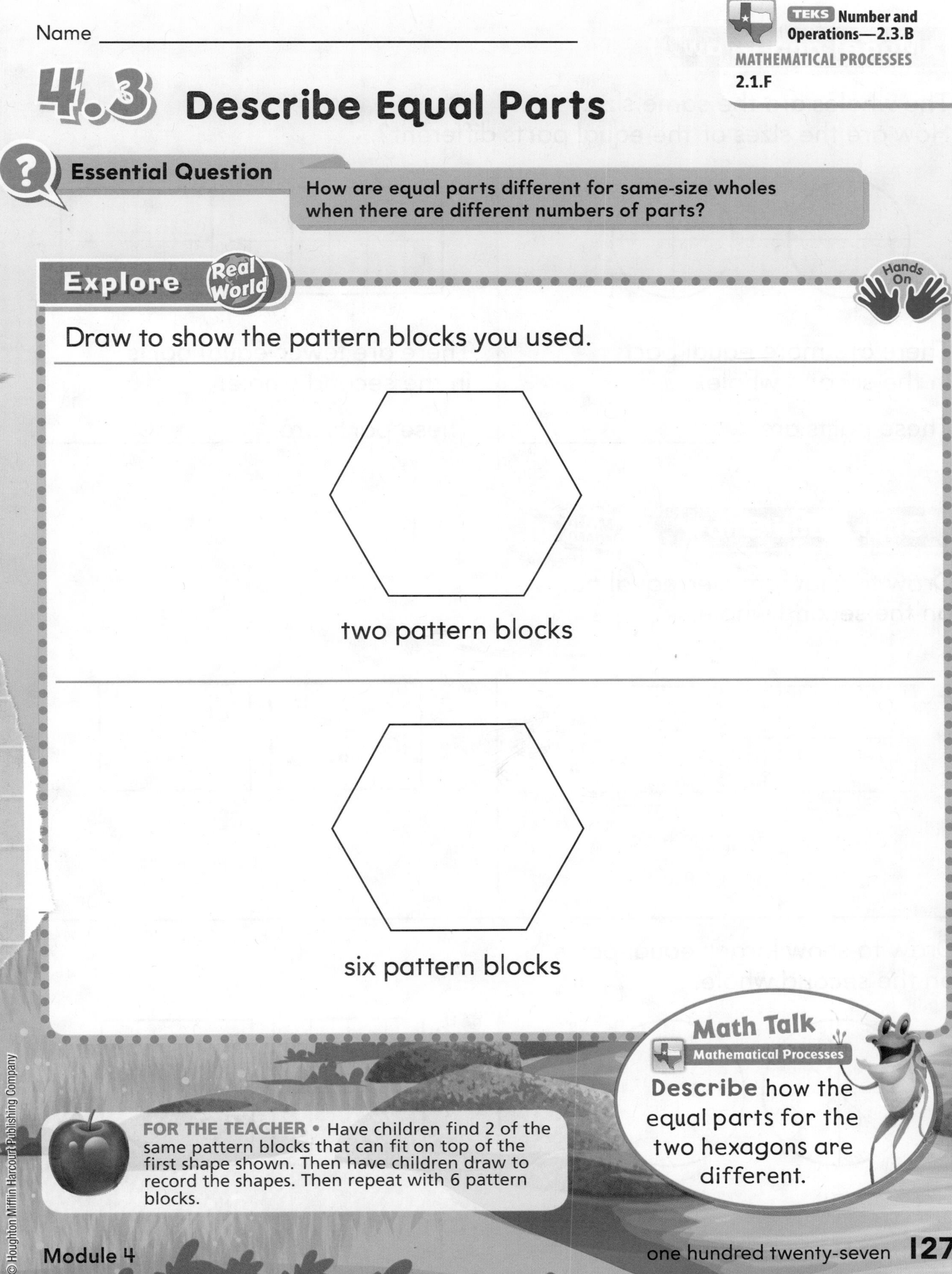

Explore Real World

Hands On

Draw to show the pattern blocks you used.

two pattern blocks

six pattern blocks

Math Talk Mathematical Processes

Describe how the equal parts for the two hexagons are different.

FOR THE TEACHER • Have children find 2 of the same pattern blocks that can fit on top of the first shape shown. Then have children draw to record the shapes. Then repeat with 6 pattern blocks.

Model and Draw

The wholes are the same size.
How are the sizes of the equal parts different?

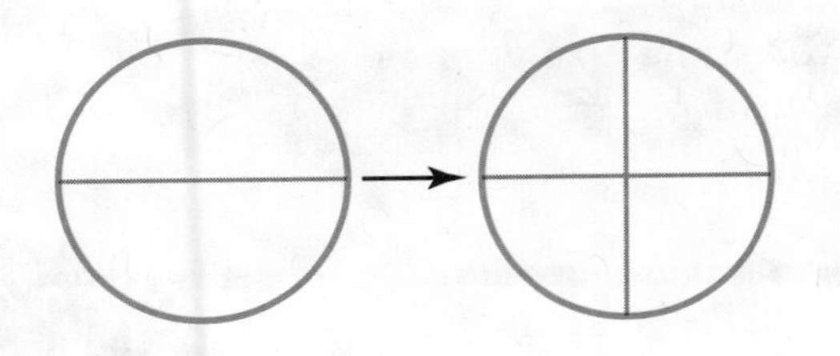

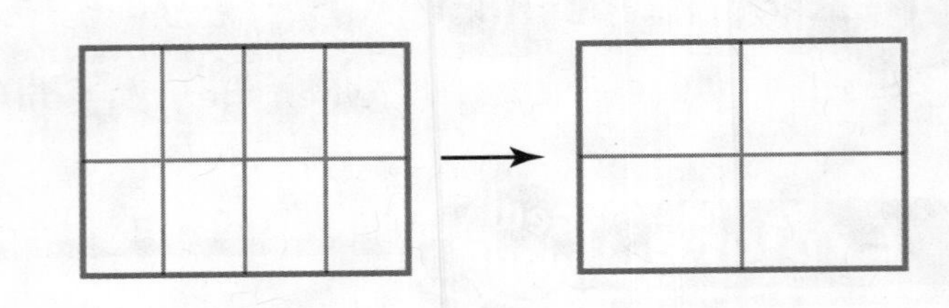

There are more equal parts in the second whole.

These parts are ________________.

There are fewer equal parts in the second whole.

These parts are ________________.

Share and Show

Draw to show smaller equal parts on the second whole.

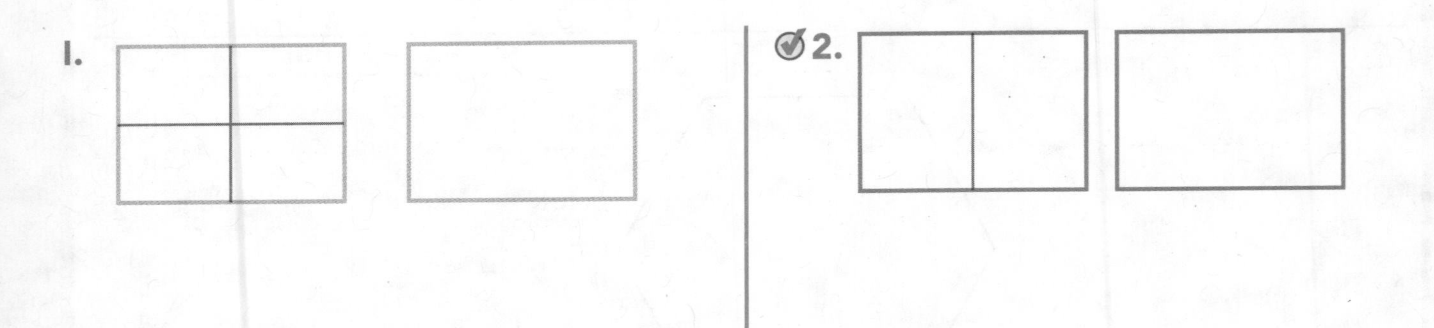

1.

2.

Draw to show larger equal parts on the second whole.

3.

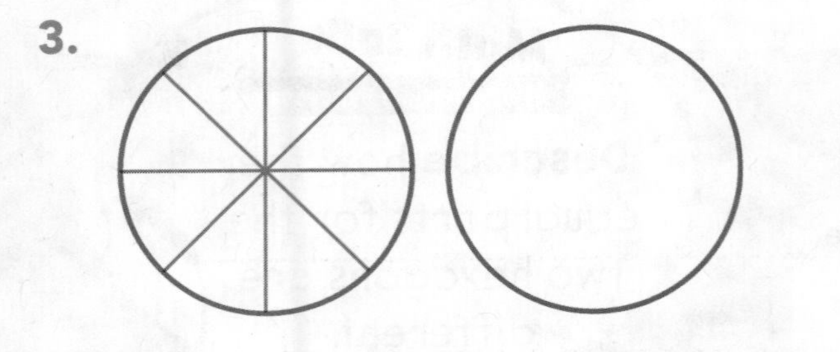

4.

Name ______________________________

Problem Solving

Read each label. Draw to show the equal parts on the second whole.

5. more equal parts

6. fewer equal parts

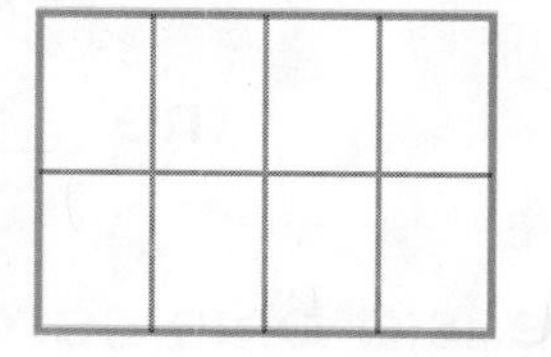

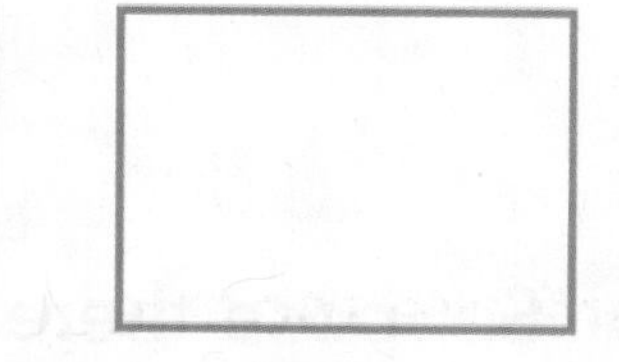

7. H.O.T. Two posters are the same size. A half of one poster is red, and a fourth of the other poster is blue.

Is the red part or the blue part larger? Draw and write to explain.

____

____

____

8. H.O.T. **Multi-Step** Three cakes are the same size. Read each label. Draw to show the cakes divided into those equal parts.

How do the sizes of the parts change when there are fewer equal parts?

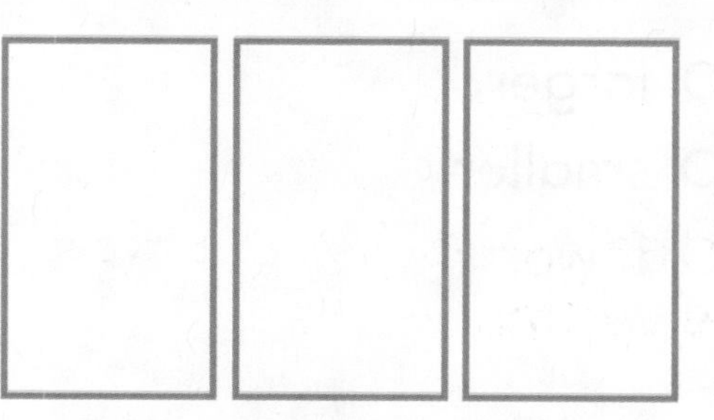

eighths fourths halves

____

____

Daily Assessment Task

Choose the correct answer.

9. **Analyze** Two cards are the same size. The red card is cut into halves. The green card is cut into fourths. Which card has more parts?

the ____________ card

Suppose there is a blue card that is the same size as the green card. If the blue card is cut into more equal parts than the green card, will blue parts be larger? Explain.

____

____

____

10. **TEXAS Test Prep** Which word completes the sentence?

The red rectangle has ____ equal parts than the blue rectangle.

- O larger
- O smaller
- O fewer

TAKE HOME ACTIVITY • Ask your child to show how he or she solved an exercise in the lesson.

Name ________________

4.3 Describe Equal Parts

Draw to show smaller equal parts on the second whole.

1.

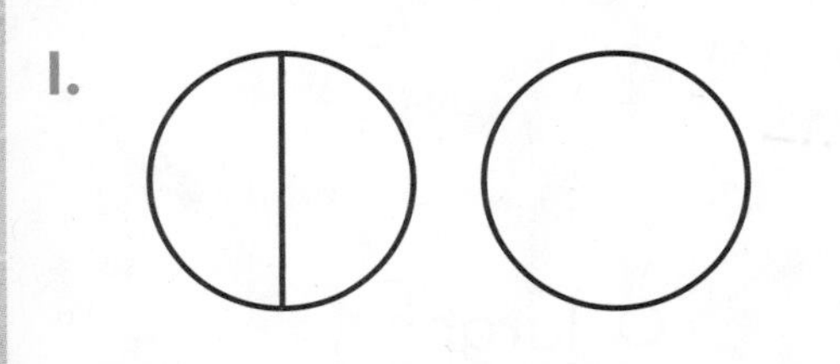

2.

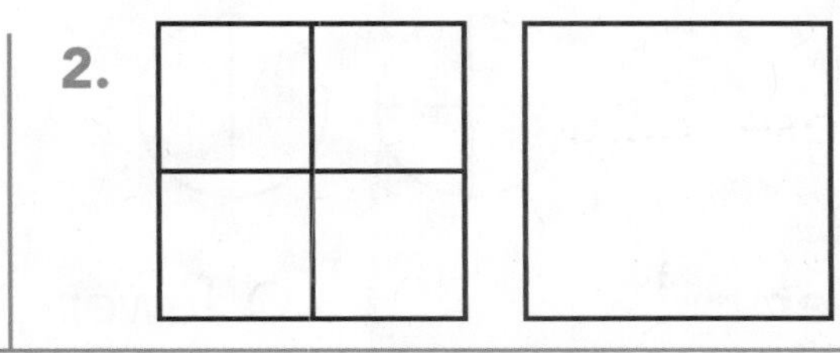

Draw to show larger equal parts on the second whole.

3.

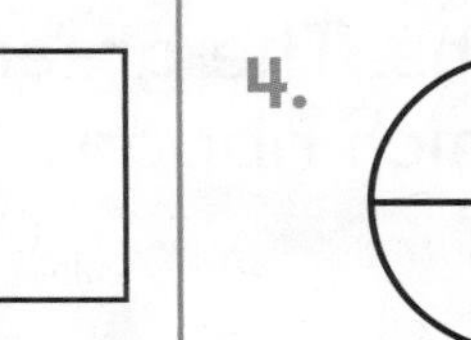

4.

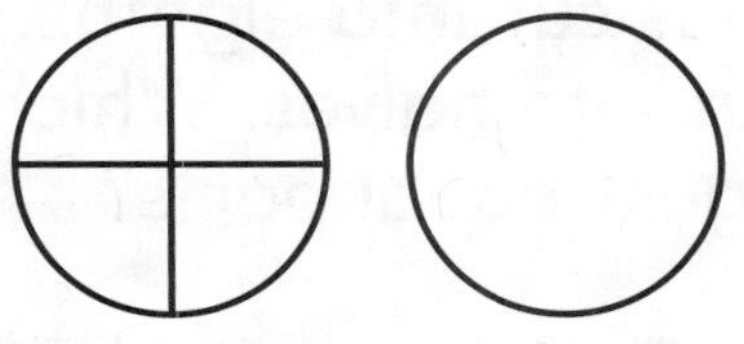

Problem Solving

Solve. Write or draw to explain.

5. **Multi-Step** Donna has three pizzas that are the same size. Read each label. Draw to show the pizzas divided into those equal parts.

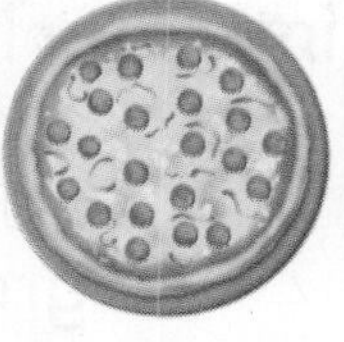
halves

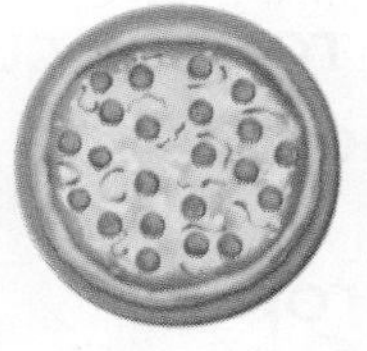
fourths

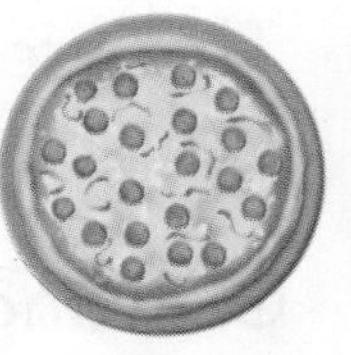
eighths

How do the sizes of the parts change when there are fewer equal parts?

____

____

____

Lesson Check

TEXAS Test Prep

Choose the correct answer.

6. Which word completes the sentence?

   The red circle has ____ equal parts than the blue circle.

   ○ smaller ○ fewer ○ larger

7. Three ribbons are the same size. The red ribbon is cut into fourths. The blue ribbon is cut into eighths. The green ribbon is cut into halves. Which ribbon has the largest equal parts?

   ○ blue ribbon ○ green ribbon ○ red ribbon

8. Three ropes are the same size. The orange rope is cut into halves. The brown rope is cut into eighths. The green rope is cut into fourths. Which rope has the smallest equal parts?

   ○ orange rope ○ green rope ○ brown rope

9. Sandy cuts three pies that are the same size. She cuts the apple pie into 6 equal slices, the peach pie into 8 equal slices, and the cherry pie into 4 equal slices. Which pie has the smallest slices?

   ○ cherry pie ○ peach pie ○ apple pie

Name ______________________________

TEKS Number and Operations—2.3.D, 2.3.C
MATHEMATICAL PROCESSES 2.1.C

4.4 Identify Parts of a Whole

Essential Question How can you name some parts of a whole?

Explore Real World

Circle the shapes that show equal parts.
Name the equal parts shown.

HOME CONNECTION • Your child completed this sorting activity with shapes to review the concept of equal parts.

Model and Draw

Can you name the shaded amount as some equal parts?

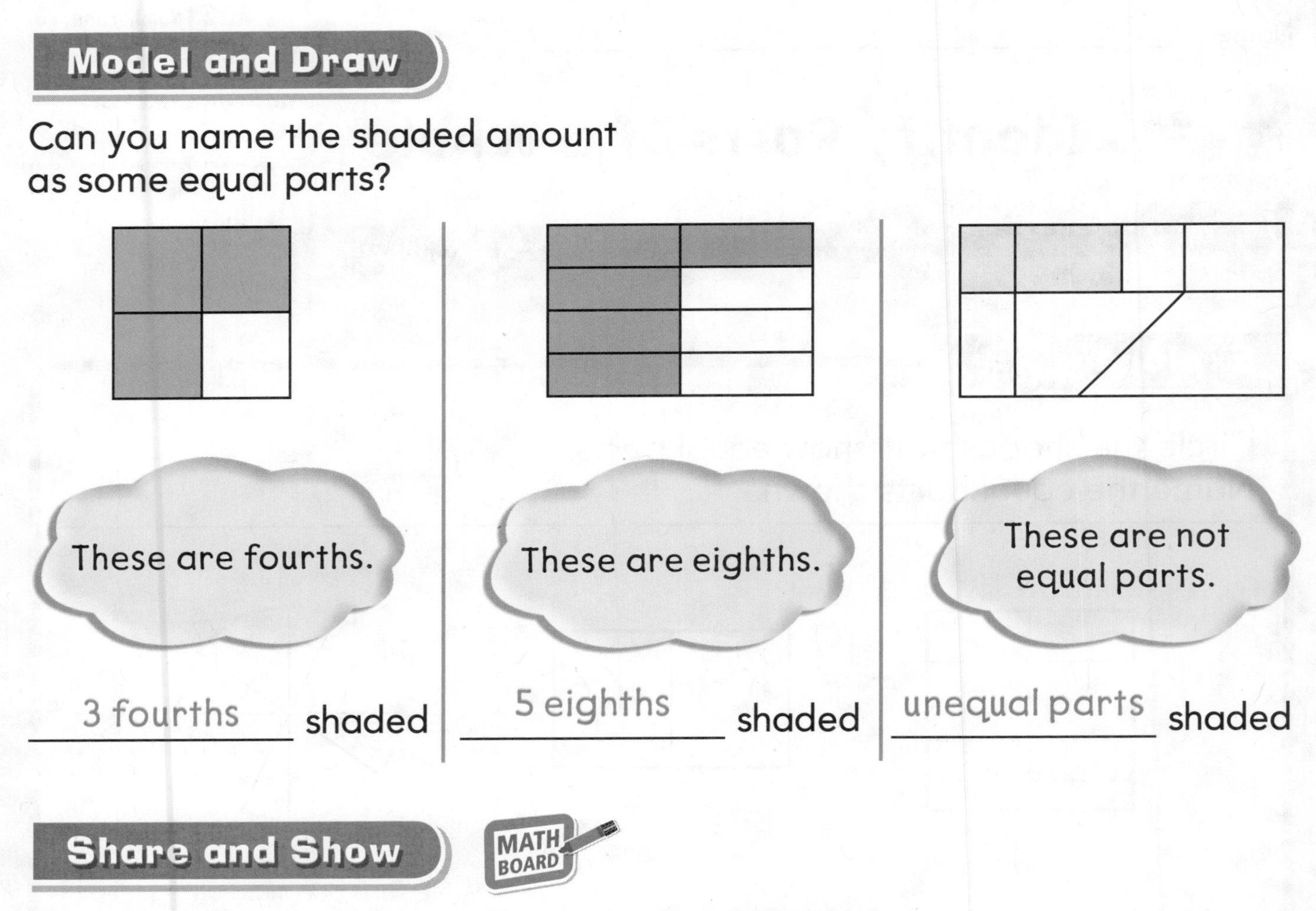

Share and Show

MATH BOARD

If there are equal parts, write the amount shaded.
If the parts are not equal, write **unequal parts**.

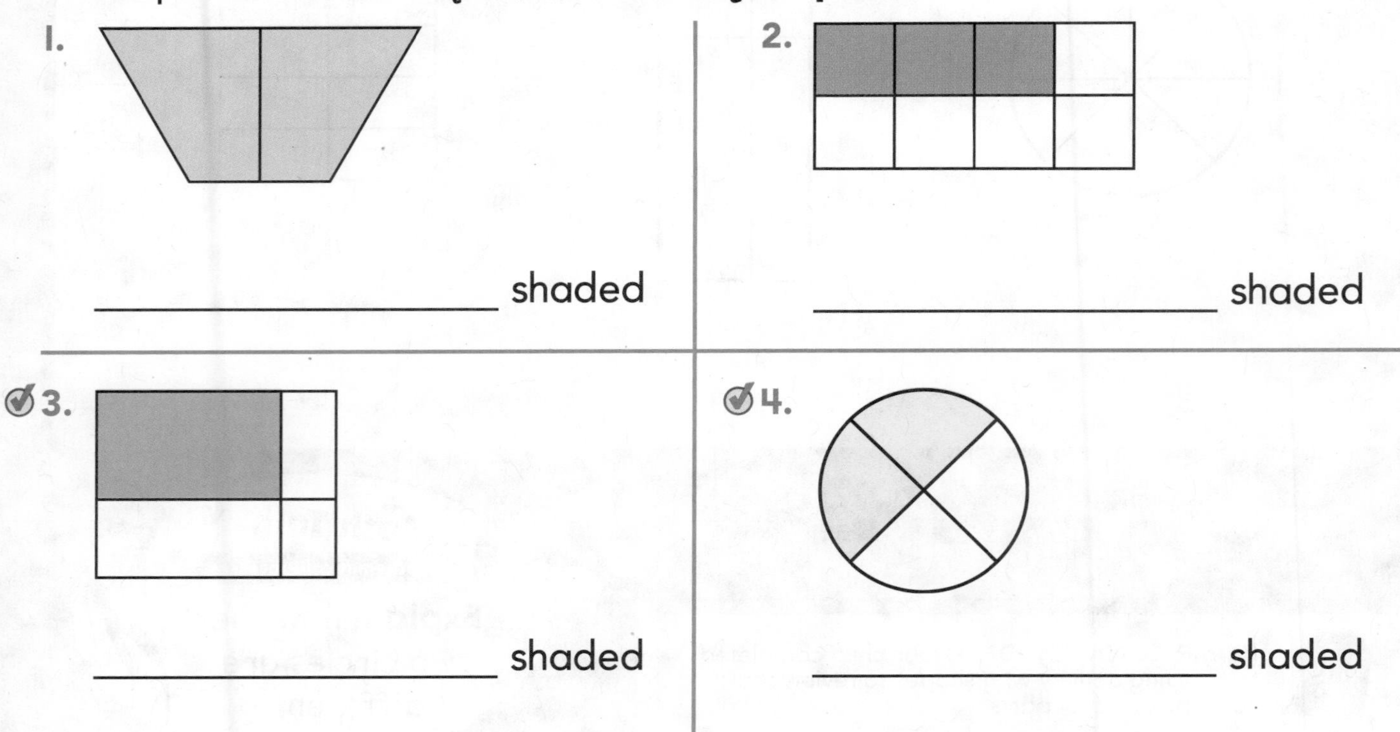

Name ______________________

Problem Solving

If there are equal parts, write the amount shaded.
If the parts are not equal, write **unequal parts**.

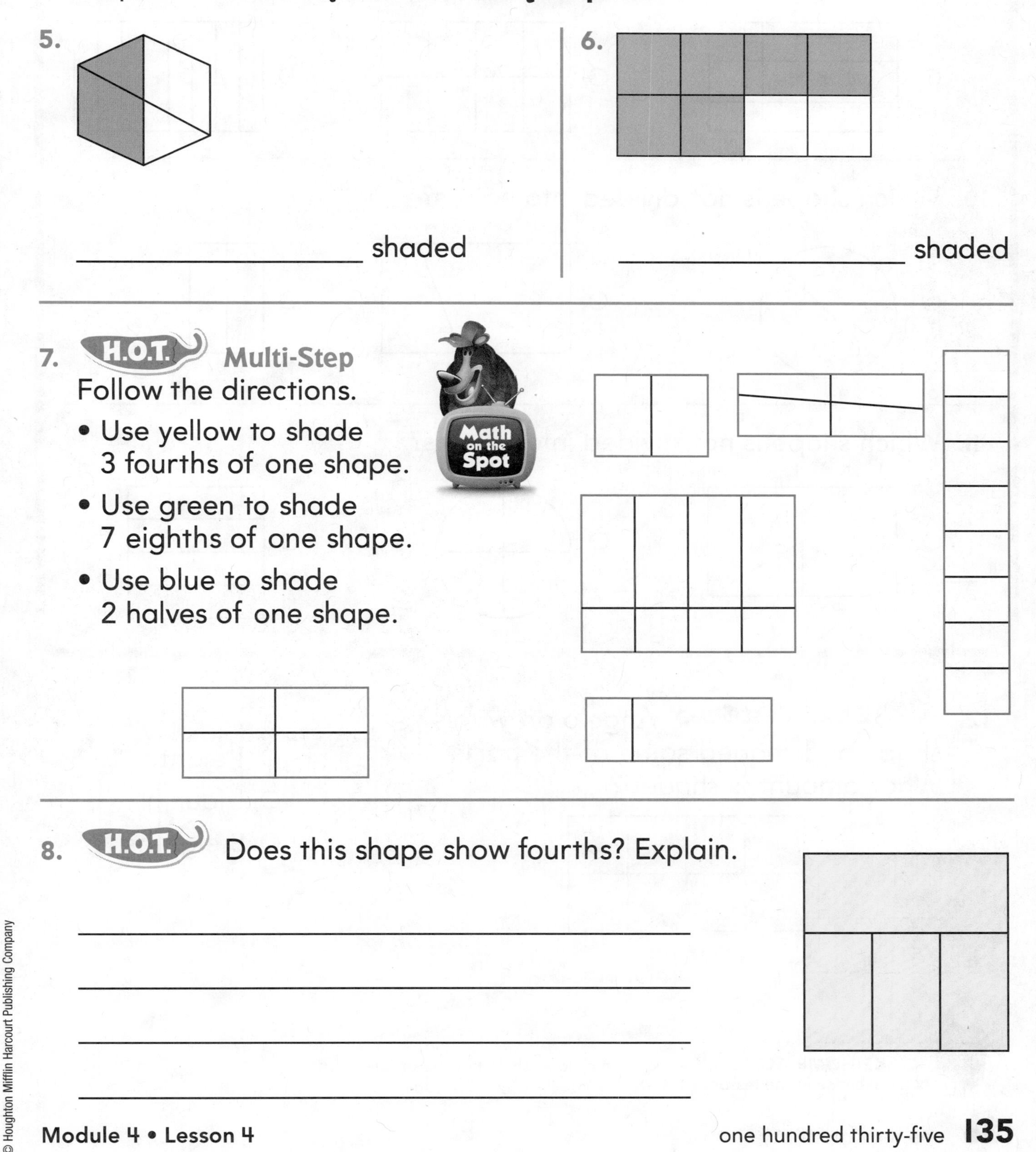

5. ______________ shaded

6. ______________ shaded

7. H.O.T. **Multi-Step**

Follow the directions.

- Use yellow to shade 3 fourths of one shape.
- Use green to shade 7 eighths of one shape.
- Use blue to shade 2 halves of one shape.

8. H.O.T. Does this shape show fourths? Explain.

____

____

____

____

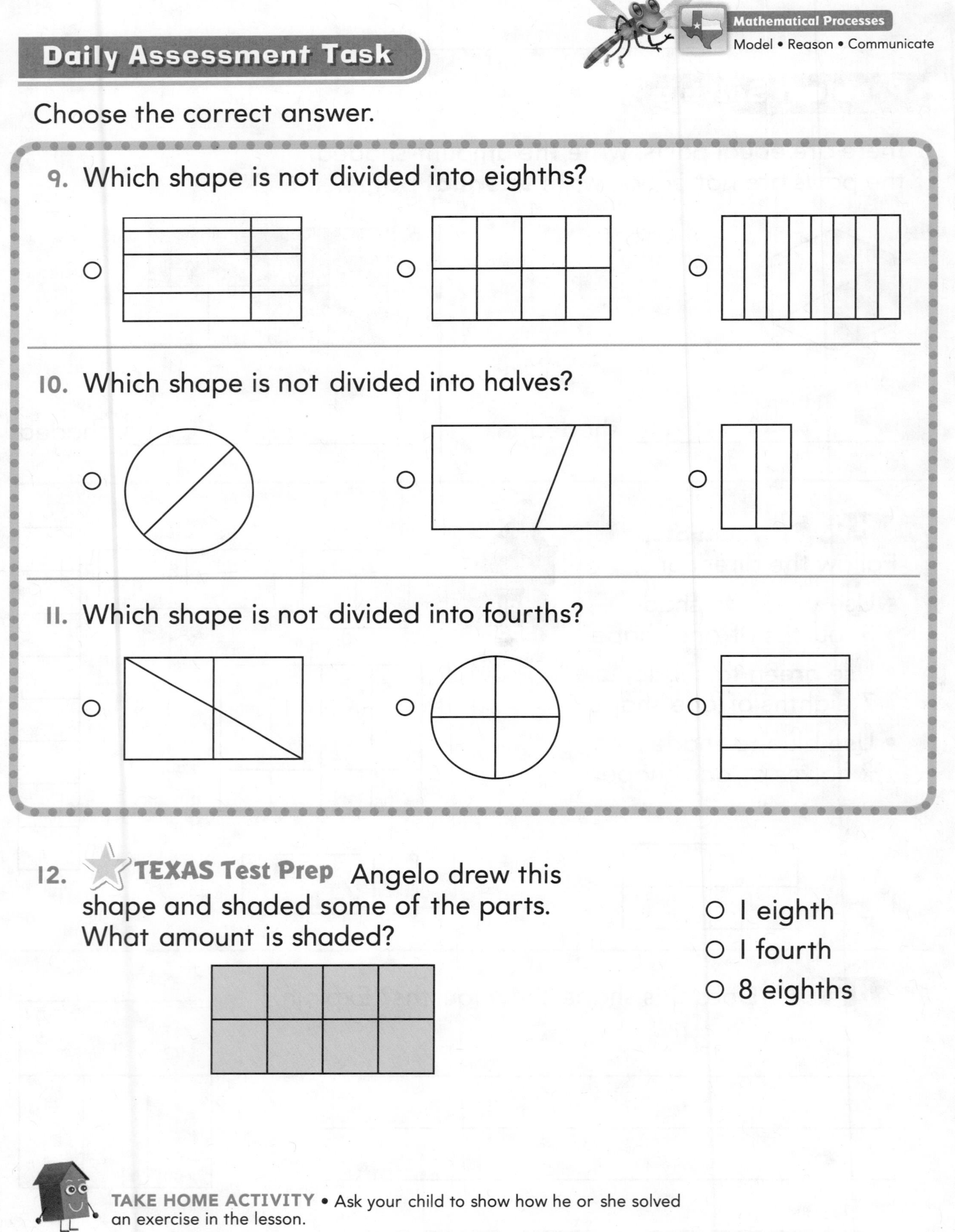

Mathematical Processes
Model • Reason • Communicate

Daily Assessment Task

Choose the correct answer.

9. Which shape is not divided into eighths?

○ ○ ○

10. Which shape is not divided into halves?

○ ○ ○

11. Which shape is not divided into fourths?

○ ○ ○

12. **TEXAS Test Prep** Angelo drew this shape and shaded some of the parts. What amount is shaded?

○ 1 eighth
○ 1 fourth
○ 8 eighths

TAKE HOME ACTIVITY • Ask your child to show how he or she solved an exercise in the lesson.

Name ____________________

4.4 Identify Parts of a Whole

If there are equal parts, write the amount shaded.
If the parts are not equal, write *unequal parts*.

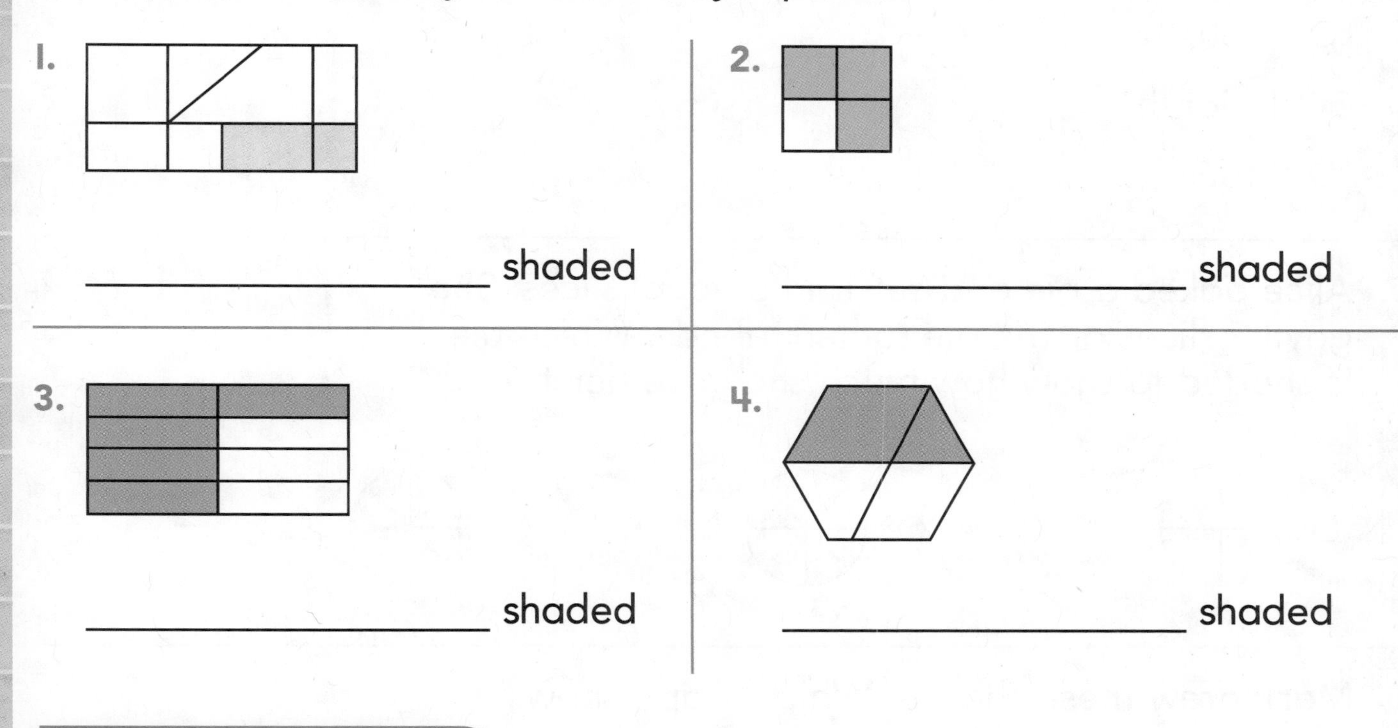

1. ____________ shaded

2. ____________ shaded

3. ____________ shaded

4. ____________ shaded

Problem Solving

Follow directions.

5. **Multi-Step**
   - Use yellow to shade 5 eighths of one shape.
   - Use green to shade 2 halves of one shape.
   - Use blue to shade 3 fourths of one shape.

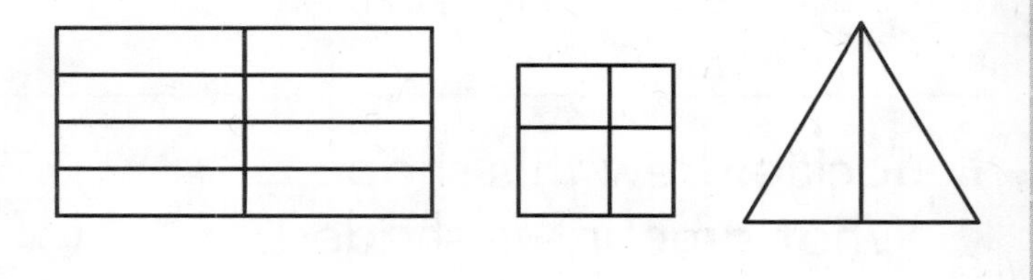

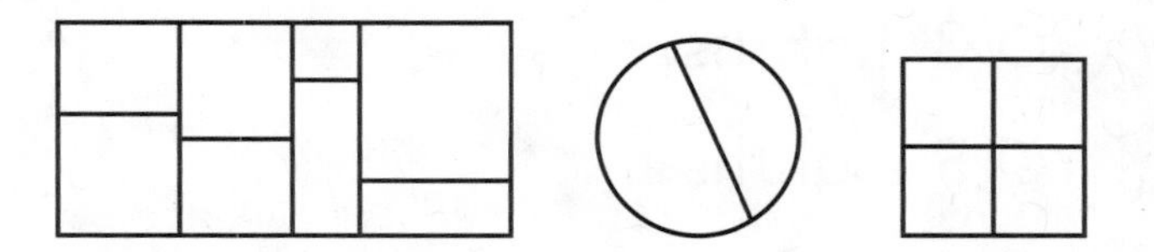

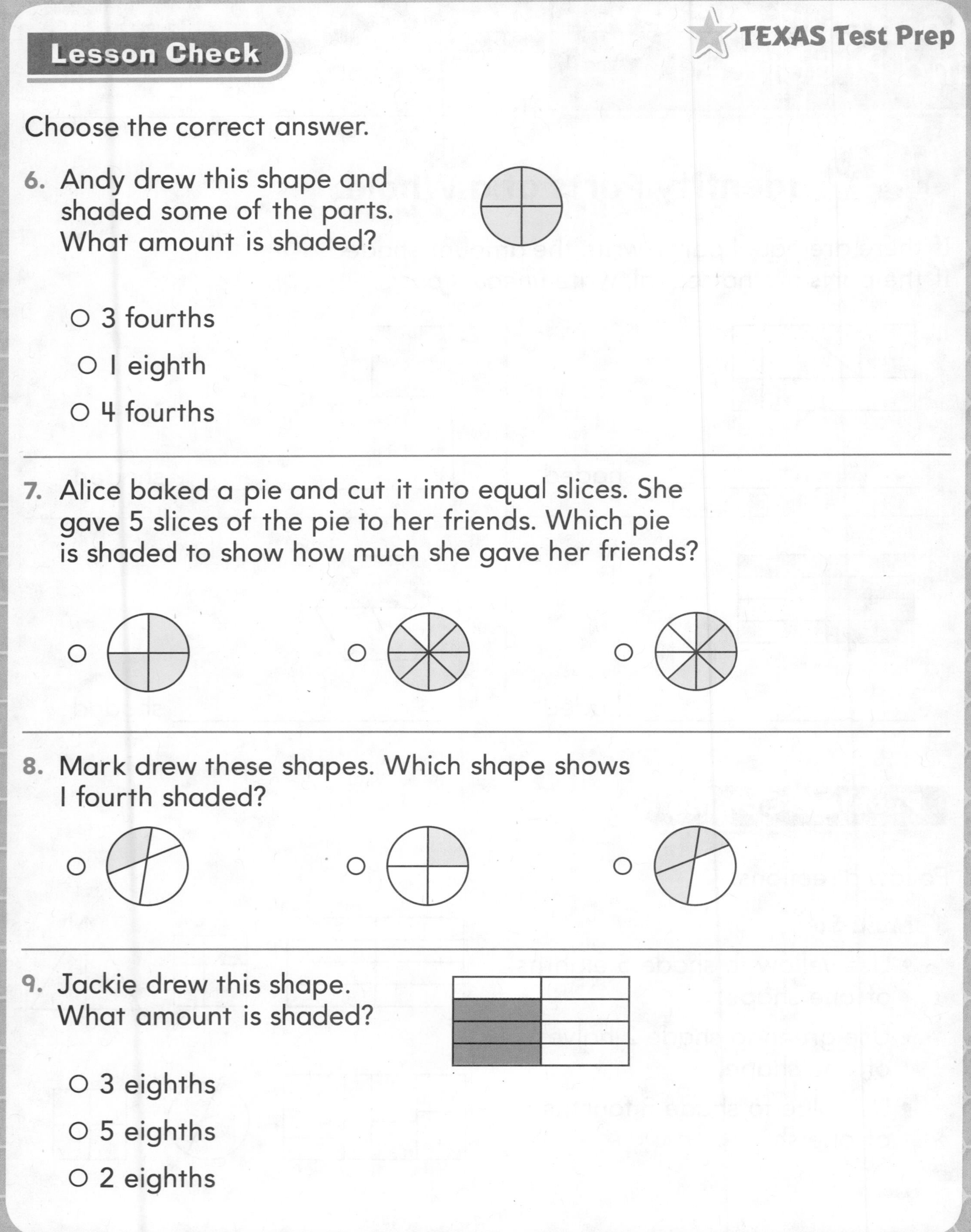

Lesson Check

TEXAS Test Prep

Choose the correct answer.

6. Andy drew this shape and shaded some of the parts. What amount is shaded?

○ 3 fourths

○ 1 eighth

○ 4 fourths

7. Alice baked a pie and cut it into equal slices. She gave 5 slices of the pie to her friends. Which pie is shaded to show how much she gave her friends?

○ ○ ○

8. Mark drew these shapes. Which shape shows 1 fourth shaded?

○ ○ ○

9. Jackie drew this shape. What amount is shaded?

○ 3 eighths

○ 5 eighths

○ 2 eighths

Name ____________________

4.5 PROBLEM SOLVING • Counting with Equal Parts

Essential Question How can I name a fractional amount that is greater than 1 whole?

Unlock the Problem (Real World) (Hands On)

Aria has 2 same-size ribbons. She cuts each ribbon into 8 equal parts. She uses 14 parts. What is another way to write the amount of ribbon she used?

Read

What information am I given?

There are _____ ribbons that are cut into _____ equal parts.

Aria uses _______ parts.

What is my plan or strategy?

I can use fraction strips to ____________________ the problem.

Solve

Show how you solve the problem.
Shade to model the parts of the ribbons she used.

1 eighth	2 eighths	3 eighths	4 eighths	5 eighths	6 eighths	7 eighths	8 eighths

8 eighths is 1 whole.

Aria used ______________________________ ribbons.

HOME CONNECTION • Your child used fraction strips to count fractional parts and name the amount in different ways.

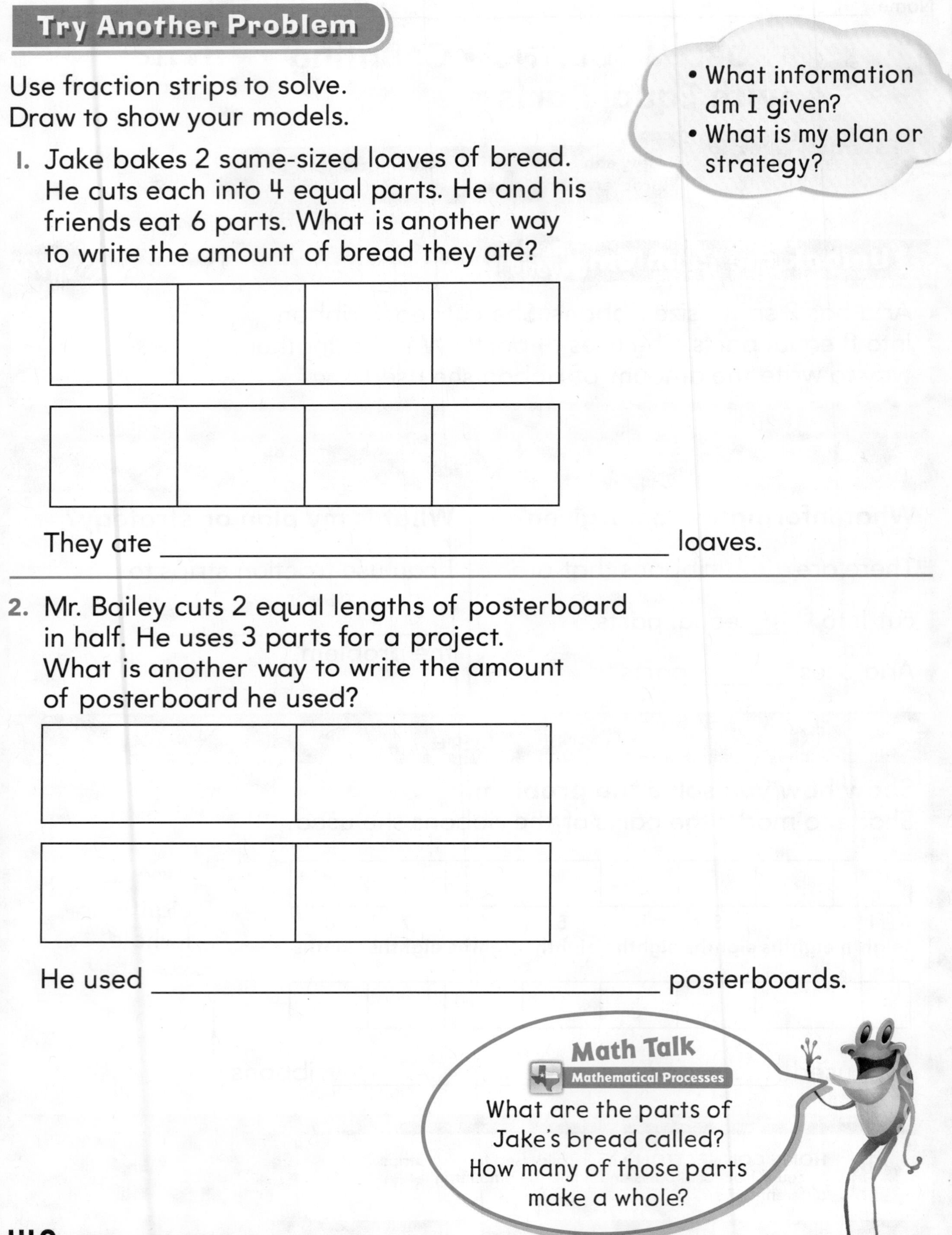

Try Another Problem

Use fraction strips to solve.
Draw to show your models.

- What information am I given?
- What is my plan or strategy?

1. Jake bakes 2 same-sized loaves of bread. He cuts each into 4 equal parts. He and his friends eat 6 parts. What is another way to write the amount of bread they ate?

They ate ______________________ loaves.

2. Mr. Bailey cuts 2 equal lengths of posterboard in half. He uses 3 parts for a project. What is another way to write the amount of posterboard he used?

He used ______________________ posterboards.

Math Talk
Mathematical Processes

What are the parts of Jake's bread called? How many of those parts make a whole?

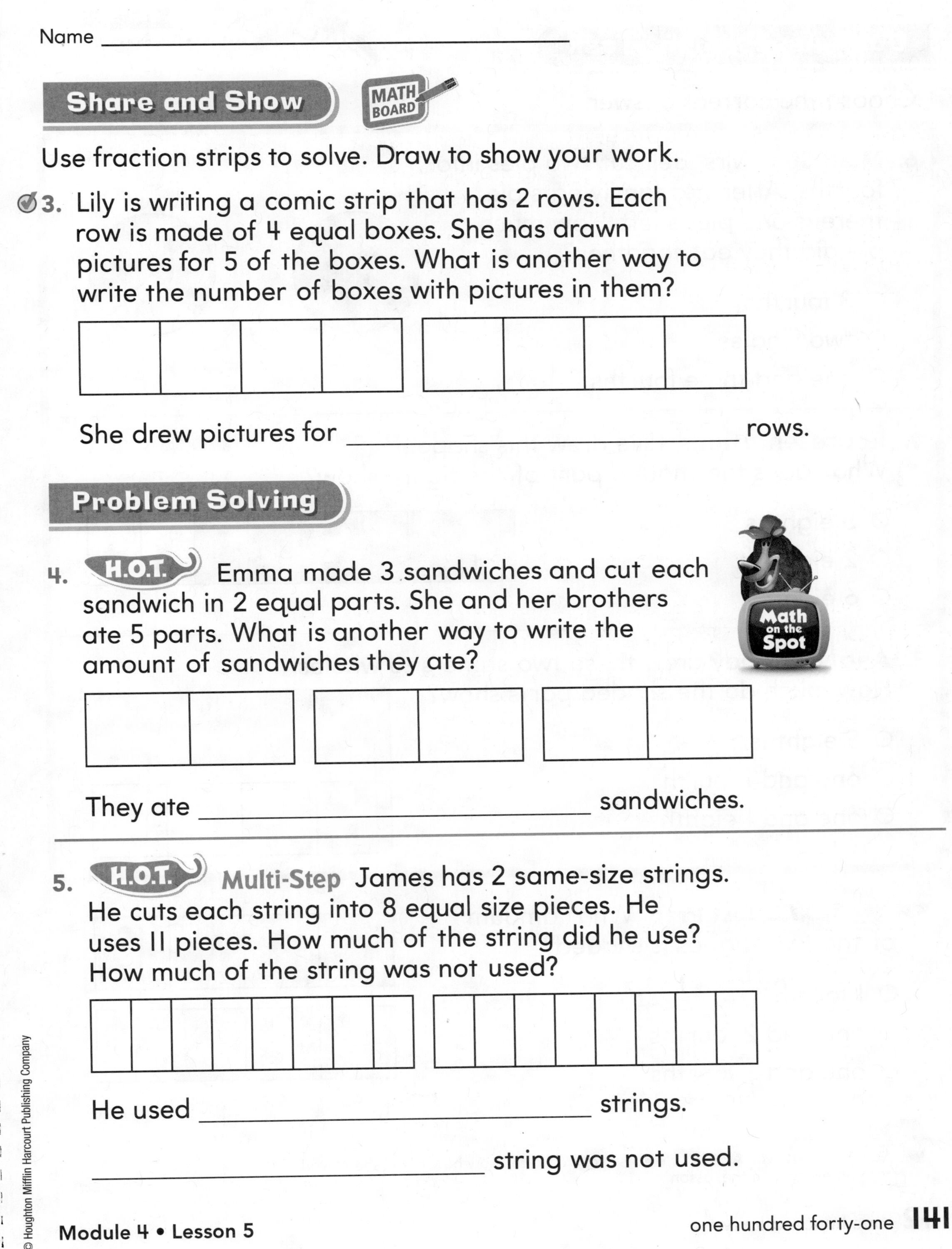

Name ______________________

Share and Show

MATH BOARD

Use fraction strips to solve. Draw to show your work.

3. Lily is writing a comic strip that has 2 rows. Each row is made of 4 equal boxes. She has drawn pictures for 5 of the boxes. What is another way to write the number of boxes with pictures in them?

She drew pictures for ______________________ rows.

Problem Solving

4. **H.O.T.** Emma made 3 sandwiches and cut each sandwich in 2 equal parts. She and her brothers ate 5 parts. What is another way to write the amount of sandwiches they ate?

Math on the Spot

They ate ______________________ sandwiches.

5. **H.O.T.** **Multi-Step** James has 2 same-size strings. He cuts each string into 8 equal size pieces. He uses 11 pieces. How much of the string did he use? How much of the string was not used?

He used ______________________ strings.

______________________ string was not used.

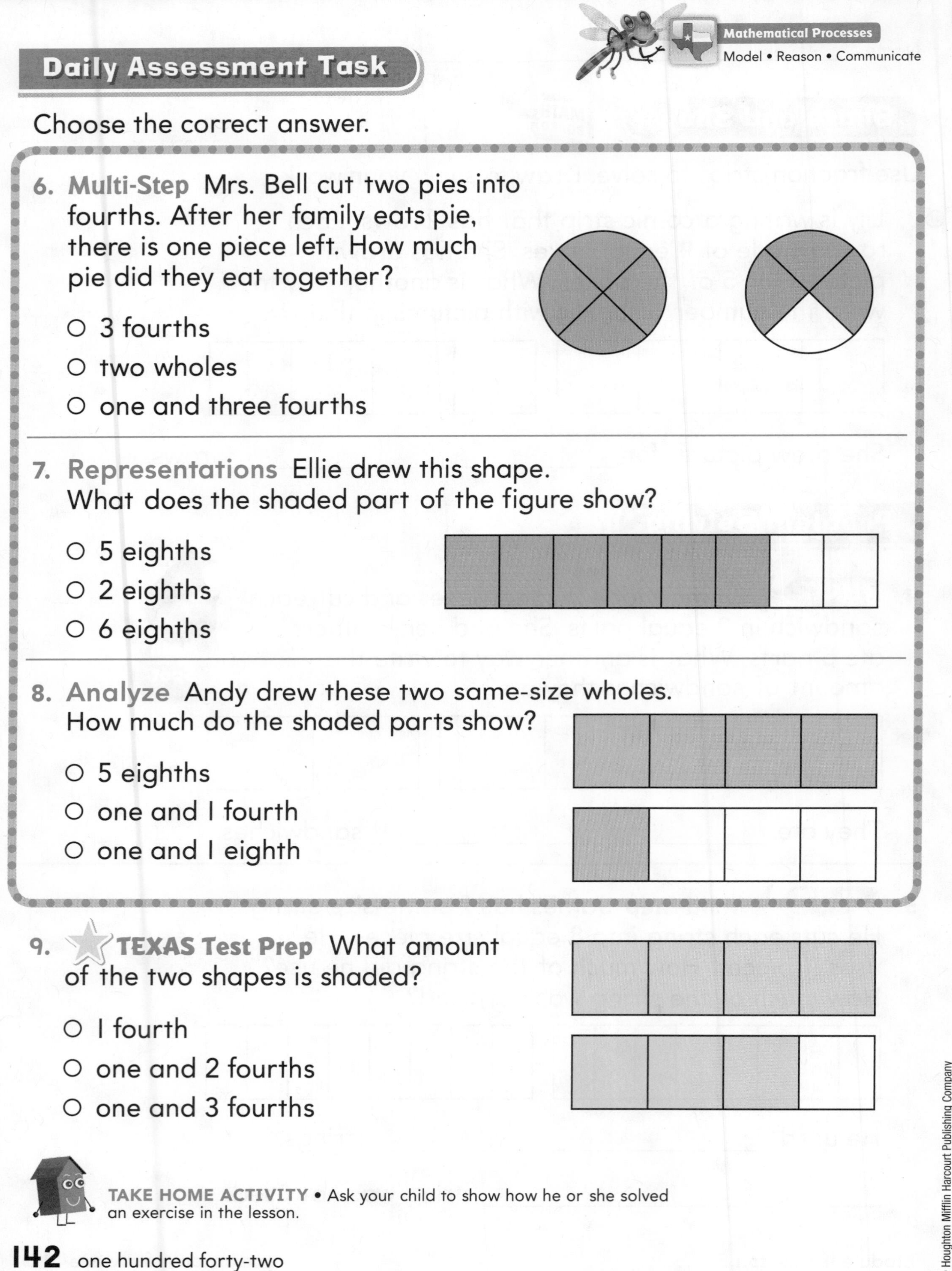

Daily Assessment Task

Choose the correct answer.

6. **Multi-Step** Mrs. Bell cut two pies into fourths. After her family eats pie, there is one piece left. How much pie did they eat together?

   ○ 3 fourths
   ○ two wholes
   ○ one and three fourths

7. **Representations** Ellie drew this shape. What does the shaded part of the figure show?

   ○ 5 eighths
   ○ 2 eighths
   ○ 6 eighths

8. **Analyze** Andy drew these two same-size wholes. How much do the shaded parts show?

   ○ 5 eighths
   ○ one and I fourth
   ○ one and I eighth

9. **TEXAS Test Prep** What amount of the two shapes is shaded?

   ○ I fourth
   ○ one and 2 fourths
   ○ one and 3 fourths

TAKE HOME ACTIVITY • Ask your child to show how he or she solved an exercise in the lesson.

Name ______________________

4.5 PROBLEM SOLVING • Counting with Equal Parts

Use fraction strips to solve. Draw to show your work.

1. Tim cuts 2 same-size pieces of wood into 2 equal parts. He uses 3 parts for a project. What is another way to write the amount of wood he used?

   ____

2. Amelia is making 2 booklets. Each booklet is made of 4 equal pages. She has drawn pictures for 5 of the pages. What is another way to write the number of pages with pictures on them?

   She drew pictures for ______________ booklets.

Problem Solving

3. **Multi-Step** Kelly has 2 ribbons of the same length. She cuts each ribbon into 8 equal size pieces. She uses 13 pieces. What is another way to write the amount of ribbon she used? How much of the ribbon was not used?

   She used ______________ ribbons.

   ______________ ribbon was not used.

Lesson Check

Choose the correct answer.

4. What amount of the two shapes is shaded?

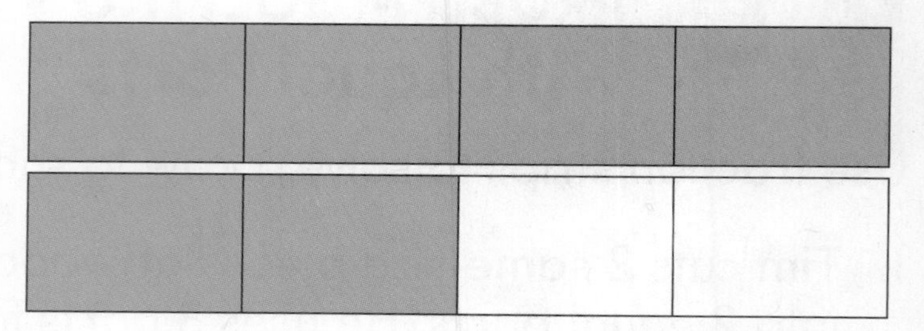

- ○ one and 2 fourths
- ○ one and 3 fourths
- ○ 2 fourths

5. Adam drew this shape. What does the shaded part of the figure show?

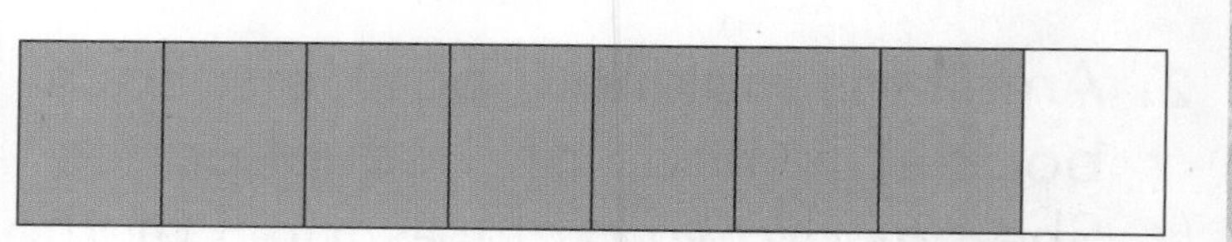

- ○ 1 eighth
- ○ 7 eighths
- ○ 6 eighths

6. Nate drew these two same-size wholes. How much do the shaded parts show?

- ○ 3 eighths
- ○ one and three fourths
- ○ one and one fourth

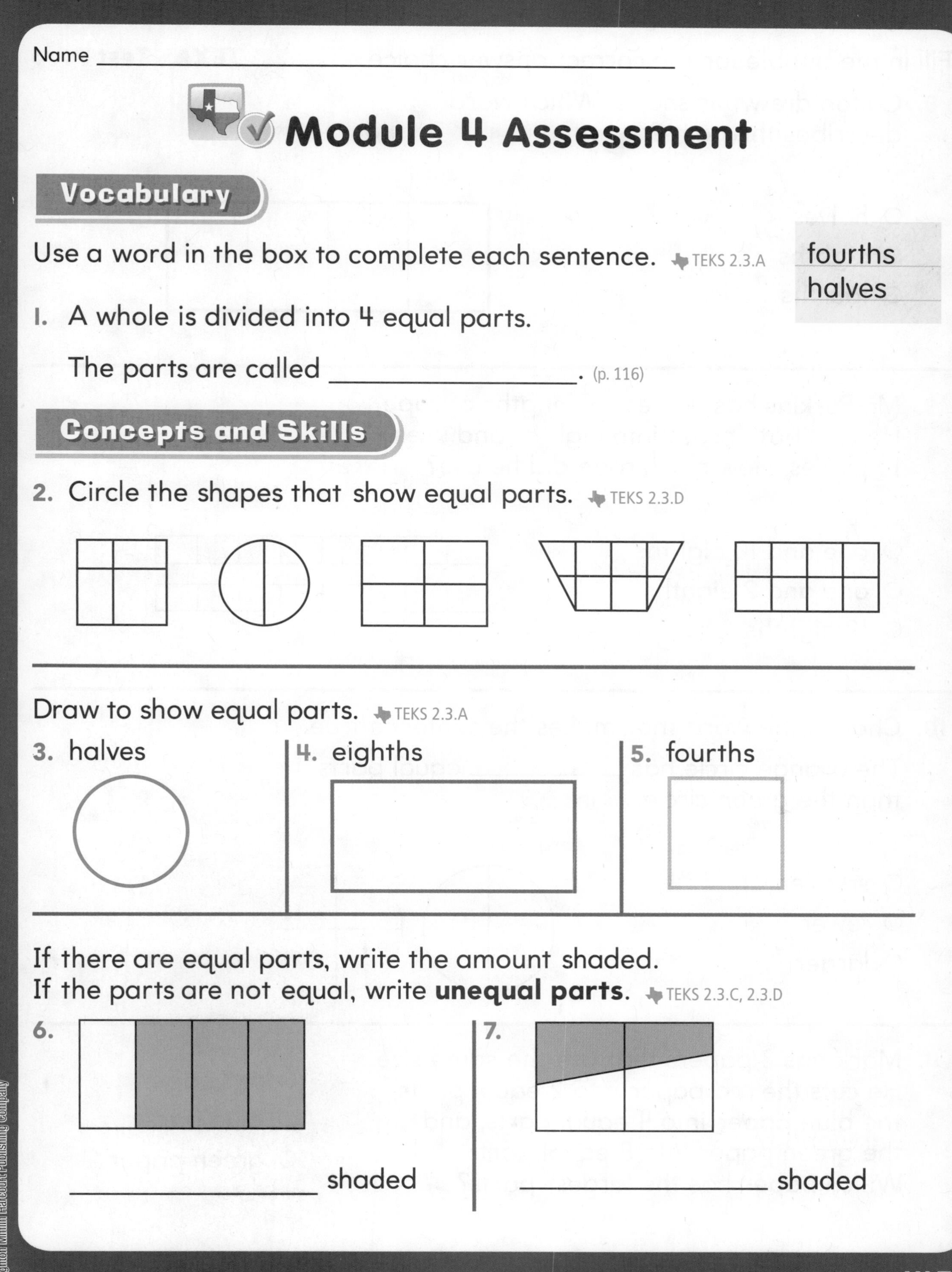

Name ____________________

Module 4 Assessment

Vocabulary

Use a word in the box to complete each sentence. TEKS 2.3.A

fourths
halves

1. A whole is divided into 4 equal parts.

   The parts are called ____________. (p. 116)

Concepts and Skills

2. Circle the shapes that show equal parts. TEKS 2.3.D

Draw to show equal parts. TEKS 2.3.A

3. halves

4. eighths

5. fourths

If there are equal parts, write the amount shaded.
If the parts are not equal, write **unequal parts**. TEKS 2.3.C, 2.3.D

6. ____________ shaded

7. ____________ shaded

Fill in the bubble for the correct answer choice. TEXAS Test Prep

8. Colton drew this shape. Which word describes the parts? TEKS 2.3.A

- ○ halves
- ○ eighths
- ○ fourths

---

9. Mr. Perkins has two equal lengths of rope. He cuts both ropes into eighths and uses 10 pieces. How much rope did he use? TEKS 2.3.C

- ○ one and 10 eighths
- ○ one and 2 eighths
- ○ 12 eighths

---

10. Choose the word that makes the sentence true.

The orange circle has __________ equal parts than the green circle. TEKS 2.3.B

- ○ smaller
- ○ fewer
- ○ larger

---

11. Mark has 3 papers that are the same size. He cuts the red paper into 2 equal parts, the blue paper into 4 equal parts, and the green paper into 8 equal parts. Which paper has the largest parts? TEKS 2.3.B

- ○ red paper
- ○ blue paper
- ○ green paper

Name ___________________________

TEKS Number and Operations—2.4.A
MATHEMATICAL PROCESSES 2.1.C

5.1 Addition Strategies

Essential Question
What strategies can be used to remember sums for basic facts?

Explore (Real World) (Hands On)

Draw a picture to show the problem. Then write an addition sentence for the problem.

____

_______ toy cars

FOR THE TEACHER • Read the following problem and have children draw a picture for the problem. Nick has 4 toy cars. Adrian gives Nick 4 more toy cars. How many toy cars does Nick have now? After children draw pictures, have them write a number sentence for the problem.

Math Talk Mathematical Processes

Explain why 3 + 3 = 6 is called a doubles fact.

Model and Draw

Doubles facts can be used to find other **sums**.

$5 + 5 = 10$

$5 + 6 =$ ____

Think: $10 + 1$

$5 + 4 =$ ____

Think: $10 - 1$

Changing the order of **addends** does not change the sum.

$7 + 1 = 8$

$1 + 7 = 8$

$3 + 6 =$ ____

$6 + 3 =$ ____

Share and Show

MATH BOARD

Write the sum.

1. $3 + 4 =$ ____	2. $7 + 0 =$ ____	3. ____ $= 1 + 8$
4. $2 + 3 =$ ____	5. ____ $= 5 + 1$	6. $4 + 2 =$ ____
✓7. $5 + 3 =$ ____	8. $4 + 4 =$ ____	9. ____ $= 6 + 3$
10. $3 + 3$	✓11. $6 + 4$	12. $0 + 8$

Problem Solving

Write the sum.

13. $3 + 7 =$ ____	14. ____ $= 5 + 5$	15. $6 + 7 =$ ____
16. $6 + 5 =$ ____	17. $4 + 5 =$ ____	18. ____ $= 9 + 1$
19. $\begin{array}{r} 10 \\ +\ 10 \\ \hline \end{array}$	20. $\begin{array}{r} 4 \\ +\ 7 \\ \hline \end{array}$	21. $\begin{array}{r} 7 \\ +\ 8 \\ \hline \end{array}$

Solve. Write or draw to explain.

22. **H.O.T.** Mr. Carter wrote a doubles fact. It has a sum greater than 6. The addends are each less than 6. What fact might he have written?

____

23. **H.O.T.** **Multi-Step** Thomas painted 4 pictures. Maria painted twice as many pictures as Thomas. How many pictures did they paint?

____ pictures

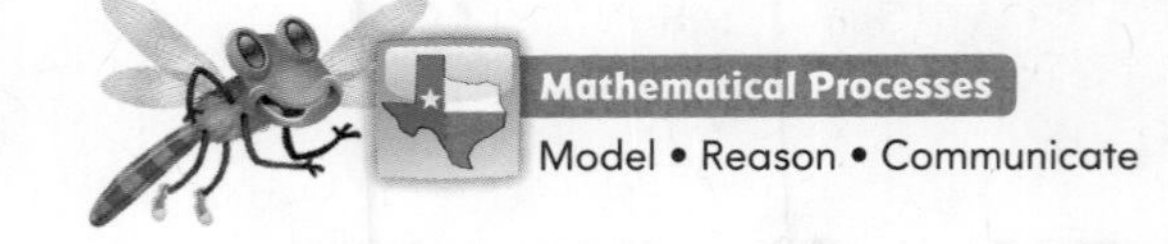

Daily Assessment Task

Choose the correct answer.

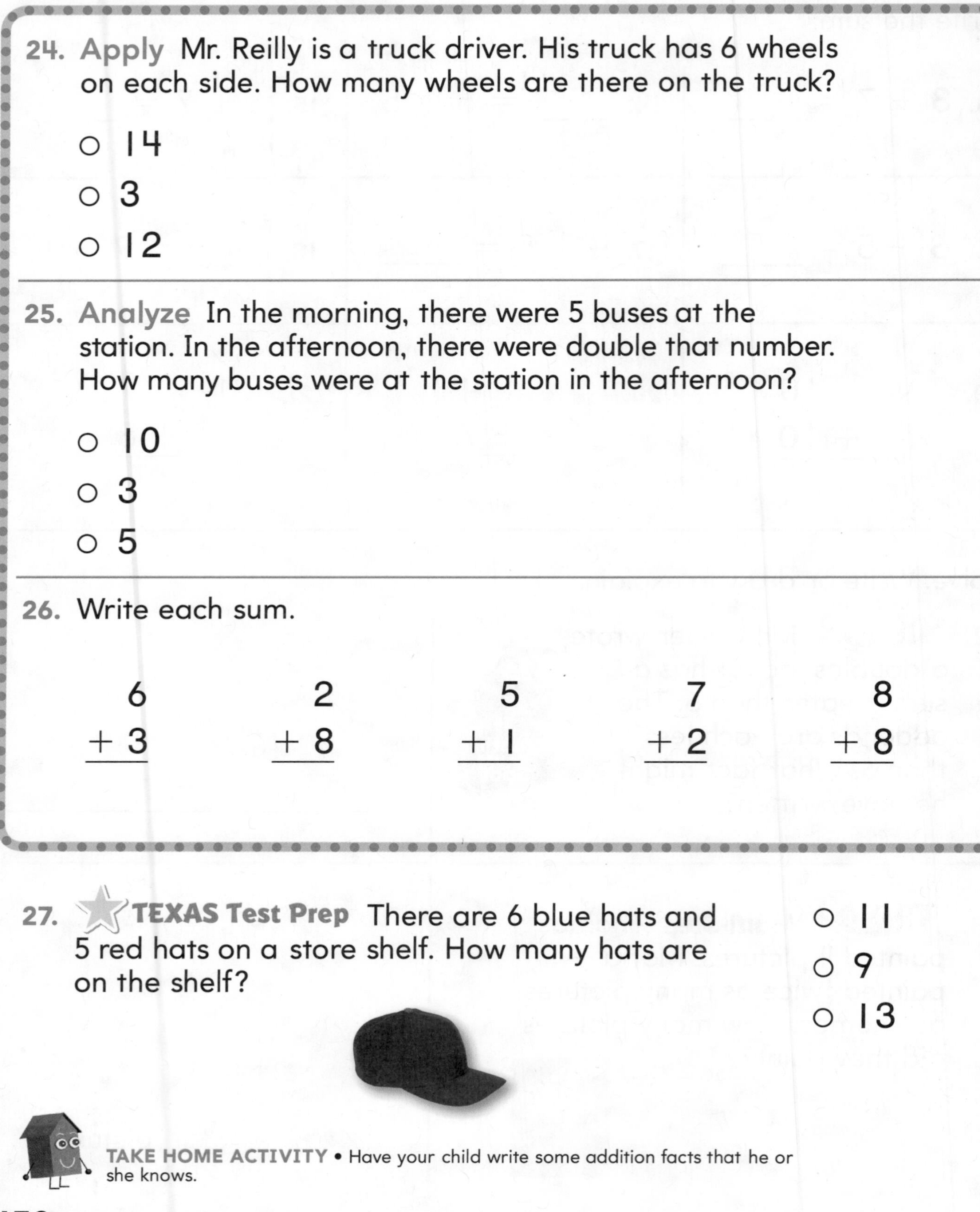

24. **Apply** Mr. Reilly is a truck driver. His truck has 6 wheels on each side. How many wheels are there on the truck?

- ○ 14
- ○ 3
- ○ 12

25. **Analyze** In the morning, there were 5 buses at the station. In the afternoon, there were double that number. How many buses were at the station in the afternoon?

- ○ 10
- ○ 3
- ○ 5

26. Write each sum.

$$\begin{array}{r} 6 \\ +\ 3 \\ \hline \end{array} \qquad \begin{array}{r} 2 \\ +\ 8 \\ \hline \end{array} \qquad \begin{array}{r} 5 \\ +\ 1 \\ \hline \end{array} \qquad \begin{array}{r} 7 \\ +\ 2 \\ \hline \end{array} \qquad \begin{array}{r} 8 \\ +\ 8 \\ \hline \end{array}$$

27. **TEXAS Test Prep** There are 6 blue hats and 5 red hats on a store shelf. How many hats are on the shelf?

- ○ 11
- ○ 9
- ○ 13

TAKE HOME ACTIVITY • Have your child write some addition facts that he or she knows.

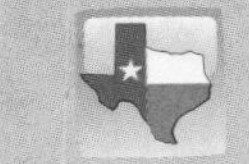

TEKS Number and Operations—2.4.A
MATHEMATICAL PROCESSES 2.1.C

Name ______________________

5.1 Addition Strategies

Write the sum.

1. $2 + 2 =$ ____	2. ____ $= 9 + 3$	3. $8 + 1 =$ ____
4. $7 + 4 =$ ____	5. $4 + 3 =$ ____	6. ____ $= 5 + 7$
7. $\begin{array}{r} 6 \\ + 1 \\ \hline \end{array}$	8. $\begin{array}{r} 2 \\ + 5 \\ \hline \end{array}$	9. $\begin{array}{r} 3 \\ + 8 \\ \hline \end{array}$

Problem Solving Real World

Solve. Write or draw to explain.

10. Sue wrote a doubles fact. It has a sum less than 10 and greater than 4. The addends are each less than 5. What fact might she have written?

____

____

11. **Multi-Step** Ron sees 3 dogs at the park. Hal sees twice as many dogs as Ron. How many dogs do they see in all?

____

Lesson Check

TEXAS Test Prep

Choose the correct answer.

12. There are 5 kittens and 8 puppies at the pet store. How many kittens and puppies are there in all?

○ 3 ○ 12 ○ 13

13. In the morning, there were 7 cars parked at a parking lot. In the afternoon, there were double that number. How many cars were parked at the parking lot in the afternoon?

○ 7 ○ 14 ○ 12

14. Jacob is a bus driver. His bus has 8 wheels on each side. How many wheels are there on the bus?

○ 4 ○ 16 ○ 18

15. Gary has twice as many crayons as Beth. Beth has 6 crayons in her box. How many crayons does Gary have?

○ 12 ○ 7 ○ 14

16. **Multi-Step** Ed picks 3 green apples and 6 red apples. Then he picks 3 more green apples. How many apples does Ed pick?

○ 11 ○ 9 ○ 12

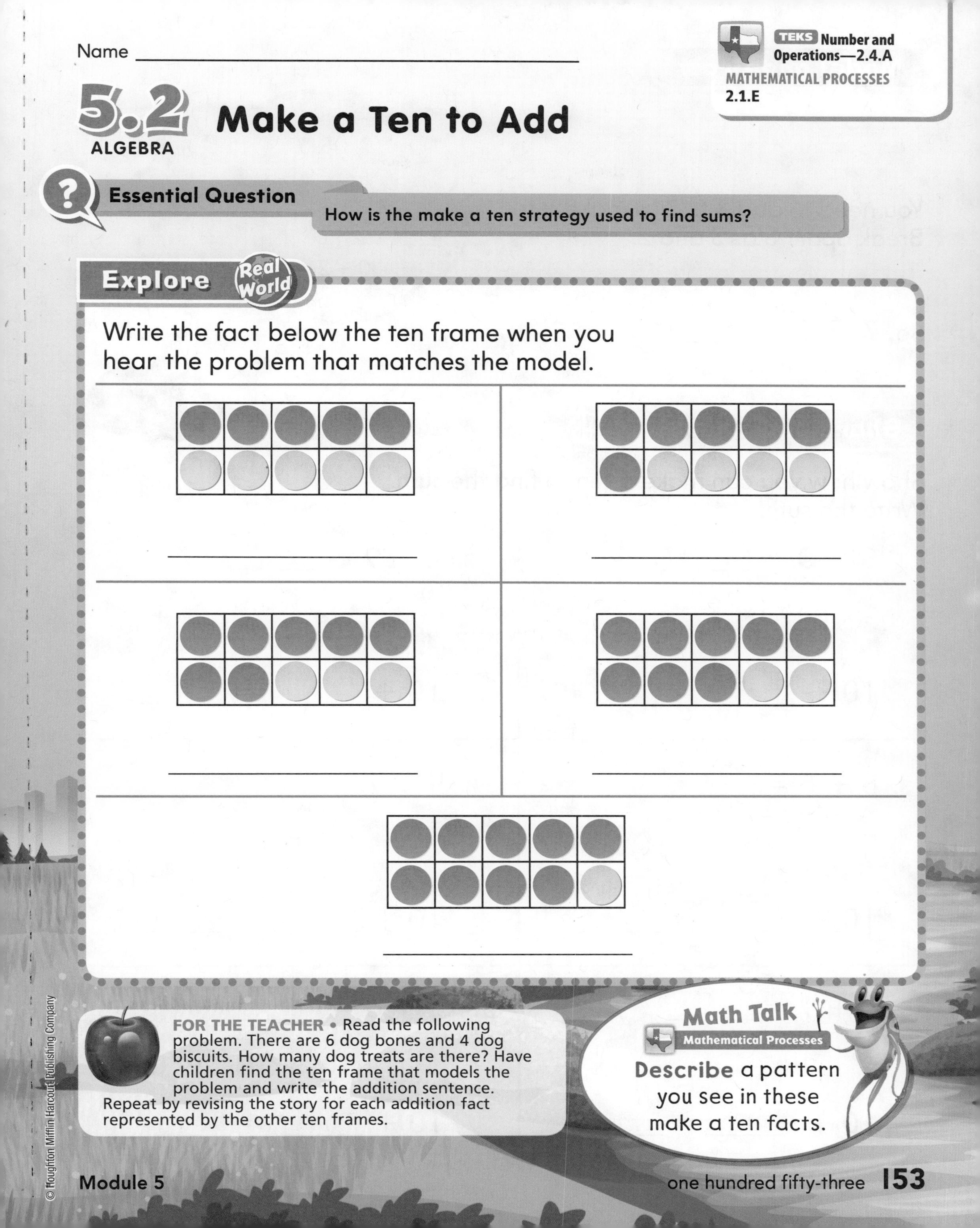

Name ______________________________

5.2 ALGEBRA Make a Ten to Add

Essential Question How is the make a ten strategy used to find sums?

Explore Real World

Write the fact below the ten frame when you hear the problem that matches the model.

____

____

____

____

____

FOR THE TEACHER • Read the following problem. There are 6 dog bones and 4 dog biscuits. How many dog treats are there? Have children find the ten frame that models the problem and write the addition sentence. Repeat by revising the story for each addition fact represented by the other ten frames.

Math Talk Mathematical Processes

Describe a pattern you see in these make a ten facts.

Model and Draw

$7 + 5 = ?$

You need to add 3 to 7 to make a ten.
Break apart 5 as 3 and 2.

So, $7 + 5 =$ ______.

Share and Show

MATH BOARD

Show how you can make a ten to find the sum.
Write the sum.

1. $8 + 3 =$ ______

   $10 +$ ______ $=$ ______

2. $2 + 9 =$ ______

   $10 +$ ______ $=$ ______

3. $8 + 5 =$ ______

   $10 +$ ______ $=$ ______

4. $4 + 7 =$ ______

   $10 +$ ______ $=$ ______

5. $3 + 9 =$ ______

   $10 +$ ______ $=$ ______

6. $7 + 6 =$ ______

   $10 +$ ______ $=$ ______

Name ___________________________

Problem Solving

Make a ten to find the sum. Write the sum.

7. $4 + 9 =$ ______

$10 +$ ______ $=$ ______

8. $9 + 8 =$ ______

$10 +$ ______ $=$ ______

9. $8 + 6 =$ ______

$10 +$ ______ $=$ ______

10. $5 + 9 =$ ______

$10 +$ ______ $=$ ______

11. $9 + 9 =$ ______

$10 +$ ______ $=$ ______

12. $8 + 4 =$ ______

$10 +$ ______ $=$ ______

Solve. Write or draw to explain.

13. **H.O.T.** There were 5 bees in a hive. How many more bees need to go in the hive for there to be 14 bees?

______ more bees

14. **H.O.T.** **Multi-Step** Max is thinking of a doubles fact. The sum is greater than the sum of $6 + 4$ but less than the sum of $8 + 5$. What fact is Max thinking of?

______ $+$ ______ $=$ ______

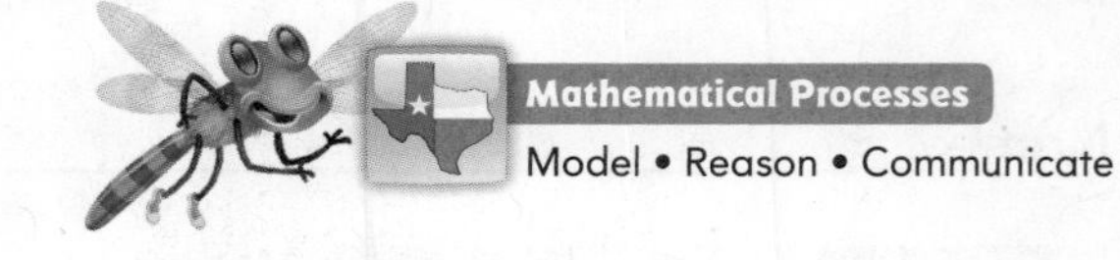

Daily Assessment Task

Choose the correct answer.

15. **Multi-Step** Peter and his dad played a game of Ball Toss. Peter scored 8 points and 7 points. His dad scored 9 points and 5 points. Who scored more points?

- ○ Peter
- ○ Peter's dad
- ○ They scored the same number of points.

16. There were 9 girls and 7 boys standing in line to play a game. How many children were standing in line?

- ○ 15
- ○ 13
- ○ 16

17. **Connect** Winston has 8 tokens and Shelly has 5 tokens. Which of the following could you use to find how many tokens they have?

- ○ $10 + 4$
- ○ $10 + 3$
- ○ $10 + 7$

18. **TEXAS Test Prep** Natasha had 8 shells. Then she found 5 more shells. How many shells does she have now?

- ○ 12
- ○ 13
- ○ 3

TAKE HOME ACTIVITY • Ask your child to name pairs of numbers that have sums of 10. Then have him or her write the addition sentences.

Name ______________________

5.2 Make a Ten to Add

ALGEBRA

Make a ten to find the sum. Write the sum.

1. $7 + 7 =$ ______

   $10 +$ ______ $=$ ______

2. $9 + 7 =$ ______

   $10 +$ ______ $=$ ______

3. $6 + 7 =$ ______

   $10 +$ ______ $=$ ______

4. $8 + 9 =$ ______

   $10 +$ ______ $=$ ______

Problem Solving Real World

Solve. Write or draw to explain.

5. How many more frogs are needed for there to be 13 frogs?

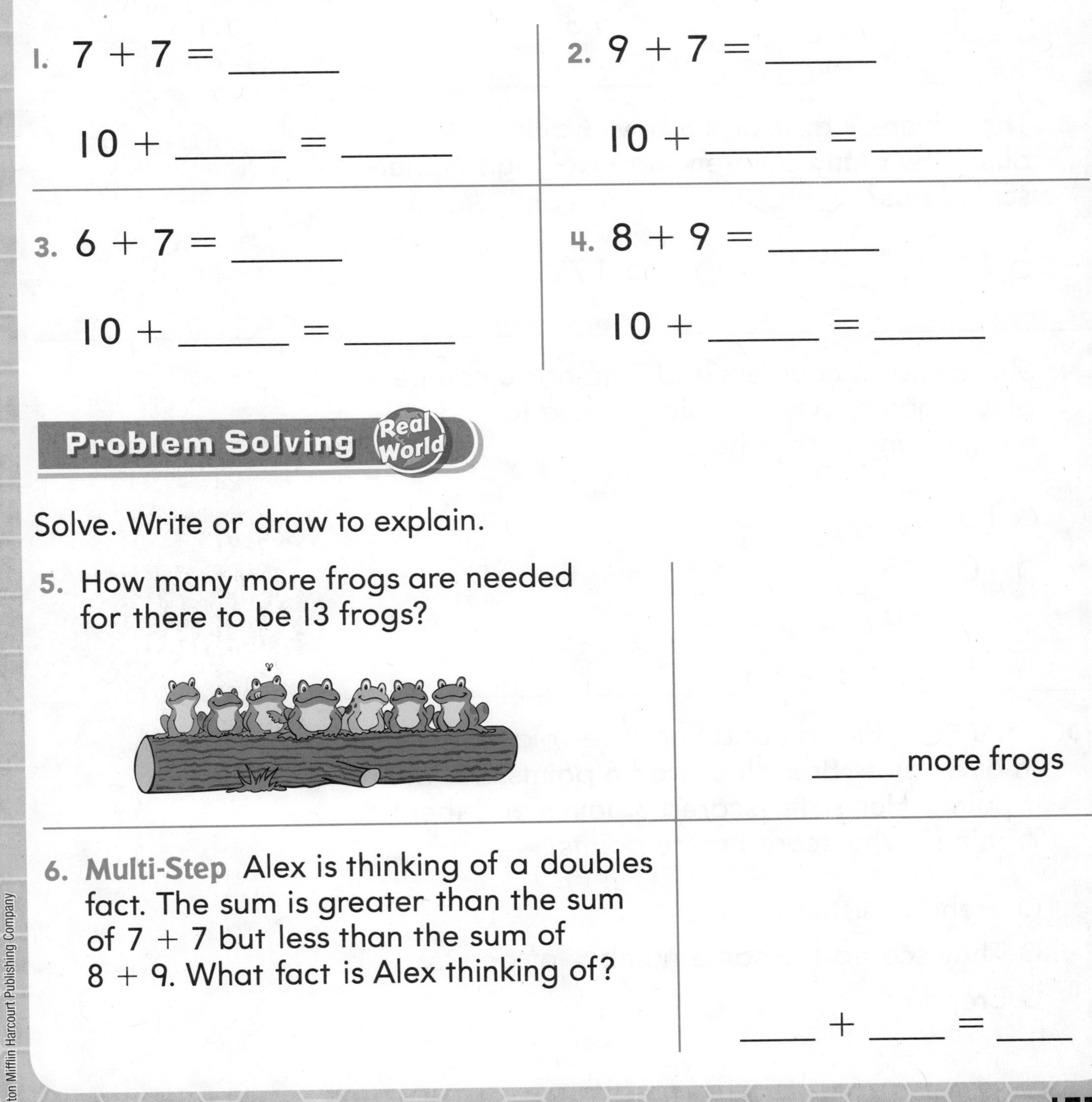

______ more frogs

6. **Multi-Step** Alex is thinking of a doubles fact. The sum is greater than the sum of $7 + 7$ but less than the sum of $8 + 9$. What fact is Alex thinking of?

____ $+$ ____ $=$ ____

Lesson Check

TEXAS Test Prep

Choose the correct answer.

7. Leon saw 5 birds in the morning. Then he saw 6 more birds in the afternoon. How many birds did he see in all?

○ 11 ○ 13 ○ 1

8. There were 9 girls and 8 boys waiting for the school bus. How many children were waiting for the school bus?

○ 19 ○ 17 ○ 15

9. Shirley has 6 counters and Sam has 8 counters to play a game. Which could you use to find how many counters they have?

○ $10 + 7$
○ $10 + 5$
○ $10 + 4$

10. **Multi-Step** Brenda and her sister played a game. In one game, Brenda scored 6 points and then 9 points. Her sister scored 8 points and then 7 points. Who scored more points?

○ Brenda's sister
○ They scored the same number of points.
○ Brenda

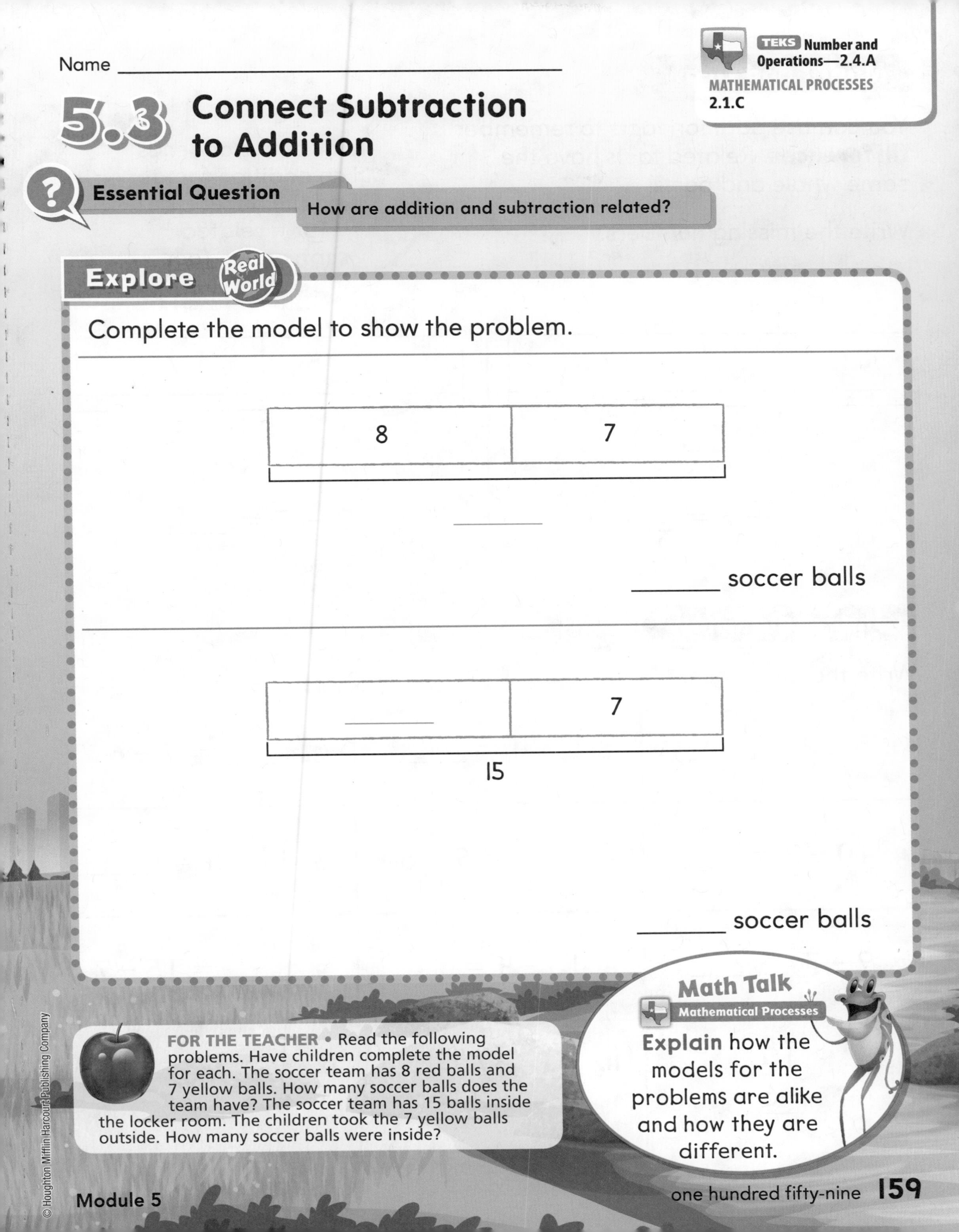

Name ___________________________

TEKS Number and Operations—2.4.A
MATHEMATICAL PROCESSES 2.1.C

5.3 Connect Subtraction to Addition

Essential Question How are addition and subtraction related?

Explore Real World

Complete the model to show the problem.

8	7

______

______ soccer balls

______	7

15

______ soccer balls

FOR THE TEACHER • Read the following problems. Have children complete the model for each. The soccer team has 8 red balls and 7 yellow balls. How many soccer balls does the team have? The soccer team has 15 balls inside the locker room. The children took the 7 yellow balls outside. How many soccer balls were inside?

Math Talk Mathematical Processes

Explain how the models for the problems are alike and how they are different.

Model and Draw

You can use addition facts to remember **differences**. Related facts have the same whole and parts.

Write the missing numbers.

Think of the addends in an addition fact to find the difference for a related subtraction fact.

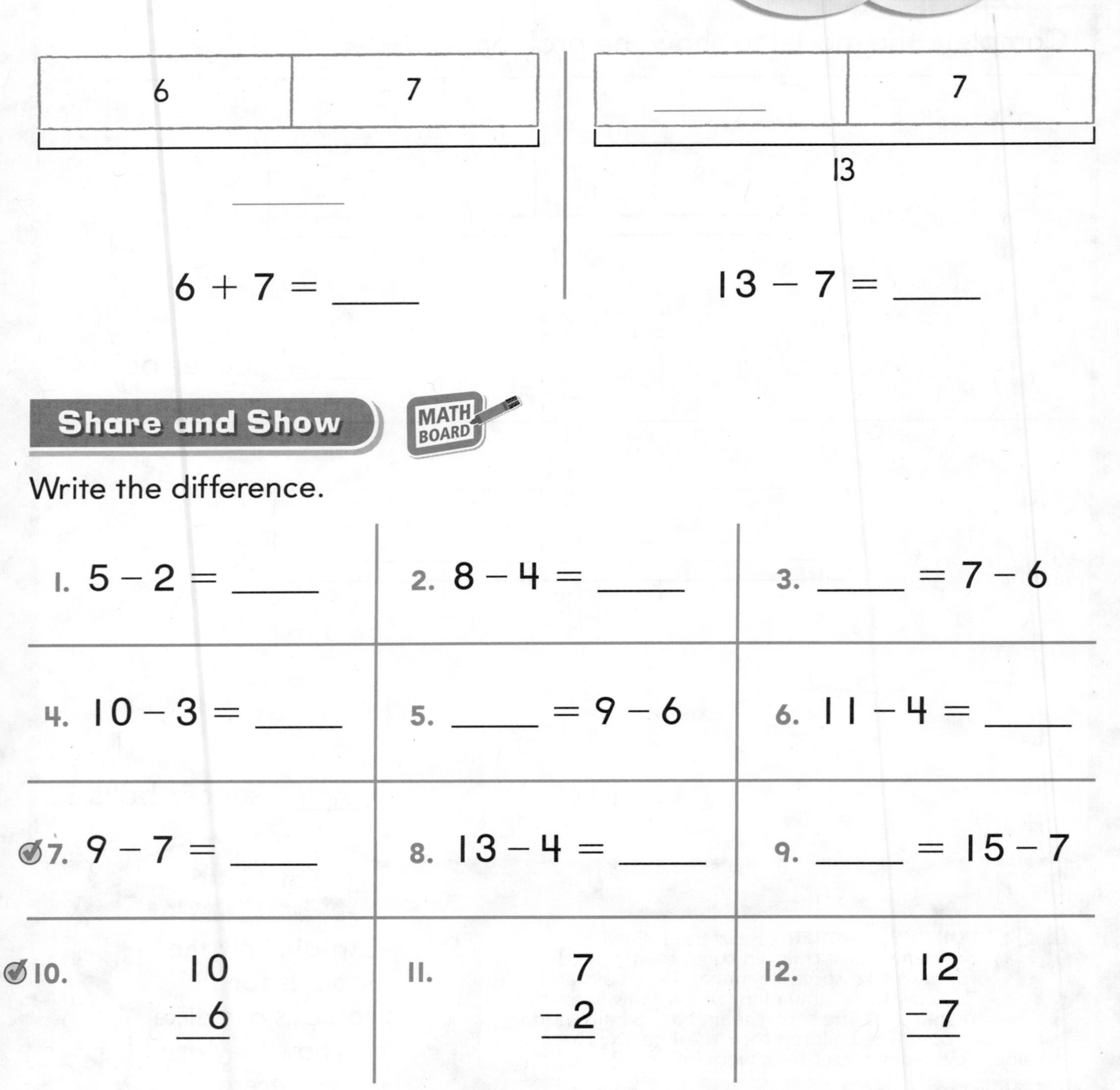

$6 + 7 =$ ____

$13 - 7 =$ ____

Share and Show

MATH BOARD

Write the difference.

1. $5 - 2 =$ ____	2. $8 - 4 =$ ____	3. ____ $= 7 - 6$
4. $10 - 3 =$ ____	5. ____ $= 9 - 6$	6. $11 - 4 =$ ____
7. $9 - 7 =$ ____	8. $13 - 4 =$ ____	9. ____ $= 15 - 7$
10. $\begin{array}{r} 10 \\ - 6 \\ \hline \end{array}$	11. $\begin{array}{r} 7 \\ - 2 \\ \hline \end{array}$	12. $\begin{array}{r} 12 \\ - 7 \\ \hline \end{array}$

Name ______________________

Problem Solving

Write the difference.

13. $14 - 8 =$ ____	14. ____ $= 8 - 3$	15. $11 - 6 =$ ____
16. $8 - 3 =$ ____	17. $12 - 4 =$ ____	18. ____ $= 16 - 9$
19. $\begin{array}{r} 7 \\ -\ 4 \\ \hline \end{array}$	20. $\begin{array}{r} 20 \\ -\ 10 \\ \hline \end{array}$	21. $\begin{array}{r} 10 \\ -\ 2 \\ \hline \end{array}$

Solve. Write or draw to explain.

22. H.O.T. Carmen had some balloons. She gave 9 balloons to Mark. She has 4 balloons now. How many balloons did she have to start?

____ balloons

23. H.O.T. **Multi-Step** Mr. Davis has a bag of 8 apples and a bag of 7 apples. His family eats 5 apples. How many apples does he have now?

____ apples

Mathematical Processes
Model • Reason • Communicate

Daily Assessment Task

Choose the correct answer.

24. Grant has 10 newspapers to deliver. He has delivered 4 newspapers. How many more newspapers does he need to deliver?
    - ○ 6
    - ○ 4
    - ○ 8

25. **Analyze** Kendra saw 14 deer. That is 5 more deer than Sam saw. How many deer did Sam see?
    - ○ 5
    - ○ 11
    - ○ 9

26. Write each difference.

$$\begin{array}{r} 8 \\ -\ 4 \\ \hline \end{array} \quad \begin{array}{r} 7 \\ -\ 1 \\ \hline \end{array} \quad \begin{array}{r} 14 \\ -\ 6 \\ \hline \end{array} \quad \begin{array}{r} 11 \\ -\ 3 \\ \hline \end{array} \quad \begin{array}{r} 13 \\ -\ 6 \\ \hline \end{array}$$

27. **TEXAS Test Prep** The children have 10 songs to play. After they play 6 songs, how many more songs do they still need to play?
    - ○ 8
    - ○ 14
    - ○ 4

TAKE HOME ACTIVITY • Have your child explain how he or she solved one of the problems in this lesson.

Homework and Practice

TEKS Number and Operations—2.4.A
MATHEMATICAL PROCESSES 2.1.C

Name ______________________

Connect Subtraction to Addition

Write the difference.

1. $6 - 2 =$ ____	2. $8 - 7 =$ ____	3. $16 - 7 =$ ____
4. $18 - 9 =$ ____	5. $13 - 8 =$ ____	6. $9 - 3 =$ ____

Problem Solving Real World

Solve. Write or draw to explain.

7. Will had some star stickers. He gave 6 stickers to James. He has 9 stickers now. How many star stickers did he have to start?

_______ star stickers

8. **Multi-Step** Ellen has one bunch of 6 bananas and another bunch with the same number of bananas. She gave away 4 bananas. How many bananas does she have now?

_______ bananas

Lesson Check

★ TEXAS Test Prep

Choose the correct answer.

9. On Monday, the pet store had 12 pets. By Wednesday, there were 7 pets. How many pets were bought from the pet store?

○ 6　　○ 19　　○ 5

10. There are 13 people in the lake. Six of them are adults. The rest are children. How many children are in the lake?

○ 19　　○ 7　　○ 8

11. Saul and Kim counted cars while riding in their family car. Saul saw 15 red cars. That is 6 more red cars than Kim saw. How many red cars did Kim see?

○ 9　　○ 11　　○ 8

12. Rita saw 16 monkeys and 9 lions at the zoo. How many more monkeys than lions did she see?

○ 3　　○ 7　　○ 6

13. **Multi-Step** Alex has 12 coins. He uses 3 coins to pay for a pencil. Then his friend gives him 4 more coins. How many coins does Alex have now?

○ 9　　○ 14　　○ 13

Name ______________________________

5.4 Use Ten to Subtract

Essential Question How does getting to 10 in subtraction help when finding differences?

Explore Real World

Circle to show the amount you subtract for each problem.

FOR THE TEACHER • Read the following problem. Scott has 13 crayons. He gives 3 crayons to Tyler. How many crayons does Scott have now? Have children circle the part of the blue line segment that shows what is subtracted from the total. Repeat for two more problems.

Math Talk Mathematical Processes

Describe a pattern in the three problems and answers.

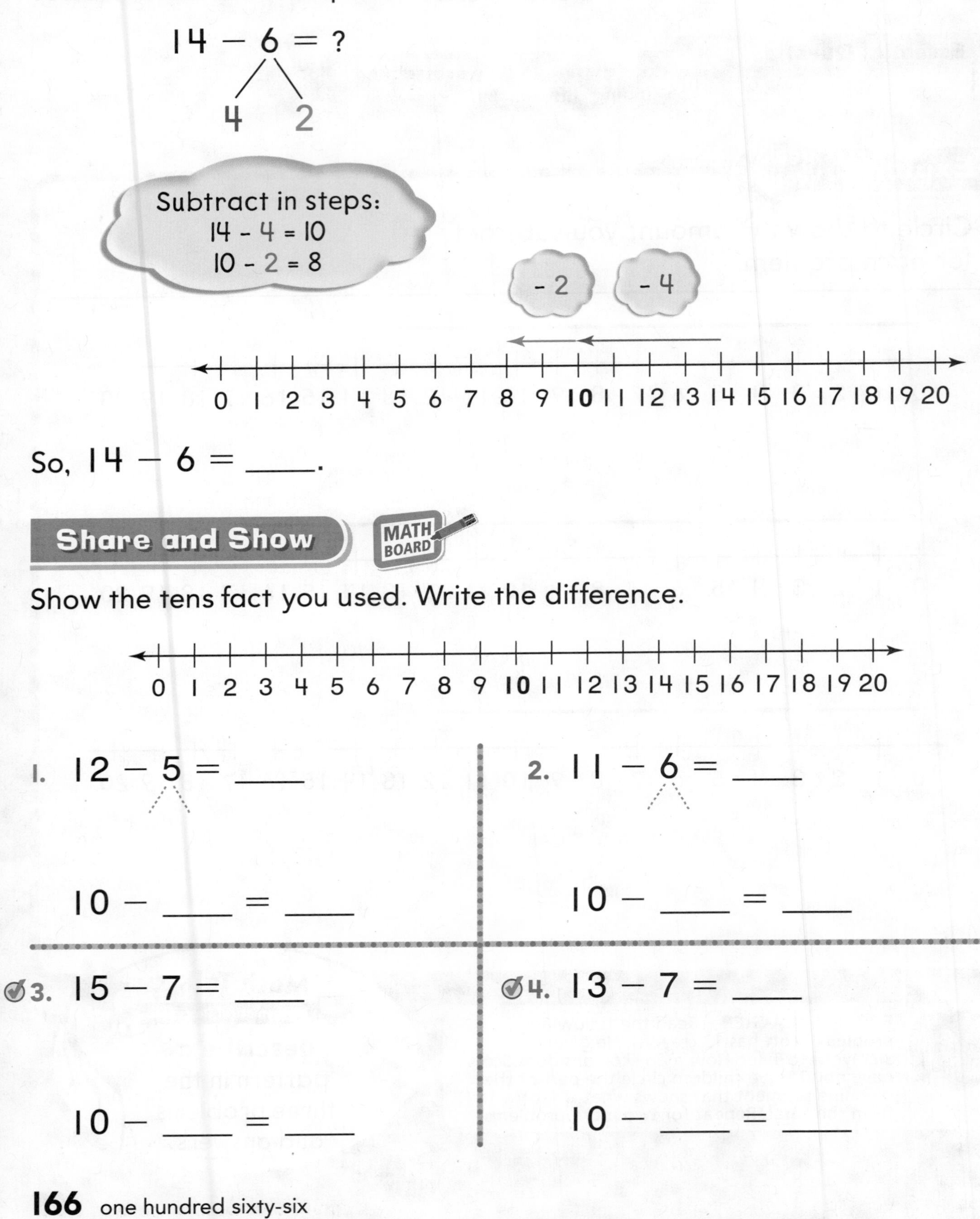

Model and Draw

You can subtract in steps to use a tens fact.

$14 - 6 = ?$

4 2

Subtract in steps:
$14 - 4 = 10$
$10 - 2 = 8$

- 2
- 4

0 1 2 3 4 5 6 7 8 9 **10** 11 12 13 14 15 16 17 18 19 20

So, $14 - 6 =$ ____.

Share and Show

MATH BOARD

Show the tens fact you used. Write the difference.

0 1 2 3 4 5 6 7 8 9 **10** 11 12 13 14 15 16 17 18 19 20

1. $12 - 5 =$ ____

   $10 -$ ____ $=$ ____

2. $11 - 6 =$ ____

   $10 -$ ____ $=$ ____

3. $15 - 7 =$ ____

   $10 -$ ____ $=$ ____

4. $13 - 7 =$ ____

   $10 -$ ____ $=$ ____

Name ______________________

Problem Solving

Show the tens fact you used. Write the difference.

0 1 2 3 4 5 6 7 8 9 **10** 11 12 13 14 15 16 17 18 19 20

5. 13 − 5 = ____

10 − ____ = ____

6. 15 − 6 = ____

10 − ____ = ____

7. 12 − 8 = ____

10 − ____ = ____

8. 14 − 8 = ____

10 − ____ = ____

Solve. Write or draw to explain.

9. **H.O.T.** Beth has a box of 16 crayons. She gives 3 crayons to Jake and 7 crayons to Wendy. How many crayons does Beth have now?

____ crayons

10. **H.O.T.** **Multi-Step** Chris had 15 stickers. He gave Ann and Suzy each the same number of stickers. Now Chris has 7 stickers. How many stickers did he give to each girl?

____ stickers

Daily Assessment Task

Choose the correct answer.

11. **Analyze** Tasha found two sea stars. The first sea star had 12 arms. The second sea star had 7 arms. How many more arms did the first sea star have?

- ○ 6
- ○ 5
- ○ 9

12. **Apply** Mr. Cruz wants to buy 11 postcards. So far, he has found 8 postcards. How many more postcards does Mr. Cruz need to find?

- ○ 10
- ○ 11
- ○ 3

13. Meg has 14 shells. That is 6 more shells than Lia has. How many shells does Lia have?

- ○ 6
- ○ 20
- ○ 8

14. **TEXAS Test Prep** Andy scored 13 points in the first game and 7 points in the second game. How many more points did he score in the first game than in the second game?

- ○ 6
- ○ 4
- ○ 20

TAKE HOME ACTIVITY • Ask your child to name pairs of numbers that have a difference of 10. Then have him or her write the number sentences.

Name ______

5.4 Use Ten to Subtract

Show the tens fact you used. Write the difference.

0 1 2 3 4 5 6 7 8 9 10 11 12 13 14 15 16 17 18 19 20

1. 11 − 5 = ____

   10 − ____ = ____

2. 14 − 7 = ____

   10 − ____ = ____

3. 15 − 8 = ____

   10 − ____ = ____

4. 18 − 9 = ____

   10 − ____ = ____

Problem Solving Real World

Solve. Write or draw to explain.

5. Joan has a box of 14 blue beads. She gives 5 beads to Judy and 5 beads to Sara. How many beads does Joan have now?

   ______ beads

6. **Multi-Step** Jake had 17 toy cars. He gave Dan and Andy each the same number of toy cars. Now Jake has 5 toy cars. How many toy cars did he give to each friend?

   ______ toy cars

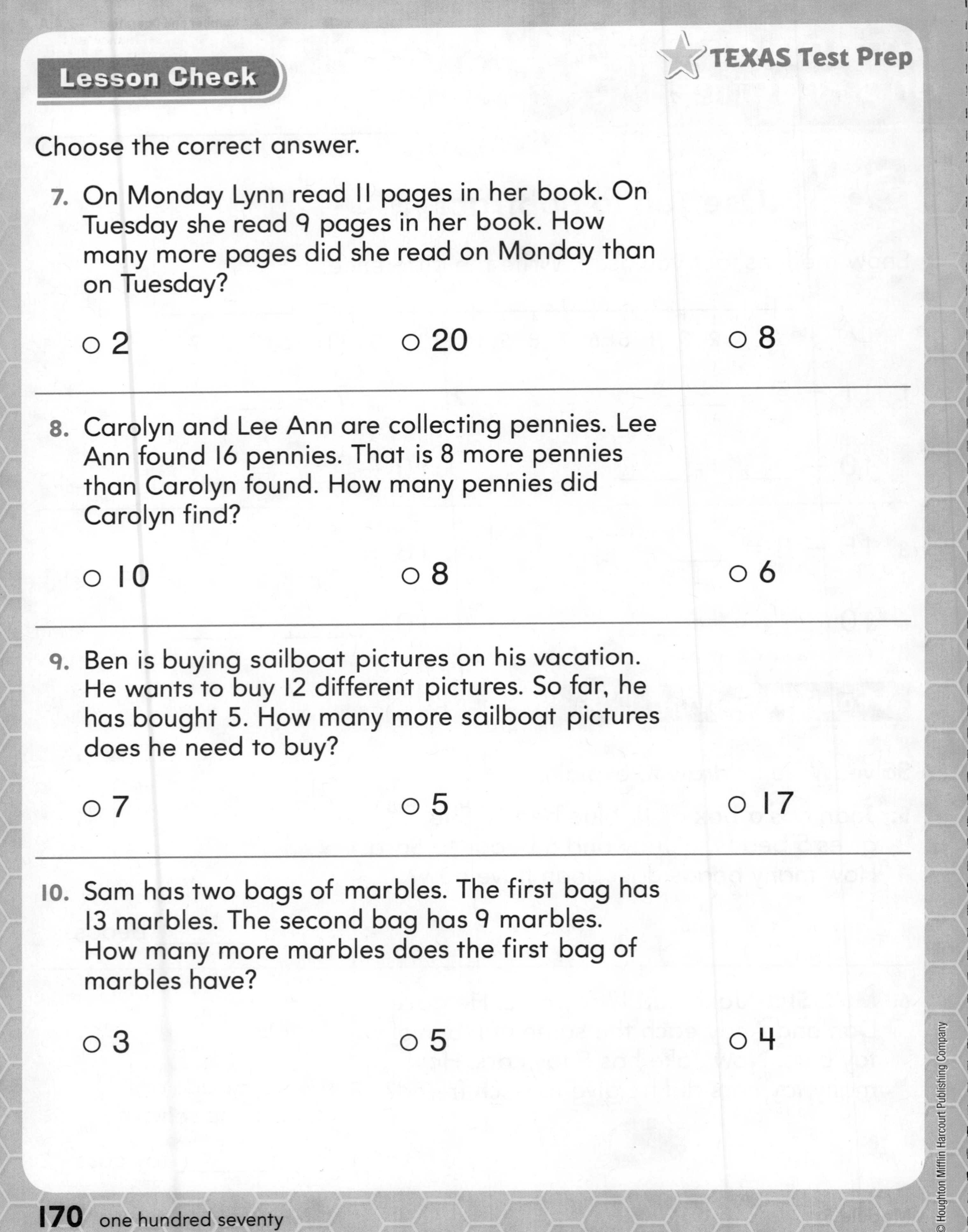

Lesson Check

TEXAS Test Prep

Choose the correct answer.

7. On Monday Lynn read 11 pages in her book. On Tuesday she read 9 pages in her book. How many more pages did she read on Monday than on Tuesday?

   ○ 2 ○ 20 ○ 8

8. Carolyn and Lee Ann are collecting pennies. Lee Ann found 16 pennies. That is 8 more pennies than Carolyn found. How many pennies did Carolyn find?

   ○ 10 ○ 8 ○ 6

9. Ben is buying sailboat pictures on his vacation. He wants to buy 12 different pictures. So far, he has bought 5. How many more sailboat pictures does he need to buy?

   ○ 7 ○ 5 ○ 17

10. Sam has two bags of marbles. The first bag has 13 marbles. The second bag has 9 marbles. How many more marbles does the first bag of marbles have?

    ○ 3 ○ 5 ○ 4

Name ______________________________

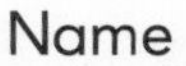

5.5 ALGEBRA Use Equations to Represent Problems

TEKS Number and Operations—2.4.A, 2.4.C
MATHEMATICAL PROCESSES 2.1.A

Essential Question How are number sentences used to show addition and subtraction situations?

Explore Real World

Write a story problem that could be solved using this model.

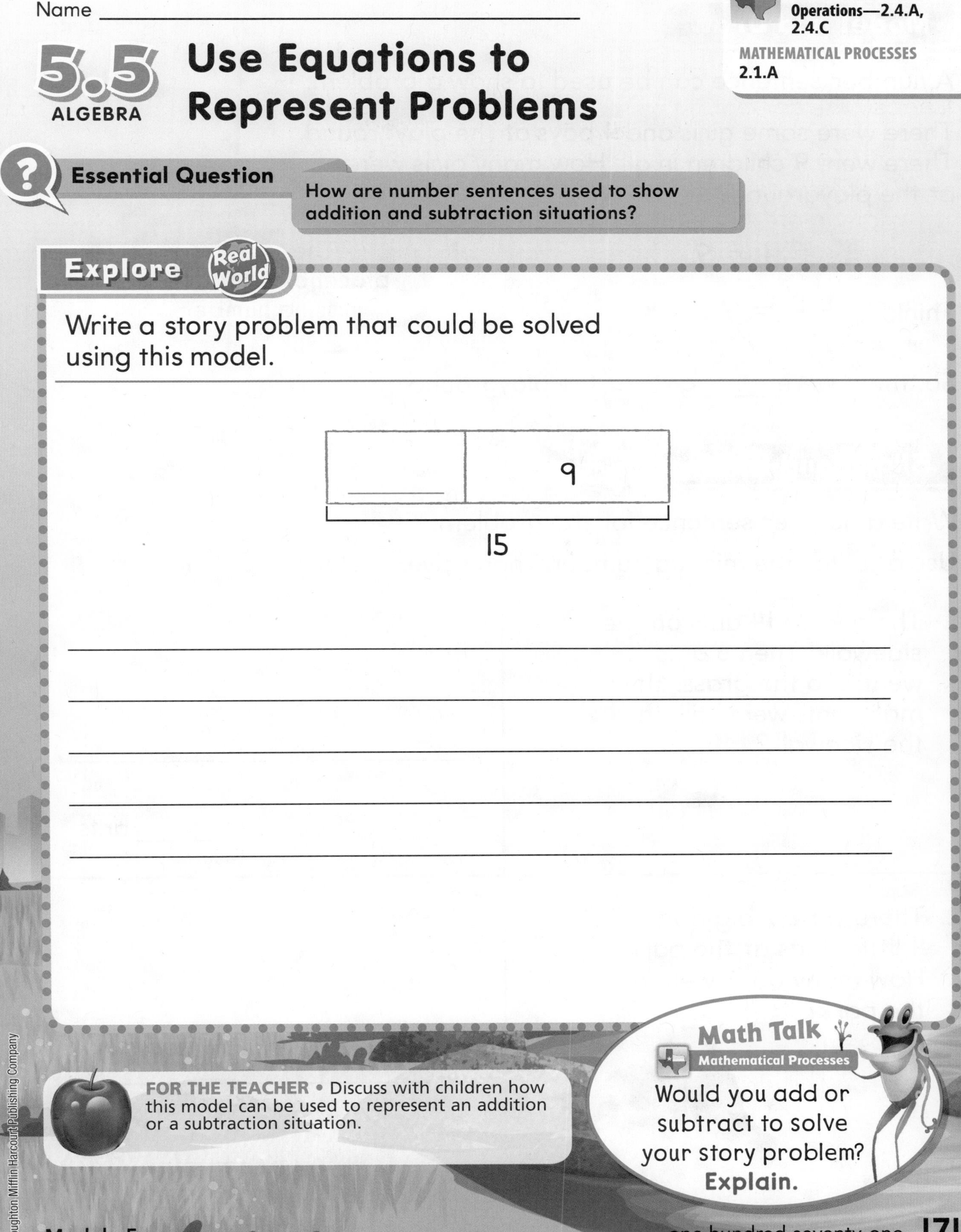

FOR THE TEACHER • Discuss with children how this model can be used to represent an addition or a subtraction situation.

Model and Draw

A number sentence can be used to show a problem.

There were some girls and 4 boys at the playground. There were 9 children in all. How many girls were at the playground?

$■ + 4 = 9$

Think: $5 + 4 = 9$

The ■ is a placeholder for the missing number.

So, there were _____ girls at the playground.

Share and Show

Write a number sentence for the problem.
Use a ■ for the missing number. Then solve.

1. There were 14 ants on the sidewalk. Then 6 ants went into the grass. How many ants were still on the sidewalk?

____

_______ ants

2. There were 7 big dogs and 4 little dogs at the park. How many dogs were at the park?

____

_______ dogs

Name ______________________________

Problem Solving

Write a number sentence for the problem.

Use a ■ for the missing number. Then solve.

3. There were 13 girls flying kites. Some of the girls went home. Then there were 7 girls flying kites. How many girls went home?

____

______ girls

4. There are 18 boys at the field. 9 of the boys are playing soccer. How many boys are not playing soccer?

____

______ boys

Solve. Write or draw to explain.

5. **H.O.T.** There were some ducks in a pond. Four more ducks joined them. Then there were 12 ducks in the pond. How many ducks were in the pond at first?

______ ducks

6. **H.O.T.** **Multi-Step** Matthew found 13 acorns. He traded 4 of his acorns for 7 acorns that Greg had. How many acorns does Matthew have now?

______ acorns

Daily Assessment Task

Choose the correct answer.

7. **Apply** Kent and Clark are playing a game. Clark has 11 points. That is 5 points more than Kent has. How many points does Kent have?

   ○ 7
   ○ 16
   ○ 6

8. **Multi-Step** 4 children are playing soccer, 6 children are playing basketball and 3 children are playing catch. How many children are playing games?

   ○ 10
   ○ 13
   ○ 9

9. There are 5 children and 9 adults watching a game. How many people are watching the game?

   ○ 12
   ○ 16
   ○ 14

10. **TEXAS Test Prep** Jon counted 12 butterflies. Tessa counted 7 butterflies. How many fewer butterflies did Tessa count than Jon?

   ○ 7
   ○ 5
   ○ 19

TAKE HOME ACTIVITY • Ask your child to explain how he or she solved one of the problems on this page.

Homework and Practice

TEKS Number and Operations—2.4.A, 2.4.C
MATHEMATICAL PROCESSES 2.1.A

Name ____________________

5.5 ALGEBRA Use Equations to Represent Problems

Write a number sentence for the problem.
Use a ■ for the missing number. Then solve.

1. There were 11 boys riding bikes. Some of the boys left to drink water. Then there were 5 boys riding bikes. How many boys went to drink water?

   ____

   _____ boys

2. There are 7 runners at the track. Then walkers came to the track. Now there are 14 people at the track. How many walkers came to the track?

   ____

   _____ walkers

Problem Solving Real World

Solve. Write or draw to explain.

3. There were some apples on the ground. Five more apples fell to the ground. Then there were 14 apples on the ground. How many apples were there on the ground first?

   _____ apples

4. **Multi-Step** Kayla found 10 coins in a jar. She gave 3 coins to her sister. Then Kayla found 6 more coins on a table. How many coins does Kayla have now?

   _____ coins

Lesson Check

TEXAS Test Prep

Choose the correct answer.

5. Jan counted 14 water bottles and Rita counted 6 water bottles. How many fewer water bottles did Rita count than Jan?

○ 8 ○ 7 ○ 20

6. There are 7 children and 6 adults at the dinner table. How many people are having dinner?

○ 7 ○ 13 ○ 12

7. Elliot and David are playing basketball. David won the game with 15 points. That was 7 points more than Elliot had. How many points did Elliot have?

○ 8
○ 1
○ 9

8. **Multi-Step** At the beach, 7 children are swimming and 5 children are playing in the sand. There are 4 other children who are reading. How many children are at beach?

○ 12
○ 16
○ 9

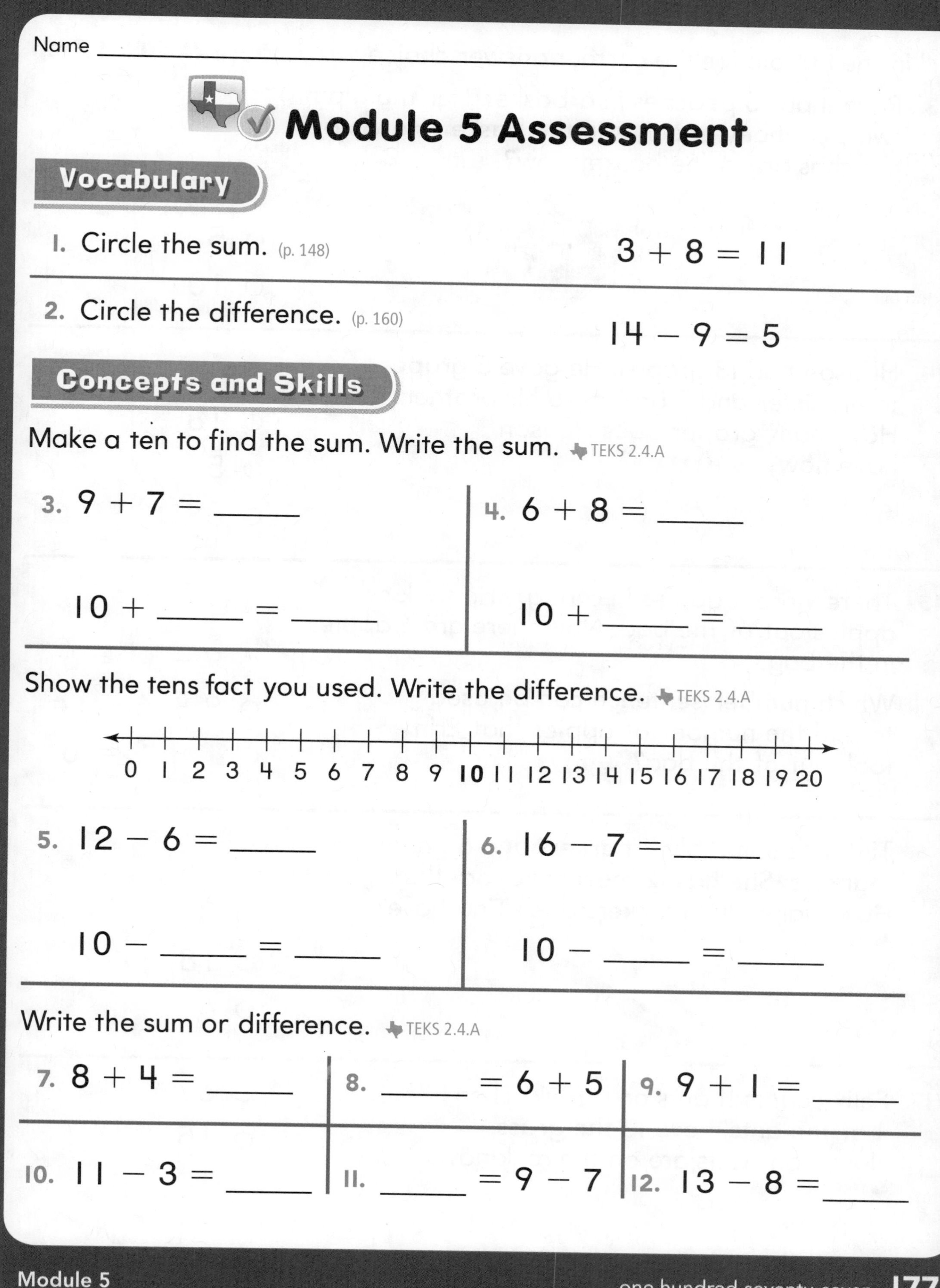

Name ______________________________

Module 5 Assessment

Vocabulary

1. Circle the sum. (p. 148) $3 + 8 = 11$

2. Circle the difference. (p. 160) $14 - 9 = 5$

Concepts and Skills

Make a ten to find the sum. Write the sum. TEKS 2.4.A

3. $9 + 7 =$ ______

   $10 +$ ______ $=$ ______

4. $6 + 8 =$ ______

   $10 +$ ______ $=$ ______

Show the tens fact you used. Write the difference. TEKS 2.4.A

5. $12 - 6 =$ ______

   $10 -$ ______ $=$ ______

6. $16 - 7 =$ ______

   $10 -$ ______ $=$ ______

Write the sum or difference. TEKS 2.4.A

7. $8 + 4 =$ ______

8. ______ $= 6 + 5$

9. $9 + 1 =$ ______

10. $11 - 3 =$ ______

11. ______ $= 9 - 7$

12. $13 - 8 =$ ______

Fill in the bubble for the correct answer choice.

TEXAS Test Prep

13. Rachel put 5 peaches in a basket. Her mom put twice as many peaches in the basket. How many peaches are in the basket now? TEKS 2.4.A

- ○ 15
- ○ 5
- ○ 10

14. Hudson had 13 grapes. He gave 5 grapes to his sister and 3 grapes to his brother. How many grapes does Hudson have now? TEKS 2.4.A

- ○ 18
- ○ 5
- ○ 8

15. There were 9 apples in a bag. Erin took some apples out of the bag. Now there are 6 apples in the bag.
Which number sentence can be used to find the number of apples that Erin took out of the bag? TEKS 2.4.A, 2.4.C

- ○ $9 - ■ = 6$
- ○ $9 + 6 = ■$
- ○ $■ + 2 = 6$

16. Tina has some blue markers and 6 green markers. She has 12 markers altogether. How many blue markers does Tina have? TEKS 2.4.A

- ○ 8
- ○ 18
- ○ 6

17. Felix counts 11 ants on a rock. Then 4 of the ants move to the grass. How many ants are on the rock now? TEKS 2.4.A

- ○ 6
- ○ 15
- ○ 7

Name ______________________________

TEKS Number and Operations—2.4.B
MATHEMATICAL PROCESSES
2.1.C, 2.1.E, 2.1.F

6.1 Break Apart Ones to Add

Essential Question How does breaking apart a number make it easier to add?

Explore — Real World — Hands On

Use [tens block] [ones block]. Draw to show what you did.

FOR THE TEACHER • Read the following problem. Have children use blocks to solve. Griffin read 27 books about animals and 6 books about space. How many books did he read?

Math Talk — Mathematical Processes

Describe what you did with the blocks.

Model and Draw

Break apart ones to make a ten.
Use this as a way to add.

$27 + 8 =$ ___?___

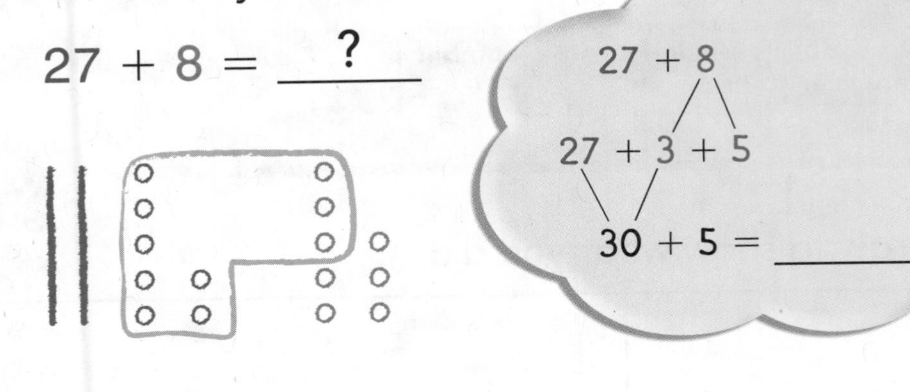

27 + 8

27 + 3 + 5

30 + 5 = ______

$27 + 8 =$ ______

Share and Show

Draw quick pictures. Break apart ones to make a ten. Then add and write the sum.

1. $15 + 7 =$ ______

2. $5 + 26 =$ ______

3. $37 + 8 =$ ______

4. $28 + 6 =$ ______

Name ___________________________

Problem Solving

Break apart ones to make a ten.
Then add and write the sum.

5. $23 + 9 =$ ______

6. $48 + 5 =$ ______

7. $7 + 58 =$ ______

8. $33 + 9 =$ ______

9. $6 + 27 =$ ______

10. $49 + 4 =$ ______

Solve. Write or draw to explain.

11. H.O.T. **Multi-Step** Bruce sees 29 oak trees and 4 maple trees at the park. Then he sees double the number of pine trees as maple trees. How many trees does Bruce see?

Math on the Spot

______ trees

12. H.O.T. Jamal has a box with some toy cars in it. He puts 3 more toy cars into the box. Now there are 22 toy cars in the box. How many toy cars were in the box before?

______ toy cars

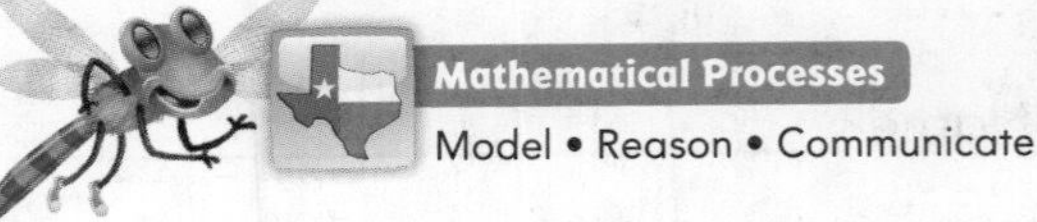

Daily Assessment Task

Choose the correct answer.

13. **Connect** Devon saw 19 adults wearing hats and 3 children wearing hats. How many people did Devon see wearing hats?

- ○ 22
- ○ 21
- ○ 23

14. Draw quick pictures to show how to break apart ones to make a ten. Then find the sum.

$27 + 8 =$ _____

15. **TEXAS Test Prep** Alicia puts 25 books on the shelf. Trenton puts 8 books on the shelf. How many books do they put on the shelf?

- ○ 28
- ○ 23
- ○ 33

TAKE HOME ACTIVITY • Say a number from 0 to 9. Have your child name a number to add to yours to have a sum of 10.

Homework and Practice

TEKS Number and Operations—2.4.B
MATHEMATICAL PROCESSES 2.1.C, 2.1.E, 2.1.F

Name ______________________

6.1 Break Apart Ones to Add

Draw quick pictures. Break apart ones to make a ten. Then add and write the sum.

1. 18 + 5 = ______

2. 34 + 8 = ______

3. 56 + 7 = ______

4. 6 + 49 = ______

Problem Solving Real World

Solve. Write or draw to explain.

5. **Multi-Step** Alex sets up 32 small tables and 9 large tables in a room. Then he sets up 5 more large tables along a wall. How many tables does Alex set up?

______ tables

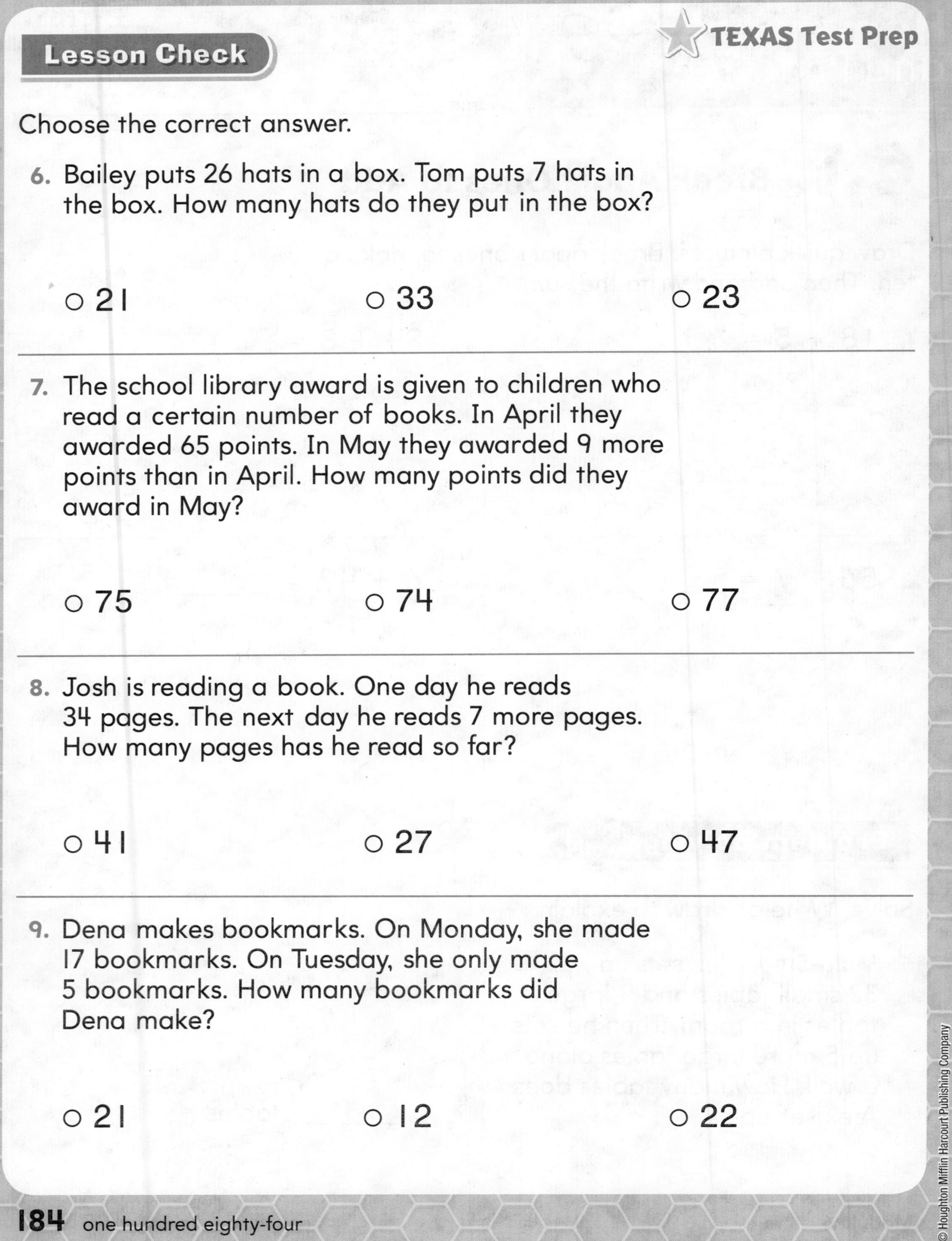

Lesson Check

TEXAS Test Prep

Choose the correct answer.

6. Bailey puts 26 hats in a box. Tom puts 7 hats in the box. How many hats do they put in the box?

○ 21 ○ 33 ○ 23

7. The school library award is given to children who read a certain number of books. In April they awarded 65 points. In May they awarded 9 more points than in April. How many points did they award in May?

○ 75 ○ 74 ○ 77

8. Josh is reading a book. One day he reads 34 pages. The next day he reads 7 more pages. How many pages has he read so far?

○ 41 ○ 27 ○ 47

9. Dena makes bookmarks. On Monday, she made 17 bookmarks. On Tuesday, she only made 5 bookmarks. How many bookmarks did Dena make?

○ 21 ○ 12 ○ 22

Name ______________________________

6.2 Use Compensation

Essential Question How can you make an addend a ten to help solve an addition problem?

Hands On

Draw quick pictures to show the problems.

FOR THE TEACHER • Have children draw quick pictures to solve this problem. Kara has 47 stickers. She buys 20 more stickers. How many stickers does she have now? Repeat for this problem. Tyrone has 30 stickers and buys 52 more stickers. How many stickers does he have now?

Math Talk Mathematical Processes

Describe how you found how many stickers Tyrone has.

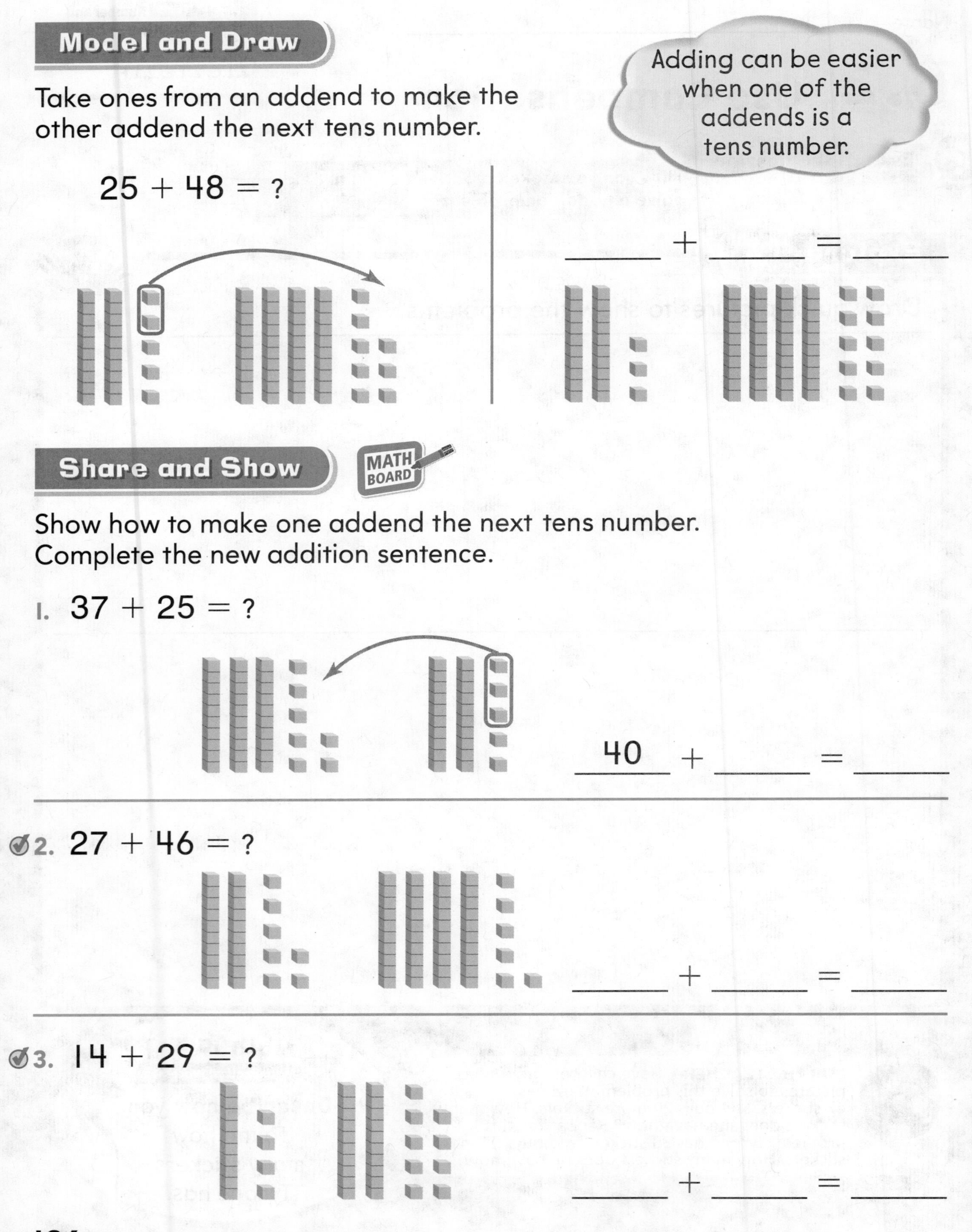

Model and Draw

Take ones from an addend to make the other addend the next tens number.

Adding can be easier when one of the addends is a tens number.

$25 + 48 = ?$

____ + ____ = ____

Share and Show

MATH BOARD

Show how to make one addend the next tens number. Complete the new addition sentence.

1. $37 + 25 = ?$

40 + ____ = ____

2. $27 + 46 = ?$

____ + ____ = ____

3. $14 + 29 = ?$

____ + ____ = ____

Name ______________________________

Problem Solving

Show how to make one addend the next tens number.
Complete the new addition sentence.

4. 24 + 18 = ?

_____ + _____ = _____

5. 27 + 24 = ?

_____ + _____ = _____

Solve. Write or draw to explain.

6. H.O.T. **Multi-Step** Zach finds 38 twigs. Kelly finds 27 twigs. How many more twigs do the two children still need if they want 70 twigs in all?

Math on the Spot

_____ more twigs

7. H.O.T. **Multi-Step** The chart shows the leaves that Philip collected. He wants a collection of 52 leaves, using only two colors. Which two colors of leaves should he use?

Leaves Collected

Color	Number
green	27
brown	29
yellow	25

__________ and __________

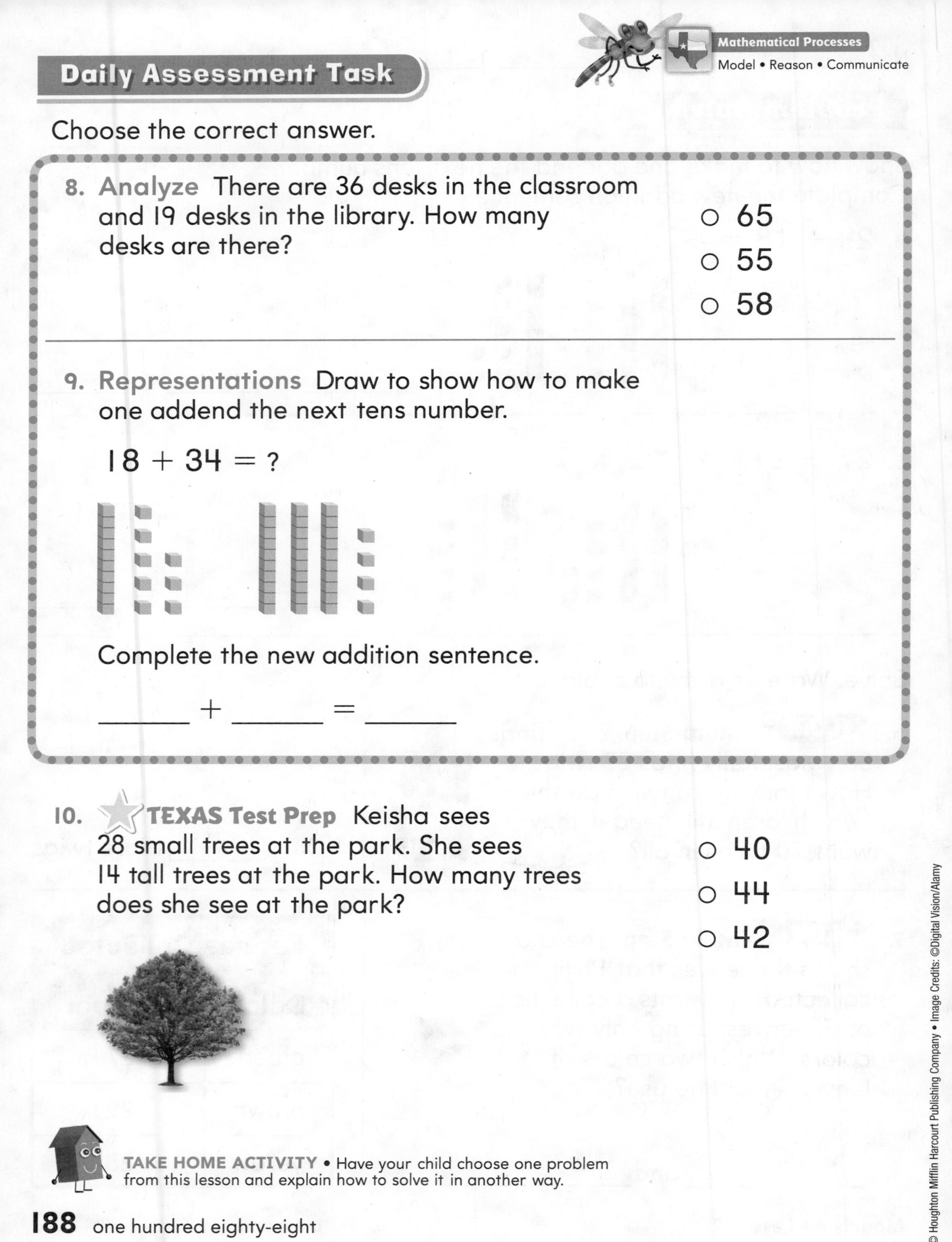

Daily Assessment Task

Mathematical Processes
Model • Reason • Communicate

Choose the correct answer.

8. **Analyze** There are 36 desks in the classroom and 19 desks in the library. How many desks are there?

- ○ 65
- ○ 55
- ○ 58

9. **Representations** Draw to show how to make one addend the next tens number.

18 + 34 = ?

Complete the new addition sentence.

______ + ______ = ______

10. **TEXAS Test Prep** Keisha sees 28 small trees at the park. She sees 14 tall trees at the park. How many trees does she see at the park?

- ○ 40
- ○ 44
- ○ 42

TAKE HOME ACTIVITY • Have your child choose one problem from this lesson and explain how to solve it in another way.

TEKS Number and Operations—2.4.B
MATHEMATICAL PROCESSES 2.1.C, 2.1.E, 2.1.F

Name ______________________

6.2 Use Compensation

Show how to make one addend the next tens number.
Complete the new addition sentence.

1. 26 + 27 = ?

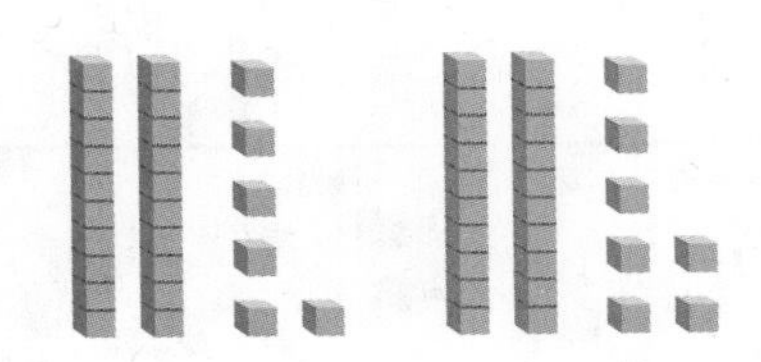

_____ + _____ = _____

2. 38 + 45 = ?

_____ + _____ = _____

Problem Solving Real World

Solve. Write or draw to explain.

3. **Multi-Step** Lee finds 44 shells. Wayne finds 39 shells. How many shells do they still need if they want 90 shells in all?

_____ shells

Lesson Check

TEXAS Test Prep

Choose the correct answer.

4. Marianne picks up 24 acorns at the park. Then she finds and picks up 19 more acorns. How many acorns does she pick up?

   ○ 39
   ○ 43
   ○ 42

---

5. There are 18 long coats in the closet and 34 short coats in the closet. How many coats are there?

   ○ 52
   ○ 42
   ○ 54

---

6. A sports store has 45 red bikes and 47 black bikes. How many bikes does the store have altogether?

   ○ 93
   ○ 97
   ○ 92

---

7. **Multi-Step** The coach buys 16 short hockey sticks and 19 long hockey sticks. The he buys 3 more short sticks. How many hockey sticks did he buy?

   ○ 35
   ○ 28
   ○ 38

Name ___________________________

6.3 Break Apart Addends as Tens and Ones

Essential Question How do you break apart addends to add tens and then add ones?

Explore

Write the number. Then write the number as tens plus ones.

[ ] ____ + ____

[ ] ____ + ____

[ ] ____ + ____

FOR THE TEACHER • Direct children's attention to the orange box. Have children write 25 inside the large rectangle. Then ask children to write 25 as tens plus ones. Repeat the activity for 36 and 42.

Math Talk Mathematical Processes

What is the value of the 6 in the number 63? **Explain.**

Model and Draw

Break apart the addends into tens and ones.
Add the tens. Add the ones. Find the sum.

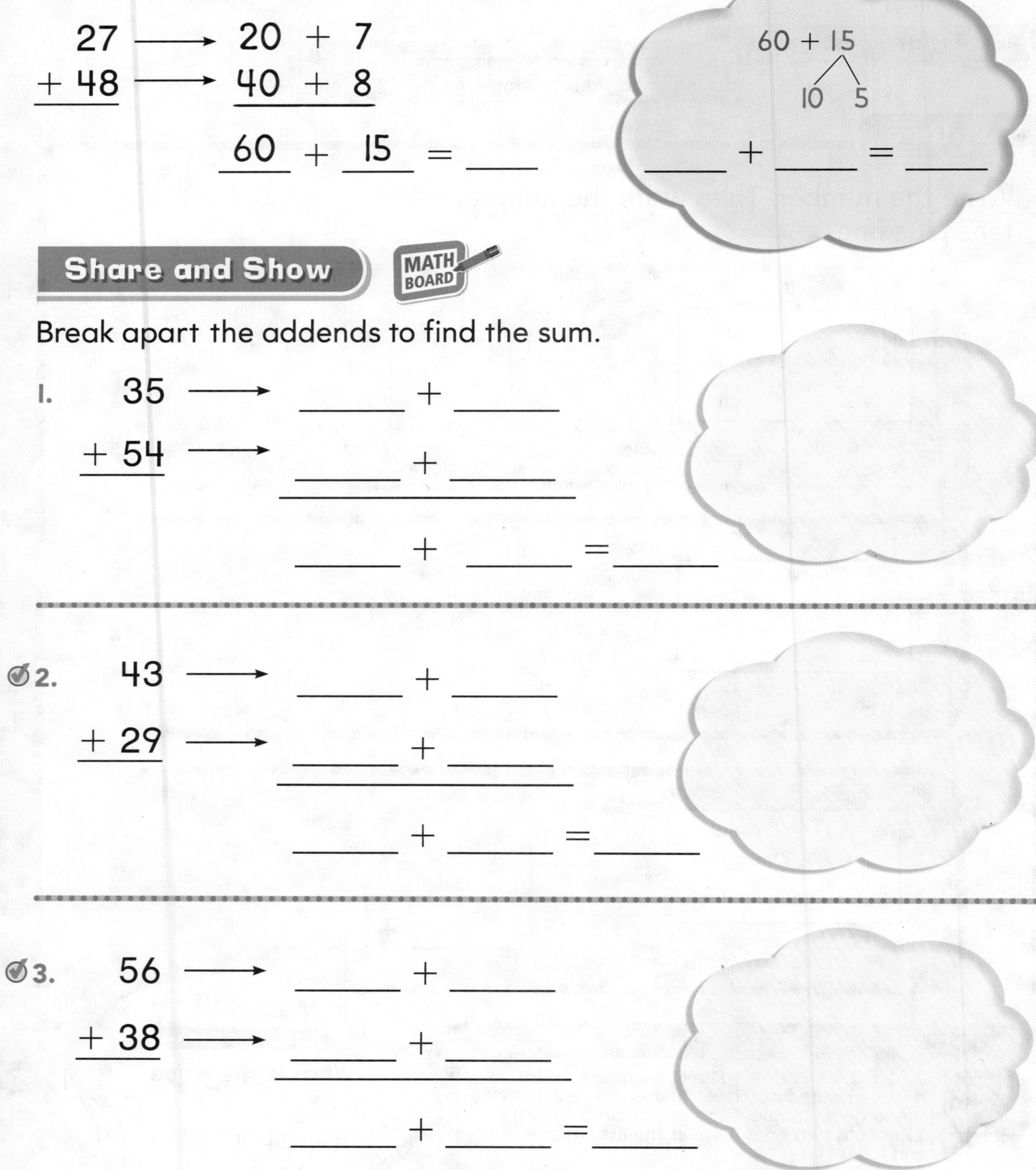

27 → 20 + 7
+ 48 → 40 + 8

60 + 15 = ____

60 + 15
10 5

____ + ____ = ____

Share and Show

MATH BOARD

Break apart the addends to find the sum.

1. 35 → ____ + ____
+ 54 → ____ + ____

____ + ____ = ____

2. 43 → ____ + ____
+ 29 → ____ + ____

____ + ____ = ____

3. 56 → ____ + ____
+ 38 → ____ + ____

____ + ____ = ____

Name ______________________________

Problem Solving

Break apart the addends to find the sum.

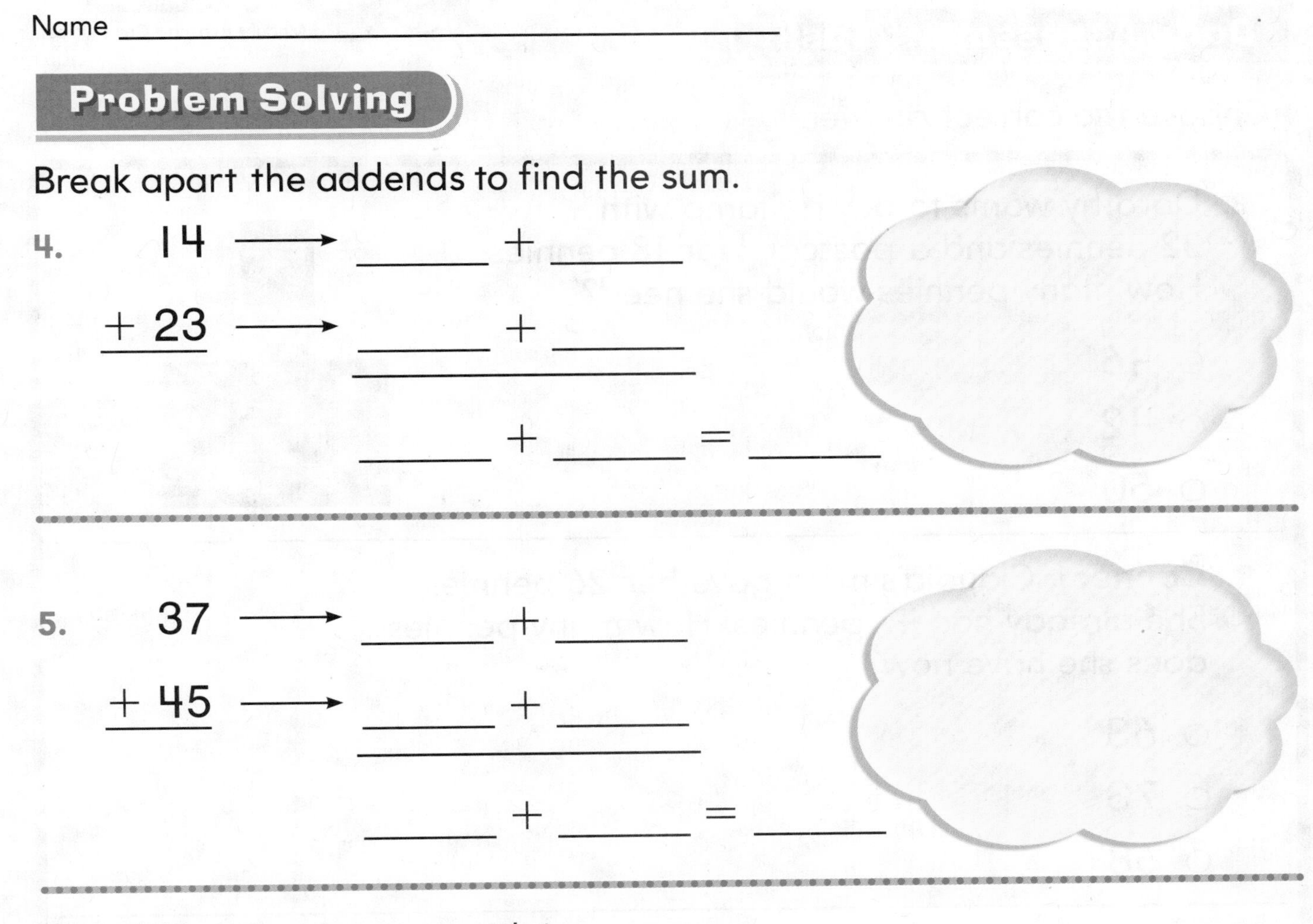

4. 14 → ____ + ____

+ 23 → ____ + ____

____ + ____ = ____

5. 37 → ____ + ____

+ 45 → ____ + ____

____ + ____ = ____

Solve. Write or draw to explain.

6. **H.O.T.** **Multi-Step** Julie read 18 pages of her book in the morning. She read the same number of pages in the afternoon. How many pages did she read?

____ pages

7. **H.O.T.** **Multi-Step** Chris read 15 pages of his book. Tony read 4 more pages than Chris. How many pages did Chris and Tony read?

____ pages

Mathematical Processes
Model • Reason • Communicate

Daily Assessment Task

Choose the correct answer.

8. Dorothy wants to buy a stamp with 32 pennies and a postcard for 18 pennies. How many pennies would she need?

- ○ 46
- ○ 42
- ○ 50

9. **Connect** Claudia's mom gave her 26 pennies. She already had 47 pennies. How many pennies does she have now?

- ○ 63
- ○ 73
- ○ 68

10. **Analyze** Mr. Green has 48 books on one shelf. He has 34 books on another shelf. How many books are on the two shelves?

- ○ 84
- ○ 70
- ○ 82

11. **TEXAS Test Prep** Tomás has 17 art pencils. He buys 26 more art pencils. How many art pencils does Tomás have now?

- ○ 43
- ○ 33
- ○ 41

TAKE HOME ACTIVITY • Write 32 + 48 on a sheet of paper. Have your child break apart the numbers and find the sum.

Homework and Practice

TEKS Number and Operations—2.4.B
MATHEMATICAL PROCESSES 2.1.C, 2.1.E, 2.1.F

Name ______________________

6.3 Break Apart Addends as Tens and Ones

Break apart the addends to find the sum.

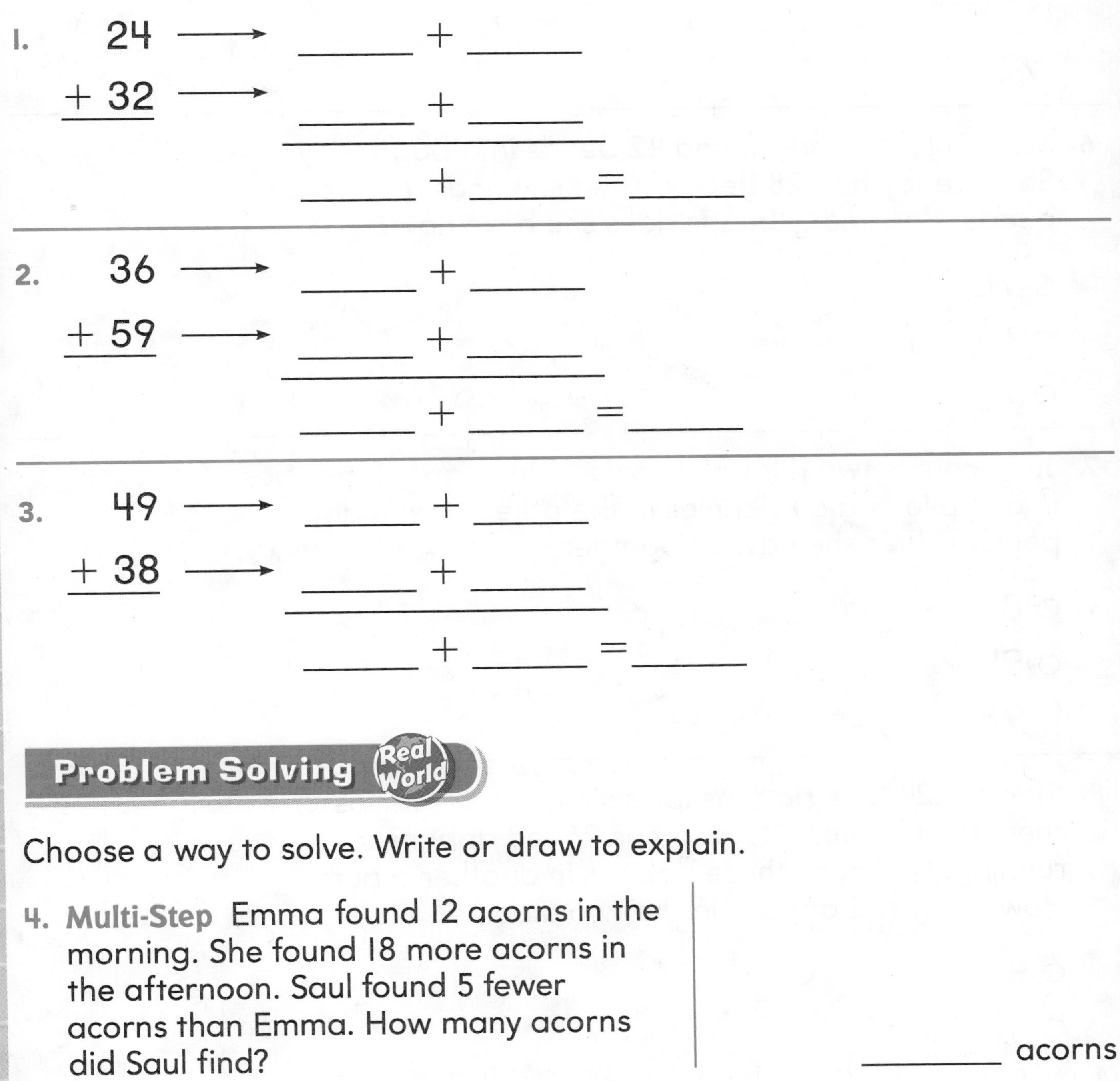

1. 24 → ____ + ____
   + 32 → ____ + ____
   ____ + ____ = ____

2. 36 → ____ + ____
   + 59 → ____ + ____
   ____ + ____ = ____

3. 49 → ____ + ____
   + 38 → ____ + ____
   ____ + ____ = ____

Problem Solving Real World

Choose a way to solve. Write or draw to explain.

4. **Multi-Step** Emma found 12 acorns in the morning. She found 18 more acorns in the afternoon. Saul found 5 fewer acorns than Emma. How many acorns did Saul find?

   ____ acorns

Lesson Check

Choose the correct answer.

5. Ray has 19 marbles. He buys 35 more marbles. How many marbles does Ray have now?

   - ○ 54
   - ○ 44
   - ○ 55

---

6. **Multi-Step** Melinda found 42 beads in a bag today. She already had 28 beads. Then she finds 9 more beads. How many beads does she have now?

   - ○ 70
   - ○ 69
   - ○ 79

---

7. Julia counts two piles of pennies. There are 25 pennies in one pile and 69 pennies in the other. How many pennies does she have altogether?

   - ○ 84
   - ○ 94
   - ○ 95

---

8. Rick has 24 blue ribbons for swimming. He keeps them in an album. He also has 26 red ribbons for running. He keeps those ribbons in another album. How many ribbons are in the two albums?

   - ○ 42
   - ○ 40
   - ○ 50

Name ______________________________

TEKS Number and Operations—2.4.B
MATHEMATICAL PROCESSES 2.1.D, 2.1.E, 2.1.F

6.4 Model and Record 2-Digit Addition

Essential Question How do you record 2-digit addition?

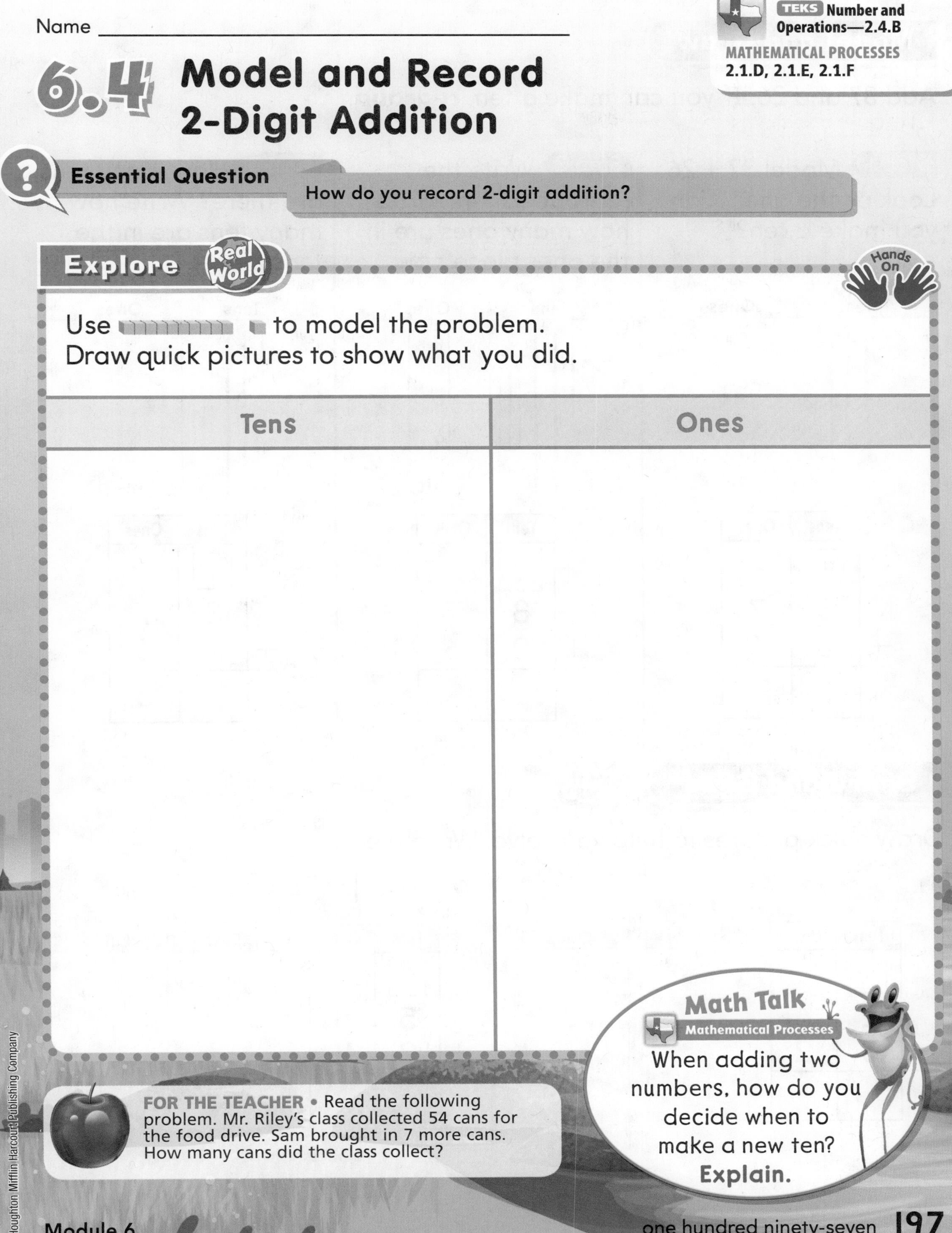

Explore Real World

Hands On

Use [tens blocks] [ones blocks] to model the problem.
Draw quick pictures to show what you did.

Tens	Ones

FOR THE TEACHER • Read the following problem. Mr. Riley's class collected 54 cans for the food drive. Sam brought in 7 more cans. How many cans did the class collect?

Math Talk
Mathematical Processes
When adding two numbers, how do you decide when to make a new ten? **Explain.**

Model and Draw

Add 37 and 26. If you can make a ten, **regroup**.

Step 1 Model 37 + 26. Look at the ones. Can you make a ten?

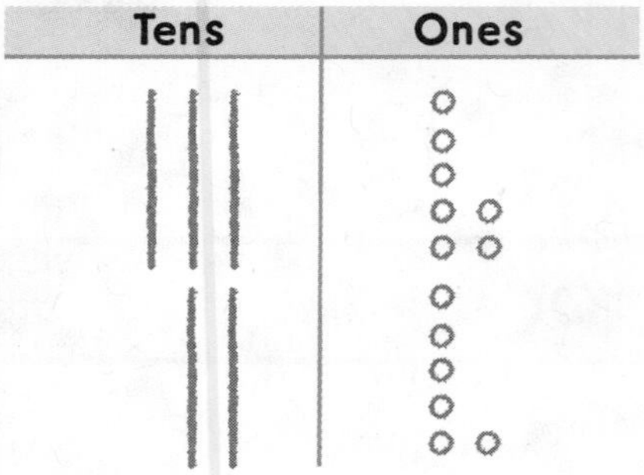

Tens	Ones
3	7
+ 2	6

Step 2 Write the regrouped ten. Write how many ones are in the ones place now.

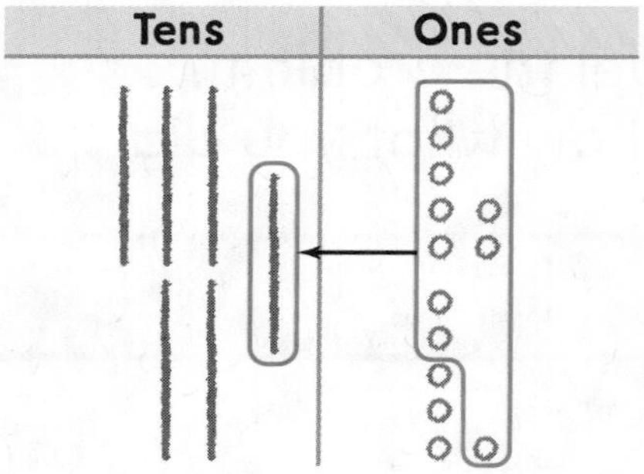

Tens	Ones
1	
3	7
+ 2	6
	3

Step 3 How many tens are there? Write how many tens are in the tens place.

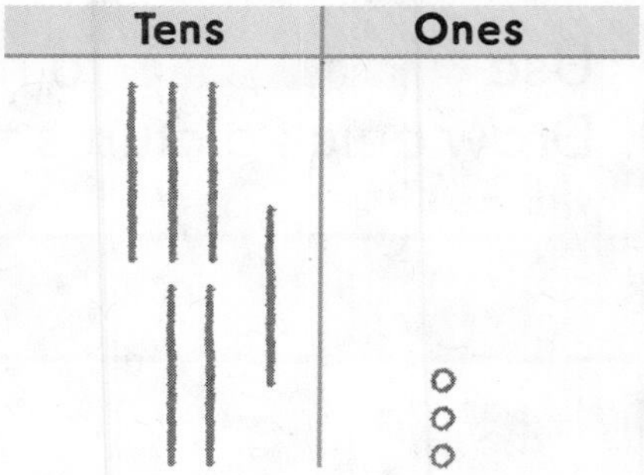

Tens	Ones
1	
3	7
+ 2	6
6	3

Share and Show

MATH BOARD

Draw quick pictures to help you solve. Write the sum.

1.

Tens	Ones
2	6
+ 3	2

Tens	Ones

2.

Tens	Ones
5	8
+ 2	4

Tens	Ones

Homework and Practice

Name ______________________

6.4 Model and Record 2-Digit Addition

Draw quick pictures to help you solve. Write the sum.

1.

	Tens	Ones
	☐	
	3	6
+	2	8

Tens	Ones

2.

	Tens	Ones
	☐	
	5	3
+	3	2

Tens	Ones

3.

	Tens	Ones
	☐	
	2	9
+	2	7

Tens	Ones

4.

	Tens	Ones
	☐	
	6	8
+	1	3

Tens	Ones

Problem Solving Real World

Choose a way to solve. Write or draw to explain.

5. **Multi-Step** A baker wants to sell 100 muffins. So far the baker has sold 48 corn muffins and 42 bran muffins. How many more muffins does the baker need to sell?

_______ more muffins

Lesson Check

TEXAS Test Prep

Choose the correct answer.

6. Darla made 27 drawings. Sue Ann made 34 drawings. How many drawings did they make in all?

○ 61 ○ 53 ○ 41

7. Tim and his family spent the day hiking. In the morning Tim counted 35 birds. In the afternoon he counted 36 birds. How many birds did Tim count?

○ 71 ○ 61 ○ 72

8. Rose brings 59 bottles to the recycling center on Friday. On Saturday Rose brings 33 more bottles to the recycling center. How many bottles does she bring to the recycling center on those two days?

○ 96
○ 92
○ 82

9. **Multi-Step** Ryan counted 29 bricks. Amanda counted 47 bricks and then counted 10 more. How many bricks did they count altogether?

○ 72
○ 66
○ 86

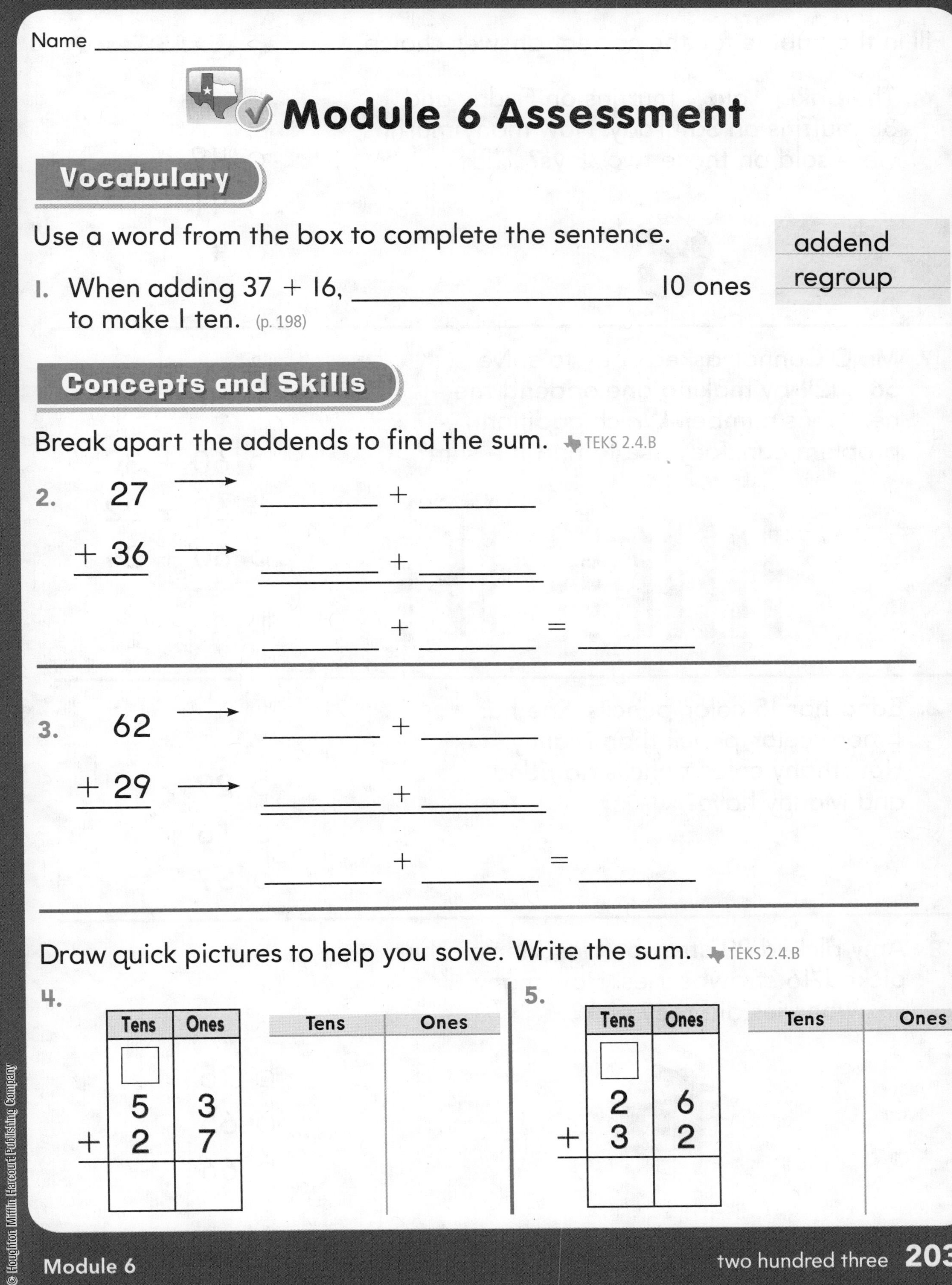

Name ______________________

Module 6 Assessment

Vocabulary

Use a word from the box to complete the sentence.

addend
regroup

1. When adding 37 + 16, ______________ 10 ones to make 1 ten. (p. 198)

Concepts and Skills

Break apart the addends to find the sum. TEKS 2.4.B

2.
$$\begin{array}{r} 27 \\ +\ 36 \\ \hline \end{array}$$
27 → ______ + ______
36 → ______ + ______
______ + ______ = ______

3.
$$\begin{array}{r} 62 \\ +\ 29 \\ \hline \end{array}$$
62 → ______ + ______
29 → ______ + ______
______ + ______ = ______

Draw quick pictures to help you solve. Write the sum. TEKS 2.4.B

4.

	Tens	Ones
	□	
	5	3
+	2	7

Tens	Ones

5.

	Tens	Ones
	□	
	2	6
+	3	2

Tens	Ones

Fill in the bubble for the correct answer choice. TEXAS Test Prep

6. The baker sold 9 muffins on Friday and 38 muffins on Saturday. How many muffins were sold on those two days? TEKS 2.4.B

- ○ 49
- ○ 41
- ○ 47

7. Mr. O'Connor asked Joey to solve 58 + 24 by making one addend the next tens number. Which addition problem can Joey use to find the sum? TEKS 2.4.B

- ○ 60 + 30
- ○ 60 + 22
- ○ 60 + 24

8. Edna has 15 color pencils. She has 1 more color pencil than Manny. How many color pencils do Edna and Manny have? TEKS 2.4.B

- ○ 29
- ○ 16
- ○ 39

9. Amy picked 29 strawberries. Her mother picked 46 strawberries. How many strawberries did they pick? TEKS 2.4.B

- ○ 75
- ○ 65
- ○ 66

Name ______________________________

TEKS Number and Operations—2.4.B
MATHEMATICAL PROCESSES 2.1.D, 2.1.E

7.1 2-Digit Addition

Essential Question How do you record the steps when adding 2-digit numbers?

Explore Real World

Hands On

Draw quick pictures to model each problem.

Tens	Ones

Tens	Ones

FOR THE TEACHER • Read the following problem and have children draw quick pictures to solve. The animal shelter has 35 dogs and 47 cats for adoption. How many pets are at the shelter? Repeat the activity with this problem. After a pet fair, there are only 18 dogs and 21 cats at the shelter. How many pets are at the shelter now?

Math Talk Mathematical Processes

Explain when you need to regroup ones.

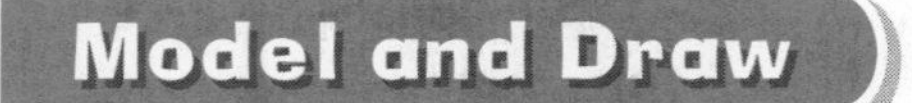

Model and Draw

Add 59 and 24.

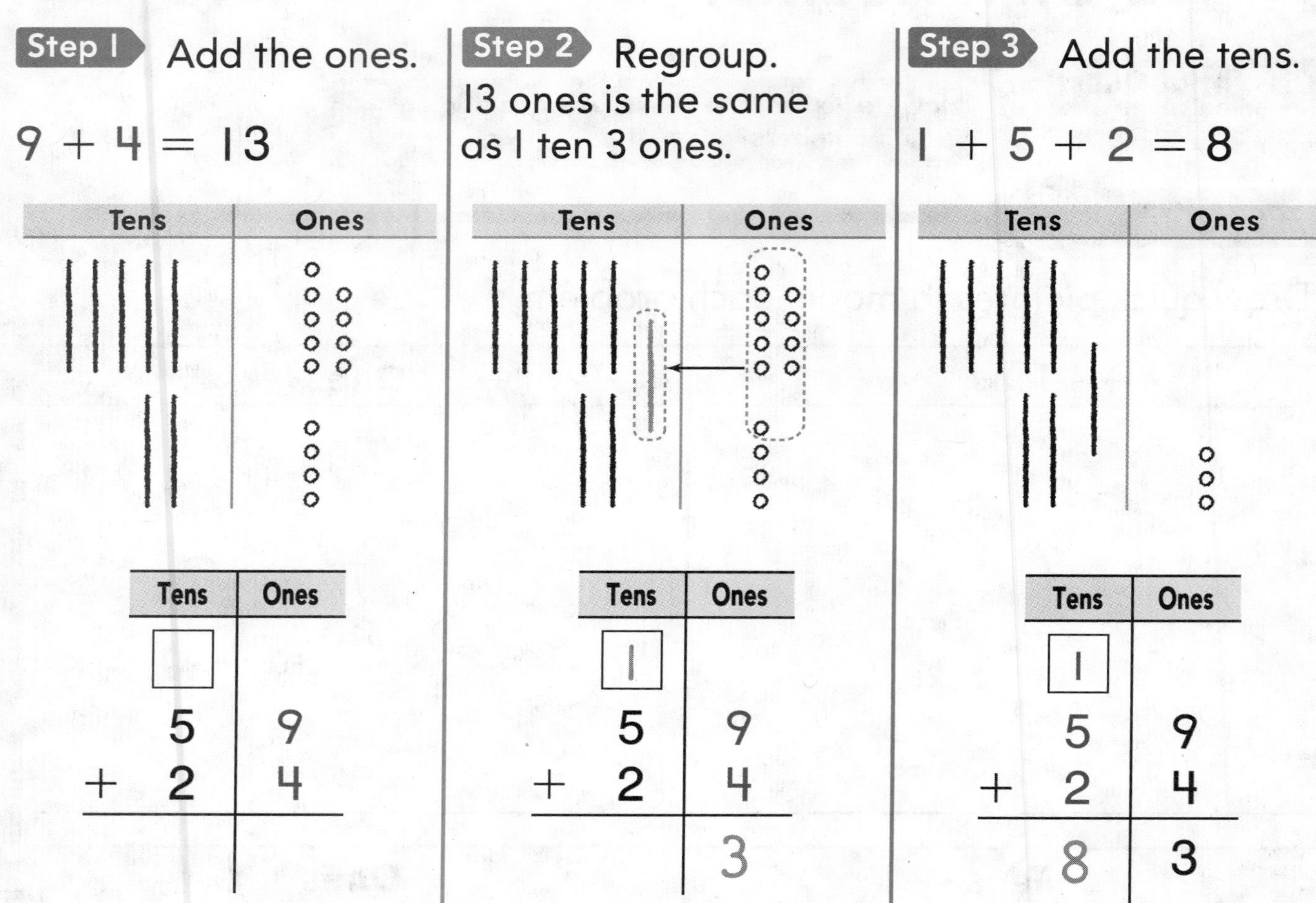

Tens	Ones
5	9
+ 2	4

Tens	Ones
1	
5	9
+ 2	4
	3

Tens	Ones
1	
5	9
+ 2	4
8	3

Share and Show

Regroup if you need to. Write the sum.

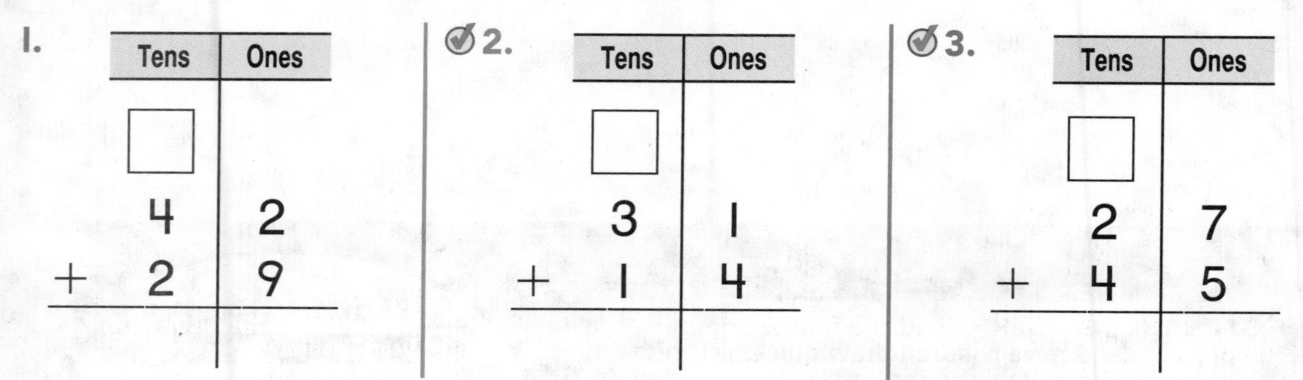

1.

Tens	Ones
4	2
+ 2	9

2.

Tens	Ones
3	1
+ 1	4

3.

Tens	Ones
2	7
+ 4	5

Name ____________________

Problem Solving

Regroup if you need to. Write the sum.

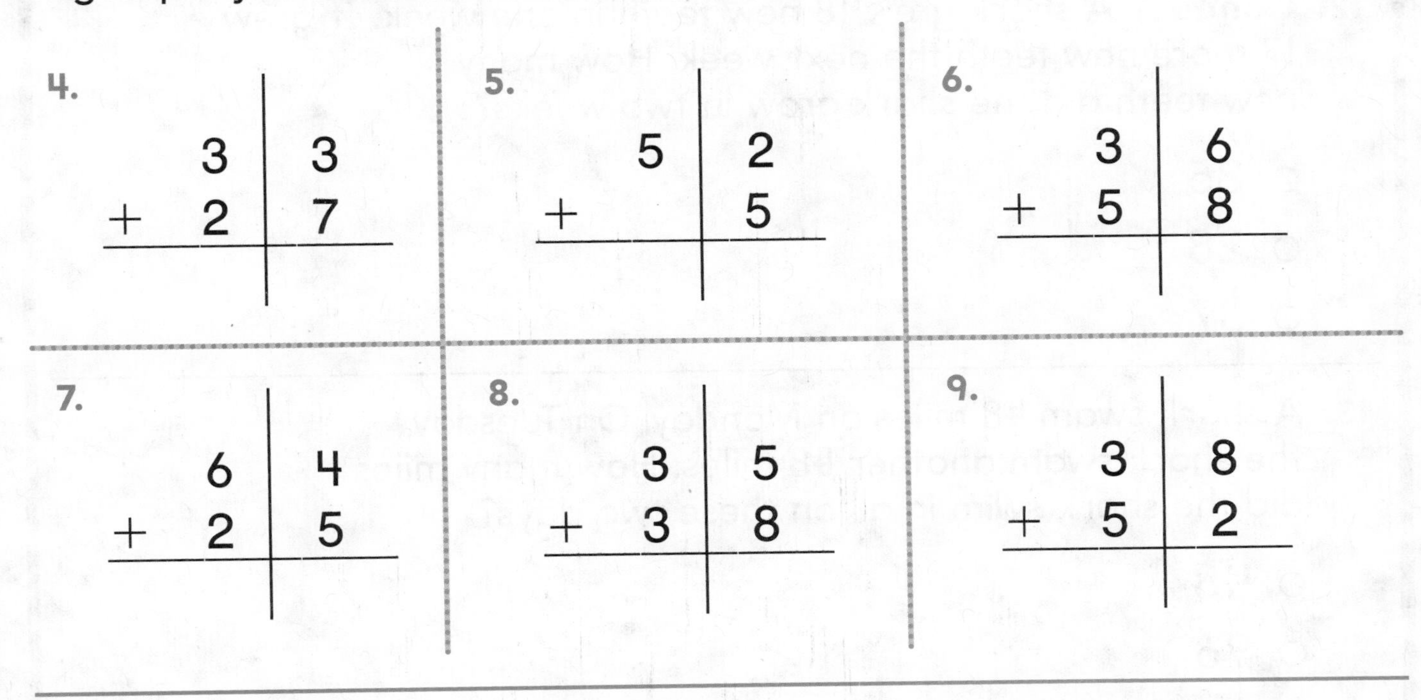

Solve. Write or draw to explain.

10. H.O.T. **Multi-Step** Jin has 31 books about cats and 19 books about dogs. He gives 5 books to his sister. How many books does Jin have now?

_______ books

11. H.O.T. Abby used a different way to add. Describe Abby's way of adding 2-digit numbers.

$$\begin{array}{r} 35 \\ +\ 48 \\ \hline 13 \\ +\ 70 \\ \hline 83 \end{array}$$

____

____

____

____

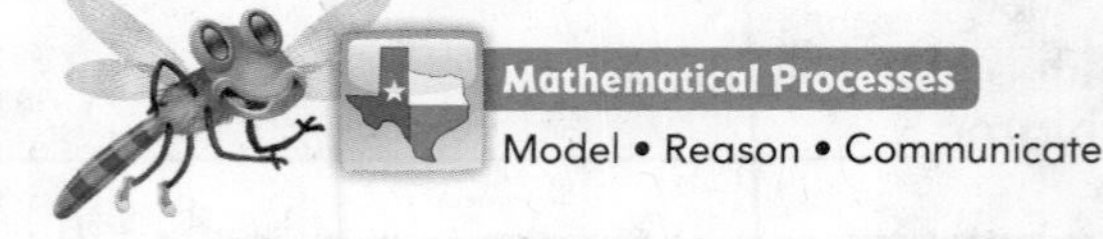

Daily Assessment Task

Choose the correct answer.

12. **Connect** A shark grew 18 new teeth in one week. It grew 17 more new teeth the next week. How many new teeth did the shark grow in two weeks?

- ○ 35
- ○ 28
- ○ 37

13. A shark swam 48 miles on Monday. On Tuesday, the shark swam another 48 miles. How many miles did the shark swim in all on these two days?

- ○ 48
- ○ 96
- ○ 86

14. **Reasoning** Anna has 31 animal cards. Roy has 49 animal cards. How many animal cards do the two children have?

- ○ 79
- ○ 70
- ○ 80

15. **TEXAS Test Prep** Carlos had 68 stamps in his collection. He bought 14 more stamps. How many stamps does he have now?

- ○ 74
- ○ 82
- ○ 56

TAKE HOME ACTIVITY • Ask your child to show you two ways to add 45 and 38.

Homework and Practice

Name ____________________

7.1 2-Digit Addition

Regroup if you need to. Write the sum.

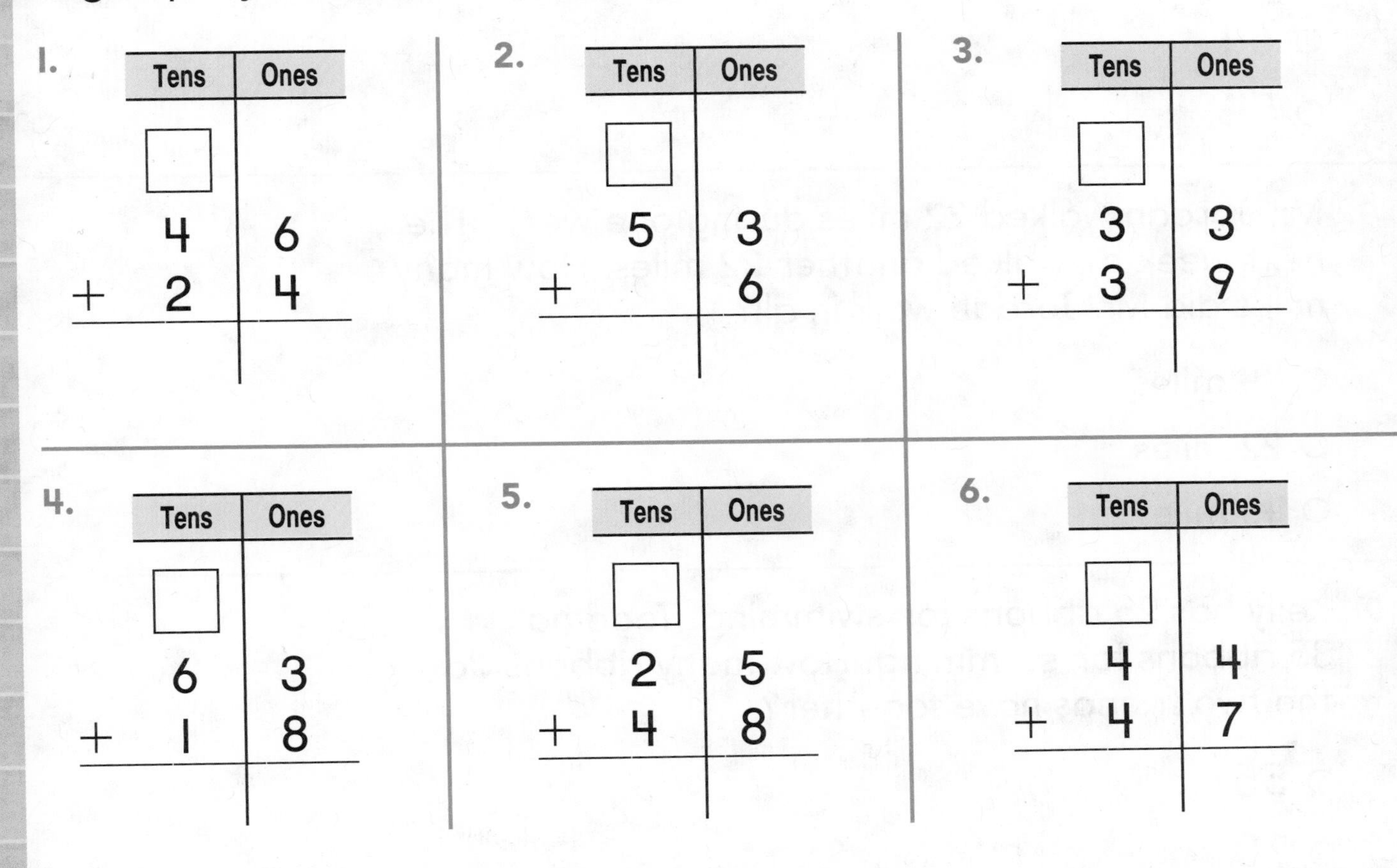

Problem Solving Real World

Solve. Write or draw to explain.

7. Keith has 22 sun stickers and 28 star stickers. How many stickers does Keith have now?

_______ stickers

Lesson Check

Choose the correct answer.

8. Olivia had 48 shells. She found 16 more shells at the beach. How many shells does she have now?

   ○ 62

   ○ 64

   ○ 54

---

9. Mr. Jordan walked 22 miles during one week. The next week he walked another 22 miles. How many miles did Mr. Jordan walk in all?

   ○ 44 miles

   ○ 22 miles

   ○ 46 miles

---

10. Kelly has 25 ribbons for swimming. Todd has 35 ribbons for swimming. How many ribbons do the two friends have together?

    ○ 55

    ○ 70

    ○ 60

---

11. **Multi-Step** Marie counts 14 turtles at the pond. Scott counts double that number of fish in the pond. How many turtles and fish did they see at the pond?

    ○ 32

    ○ 42

    ○ 28

Name ______________________________

7.2 Practice 2-Digit Addition

How do you record the steps when adding 2-digit numbers?

Explore Real World

Hands On

Choose a tool for solving the problem.
You could use real objects, blocks, or paper and pencil. Then draw or write to show what you did.

FOR THE TEACHER • Read the following problem. There were 27 boys and 18 girls who ran in the race. How many children ran in the race?

Math Talk Mathematical Processes

Explain your choice for solving the problem.

Model and Draw

Mrs. Meyers sold 47 snacks before the game. Then she sold 85 snacks during the game. How many snacks did she sell?

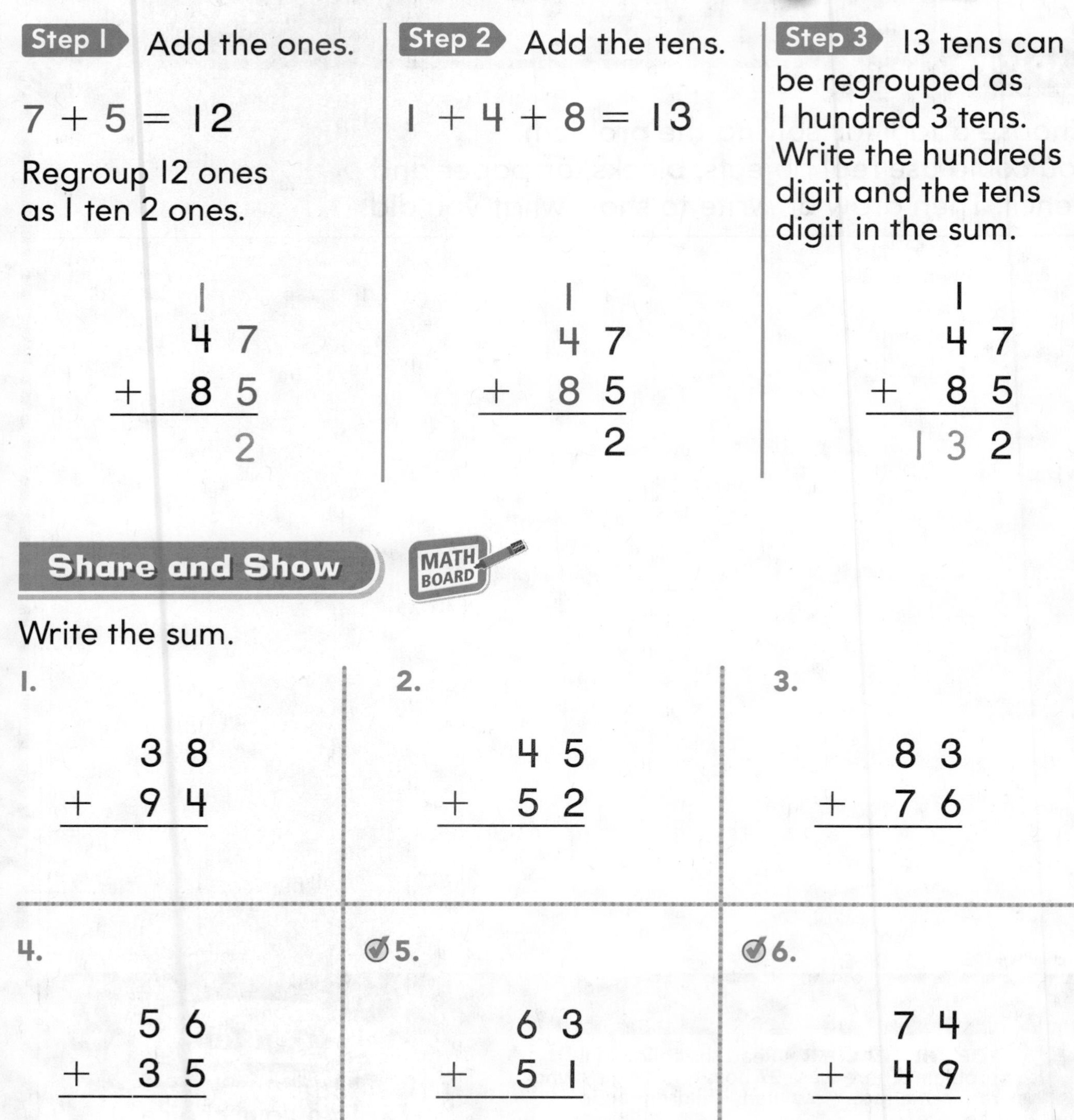

Step 1 Add the ones.

$7 + 5 = 12$

Regroup 12 ones as 1 ten 2 ones.

$$\begin{array}{r} {}^{1} \\ 47 \\ +\ 85 \\ \hline 2 \end{array}$$

Step 2 Add the tens.

$1 + 4 + 8 = 13$

$$\begin{array}{r} {}^{1} \\ 47 \\ +\ 85 \\ \hline 2 \end{array}$$

Step 3 13 tens can be regrouped as 1 hundred 3 tens. Write the hundreds digit and the tens digit in the sum.

$$\begin{array}{r} {}^{1} \\ 47 \\ +\ 85 \\ \hline 132 \end{array}$$

Share and Show

MATH BOARD

Write the sum.

1. $\begin{array}{r} 38 \\ +\ 94 \\ \hline \end{array}$

2. $\begin{array}{r} 45 \\ +\ 52 \\ \hline \end{array}$

3. $\begin{array}{r} 83 \\ +\ 76 \\ \hline \end{array}$

4. $\begin{array}{r} 56 \\ +\ 35 \\ \hline \end{array}$

✓5. $\begin{array}{r} 63 \\ +\ 51 \\ \hline \end{array}$

✓6. $\begin{array}{r} 74 \\ +\ 49 \\ \hline \end{array}$

Name ____________________

Problem Solving

Write the sum.

7.
$$\begin{array}{r} 52 \\ +\ 37 \\ \hline \end{array}$$

8.
$$\begin{array}{r} 88 \\ +\ 21 \\ \hline \end{array}$$

9.
$$\begin{array}{r} 74 \\ +\ 67 \\ \hline \end{array}$$

10.
$$\begin{array}{r} 93 \\ +\ 54 \\ \hline \end{array}$$

11.
$$\begin{array}{r} 25 \\ +\ 49 \\ \hline \end{array}$$

12.
$$\begin{array}{r} 92 \\ +\ 78 \\ \hline \end{array}$$

Solve. Write or draw to explain.

13. H.O.T. **Multi-Step** Without finding the sums, circle the pairs of addends for which the sum will be greater than 100.

73 / 18

47 / 62

54 / 71

36 / 59

Explain how you decided which pairs to circle.

____

____

____

14. H.O.T. In a game, Lou scored 37 points, Becky scored 23 points, and Kevin scored 19 points. Which two players scored 56 points in all?

____________ and ____________

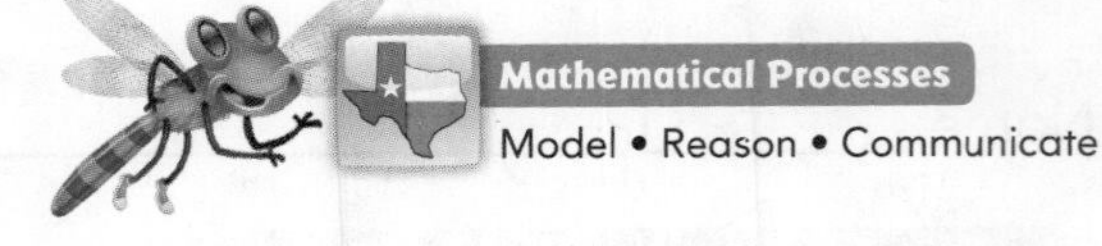

Daily Assessment Task

Choose the correct answer.

15. Elena has 27 beads in one bag. In another bag, she has 44 beads. How many beads does Elena have in the bags?

- ○ 67
- ○ 61
- ○ 71

16. **Reasoning** Dale has 29 orange beads and 14 blue beads. How many beads does Dale have?

Choose a tool for solving this problem. You can use real objects, blocks, or paper and pencil. Then draw and write to show what you did.

Dale has ________ beads.

17. **TEXAS Test Prep** Amber has 52 stickers of cats and 67 stickers of dogs. How many stickers does Amber have?

- ○ 119
- ○ 115
- ○ 129

HOME CONNECTION • Tell your child two 2-digit numbers. Have him or her write the numbers and find the sum.

TEKS Number and Operations—2.4.B
MATHEMATICAL PROCESSES 2.1.C, 2.1.D, 2.1.G

Name ____________________

7.2 Practice 2-Digit Addition

Write the sum.

1. $\begin{array}{r} 54 \\ +\ 31 \\ \hline \end{array}$

2. $\begin{array}{r} 86 \\ +\ 73 \\ \hline \end{array}$

3. $\begin{array}{r} 27 \\ +\ 99 \\ \hline \end{array}$

4. $\begin{array}{r} 47 \\ +\ 93 \\ \hline \end{array}$

5. $\begin{array}{r} 36 \\ +\ 95 \\ \hline \end{array}$

6. $\begin{array}{r} 73 \\ +\ 72 \\ \hline \end{array}$

Problem Solving Real World

Solve. Write or draw to explain.

7. **Multi-Step** In a bowling game, Sam scored 77 points, Marie scored 53 points, and Eric scored 69 points. Which two bowlers scored 130 points?

_______ and _______

Choose the correct answer.

8. Emma has 43 black marbles and 55 red marbles. How many marbles does Emma have?

   ○ 98

   ○ 108

   ○ 93

9. Jake has two bags of coins. One bag has 22 coins and the other bag has 38 coins. How many coins does he have in all?

   ○ 50

   ○ 60

   ○ 56

10. At a basketball game, Doug passed the ball 47 times. Adam passed the ball 56 times. How many times did they both pass the ball?

    ○ 93

    ○ 113

    ○ 103

11. Cindy made a necklace with colored beads. She used 64 gold beads and 48 red beads. How many beads did she use to make the necklace?

    ○ 102 beads

    ○ 112 beads

    ○ 104 beads

Name ______________________________

7.3 ALGEBRA Write Equations to Represent Addition

Essential Question How do you write a number sentence to represent a problem?

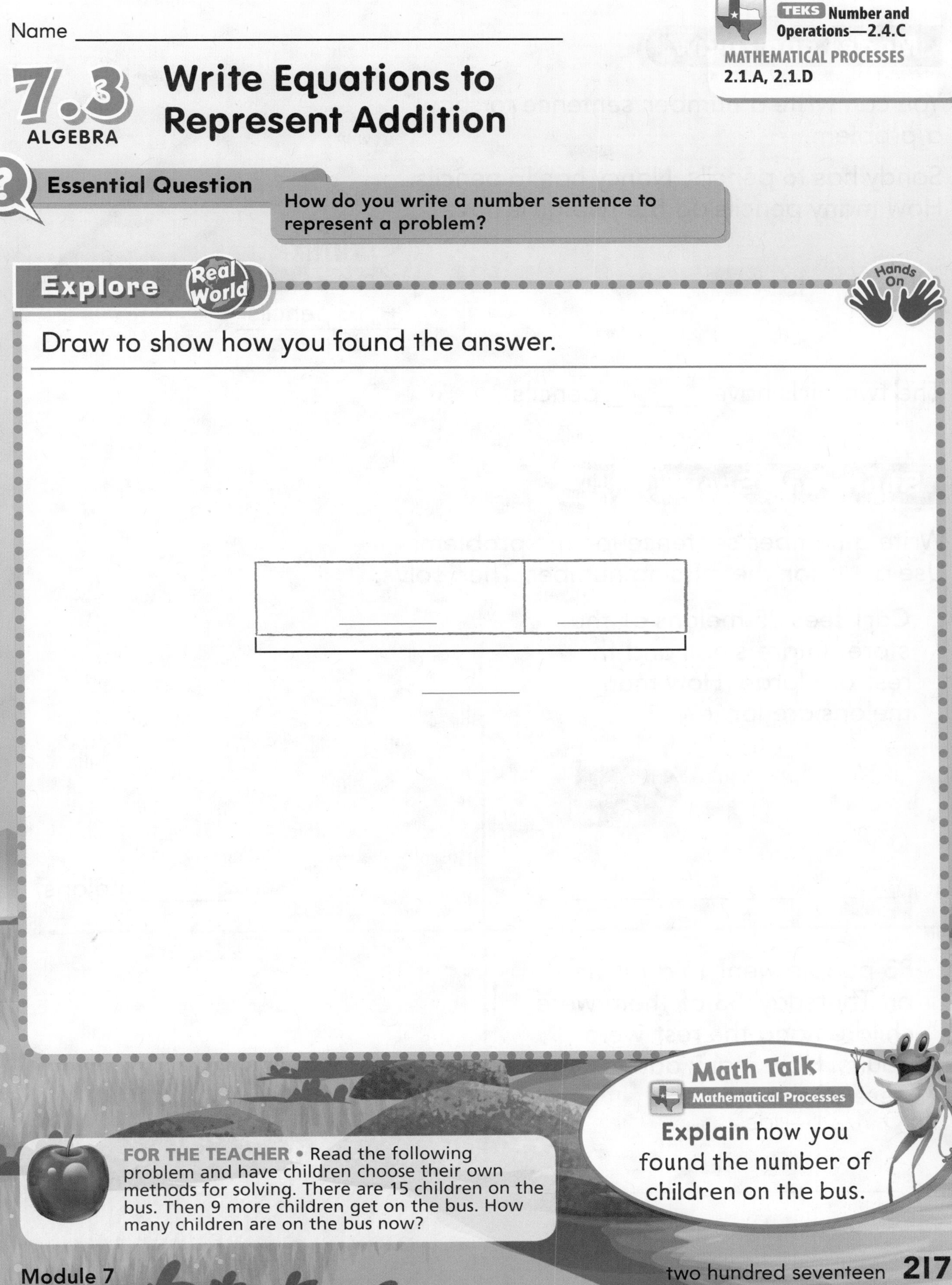

Explore Real World

Hands On

Draw to show how you found the answer.

Math Talk
Mathematical Processes
Explain how you found the number of children on the bus.

FOR THE TEACHER • Read the following problem and have children choose their own methods for solving. There are 15 children on the bus. Then 9 more children get on the bus. How many children are on the bus now?

Model and Draw

You can write a number sentence to show a problem.

Sandy has 16 pencils. Nancy has 13 pencils. How many pencils do the two girls have?

$16 + 13 = \blacksquare$

THINK:

$$\begin{array}{r} 16 \text{ pencils} \\ +\ 13 \text{ pencils} \\ \hline 29 \text{ pencils} \end{array}$$

The two girls have ______ pencils.

Write a number sentence for the problem. Use a ■ for the missing number. Then solve.

1. Carl sees 25 melons at the store. 15 are small and the rest are large. How many melons are large?

____

______ melons

2. 83 people went to a movie on Thursday. 53 of them were children and the rest were adults. How many adults were at the movie?

____

______ adults

Name ___________________________________

Problem Solving

Write a number sentence for the problem. Use a ■ for the missing number. Then solve.

3. Chris and his friends went to the zoo. In the Reptile House, they saw 9 snakes and 14 lizards. How many reptiles did they see?

____

______ reptiles

Solve. Write or draw to explain.

4. H.O.T. **Multi-Step** Braden's class went to the park. They saw 26 oak trees and 14 maple trees. They also saw 13 cardinals and 35 blue jays. Compare the total number of trees and the total number of birds that the class saw.

______ ◯ ______

5. H.O.T. Amy needs about 70 paper clips. Without adding, circle 2 boxes that would be close to the amount that she needs.

70 clips	81 clips	54 clips
19 clips	35 clips	32 clips

Explain how you made your choices.

____

____

____

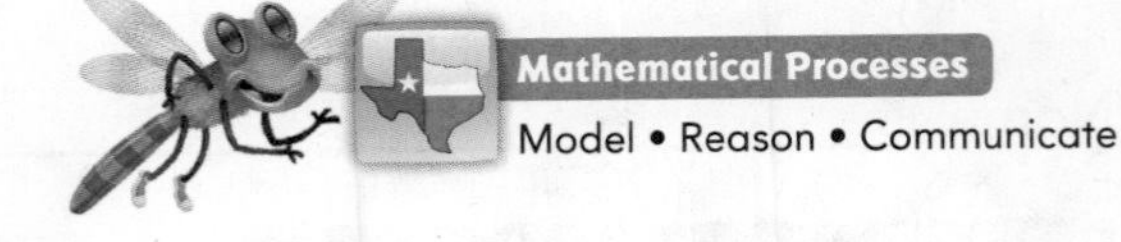

Daily Assessment Task

Choose the correct answer.

6. **Apply** There are 43 whales in the first group. There are 38 whales in the second group. How many whales are in the two groups?

○ 81
○ 78
○ 71

7. There are 43 fish in one group and 38 fish in another group. How many fish are there?

○ 75
○ 88
○ 81

8. **Reasoning** In April, Robert counted 49 boats in the lake. Robert counted 47 boats in May. How many boats did Robert count in the two months?

○ 96
○ 86
○ 99

9. **TEXAS Test Prep** Mr. Walton baked 54 cookies last week. He baked 38 cookies this week. How many cookies did he bake in the two weeks?

○ 16
○ 92
○ 82

TAKE HOME ACTIVITY • Have your child explain how he or she solved one of the exercises in this lesson.

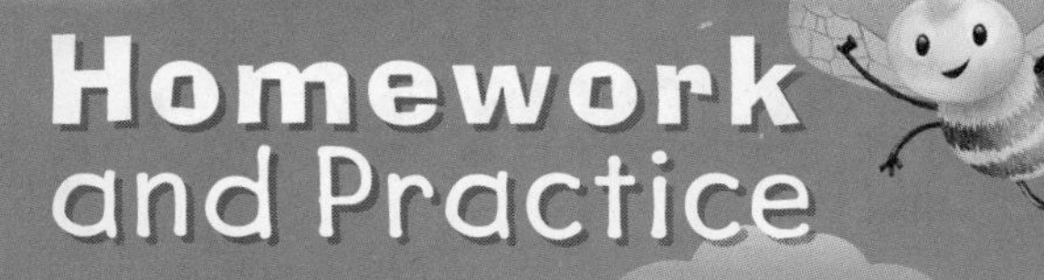

Name ____________________

Write Equations to Represent Addition

Write a number sentence for the problem. Use a ▢ for the missing number. Then solve.

1. A group of friends went to the town fair. They saw 35 pumpkins. Some are large pumpkins and 16 are smaller pumpkins. How many pumpkins are large?

____

_______ large pumpkins

2. Ben sees 90 people at the park. 46 are children and the rest are young adults. How many people are young adults?

____

_______ young adults

Problem Solving Real World

Solve. Write or draw to explain.

3. **Multi-Step** Amy's class went to the fair. They saw 22 horses and 18 ponies. They also saw 18 rabbits and 37 hares. Compare the number of horses and ponies to the number of rabbits and hares that the class saw.

_______ ◯ _______

TEXAS Test Prep

Choose the correct answer.

4. A bakery made 36 pies last week. This week the same bakery made 27 pies. How many pies did the bakery make in the two weeks?

   ○ 63
   ○ 43
   ○ 51

5. One class collects 37 coats for a coat drive. Another class collects 39 coats. How many coats do the two classes collect?

   ○ 62
   ○ 76
   ○ 72

6. Two groups of ducks swim in a large pond. One group has 23 ducks. The second group has 28 ducks. How many ducks are in the two groups?

   ○ 55
   ○ 41
   ○ 51

7. **Multi-Step** Pat's garden has 24 red tomato plants and twice as many green tomato plants as red tomato plants. How many tomato plants are in her garden?

   ○ 62 ○ 72 ○ 48

Name ______________________

Problem Solving

Add.

9.	10.	11.	12.
40 17 + 32	25 25 + 25	19 65 + 24	73 4 + 16

Solve. Write or draw to explain.

13. H.O.T. **Multi-Step** Sophia had 44 marbles. She bought 24 more marbles. Then John gave her 35 marbles. How many marbles does Sophia have now?

_____ marbles

14. H.O.T. Write a story problem that could be solved using this number sentence.

$$24 + 16 + \blacksquare = 55$$

____

____

____

____

____

Mathematical Processes
Model • Reason • Communicate

Daily Assessment Task

Choose the correct answer.

15. **Multi-Step** There were 27 hats, 10 stickers, and 18 posters sold during the parade. How many items were sold at the parade?

    ○ 55
    ○ 37
    ○ 45

16. **Analyze** In a parade, there are 21 firefighters, 18 police officers, and 28 musicians. How many people are in the parade?

    ○ 39
    ○ 67
    ○ 57

17. **Analyze** Before the parade, 20 snacks were sold. During the parade 23 snacks were sold. After the parade, 39 snacks were sold. How many snacks were sold?

    ○ 82
    ○ 72
    ○ 62

18. **TEXAS Test Prep** Mrs. Shaw has 23 red notebooks, 15 blue notebooks, and 27 green notebooks. How many notebooks does she have?

    ○ 42
    ○ 38
    ○ 65

TAKE HOME ACTIVITY • Ask your child to show you two ways to add 17, 13, and 24.

TEKS Number and Operations—2.4.B
MATHEMATICAL PROCESSES 2.1.F

Name ____________________

7.4 ALGEBRA Find Sums for 3 Addends

Add.

1. $\begin{array}{r} 33 \\ 45 \\ +\ 13 \\ \hline \end{array}$

2. $\begin{array}{r} 12 \\ 58 \\ +\ 27 \\ \hline \end{array}$

3. $\begin{array}{r} 31 \\ 52 \\ +\ 19 \\ \hline \end{array}$

4. $\begin{array}{r} 25 \\ 20 \\ +\ 22 \\ \hline \end{array}$

5. $\begin{array}{r} 19 \\ 27 \\ +\ 63 \\ \hline \end{array}$

6. $\begin{array}{r} 24 \\ 36 \\ +\ 45 \\ \hline \end{array}$

7. $\begin{array}{r} 33 \\ 33 \\ +\ 33 \\ \hline \end{array}$

8. $\begin{array}{r} 74 \\ 8 \\ +\ 22 \\ \hline \end{array}$

Problem Solving

Solve. Write or draw to explain.

9. Wendy had 35 stickers. She bought 36 more stickers. Then Kyle gave her 23 stickers. How many stickers does Wendy have now?

____

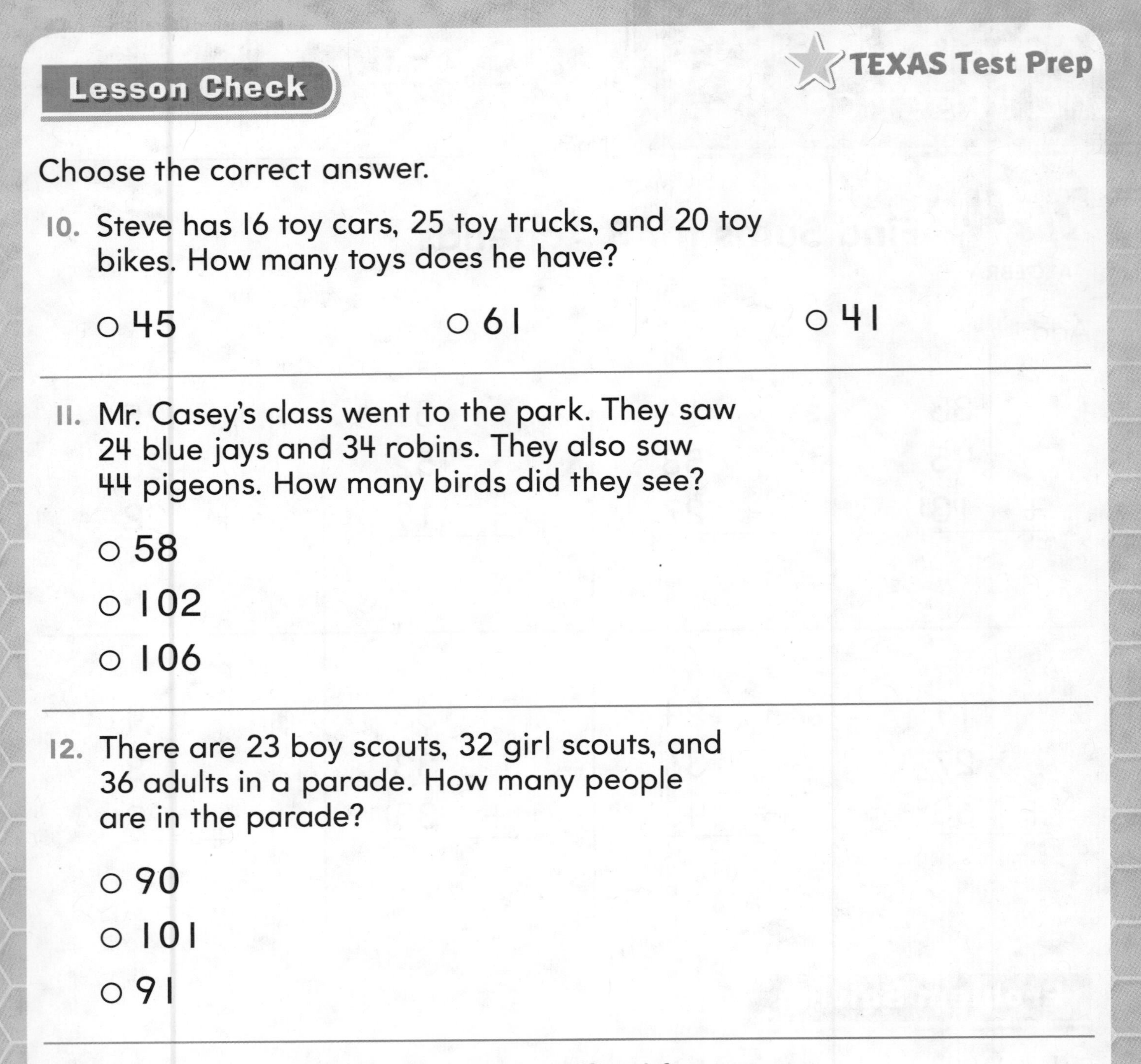

Lesson Check

TEXAS Test Prep

Choose the correct answer.

10. Steve has 16 toy cars, 25 toy trucks, and 20 toy bikes. How many toys does he have?

- ○ 45
- ○ 61
- ○ 41

11. Mr. Casey's class went to the park. They saw 24 blue jays and 34 robins. They also saw 44 pigeons. How many birds did they see?

- ○ 58
- ○ 102
- ○ 106

12. There are 23 boy scouts, 32 girl scouts, and 36 adults in a parade. How many people are in the parade?

- ○ 90
- ○ 101
- ○ 91

13. **Multi-Step** Mrs. Carson is making food for a party. She makes 20 ham sandwiches, 34 turkey sandwiches, and 38 tuna salad sandwiches. How many sandwiches does she make for the party?

- ○ 72
- ○ 92
- ○ 94

Name ______________________________

7.5 Find Sums for 4 Addends

ALGEBRA

Essential Question What are some ways to add 4 numbers?

Explore Real World

Hands On

Show how you solved each problem.

FOR THE TEACHER • Read this problem and have children choose a way to solve it. Shelly counts 16 ants in her ant farm. Pedro counts 22 ants in his farm. Tara counts 14 ants in her farm. How many ants do the 3 children count? Repeat for another problem.

Math Talk

Mathematical Processes

Describe how you found the answer to the first problem.

Model and Draw

You can add digits within a column in any order.
Add the ones first. Then add the tens.

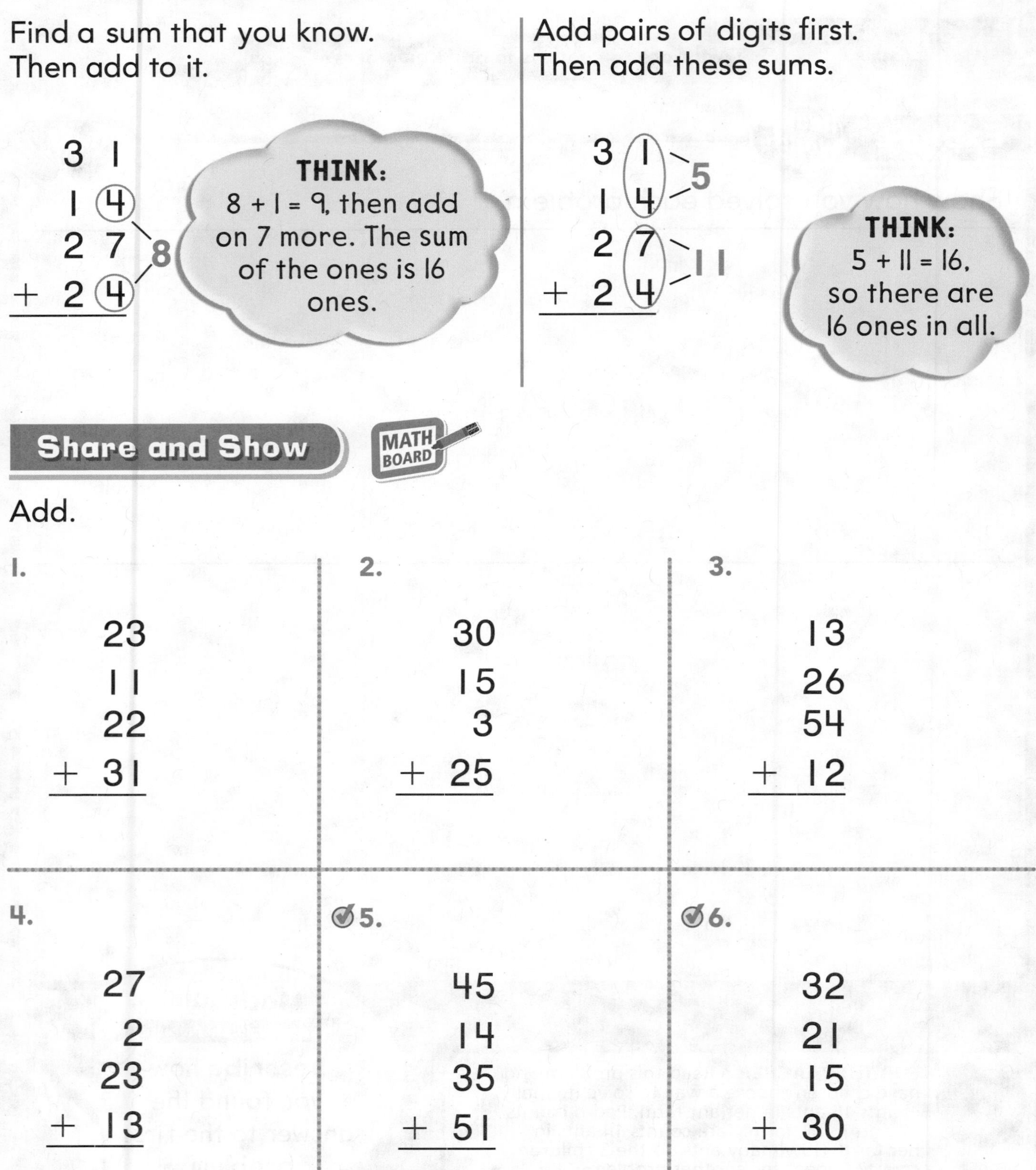

Find a sum that you know.
Then add to it.

$$\begin{array}{r} 31 \\ 14 \\ 27 \\ +\ 24 \\ \hline \end{array}$$

Add pairs of digits first.
Then add these sums.

$$\begin{array}{r} 31 \\ 14 \\ 27 \\ +\ 24 \\ \hline \end{array}$$

Share and Show

MATH BOARD

Add.

1.
$$\begin{array}{r} 23 \\ 11 \\ 22 \\ +\ 31 \\ \hline \end{array}$$

2.
$$\begin{array}{r} 30 \\ 15 \\ 3 \\ +\ 25 \\ \hline \end{array}$$

3.
$$\begin{array}{r} 13 \\ 26 \\ 54 \\ +\ 12 \\ \hline \end{array}$$

4.
$$\begin{array}{r} 27 \\ 2 \\ 23 \\ +\ 13 \\ \hline \end{array}$$

5.
$$\begin{array}{r} 45 \\ 14 \\ 35 \\ +\ 51 \\ \hline \end{array}$$

6.
$$\begin{array}{r} 32 \\ 21 \\ 15 \\ +\ 30 \\ \hline \end{array}$$

Name ______________________

Problem Solving

Add.

7.
$$\begin{array}{r} 36 \\ 12 \\ 21 \\ +\ 26 \\ \hline \end{array}$$

8.
$$\begin{array}{r} 14 \\ 23 \\ 20 \\ +\ 11 \\ \hline \end{array}$$

9.
$$\begin{array}{r} 22 \\ 13 \\ 15 \\ +\ 27 \\ \hline \end{array}$$

10.
$$\begin{array}{r} 45 \\ 12 \\ 41 \\ +\ 22 \\ \hline \end{array}$$

11.
$$\begin{array}{r} 59 \\ 31 \\ 51 \\ +\ 73 \\ \hline \end{array}$$

12.
$$\begin{array}{r} 34 \\ 10 \\ 31 \\ +\ 22 \\ \hline \end{array}$$

Solve. Write or draw to explain.

13. H.O.T. **Multi-Step** Laney added four numbers which have a total of 128. She spilled some juice over one number. What is that number?

$22 + 43 + \square + 30 = 128$

______

14. H.O.T. **Multi-Step** Some friends need 100 shells for a project. Kate brings 21 shells, Paul brings 44 shells, and Noah brings 27 shells. How many more shells do they need?

______ more shells

Daily Assessment Task

Choose the correct answer.

15. **Multi-Step** John sees a group of 47 butterflies, a group of 30 butterflies, a group of 55 butterflies, and a group of 26 butterflies. How many butterflies does he see?

○ 168
○ 146
○ 158

16. **Connect** At the Kite Festival there are 19 blue kites, 35 green kites, 20 yellow kites, and 23 orange kites. How many kites are there?

○ 94
○ 97
○ 87

17. **TEXAS Test Prep** There were 24 red beads, 31 blue beads, and 8 green beads in a jar. Then Sasha put 16 beads into the jar. How many beads are in the jar now?

○ 79
○ 63
○ 69

TAKE HOME ACTIVITY • Have your child explain how he or she solved one of the exercises in this lesson.

TEKS Number and Operations—2.4.B
MATHEMATICAL PROCESSES 2.1.F

Name ____________________

7.5 Find Sums for 4 Addends

ALGEBRA

Add.

1.	2.	3.
34 23 40 + 17	21 12 60 + 35	46 31 52 + 43

4.	5.	6.
22 19 41 + 63	34 10 37 + 55	12 24 53 + 30

Problem Solving Real World

7. **Multi-Step** Kate read 32 pages on Monday, 21 pages on Tuesday, and 15 pages on Wednesday. Then she read some more on Thursday. Altogether she read 88 pages. How many pages did she read on Thursday?

$$32 + 21 + 15 + \blacksquare = 88$$

_______ pages

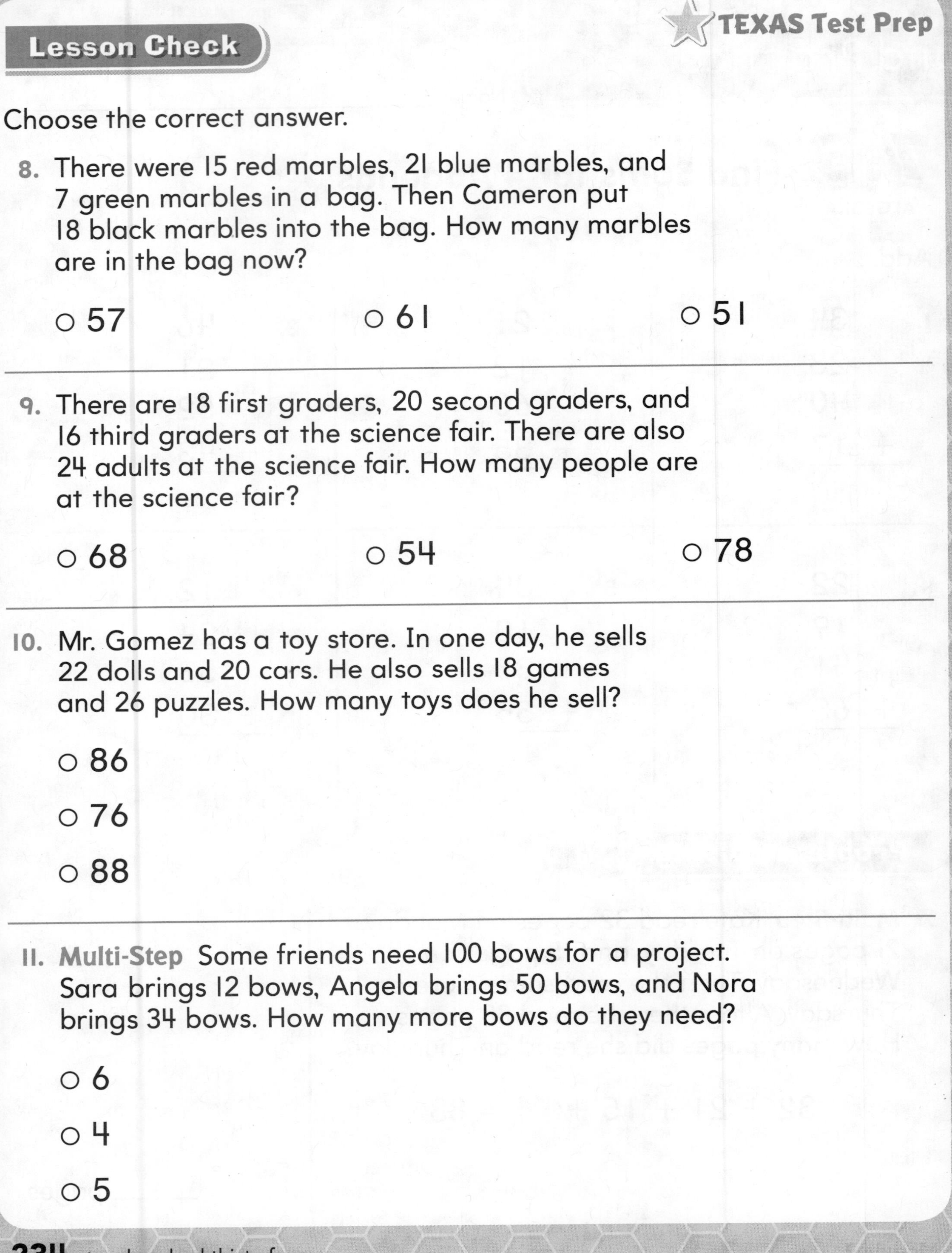

Lesson Check

TEXAS Test Prep

Choose the correct answer.

8. There were 15 red marbles, 21 blue marbles, and 7 green marbles in a bag. Then Cameron put 18 black marbles into the bag. How many marbles are in the bag now?

○ 57 ○ 61 ○ 51

9. There are 18 first graders, 20 second graders, and 16 third graders at the science fair. There are also 24 adults at the science fair. How many people are at the science fair?

○ 68 ○ 54 ○ 78

10. Mr. Gomez has a toy store. In one day, he sells 22 dolls and 20 cars. He also sells 18 games and 26 puzzles. How many toys does he sell?

○ 86

○ 76

○ 88

11. **Multi-Step** Some friends need 100 bows for a project. Sara brings 12 bows, Angela brings 50 bows, and Nora brings 34 bows. How many more bows do they need?

○ 6

○ 4

○ 5

Name ___________________________

Module 7 Assessment

Concepts and Skills

Write the sum. TEKS 2.4.B

1.
```
  56
+ 16
```

2.
```
  31
+ 45
```

3.
```
  43
+ 72
```

Write a number sentence for the problem.
Use a ■ for the missing number. Then solve. TEKS 2.4.C

4. Jake had some stamps. Then he bought 20 more stamps. Now he has 56 stamps. How many stamps did Jake have to start?

____

________ stamps

Add. TEKS 2.4.B

5.
```
  22
  27
+ 18
```

6.
```
  35
  24
+ 58
```

7.
```
  60
  15
   3
+ 21
```

8.
```
  58
  12
  24
+ 64
```

Fill in the bubble for the correct answer choice.

TEXAS Test Prep

9. Miles saw some toy cars at the store. 16 of the cars are red and 18 of the cars are green. Which number sentence could be used to find how many cars he saw? TEKS 2.4.C

○ $16 + \blacksquare = 18$

○ $16 + 18 = \blacksquare$

○ $\blacksquare + 16 = 18$

10. Avery had 46 crayons. She bought 29 more crayons. Then Edward gave her 33 crayons. How many crayons does Avery have now? TEKS 2.4.B

○ 108

○ 75

○ 95

11. Gavin has 54 coins. His sister gives him 36 coins. How many coins does he have now? TEKS 2.4.B

○ 80

○ 18

○ 90

12. Reagan made a bracelet. She used 67 blue beads and 52 green beads. How many beads did she use? TEKS 2.4.B

○ 119

○ 115

○ 129

13. Parker collected 21 shells. Katie collected 34 shells. Ella collected 15 shells. Marco collected 26 shells. How many shells did the four children collect? TEKS 2.4.B

○ 70

○ 96

○ 86

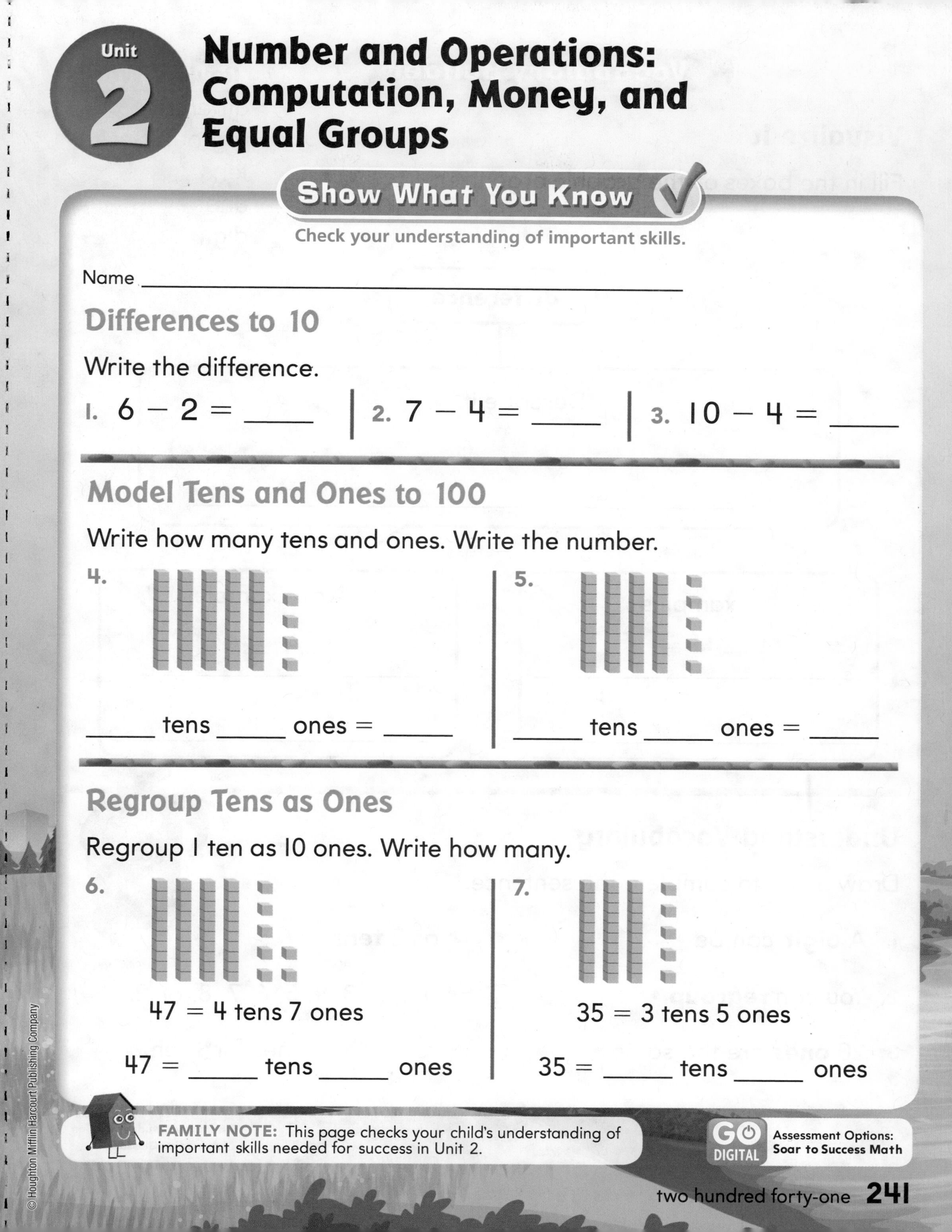

Unit 2

Number and Operations: Computation, Money, and Equal Groups

Show What You Know

Check your understanding of important skills.

Name ______________________________

Differences to 10

Write the difference.

1. 6 − 2 = ____

2. 7 − 4 = ____

3. 10 − 4 = ____

Model Tens and Ones to 100

Write how many tens and ones. Write the number.

4. ____ tens ____ ones = ____

5. ____ tens ____ ones = ____

Regroup Tens as Ones

Regroup 1 ten as 10 ones. Write how many.

6. 47 = 4 tens 7 ones

47 = ____ tens ____ ones

7. 35 = 3 tens 5 ones

35 = ____ tens ____ ones

FAMILY NOTE: This page checks your child's understanding of important skills needed for success in Unit 2.

GO DIGITAL Assessment Options: Soar to Success Math

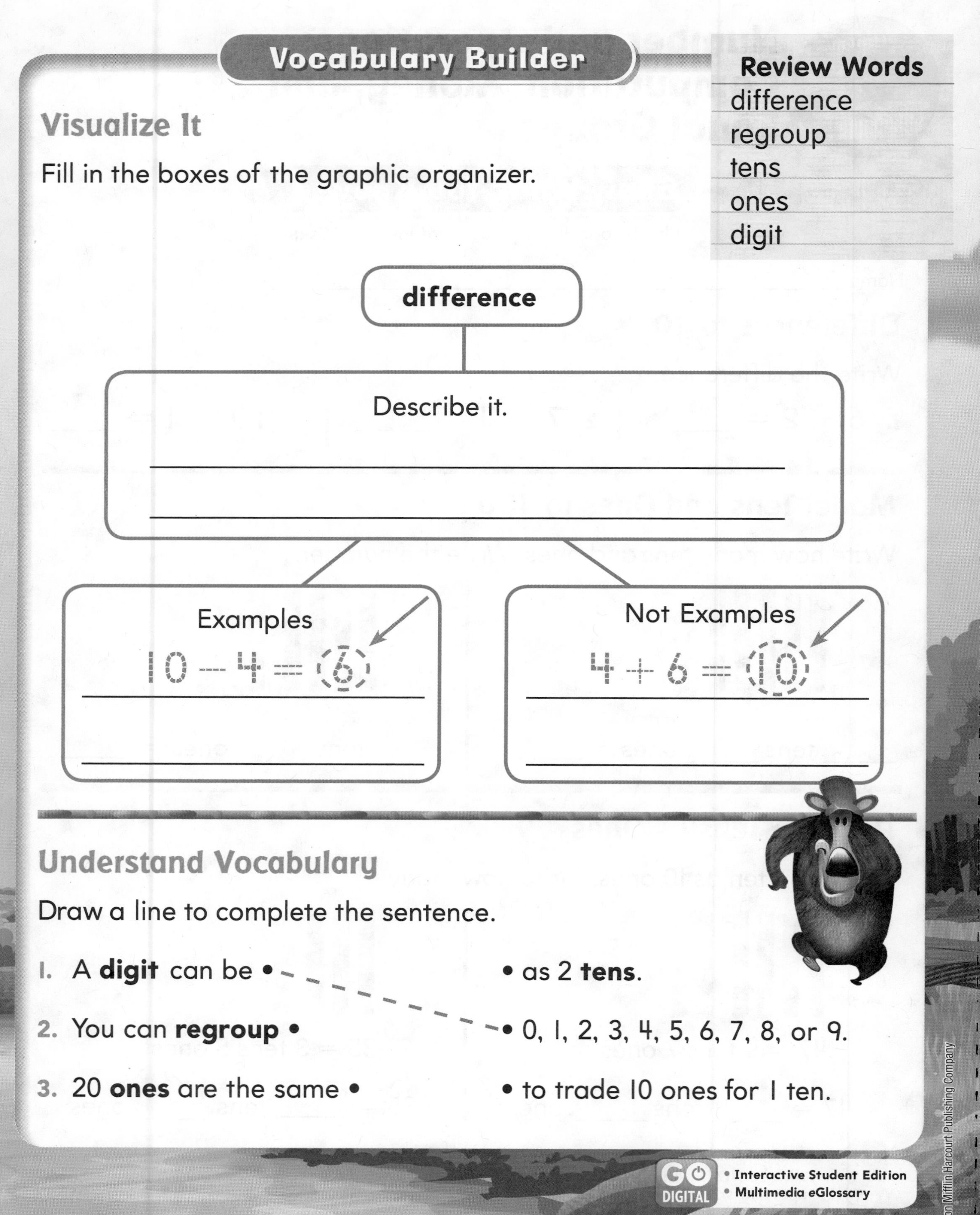

Vocabulary Builder

Review Words
- difference
- regroup
- tens
- ones
- digit

Visualize It

Fill in the boxes of the graphic organizer.

Understand Vocabulary

Draw a line to complete the sentence.

1. A **digit** can be • • as 2 **tens**.
2. You can **regroup** • • 0, 1, 2, 3, 4, 5, 6, 7, 8, or 9.
3. 20 **ones** are the same • • to trade 10 ones for 1 ten.

GO DIGITAL
- Interactive Student Edition
- Multimedia eGlossary

Vocabulary Reader

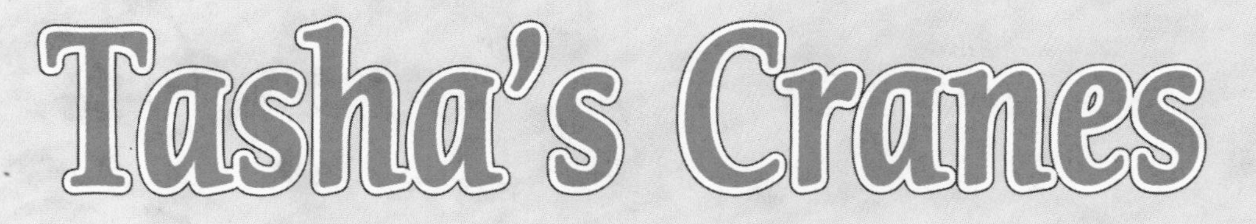

Tasha's Cranes

written by Mike Mason

This Take-Home Book belongs to

____

Reading and Writing Math

This take-home book will help you review subtraction.

MATHEMATICAL PROCESSES 2.1.A, 2.1.C, 2.1.F

Tasha folded paper cranes
For her senior center friends.
She needs 100 cranes in all.
She will make them by the tens.

Tasha started and made just 10.
Then she a short rest had to take.
She subtracted 10 from 100. Wow!
She still had 90 more to make.

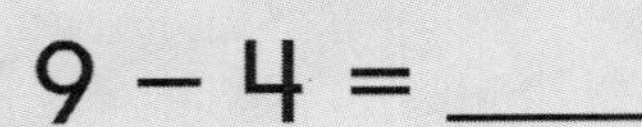

9 − 4 = _____

9 tens − 4 tens = _____ tens

90 − 40 = _____ cranes left to fold

The next day she folded 40 cranes.
How many more does she need?
Find 9 tens take away 4 tens
And you will know indeed.

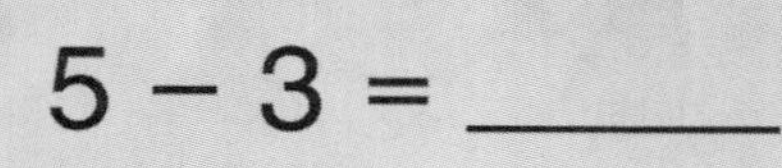

$5 - 3 =$ ______

5 tens $-$ 3 tens $=$ ______ tens

$50 - 30 =$ ______ cranes left to fold

On Friday she made
3 more sets of ten.
"Am I done?"
she wondered then.

5 tens less 3 tens
leaves 2 tens to do.
So on Saturday she made 20 more.
Finally 100 done. She was through!

At the senior center she gave away the
100 cranes—every one.
The senior citizens thanked her for what
she had done.

Name ______________________________

Write about the Math

Write Math Look at the picture. Draw and write your own story about the cranes. Include subtracting tens in your story.

Vocabulary Review
tens
subtract
take away

____

____

____

____

____

____

How Many Tens?

This picture shows the cranes that the children in Keisha's class made.

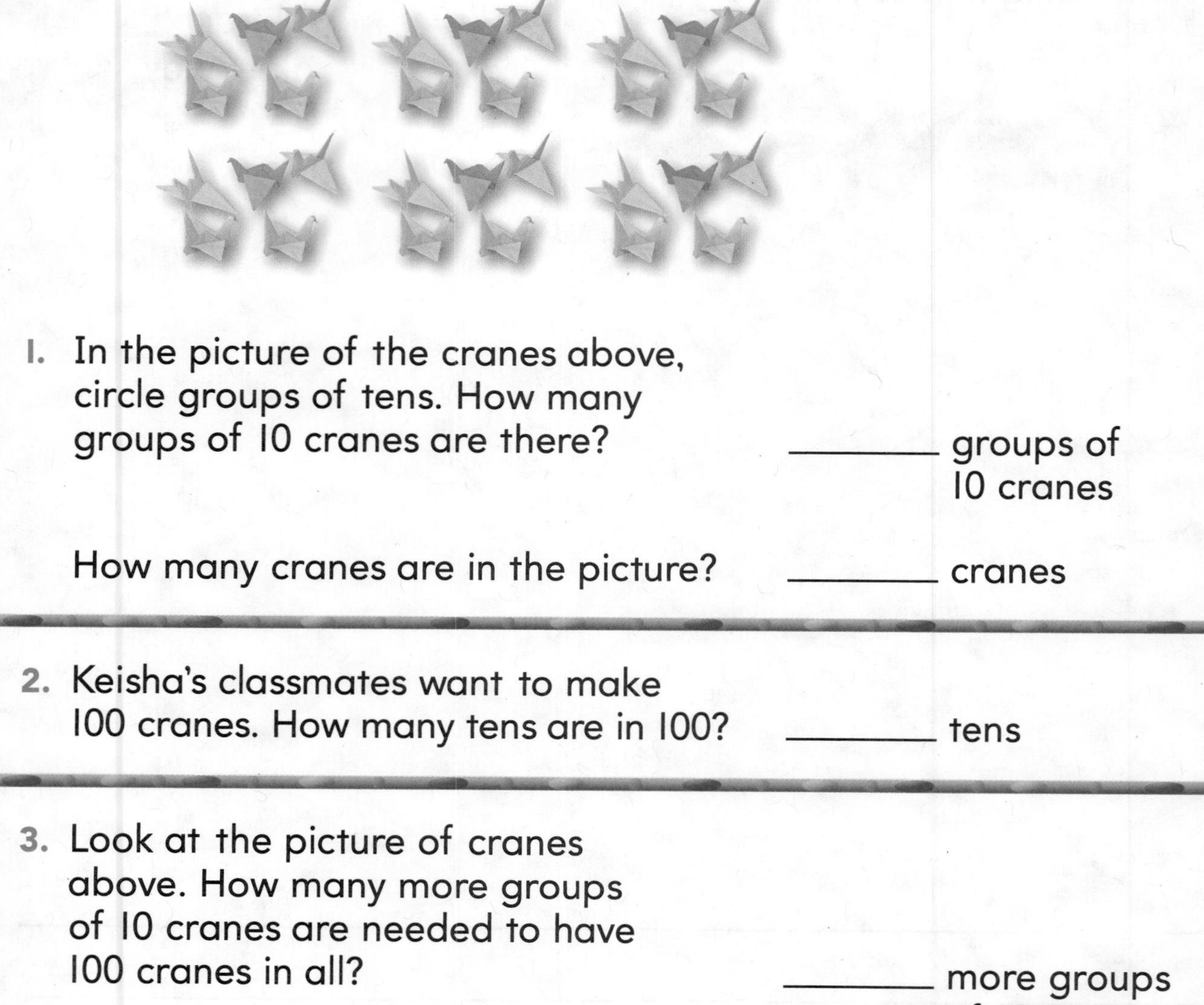

1. In the picture of the cranes above, circle groups of tens. How many groups of 10 cranes are there? _______ groups of 10 cranes

   How many cranes are in the picture? _______ cranes

2. Keisha's classmates want to make 100 cranes. How many tens are in 100? _______ tens

3. Look at the picture of cranes above. How many more groups of 10 cranes are needed to have 100 cranes in all? _______ more groups of 10 cranes

Write a question about the story that has to do with subtracting tens. Have a classmate answer your question.

Name ______________________________

TEKS Number and Operations—2.4.B
MATHEMATICAL PROCESSES 2.1.C, 2.1.E, 2.1.F

8.1 Break Apart Ones to Subtract

ALGEBRA

Essential Question How does breaking apart a number make subtracting easier?

Explore

Write two addends for each sum.

7

9

5

6

4

8

Math Talk Mathematical Processes

Describe how you chose addends for each sum.

FOR THE TEACHER • After children have recorded addends for each sum, have a class discussion about the different facts that children represented on their papers.

Model and Draw

Break apart ones. Subtract in two steps.

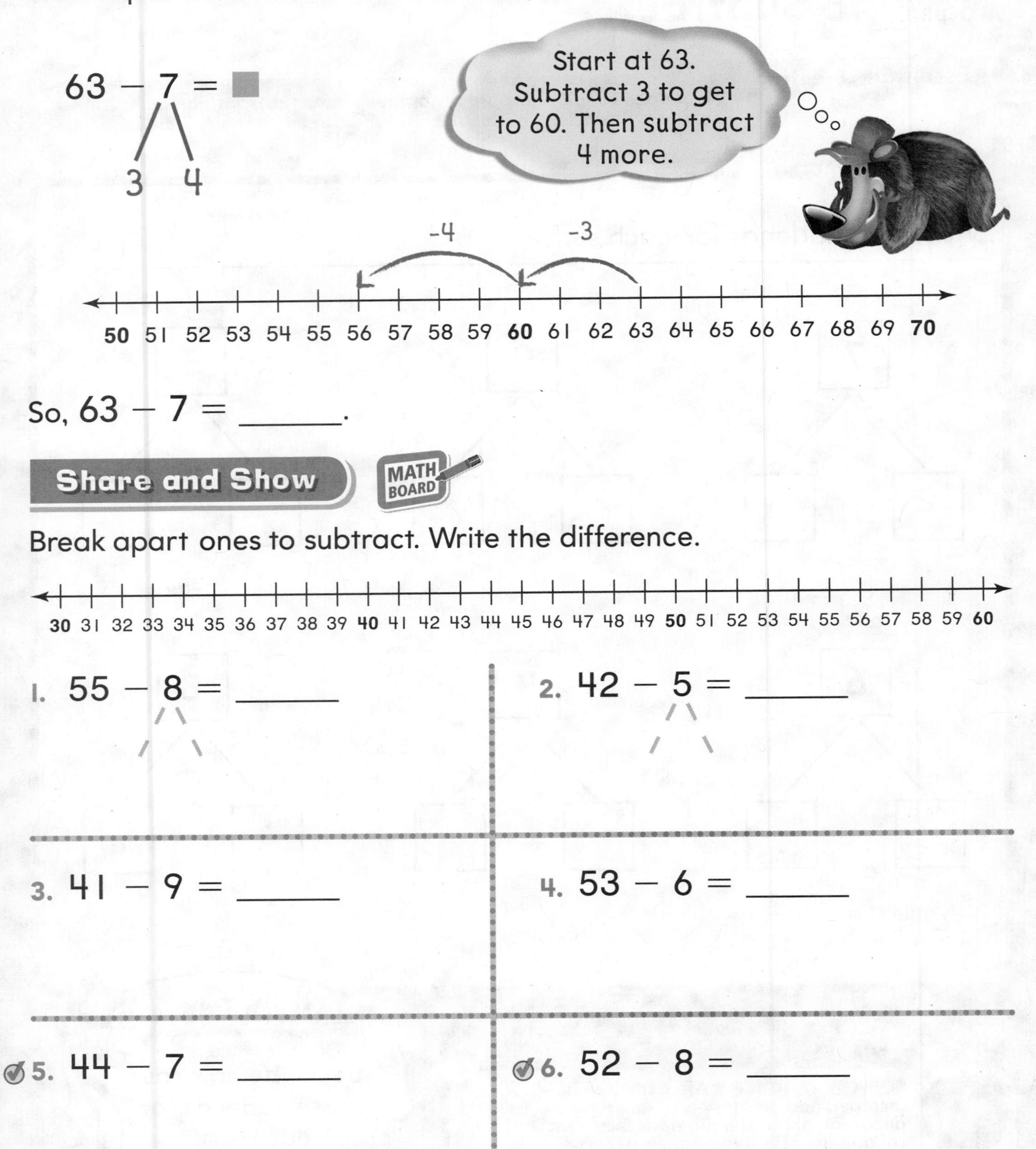

$63 - 7 = \blacksquare$

3 4

-4 -3

50 51 52 53 54 55 56 57 58 59 **60** 61 62 63 64 65 66 67 68 69 **70**

So, $63 - 7 =$ ______.

Share and Show

MATH BOARD

Break apart ones to subtract. Write the difference.

30 31 32 33 34 35 36 37 38 39 **40** 41 42 43 44 45 46 47 48 49 **50** 51 52 53 54 55 56 57 58 59 **60**

1. $55 - 8 =$ ______

2. $42 - 5 =$ ______

3. $41 - 9 =$ ______

4. $53 - 6 =$ ______

5. $44 - 7 =$ ______

6. $52 - 8 =$ ______

Name ________________________

Problem Solving

Break apart ones to subtract. Write the difference.

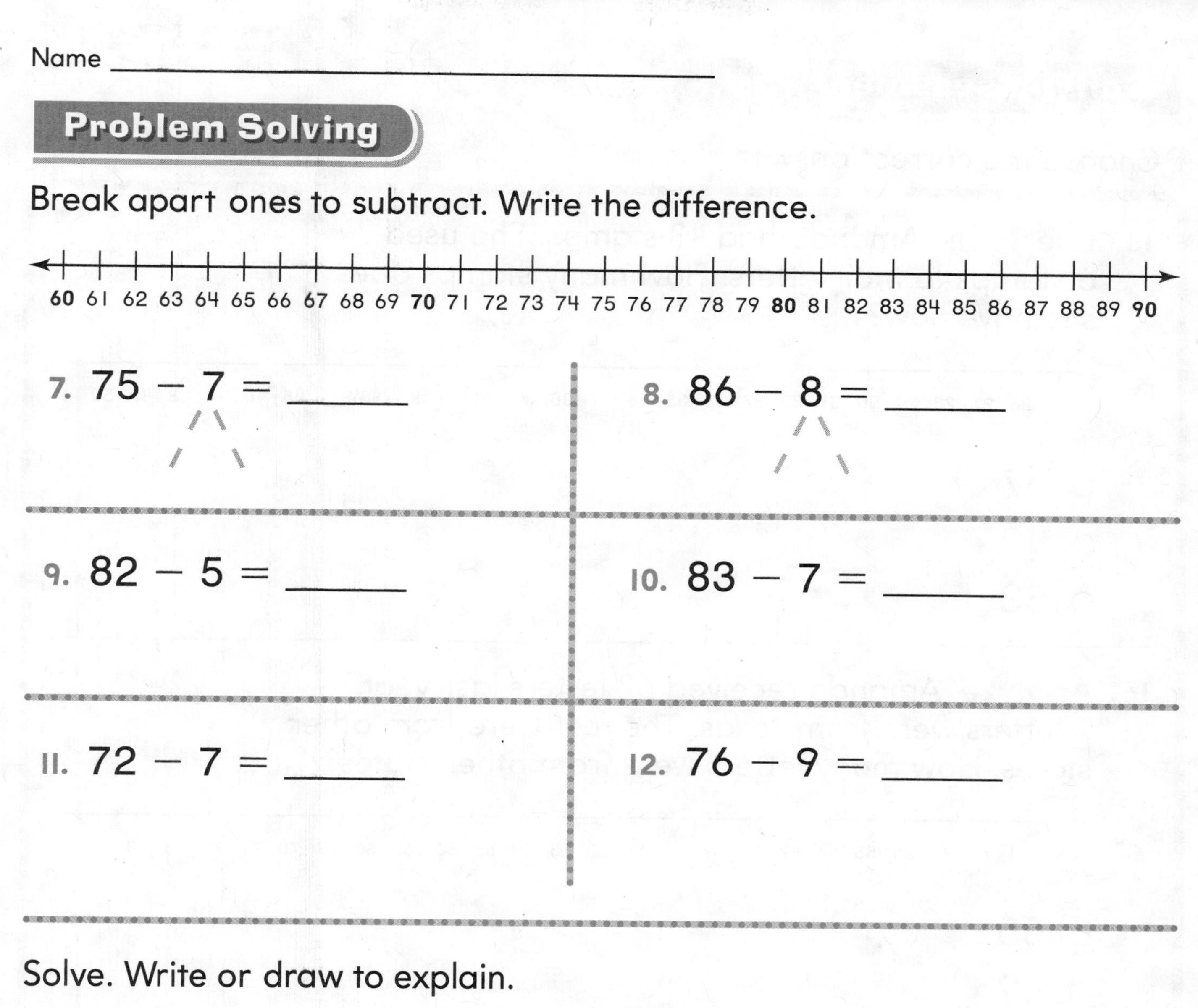

7. $75 - 7 =$ ______

8. $86 - 8 =$ ______

9. $82 - 5 =$ ______

10. $83 - 7 =$ ______

11. $72 - 7 =$ ______

12. $76 - 9 =$ ______

Solve. Write or draw to explain.

13. H.O.T. **Multi-Step** Cheryl brought 27 bagels for the bake sale. Mike brought 24 bagels. They sold all but 9 of them. How many bagels did they sell?

______ bagels

14. H.O.T. Billy has 8 fewer marbles than Sara. Sara has 45 marbles. How many marbles does Billy have?

______ marbles

Daily Assessment Task

Mathematical Processes
Model • Reason • Communicate

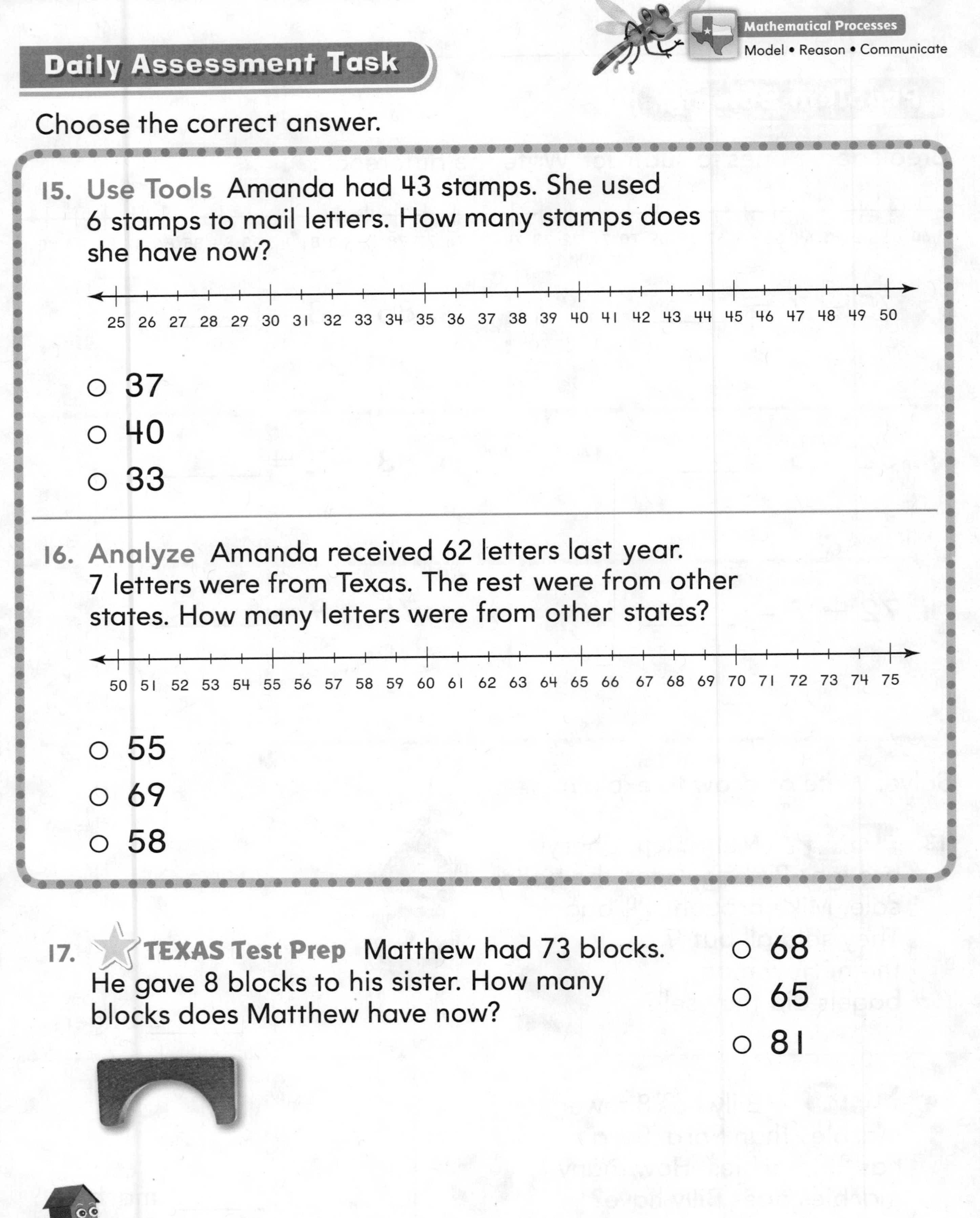

Choose the correct answer.

15. **Use Tools** Amanda had 43 stamps. She used 6 stamps to mail letters. How many stamps does she have now?

25 26 27 28 29 30 31 32 33 34 35 36 37 38 39 40 41 42 43 44 45 46 47 48 49 50

- ○ 37
- ○ 40
- ○ 33

16. **Analyze** Amanda received 62 letters last year. 7 letters were from Texas. The rest were from other states. How many letters were from other states?

50 51 52 53 54 55 56 57 58 59 60 61 62 63 64 65 66 67 68 69 70 71 72 73 74 75

- ○ 55
- ○ 69
- ○ 58

17. **TEXAS Test Prep** Matthew had 73 blocks. He gave 8 blocks to his sister. How many blocks does Matthew have now?

- ○ 68
- ○ 65
- ○ 81

TAKE HOME ACTIVITY • Ask your child to describe how to find 34 – 6.

TEKS Number and Operations—2.4.B
MATHEMATICAL PROCESSES 2.1.C, 2.1.E, 2.1.F

Name ______________________

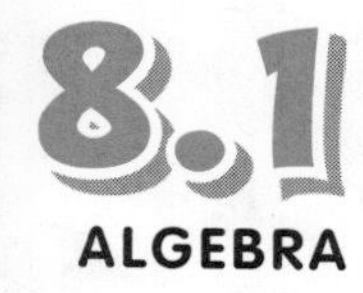

ALGEBRA

8.1 Break Apart Ones to Subtract

Break apart ones to subtract. Write the difference.

50 51 52 53 54 55 56 57 58 59 **60** 61 62 63 64 65 66 67 68 69 **70** 71 72 73 74 75 76 77 78 79 **80**

1. $65 - 6 =$ ______

2. $76 - 8 =$ ______

3. $73 - 4 =$ ______

4. $66 - 9 =$ ______

Problem Solving Real World

Choose a way to solve. Write or draw to explain.

5. Julie has 9 more crayons than Adam. Julie has 44 crayons. How many crayons does Adam have?

   ______ crayons

6. **Multi-Step** Grace brought 36 small paper cups for a science project. Cody brought 38 large paper cups. They used all but 6 of them. How many paper cups did they use?

   ______ paper cups

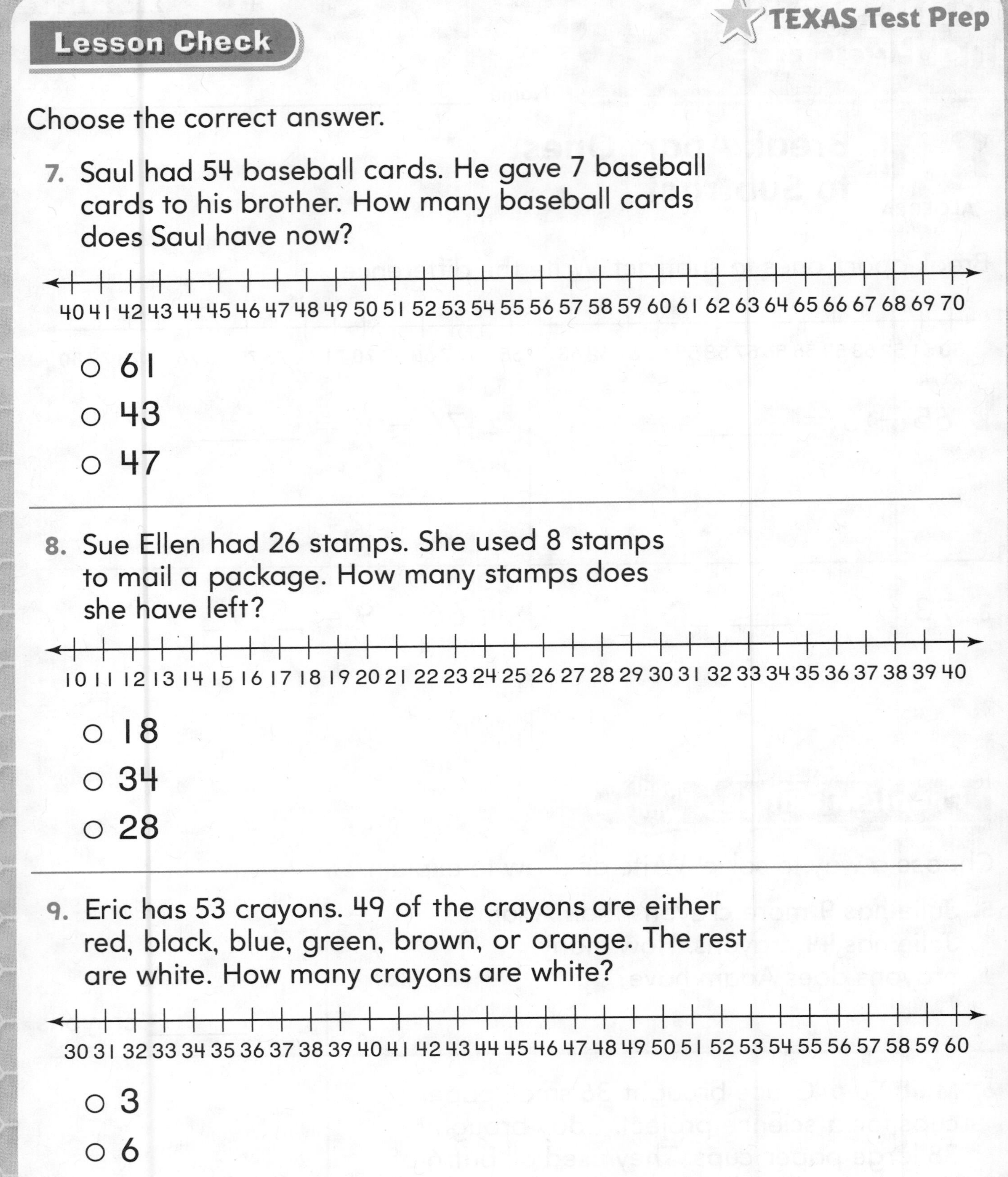

Lesson Check

TEXAS Test Prep

Choose the correct answer.

7. Saul had 54 baseball cards. He gave 7 baseball cards to his brother. How many baseball cards does Saul have now?

40 41 42 43 44 45 46 47 48 49 50 51 52 53 54 55 56 57 58 59 60 61 62 63 64 65 66 67 68 69 70

- ○ 61
- ○ 43
- ○ 47

8. Sue Ellen had 26 stamps. She used 8 stamps to mail a package. How many stamps does she have left?

10 11 12 13 14 15 16 17 18 19 20 21 22 23 24 25 26 27 28 29 30 31 32 33 34 35 36 37 38 39 40

- ○ 18
- ○ 34
- ○ 28

9. Eric has 53 crayons. 49 of the crayons are either red, black, blue, green, brown, or orange. The rest are white. How many crayons are white?

30 31 32 33 34 35 36 37 38 39 40 41 42 43 44 45 46 47 48 49 50 51 52 53 54 55 56 57 58 59 60

- ○ 3
- ○ 6
- ○ 4

Name ________________

8.2 ALGEBRA Break Apart Numbers to Subtract

TEKS Number and Operations—2.4.B
MATHEMATICAL PROCESSES 2.1.C, 2.1.E, 2.1.F

Essential Question How does breaking apart a number make subtracting easier?

Explore Real World

Hands On

Draw jumps on the number line to show how to break apart the number to subtract.

30 31 32 33 34 35 36 37 38 39 **40** 41 42 43 44 45 46 47 48 49 **50** 51 52 53 54 55 56 57 58 59 **60**

50 51 52 53 54 55 56 57 58 59 **60** 61 62 63 64 65 66 67 68 69 **70** 71 72 73 74 75 76 77 78 79 **80**

40 41 42 43 44 45 46 47 48 49 **50** 51 52 53 54 55 56 57 58 59 **60** 61 62 63 64 65 66 67 68 69 **70**

FOR THE TEACHER • Read the following problem. Have children draw jumps on the number line to solve. Mrs. Hill had 45 paintbrushes. She gave 9 paintbrushes to students in her art class. How many paintbrushes does Mrs. Hill have now? Repeat the same problem situation for 72 – 7 and 53 – 6.

Math Talk Mathematical Processes

For one of the problems, **describe** what you did.

Model and Draw

Break apart the number you are subtracting into tens and ones.

Subtract 10.
Next, subtract 2 to get to 60.
Then subtract 5 more.

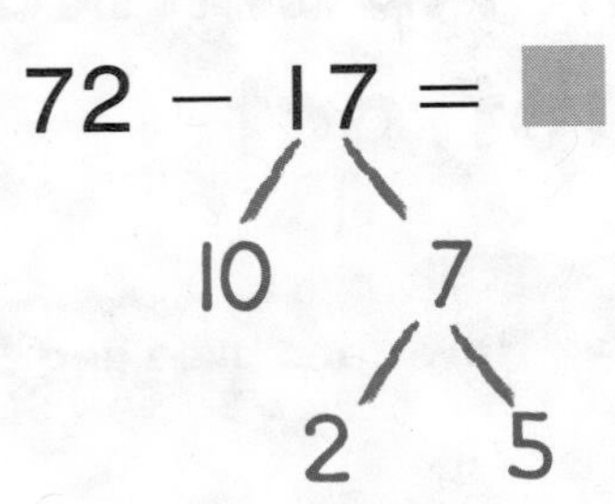

10 + 2 + 5 = 17

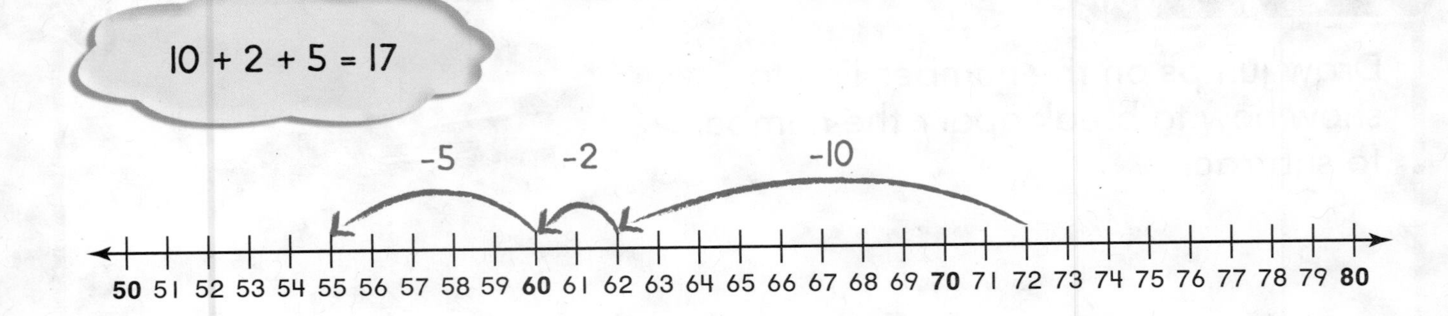

So, 72 − 17 = ______.

Share and Show

Break apart the number you are subtracting.
Write the difference.

20 21 22 23 24 25 26 27 28 29 30 31 32 33 34 35 36 37 38 39 40 41 42 43 44 45 46 47 48 49 50

1. 43 − 18 = ______

2. 45 − 14 = ______

3. 46 − 17 = ______

4. 44 − 16 = ______

Name ______

Problem Solving

Break apart the number you are subtracting.
Write the difference.

40 41 42 43 44 45 46 47 48 49 **50** 51 52 53 54 55 56 57 58 59 **60** 61 62 63 64 65 66 67 68 69 **70**

5. 57 − 15 = ______

6. 63 − 17 = ______

7. 68 − 19 = ______

8. 61 − 18 = ______

Solve. Write or draw to explain.

9. **H.O.T.** Jane has 53 toys in a box. She takes some toys out. Now there are 36 toys in the box. How many toys did Jane take out of the box?

______ toys

10. **H.O.T.** **Multi-Step** Look at Tom's steps to solve a problem. Solve this problem in the same way.

42 − 15 = ?

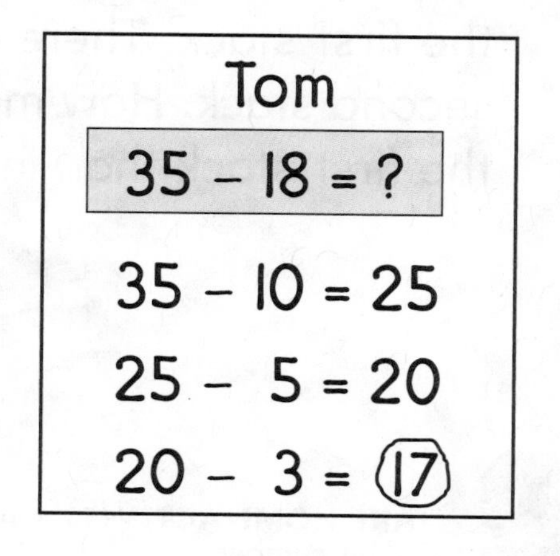

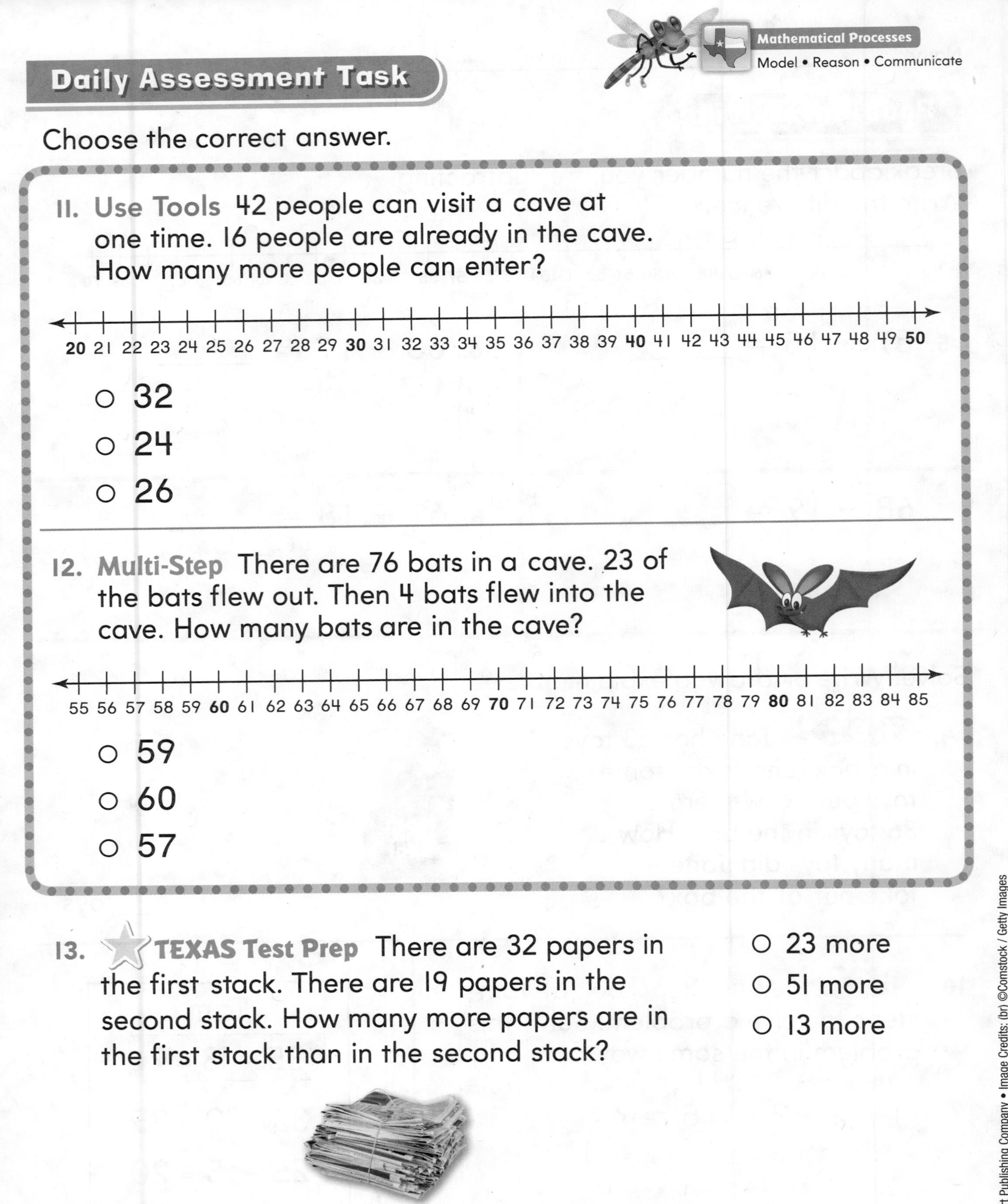

Mathematical Processes
Model • Reason • Communicate

Daily Assessment Task

Choose the correct answer.

11. **Use Tools** 42 people can visit a cave at one time. 16 people are already in the cave. How many more people can enter?

20 21 22 23 24 25 26 27 28 29 **30** 31 32 33 34 35 36 37 38 39 **40** 41 42 43 44 45 46 47 48 49 **50**

- ○ 32
- ○ 24
- ○ 26

12. **Multi-Step** There are 76 bats in a cave. 23 of the bats flew out. Then 4 bats flew into the cave. How many bats are in the cave?

55 56 57 58 59 **60** 61 62 63 64 65 66 67 68 69 **70** 71 72 73 74 75 76 77 78 79 **80** 81 82 83 84 85

- ○ 59
- ○ 60
- ○ 57

13. **TEXAS Test Prep** There are 32 papers in the first stack. There are 19 papers in the second stack. How many more papers are in the first stack than in the second stack?

- ○ 23 more
- ○ 51 more
- ○ 13 more

TAKE HOME ACTIVITY • Ask your child to write a subtraction story that uses 2-digit numbers.

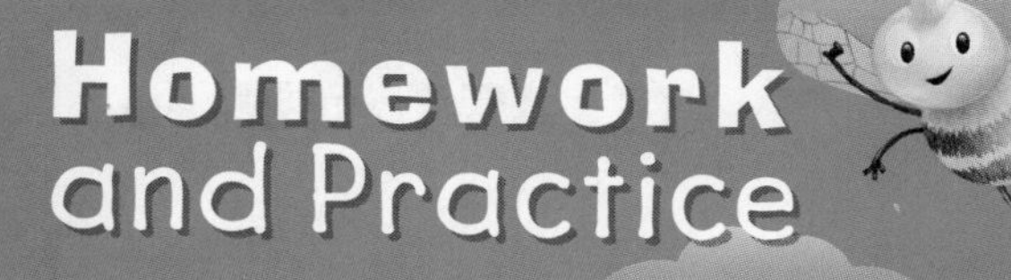

Name ____________________

ALGEBRA

Break Apart Numbers to Subtract

Break apart the number you are subtracting. Write the difference.

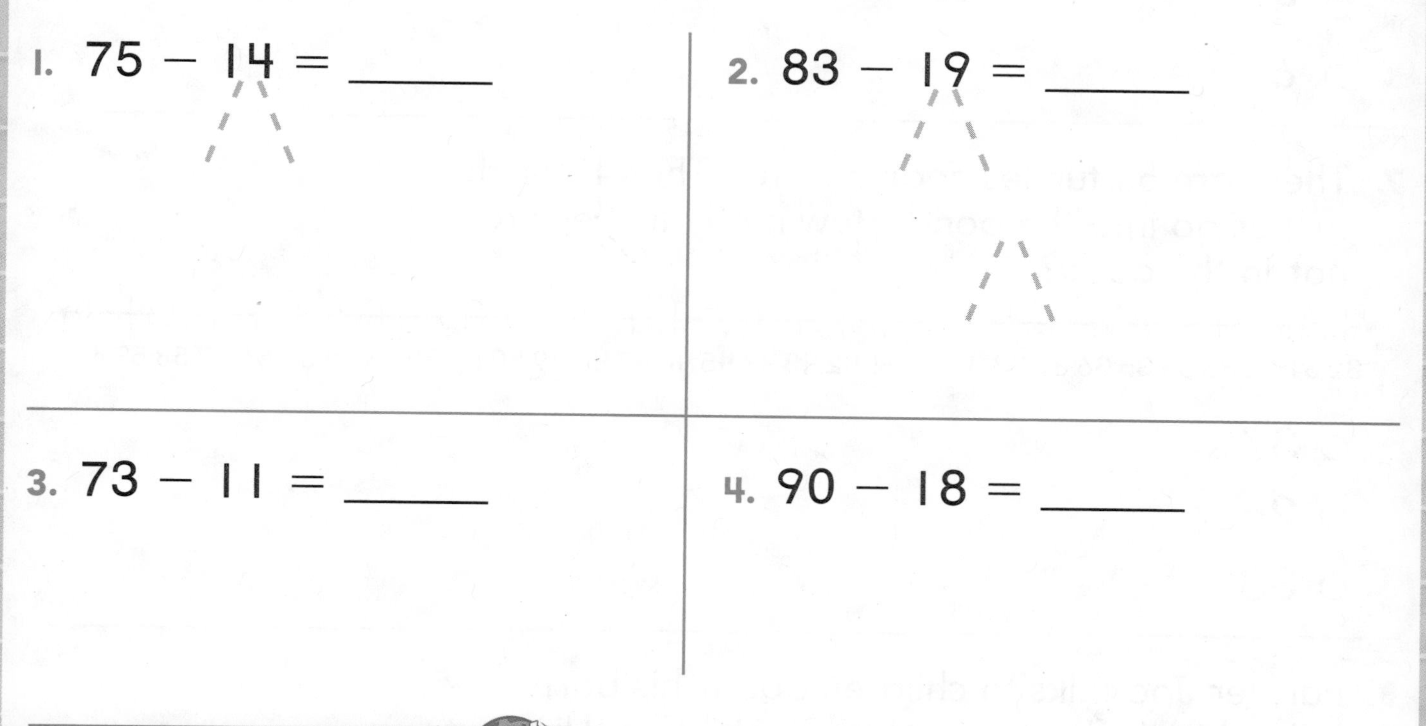

1. 75 − 14 = _____

2. 83 − 19 = _____

3. 73 − 11 = _____

4. 90 − 18 = _____

Problem Solving Real World

Choose a way to solve. Write or draw to explain.

5. **Multi-Step** Rachel has 63 buttons in a box. She takes out 9 blue buttons. Then she takes out 5 green buttons. How many buttons are in the box now?

_____ buttons

Lesson Check

TEXAS Test Prep

Choose the correct answer.

6. There are 23 books in one box. There are 17 books in a second box. How many more books are in the first box than in the second box?

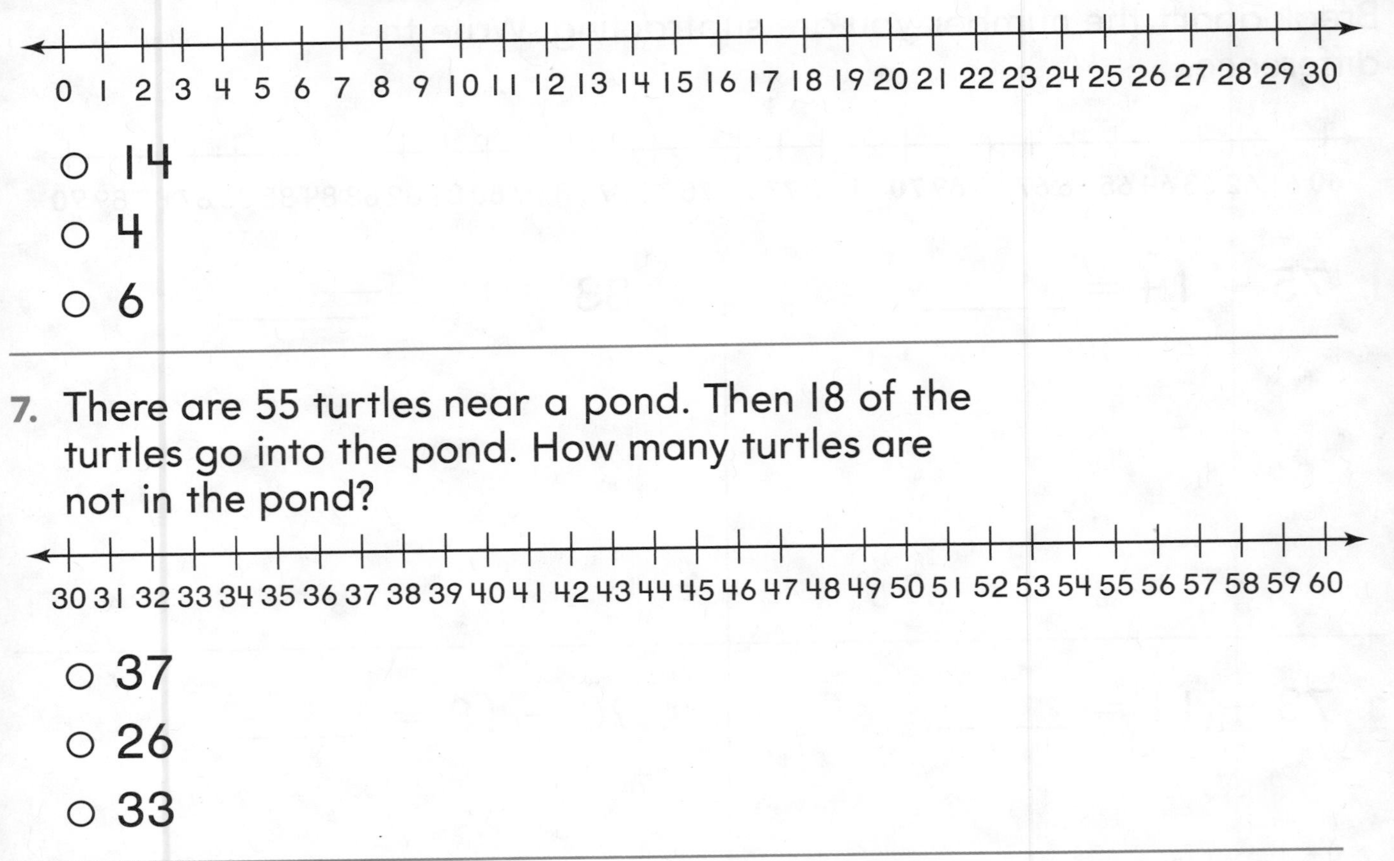

- ○ 14
- ○ 4
- ○ 6

---

7. There are 55 turtles near a pond. Then 18 of the turtles go into the pond. How many turtles are not in the pond?

30 31 32 33 34 35 36 37 38 39 40 41 42 43 44 45 46 47 48 49 50 51 52 53 54 55 56 57 58 59 60

- ○ 37
- ○ 26
- ○ 33

---

8. Farmer Joe talks to children about his barn animals. His first group has 33 children. His next group has 15 fewer children than the first. How many children are in the second group?

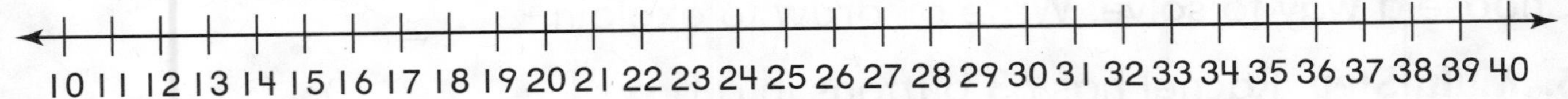

- ○ 22
- ○ 28
- ○ 18

Name ______________________________

8.3 Model and Record 2-Digit Subtraction

TEKS Number and Operations—2.4.B
MATHEMATICAL PROCESSES 2.1.D, 2.1.F

Essential Question How do you record 2-digit subtraction?

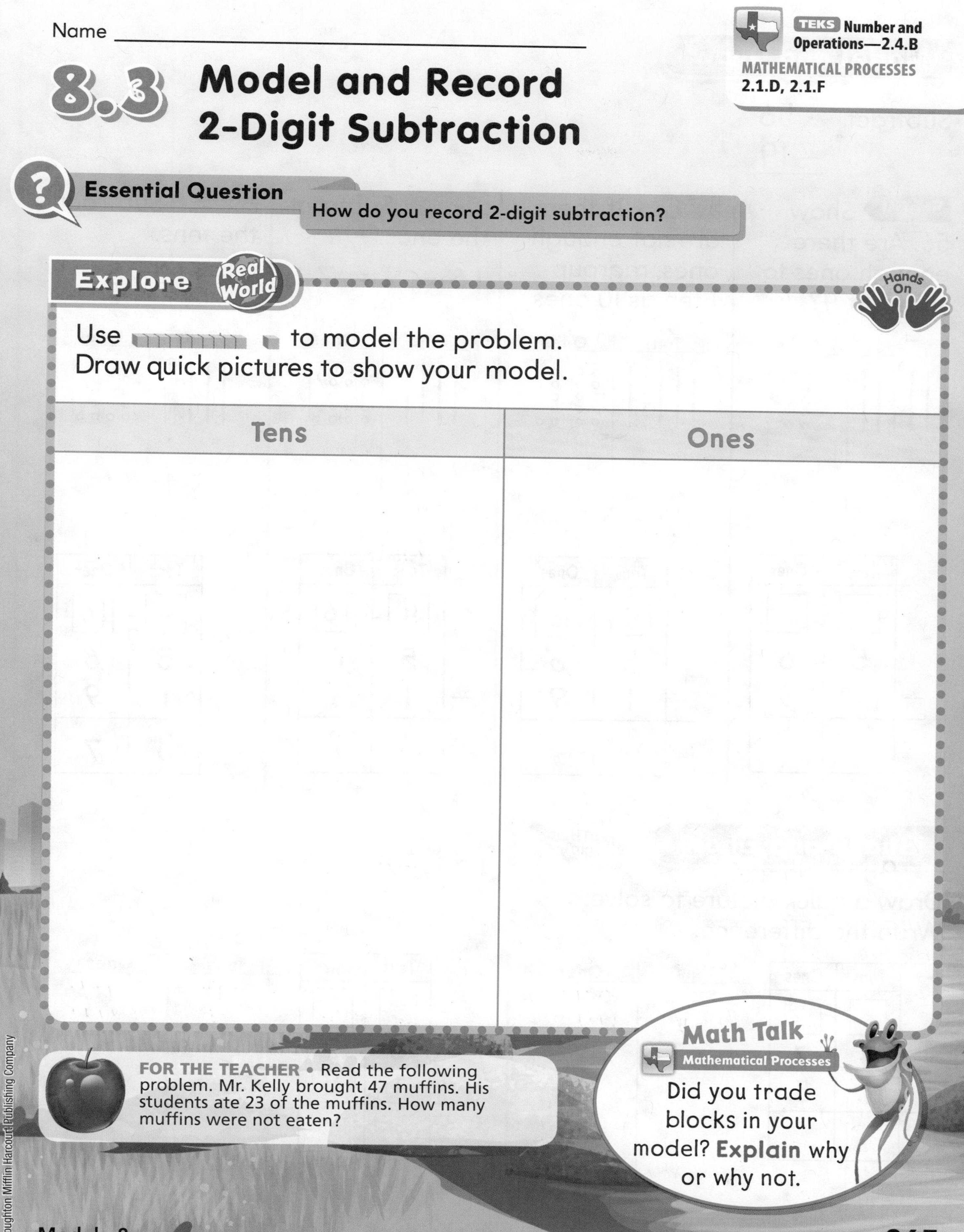

Explore Real World

Hands On

Use [tens block] [ones block] to model the problem.
Draw quick pictures to show your model.

Tens	Ones

FOR THE TEACHER • Read the following problem. Mr. Kelly brought 47 muffins. His students ate 23 of the muffins. How many muffins were not eaten?

Math Talk Mathematical Processes
Did you trade blocks in your model? **Explain** why or why not.

Model and Draw

Subtract. $\begin{array}{r} 56 \\ -\ 19 \\ \hline \end{array}$

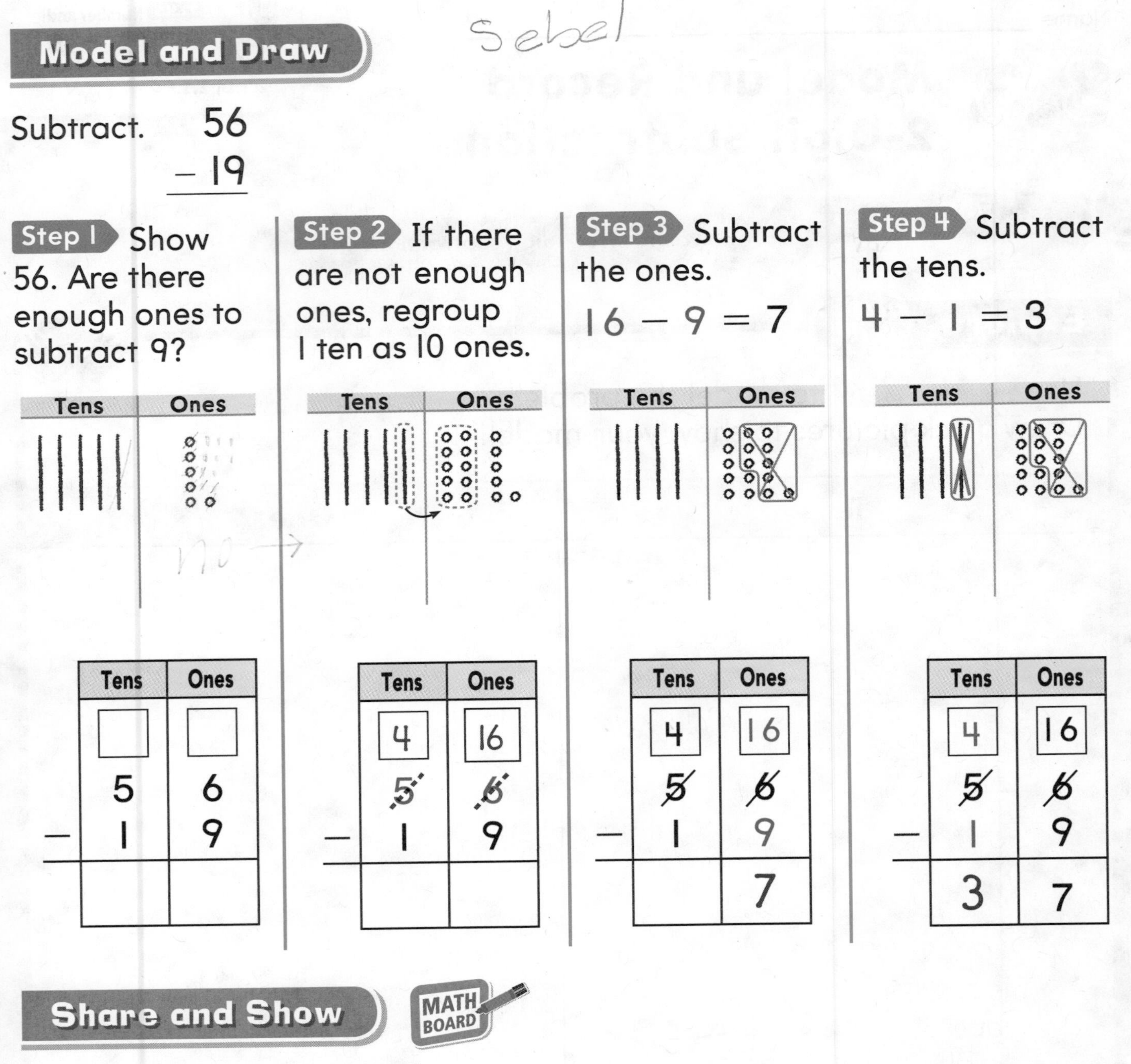

Share and Show

MATH BOARD

Draw a quick picture to solve.
Write the difference.

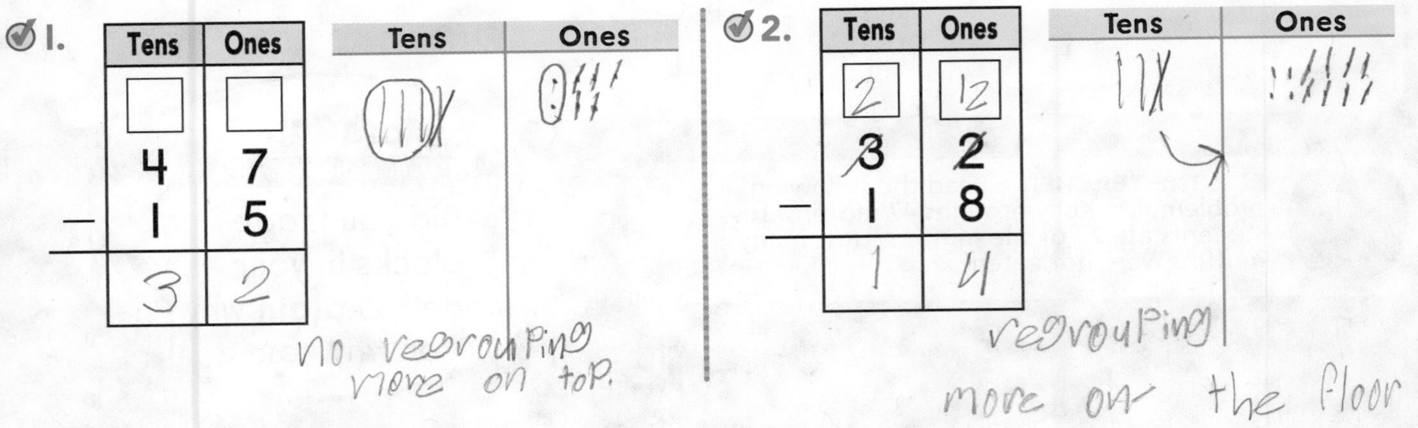

Name ____________________

TEKS Number and Operations—2.4.C

MATHEMATICAL PROCESSES 2.1.A, 2.1.B, 2.1.D

8.4 PROBLEM SOLVING • Subtraction

Essential Question How can using a model help when solving subtraction problems?

Unlock the Problem (Real World)

Jane and her mom made 33 puppets for the craft fair. They sold 14 puppets. How many puppets do they still have?

Read

What information am I given?

They made ______ puppets.

They sold ______ puppets.

Plan

What is my plan or strategy?

I can ____________________
____________________.

Solve

Show how you solve the problem.

______	______

______

33 − 14 = ■

______ puppets

HOME CONNECTION • Your child used a model and a number sentence to represent the problem. Using a model helps show what is known and what is needed to solve the problem.

Try Another Problem

- What information am I given?
- What is my plan or strategy?

Label the model. Write a number sentence with a ▇ for the unknown number. Solve.

1. Carlette had a box of 46 craft sticks. She used 28 craft sticks to make a sailboat. How many craft sticks were not used?

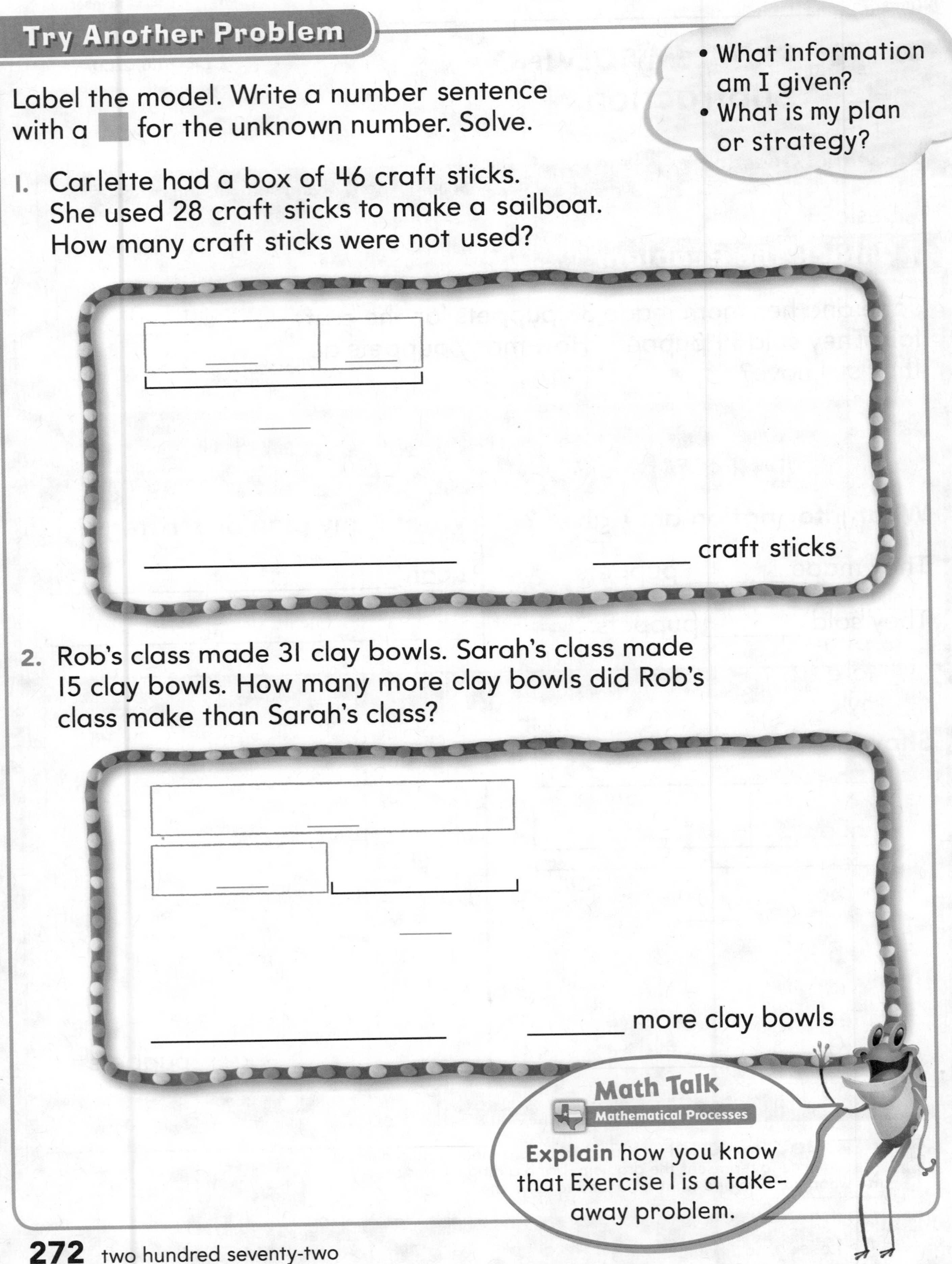

______ craft sticks

2. Rob's class made 31 clay bowls. Sarah's class made 15 clay bowls. How many more clay bowls did Rob's class make than Sarah's class?

______ more clay bowls

Math Talk

Mathematical Processes

Explain how you know that Exercise 1 is a take-away problem.

Name ______________________________

Share and Show

Label the model. Write a number sentence with a ■ for the unknown number. Solve.

3. Wesley has 21 ribbons in a box. He has 15 ribbons on the wall. How many more ribbons does he have in the box than on the wall?

_______ more ribbons

____

Solve. Write or draw to explain.

4. H.O.T. Multi-Step Jennifer wrote 9 poems at school and 11 poems at home. She wrote 5 more poems than Nell. How many poems did Nell write?

_______ poems

5. H.O.T. Multi-Step There are 70 children. 28 children are hiking and 16 are at a picnic. The rest of the children are playing soccer. How many children are playing soccer

Draw a model with bars for the problem. Describe how your drawing shows the problem. Then solve the problem.

____

____

____

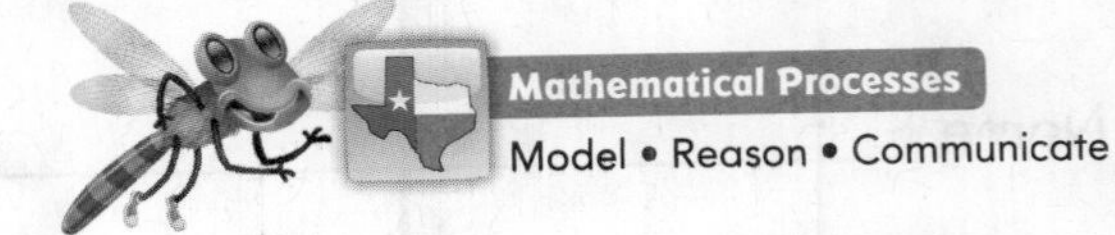

Daily Assessment Task

Choose the correct answer.

6. **Analyze** A group of 60 fish swim together. Then 25 fish swim away. How many fish are there now?

   ○ 85
   ○ 35
   ○ 45

7. There are 35 boats in a race. 12 of the boats stop racing. How many boats are still racing?

   ○ 23
   ○ 15
   ○ 20

8. **Connect** Ms. Ortiz has 70 pages in her album. 38 of the pages are filled with photos. How many pages are not filled with photos?

   ○ 40
   ○ 32
   ○ 22

9. **TEXAS Test Prep** There are 48 crackers in a bag. Children eat 25 of them. How many crackers are still in the bag?

   ○ 23
   ○ 13
   ○ 17

TAKE HOME ACTIVITY • Ask your child to explain how he or she solved one of the problems in this lesson.

Homework and Practice

TEKS Number and Operations—2.4.C
MATHEMATICAL PROCESSES 2.1.A, 2.1.B, 2.1.D

Name ______

8.4 PROBLEM SOLVING • Subtraction

Label the model. Write a number sentence with a ▢ for the unknown number. Solve.

1. Jeremy has 31 photos in his photo album. He also has 12 photos on the wall. How many more photos does he have in his album than on the wall?

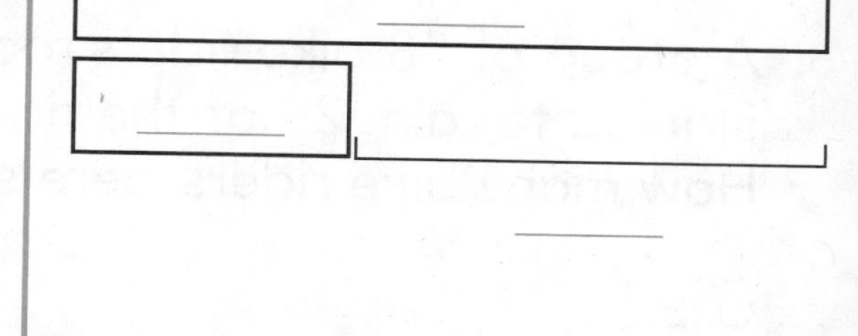

______ more photos

______

Problem Solving Real World

Solve. Write or draw to explain.

2. There are 80 children at camp. 26 of them are swimming. 24 of the children are doing crafts. The rest are on a nature hike. How many children are on a nature hike?

______ children

3. **Multi-Step** Pam made 6 drawings of cats and 13 drawings of dogs. She made 8 more drawings than Emma. How many drawings did Emma make?

______ drawings

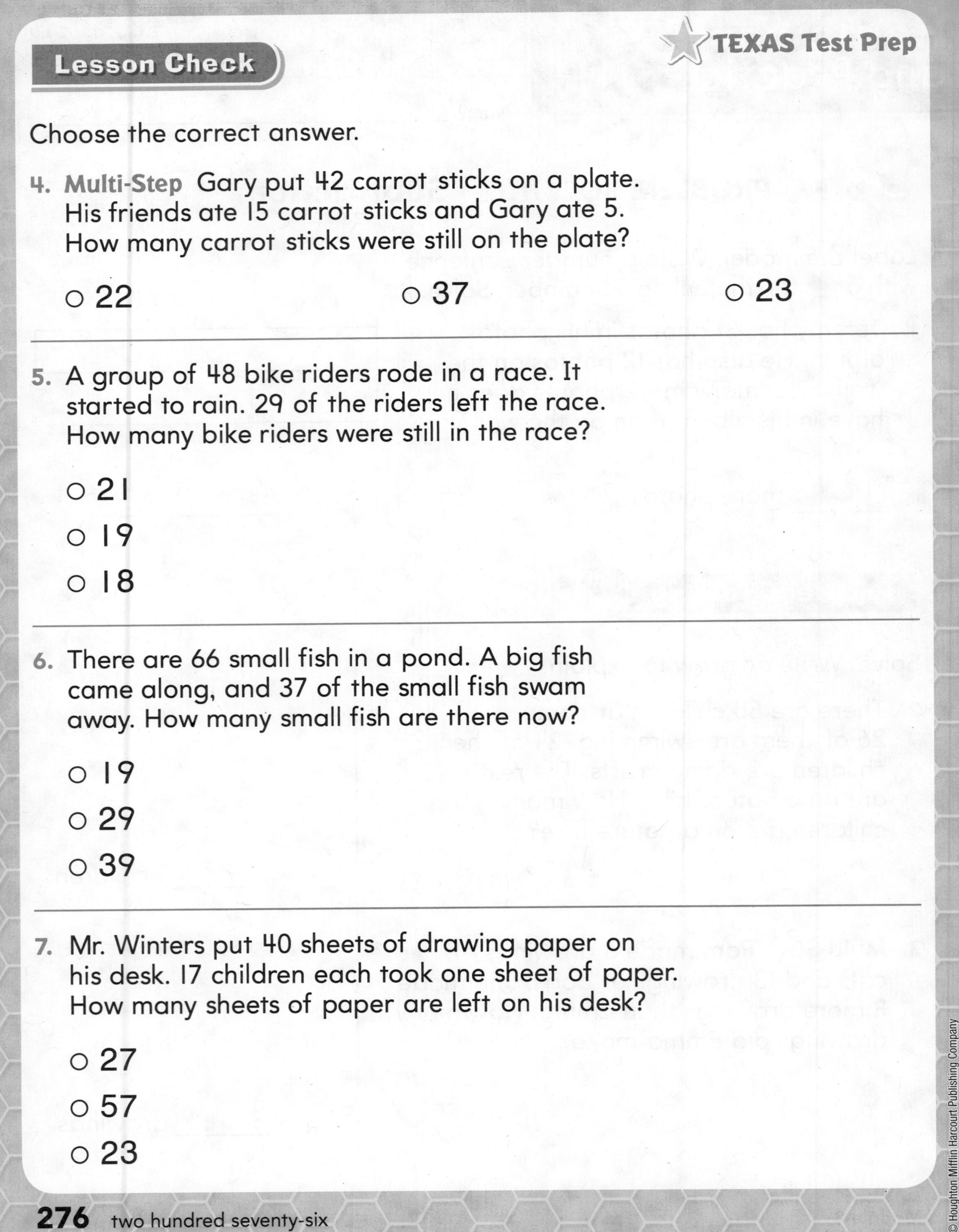

Lesson Check

TEXAS Test Prep

Choose the correct answer.

4. **Multi-Step** Gary put 42 carrot sticks on a plate. His friends ate 15 carrot sticks and Gary ate 5. How many carrot sticks were still on the plate?

   ○ 22 ○ 37 ○ 23

5. A group of 48 bike riders rode in a race. It started to rain. 29 of the riders left the race. How many bike riders were still in the race?

   ○ 21
   ○ 19
   ○ 18

6. There are 66 small fish in a pond. A big fish came along, and 37 of the small fish swam away. How many small fish are there now?

   ○ 19
   ○ 29
   ○ 39

7. Mr. Winters put 40 sheets of drawing paper on his desk. 17 children each took one sheet of paper. How many sheets of paper are left on his desk?

   ○ 27
   ○ 57
   ○ 23

Name ______________________

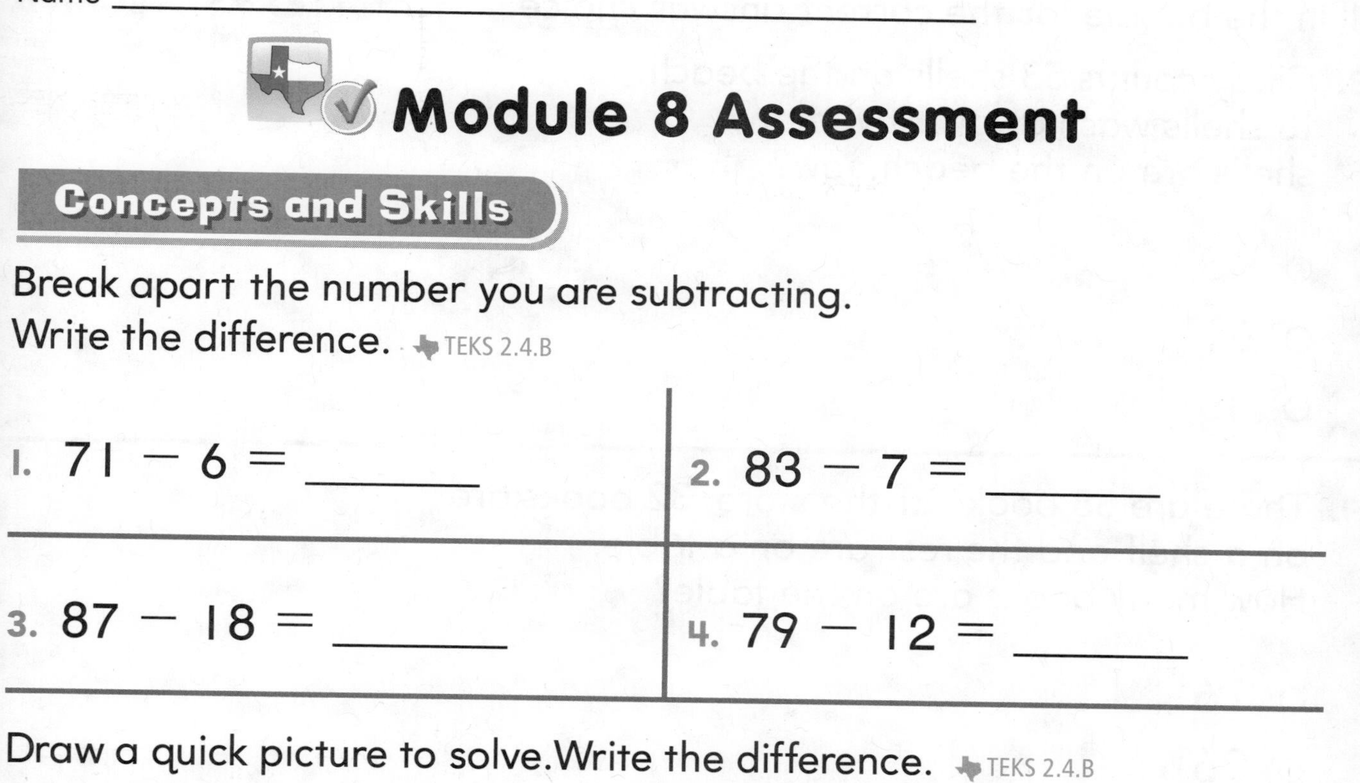

Module 8 Assessment

Concepts and Skills

Break apart the number you are subtracting.
Write the difference. TEKS 2.4.B

1. 71 − 6 = ______

2. 83 − 7 = ______

3. 87 − 18 = ______

4. 79 − 12 = ______

Draw a quick picture to solve. Write the difference. TEKS 2.4.B

5.

	Tens	Ones
	☐	☐
	4	4
−	1	7

Tens	Ones

6.

	Tens	Ones
	☐	☐
	3	8
−	1	8

Tens	Ones

7. Label the model. Write a number sentence with a ■ for the unknown number. Solve. TEKS 2.4.C

Charlie sees 35 geese in a field.
He sees 12 geese in the sky.
How many more geese does he see in the field than in the sky?

______ more geese

Fill in the bubble for the correct answer choice.

TEXAS Test Prep

8. Cindy counts 53 shells on the beach. 18 shells wash away. How many shells are on the beach now? TEKS 2.4.B

- ○ 45
- ○ 61
- ○ 35

9. There are 58 books at the store. 32 books are on a shelf and the rest are on a table. How many books are on the table? TEKS 2.4.B

- ○ 16
- ○ 26
- ○ 56

10. Children fly 61 kites at the festival. 7 kites fall to the ground. How many kites are still flying? TEKS 2.4.B

- ○ 54
- ○ 66
- ○ 13

11. There are 72 crayons in the box. Matt and Devon each take 18 crayons out of the box. How many crayons are in the box now? TEKS 2.4.B

- ○ 90
- ○ 36
- ○ 54

Name ____________________

TEKS Number and Operations—2.4.B

MATHEMATICAL PROCESSES 2.1.D, 2.1.F, 2.1.G

9.1 2-Digit Subtraction

Essential Question

How do you record the steps when subtracting 2-digit numbers?

Explore Real World

Hands On

Draw a quick picture to model each problem.

Tens	Ones

Tens	Ones

FOR THE TEACHER • Read the following problem. Devin had 36 toy robots on his shelf. He moved 12 of the robots to his closet. How many robots are on the shelf now? Repeat the activity with this problem: Devin had 54 toy cars. He gave 9 of them to his brother. How many cars does Devin have now?

Math Talk

Mathematical Processes

Explain how you know when to regroup.

Model and Draw

Subtract. $\begin{array}{r} 42 \\ -\ 15 \\ \hline \end{array}$

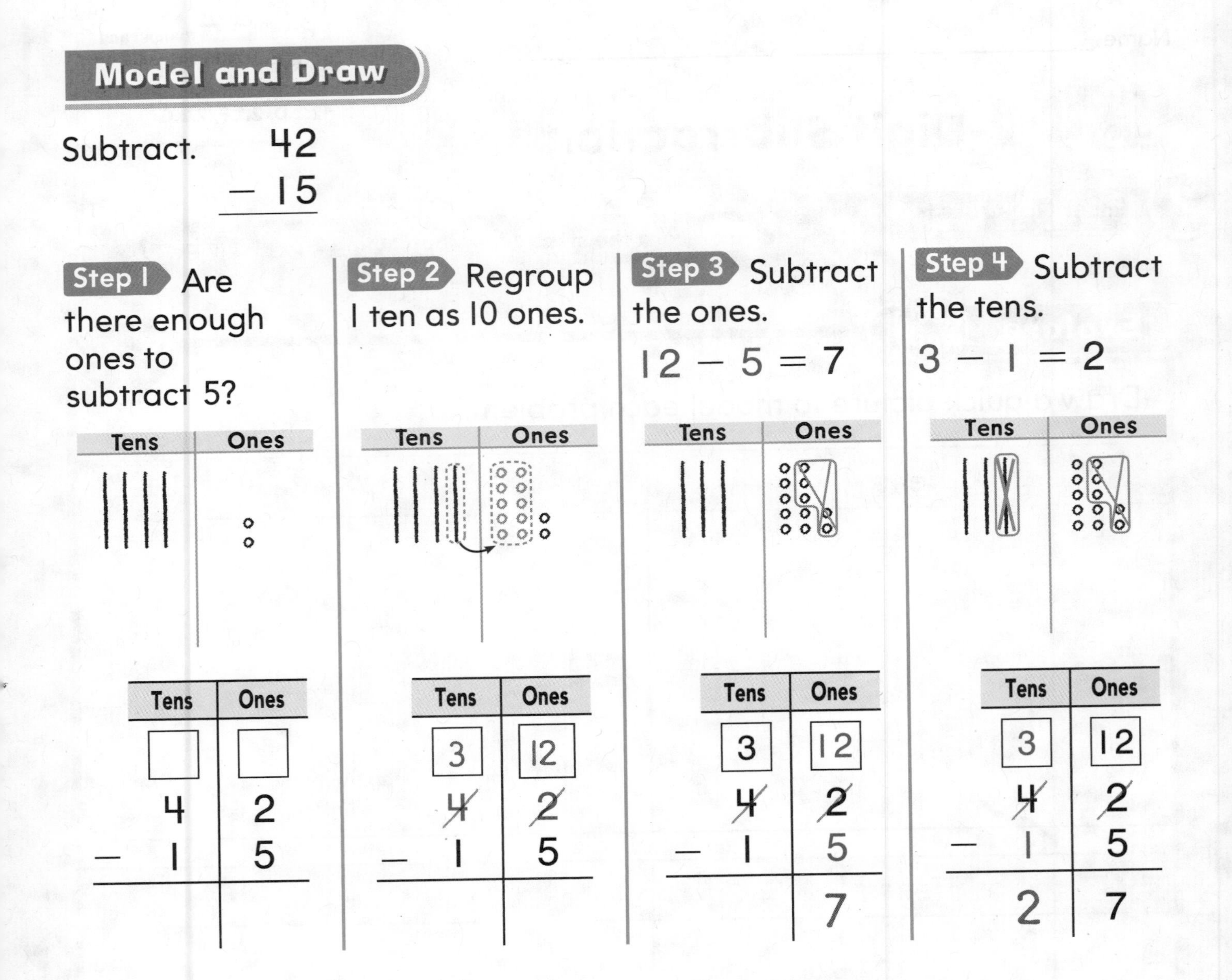

Tens	Ones
☐	☐
4	2
− 1	5

Tens	Ones
3	12
~~4~~	~~2~~
− 1	5

Tens	Ones
3	12
~~4~~	~~2~~
− 1	5
	7

Tens	Ones
3	12
~~4~~	~~2~~
− 1	5
2	7

Share and Show

Regroup if you need to. Write the difference.

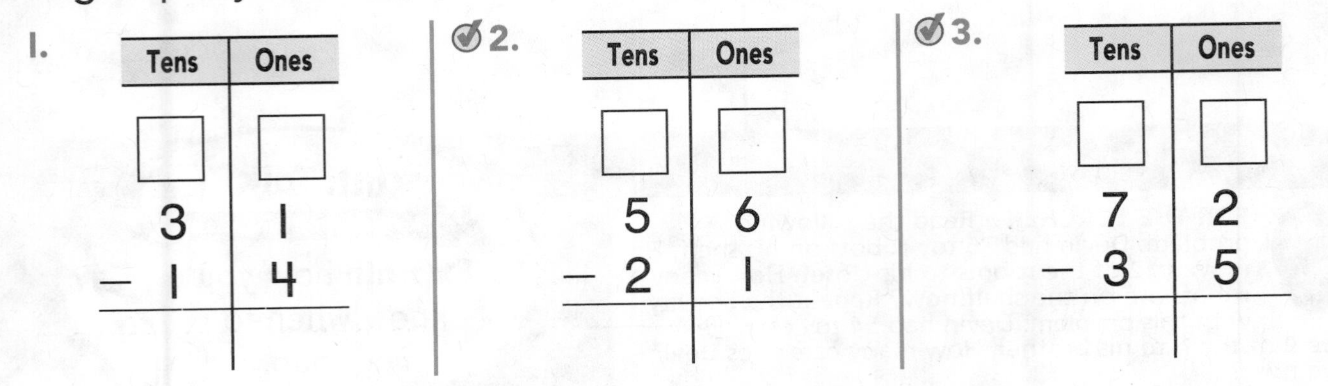

1.

Tens	Ones
☐	☐
3	1
− 1	4

2.

Tens	Ones
☐	☐
5	6
− 2	1

3.

Tens	Ones
☐	☐
7	2
− 3	5

Name ______________________

Problem Solving

Regroup if you need to. Write the difference.

4.

Tens	Ones
☐	☐
2	3
− 1	4

5.

Tens	Ones
☐	☐
8	7
− 5	7

6.

Tens	Ones
☐	☐
3	4
− 1	8

7.

Tens	Ones
☐	☐
6	1
− 1	3

8.

4	5
− 1	8

9.

5	2
− 3	6

10.

3	2
− 1	3

11.

7	5
− 4	3

12. H.O.T. Spencer wrote 5 fewer stories than Katie. Spencer wrote 18 stories. How many stories did Katie write?

_____ stories

13. Circle the problems below that you could use mental math to solve.

$54 - 10 =$ _____ $63 - 27 =$ _____ $93 - 20 =$ _____

$39 - 2 =$ _____ $41 - 18 =$ _____ $82 - 26 =$ _____

Explain your choices.

____

____

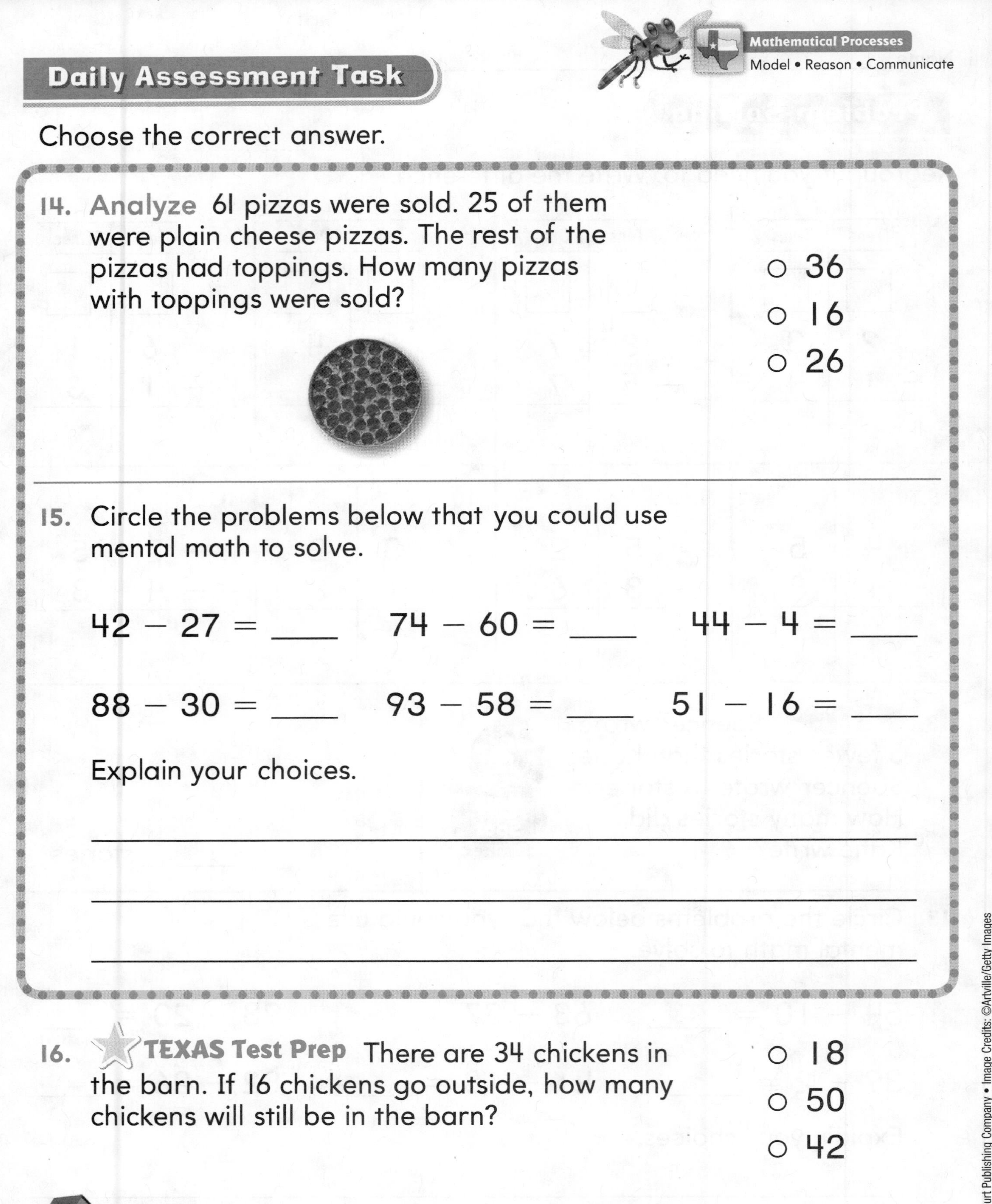

Daily Assessment Task

Choose the correct answer.

14. **Analyze** 61 pizzas were sold. 25 of them were plain cheese pizzas. The rest of the pizzas had toppings. How many pizzas with toppings were sold?

- ○ 36
- ○ 16
- ○ 26

15. Circle the problems below that you could use mental math to solve.

42 − 27 = ____ 74 − 60 = ____ 44 − 4 = ____

88 − 30 = ____ 93 − 58 = ____ 51 − 16 = ____

Explain your choices.

____

____

____

16. **TEXAS Test Prep** There are 34 chickens in the barn. If 16 chickens go outside, how many chickens will still be in the barn?

- ○ 18
- ○ 50
- ○ 42

TAKE HOME ACTIVITY • Ask your child to write a 2-digit subtraction problem with no regrouping needed. Have your child explain why he or she chose those numbers.

Name ______________________________

TEKS Number and Operations—2.4.B

MATHEMATICAL PROCESSES 2.1.C, 2.1.F

9.2 Practice 2-Digit Subtraction

Essential Question How do you record the steps when subtracting 2-digit numbers?

Explore Real World

Hands On

Choose one way to solve the problem.
Draw or write to show what you did.

FOR THE TEACHER • Read the following problem and have children choose their own methods for solving it. There are 74 books in Mr. Barron's classroom. 19 of the books are about computers. How many of the books are not about computers?

Model and Draw

Carmen had 50 game cards. Then she gave 16 game cards to Theo. How many game cards does Carmen have now?

Step 1 Look at the ones. There are not enough ones to subtract 6 from 0. So, regroup.

$$\begin{array}{r} \scriptstyle 4\ 10 \\ \not{5}\ \not{0} \\ -\ 1\ 6 \\ \hline \end{array}$$

Step 2 Subtract the ones.

$10 - 6 = 4$

$$\begin{array}{r} \scriptstyle 4\ 10 \\ \not{5}\ \not{0} \\ -\ 1\ 6 \\ \hline 4 \end{array}$$

Step 3 Subtract the tens.

$4 - 1 = 3$

$$\begin{array}{r} \scriptstyle 4\ 10 \\ \not{5}\ \not{0} \\ -\ 1\ 6 \\ \hline 3\ 4 \end{array}$$

Share and Show

MATH BOARD

Write the difference.

1. $\begin{array}{r} 38 \\ -\ 19 \\ \hline \end{array}$

2. $\begin{array}{r} 65 \\ -\ 32 \\ \hline \end{array}$

3. $\begin{array}{r} 50 \\ -\ 12 \\ \hline \end{array}$

4. $\begin{array}{r} 23 \\ -\ 0 \\ \hline \end{array}$

5. $\begin{array}{r} 70 \\ -\ 38 \\ \hline \end{array}$

6. $\begin{array}{r} 52 \\ -\ 17 \\ \hline \end{array}$

Name ______________________________

Problem Solving

Write the difference.

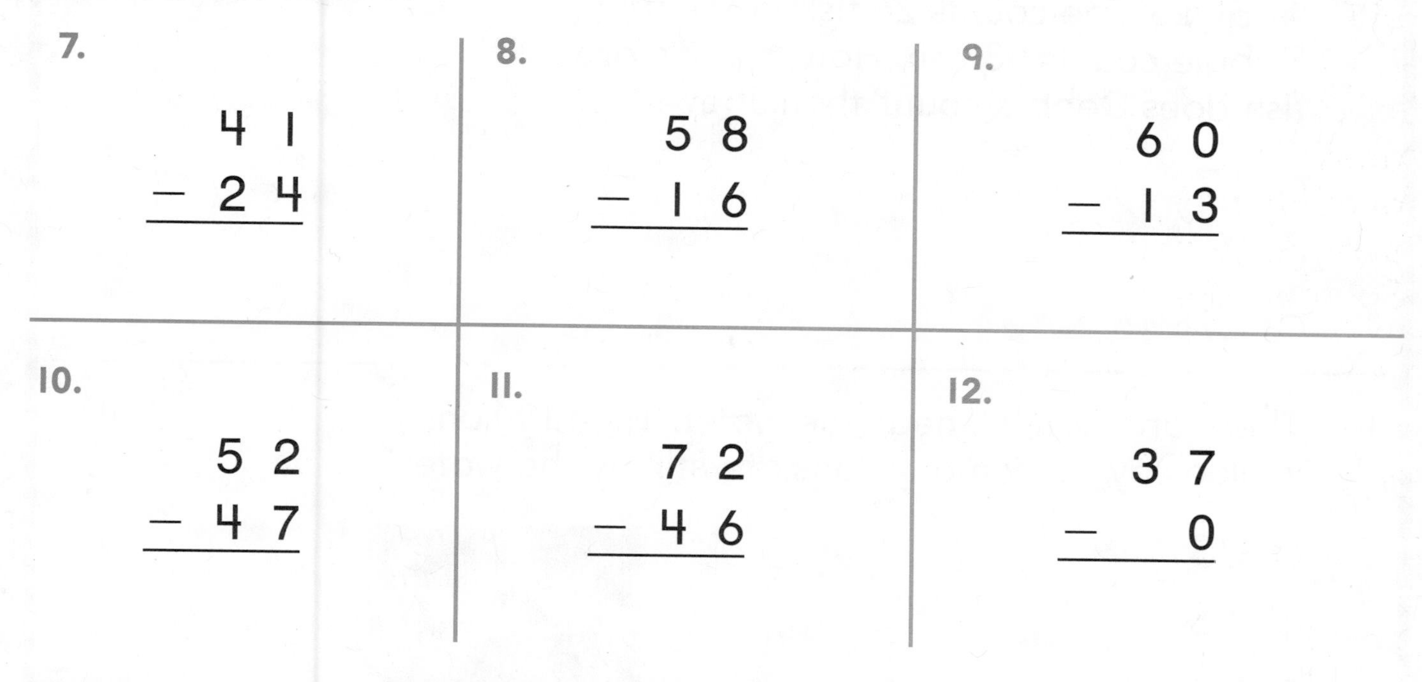

7.
$$\begin{array}{r} 41 \\ -\ 24 \\ \hline \end{array}$$

8.
$$\begin{array}{r} 58 \\ -\ 16 \\ \hline \end{array}$$

9.
$$\begin{array}{r} 60 \\ -\ 13 \\ \hline \end{array}$$

10.
$$\begin{array}{r} 52 \\ -\ 47 \\ \hline \end{array}$$

11.
$$\begin{array}{r} 72 \\ -\ 46 \\ \hline \end{array}$$

12.
$$\begin{array}{r} 37 \\ -\ \ 0 \\ \hline \end{array}$$

Solve. Write or draw to explain.

13. H.O.T. Adam takes 38 rocks out of a box. There are 23 rocks left in the box. How many rocks were in the box to start?

_______ rocks

14. H.O.T. **Multi-Step** Gwen had 70 cards. She gives 12 cards to Max and 19 cards to Kelly. How many cards does Gwen have now?

_______ cards

Daily Assessment Task

Choose the correct answer.

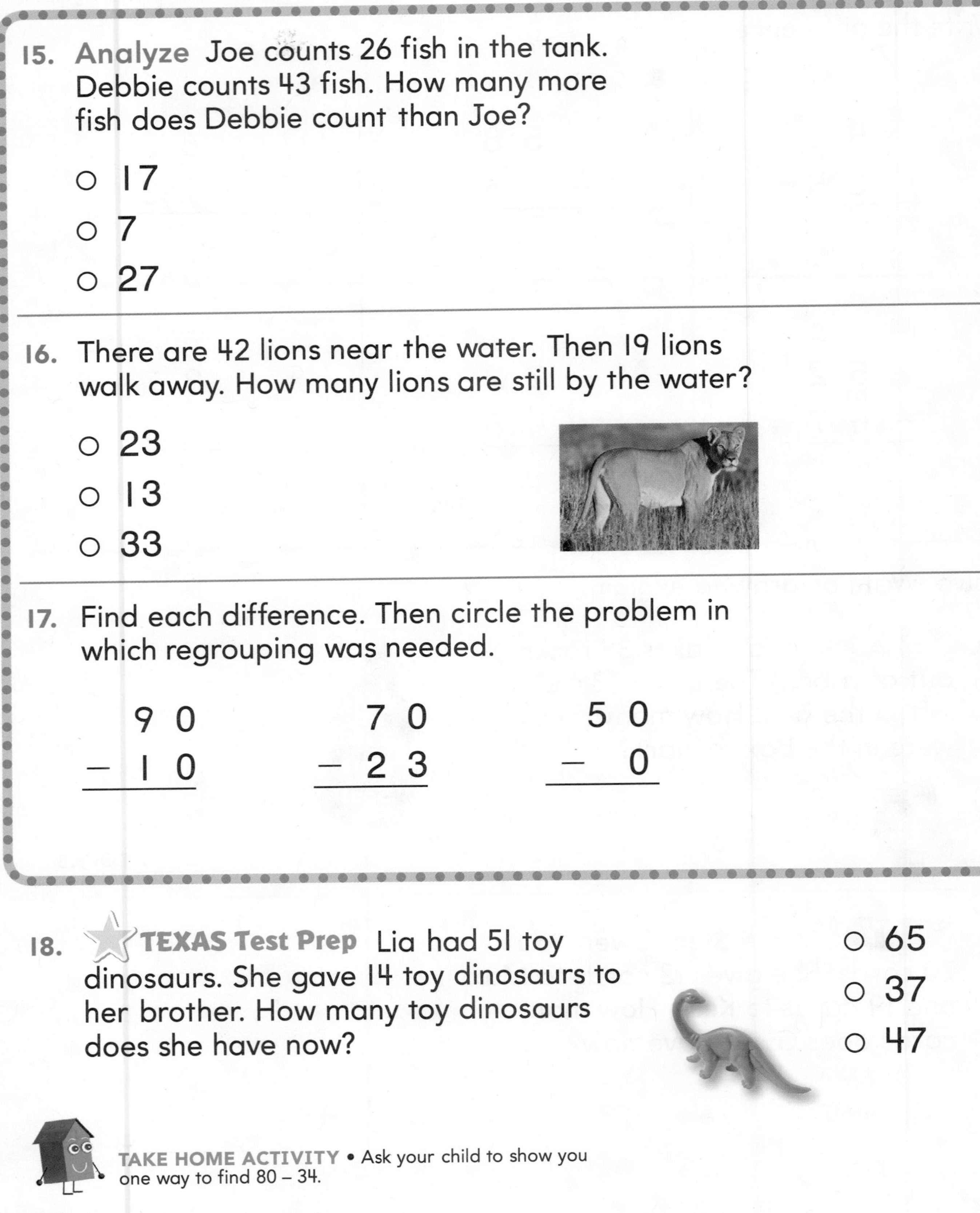

15. Analyze Joe counts 26 fish in the tank. Debbie counts 43 fish. How many more fish does Debbie count than Joe?

- ○ 17
- ○ 7
- ○ 27

16. There are 42 lions near the water. Then 19 lions walk away. How many lions are still by the water?

- ○ 23
- ○ 13
- ○ 33

17. Find each difference. Then circle the problem in which regrouping was needed.

$$\begin{array}{r} 90 \\ -\ 10 \\ \hline \end{array} \qquad \begin{array}{r} 70 \\ -\ 23 \\ \hline \end{array} \qquad \begin{array}{r} 50 \\ -\ 0 \\ \hline \end{array}$$

18. TEXAS Test Prep Lia had 51 toy dinosaurs. She gave 14 toy dinosaurs to her brother. How many toy dinosaurs does she have now?

- ○ 65
- ○ 37
- ○ 47

TAKE HOME ACTIVITY • Ask your child to show you one way to find 80 – 34.

Name ______________________

9.2 Practice 2-Digit Subtraction

Write the difference.

1.
$$\begin{array}{r} 35 \\ -\ 23 \\ \hline \end{array}$$

2.
$$\begin{array}{r} 60 \\ -\ 17 \\ \hline \end{array}$$

3.
$$\begin{array}{r} 47 \\ -\ 19 \\ \hline \end{array}$$

4.
$$\begin{array}{r} 55 \\ -\ 38 \\ \hline \end{array}$$

5.
$$\begin{array}{r} 75 \\ -\ \ 3 \\ \hline \end{array}$$

6.
$$\begin{array}{r} 86 \\ -\ 48 \\ \hline \end{array}$$

Problem Solving

Solve. Write or draw to explain.

7. Shelia has 46 blocks in her toy box. She takes out 28 blocks. How many blocks are left in the toy box?

_____ blocks

8. **Multi-Step** Vincent had 60 crayons. He gives 10 crayons to Joel and 19 crayons to Noah. How many crayons does Vincent have now?

_____ crayons

Lesson Check

TEXAS Test Prep

Choose the correct answer.

9. Gracie had 61 toy animals. She gave 17 toy animals to her sister. How many toy animals does she have now?

○ 56 ○ 78 ○ 44

10. There are 33 elephants near a stream. Then 19 elephants go into the water. How many elephants are not in the water?

○ 24 ○ 14 ○ 52

11. An elephant may live 35 years. A goat may live 8 years. How much longer can an elephant live than a goat?

○ 37 years ○ 43 years ○ 27 years

12. Ms. Keith took her class to a farm. The class saw 51 chickens and 28 pigs. How many more chickens than pigs did the class see?

○ 23 ○ 29 ○ 33

Name ______________________________

9.3 ALGEBRA Write Equations to Represent Subtraction

Essential Question How do you write a number sentence to represent a problem?

Explore Real World

Hands On

Draw to show the problem. Write a number sentence. Then solve.

____

FOR THE TEACHER • Read this problem to children. Riley has 53 crayons. He gives some crayons to Courtney. Now Riley has 38 crayons. How many crayons did Riley give to Courtney?

Math Talk Mathematical Processes

Describe how your drawing shows the problem.

Model and Draw

You can write a number sentence to show a problem.

Liza has 65 postcards. She gives 24 postcards to Wesley. How many postcards does Liza have now?

65 − 24 = ■
____

Liza has ______ postcards now.

Share and Show

Write a number sentence for the problem.

Use a ■ for the unknown number. Then solve.

1. There were 32 birds in the trees. Then 18 birds flew away. How many birds are in the trees now?

_______________ ______ birds

2. Carla read 43 pages in her book. Joe read 32 pages in his book. How many more pages did Carla read than Joe?

____

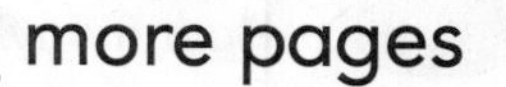

______ more pages

Name ______________________

Problem Solving

Write a number sentence for the problem.
Use a ■ for the unknown number. Then solve.

3. There were 40 ants on a rock. Some ants moved to the grass. Now there are 26 ants on the rock. How many ants moved to the grass?

____

______ ants

4. H.O.T. Keisha had a bag of ribbons. She took 29 ribbons out of the bag. Then there were 17 ribbons still in the bag. How many ribbons were in the bag to start?

____

______ ribbons

Solve.

5. H.O.T. **Multi-Step** There are 50 bees in a hive. Some bees fly out. If fewer than 20 bees are still in the hive, how many bees could have flown out?

______ bees

Use subtraction to prove your answer.

Daily Assessment Task

Choose the correct answer.

6. **Apply** Tessa is jumping rope. First she does a group of 84 jumps. Then she does a group of 99 jumps. How many fewer jumps did she do the first time?

   - ○ 170
   - ○ 15
   - ○ 48

7. Some children are playing four square. Alejo serves the ball 22 times. Hannah serves the ball 17 times. How many more times did Alejo serve than Hannah?

   - ○ 5
   - ○ 17
   - ○ 15

8. **Analyze** There are 35 students on the playground. Some students are playing a game while 19 students are waiting to play. How many students are playing the game?

   - ○ 16
   - ○ 26
   - ○ 19

9. **TEXAS Test Prep** There are 48 pictures on the zoo wall. Of these, 25 are wild cats and the rest are birds. How many of the pictures are birds?

   - ○ 13
   - ○ 37
   - ○ 23

TAKE HOME ACTIVITY • Have your child explain how he or she solved one problem in this lesson.

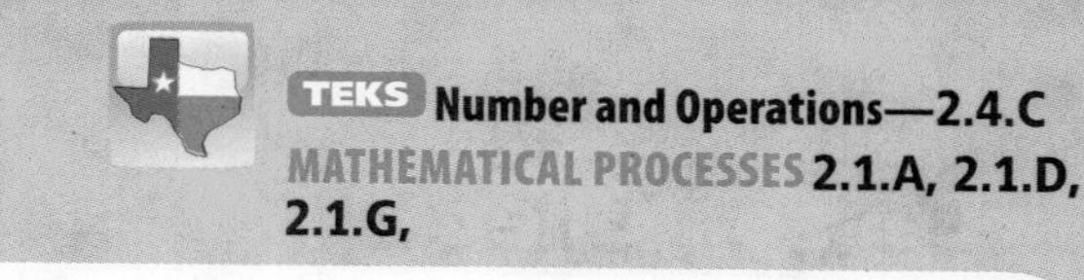

Name ______________________

9.3 ALGEBRA Write Equations to Represent Subtraction

Write a number sentence for the problem.
Use a ■ for the missing number. Then solve.

1. There were 28 coats hanging in the coat room. Some children put on their coats. Now there are 19 coats in the coat room. How many children put on their coats?

______________________ ______ children

2. Claire had a bag of marbles. She took 32 black marbles out of the bag. Now there are 15 marbles. How many marbles were in the bag to start?

______________________ ______ marbles

Problem Solving

Solve.

3. **Multi-Step** There are 30 birds in a tree. Some birds fly away. Now there are fewer than 10 birds still in the tree. How many birds could have flown away?

______ birds

Use subtraction to prove your answer.

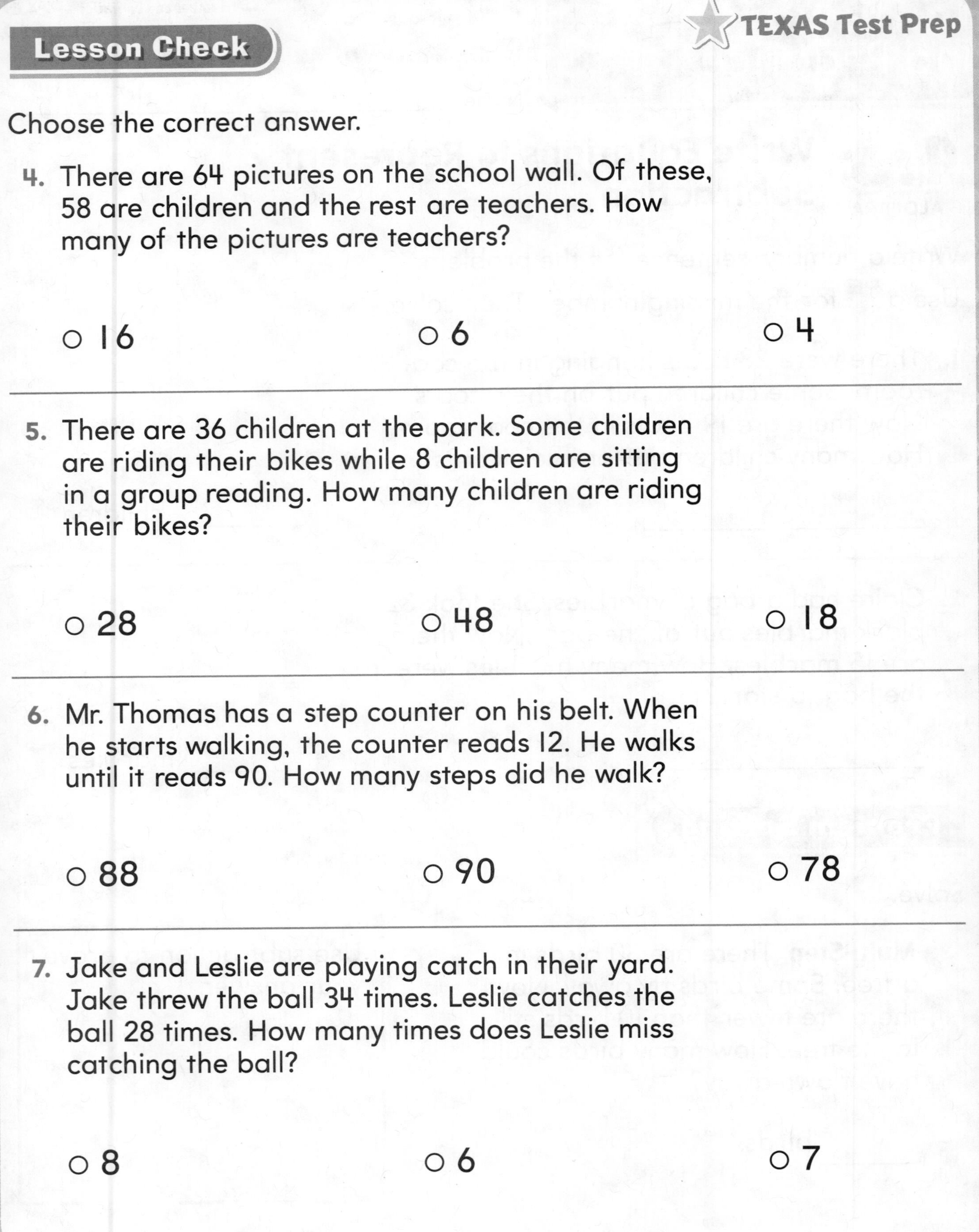

Lesson Check

TEXAS Test Prep

Choose the correct answer.

4. There are 64 pictures on the school wall. Of these, 58 are children and the rest are teachers. How many of the pictures are teachers?

○ 16 ○ 6 ○ 4

5. There are 36 children at the park. Some children are riding their bikes while 8 children are sitting in a group reading. How many children are riding their bikes?

○ 28 ○ 48 ○ 18

6. Mr. Thomas has a step counter on his belt. When he starts walking, the counter reads 12. He walks until it reads 90. How many steps did he walk?

○ 88 ○ 90 ○ 78

7. Jake and Leslie are playing catch in their yard. Jake threw the ball 34 times. Leslie catches the ball 28 times. How many times does Leslie miss catching the ball?

○ 8 ○ 6 ○ 7

Name ______________________________

9.4 Models for Multistep Problems

TEKS Number and Operations—2.4.C
MATHEMATICAL PROCESSES 2.1.A, 2.1.D, 2.1.E

Essential Question How do you decide what steps to do to solve a problem?

Explore Real World

Label the model to show each problem. Then solve.

Math Talk Mathematical Processes

Describe how the two models are different.

FOR THE TEACHER • Read this 1st problem for children. Cassie has 32 sheets of paper. She gives Jeff 9 sheets of paper. How many sheets of paper does Cassie have now? After children solve, read this 2nd problem. Cassie draws 18 pictures. Jeff draws 16 pictures. How many pictures do they draw?

Model and Draw

Models help you know what to do to solve a problem.

Ali has 27 stamps. Matt has 38 stamps. How many more stamps are needed so they will have 91 stamps?

27	38

First, find how many stamps they have now.

They have ______ stamps now.

Next, find how many more stamps they need.

91

They need ______ more stamps.

Share and Show

MATH BOARD

Complete the models for the steps you do to solve the problem.

1. Jen has 93 beads. Ana has 46 red beads and 29 blue beads. How many more beads does Ana need to have 93 beads also?

______ more beads

Name ______________________________

Problem Solving

Complete the models for the steps you do to solve the problem.

2. Max has 35 trading cards. He buys 22 more cards. Then he gives 14 cards to Rudy. How many cards does Max have now?

______ cards

Solve. Write or draw to explain.

3. H.O.T. **Multi-Step** Shelby had 32 rocks. She finds 33 more rocks at the park and gives 28 rocks to George. How many rocks does she have now?

______ rocks

4. H.O.T. **Multi-Step** Benjamin finds 31 pinecones at the park. Together, Jenna and Ellen find the same number of pinecones as Benjamin. How many pinecones could each girl have found?

Jenna: ______ pinecones

Ellen: ______ pinecones

Mathematical Processes
Model • Reason • Communicate

Daily Assessment Task

Choose the correct answer.

5. **Multi-Step** Ralph has 24 toy farm animals and 55 toy zoo animals. Of those animals, 35 are not large. How many toy animals are large?
   - ○ 20
   - ○ 79
   - ○ 44

6. **Apply** Tyler made 42 drawings at school and 25 drawings at home. He gave 11 drawings to his mother. How many drawings does he have now?
   - ○ 31
   - ○ 56
   - ○ 14

7. Mia has 12 toy bears, 21 toy rabbits, 15 toy elephants. How many toy animals does Mia have?
   - ○ 48
   - ○ 8
   - ○ 33

8. **TEXAS Test Prep** Tanya finds 22 leaves. Maurice finds 5 more leaves than Tanya finds. How many leaves do the two children find?
   - ○ 49
   - ○ 17
   - ○ 27

TAKE HOME ACTIVITY • Have your child explain how he or she solved a problem on this page.

Homework and Practice

TEKS Number and Operations—2.4.C
MATHEMATICAL PROCESSES 2.1.A, 2.1.D, 2.1.E

Name ______________________

9.4 Models for Multistep Problems

Complete the models for the steps you do to solve the problem.

1. Seth has 23 counters. He finds 15 more in a drawer. Then he gives 9 to his sister. How many counters does Seth have now?

   ______

Solve. Write or draw to explain.

2. **Multi-Step** Amber had 44 shells. She finds 26 more shells at the beach. Then she gives 25 shells to Joel. How many shells does she have now?

   _______ shells

3. **Multi-Step** Jesse has 43 pennies. Together, Ava and Lauren have the same number of pennies as Jesse. How many pennies could each girl have?

   Ava: _______ pennies

   Lauren: _______ pennies

Lesson Check

TEXAS Test Prep

Choose the correct answer.

4. Lucy finds 33 acorns. Mark finds 3 more acorns than Lucy. How many acorns do the two children find?

   ○ 69 ○ 33 ○ 36

5. Logan has 16 toy cars. He has 18 toy vans. He also has 25 toy trucks. How many toys does Logan have?

   ○ 49 ○ 34 ○ 59

6. Jada collects buttons. She has 35 gold buttons and 52 red buttons. Of those buttons, 28 are not round. How many buttons are round?

   ○ 24 ○ 59 ○ 87

7. Dylan made 36 drawings of houses. He made 9 drawings of office buildings. He gave 12 of his drawings to his brother. How many drawings does he have now?

   ○ 33 ○ 57 ○ 24

Name ______________________________

TEKS Number and Operations—2.4.D
MATHEMATICAL PROCESSES 2.1.A, 2.1.D, 2.1.F

9.5 Write Problem Situations

Essential Question How can a number sentence show a real-life problem?

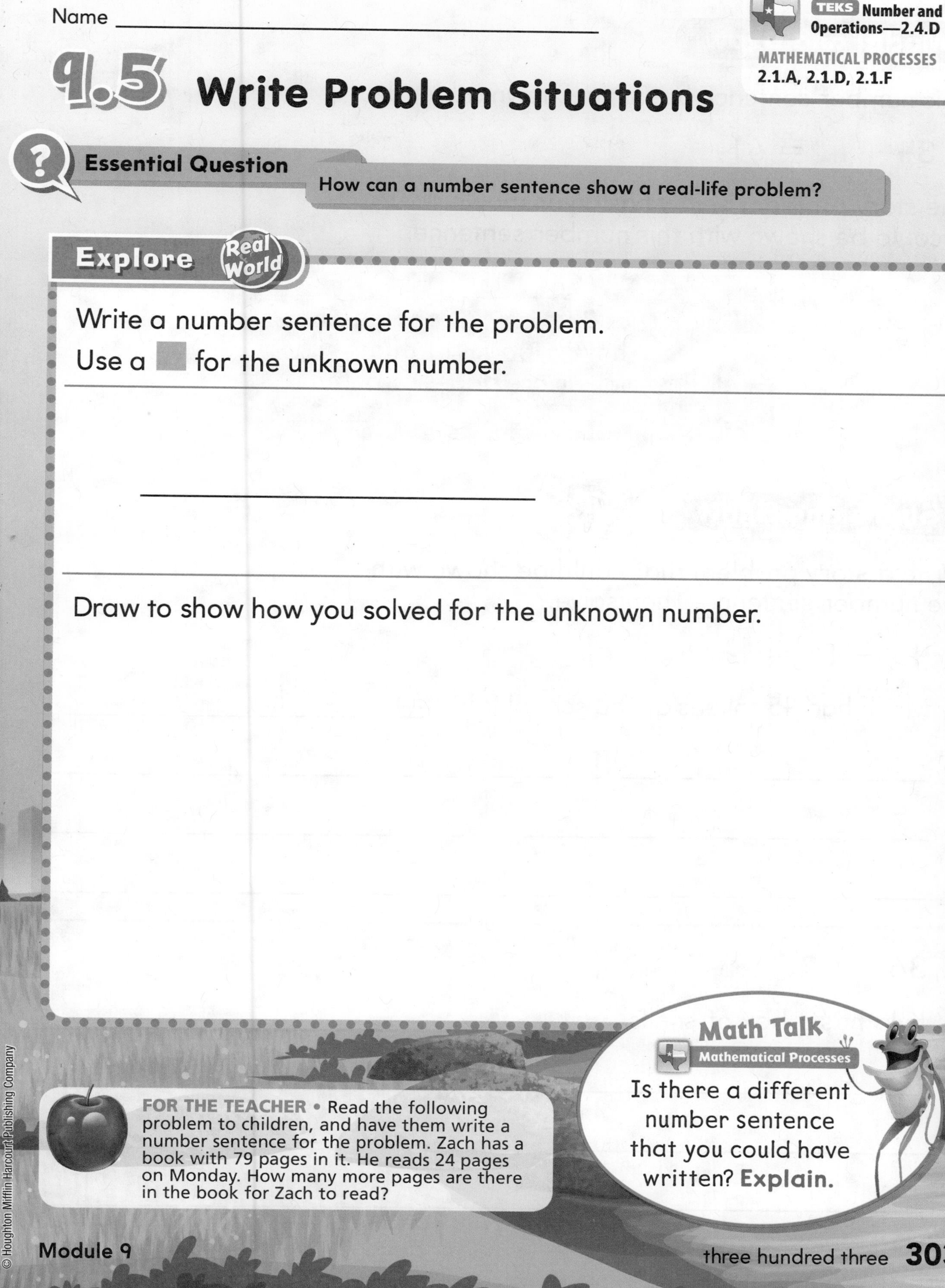

Explore Real World

Write a number sentence for the problem.
Use a ■ for the unknown number.

____

Draw to show how you solved for the unknown number.

FOR THE TEACHER • Read the following problem to children, and have them write a number sentence for the problem. Zach has a book with 79 pages in it. He reads 24 pages on Monday. How many more pages are there in the book for Zach to read?

Math Talk Mathematical Processes

Is there a different number sentence that you could have written? **Explain.**

This number sentence has an unknown addend.

$34 + \blacksquare = 61$

The story problem below has an unknown part.
It could be shown with this number sentence.

Kendra has 34 pages of photos. She wants to have 61 pages of photos in all. How many more pages of photos does she need?

Share and Show

Write a story problem that could be shown with the number sentence. Then solve.

1. $45 - 13 = \blacksquare$

Mitch had 45 tokens at the school fair. ______________________

____

____

____

2. $36 + 22 = \blacksquare$

Kyla has a box of shells. ______________________

____

____

____

Name ___________________________

Problem Solving

Write a story problem that could be shown with the number sentence. Then solve.

3. ■ + 48 = 97

____

____

____

____

4. 73 − ■ = 21

____

____

____

____

Solve. Write or draw to explain.

5. H.O.T. **Multi-Step**
Marta and Debbie each have 17 ribbons. They buy 1 package with 8 ribbons in it. How many ribbons do they have now?

_____ ribbons

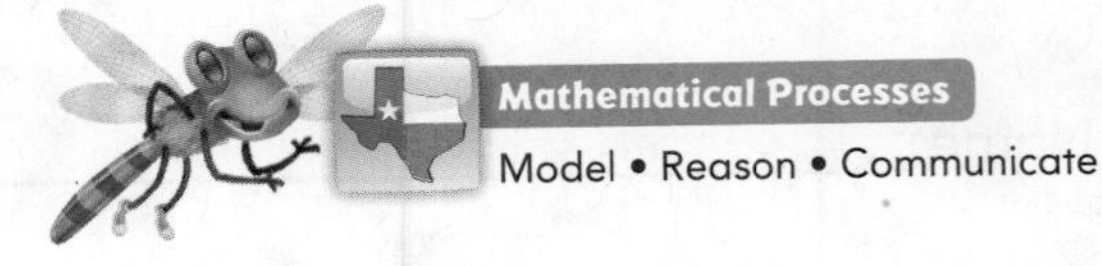

Daily Assessment Task

Choose the correct answer.

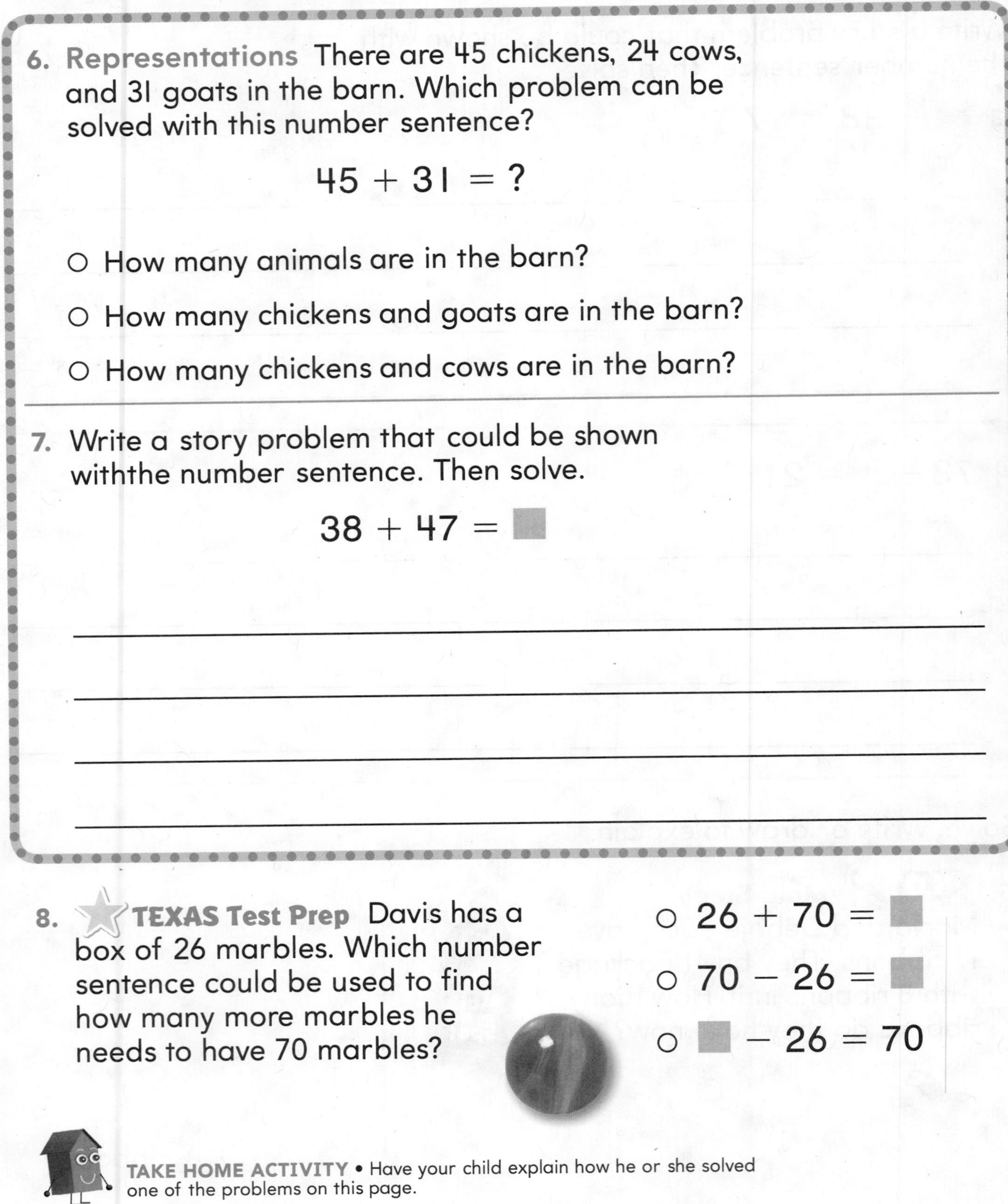

6. **Representations** There are 45 chickens, 24 cows, and 31 goats in the barn. Which problem can be solved with this number sentence?

$$45 + 31 = ?$$

- ○ How many animals are in the barn?
- ○ How many chickens and goats are in the barn?
- ○ How many chickens and cows are in the barn?

7. Write a story problem that could be shown withthe number sentence. Then solve.

$$38 + 47 = \blacksquare$$

____

____

____

____

8. **TEXAS Test Prep** Davis has a box of 26 marbles. Which number sentence could be used to find how many more marbles he needs to have 70 marbles?

- ○ $26 + 70 = \blacksquare$
- ○ $70 - 26 = \blacksquare$
- ○ $\blacksquare - 26 = 70$

TAKE HOME ACTIVITY • Have your child explain how he or she solved one of the problems on this page.

Homework and Practice

Name ____________________

9.5 Write Problem Situations

Write a story problem that could be shown with the number sentence. Then solve.

1. 64 − 32 = ■

Katie has a book with 64 pages in it.

____

____

____

____

____

Problem Solving

Solve. Write or draw to explain.

2. **Multi-Step** John and Dan each have 13 trading cards. They buy 1 package with 6 cards in it. How many trading cards do they now have now?

_______ trading cards

3. **Multi-Step** Melanie has 41 beads. She trades 8 of those beads for 12 other beads. How many beads does Melanie have now?

_______ beads

TEXAS Test Prep

Lesson Check

Choose the correct answer.

4. On a ranch, there are 46 cows, 23 pigs, and 38 horses. Which problem can be solved with this number sentence?

$$23 + 38 = ?$$

- ○ What is the total number of cows and pigs on the ranch?
- ○ What is the total number of cows and horses on the ranch?
- ○ What is the total number of pigs and horses on the ranch?

5. There are 51 children, 22 adults, and 15 pets at the town fair. Which problem can be solved with this number sentence?

$$51 + 22 = ?$$

- ○ What is the total number of people and pets at the town fair?
- ○ What is the total number of children and adults at the town fair?
- ○ What is the total number of children and pets at the town fair?

Name ____________________

Module 9 Assessment

Concepts and Skills

Write the difference. TEKS 2.4.B

1.
$$\begin{array}{r} 85 \\ -\ 64 \\ \hline \end{array}$$

2.
$$\begin{array}{r} 70 \\ -\ 38 \\ \hline \end{array}$$

3.
$$\begin{array}{r} 85 \\ -\ 68 \\ \hline \end{array}$$

Complete the models for the steps you do to solve the problem. TEKS 2.4.C

4. There are 47 oranges in one box and 36 oranges in another box. How many more oranges are needed to have 95 oranges altogether?

________ oranges

Write a story problem that could be shown with the number sentence. Then solve. TEKS 2.4.D

5. 51 − 24 = ■

Pedro put 51 markers on the art table. ____________________

____

____

____

Fill in the bubble for the correct answer choice.

TEXAS Test Prep

6. Cole saw 26 ducks on the pond. Then some ducks flew away. Now there are 17 ducks on the pond. Which number sentence can be used to find how many ducks flew away? TEKS 2.4.C

   ○ $27 - 6 = \blacksquare$
   ○ $26 + 17 = \blacksquare$
   ○ $26 - \blacksquare = 17$

7. There are 94 people in the store. If 29 people leave the store, how many people will still be in the store? TEKS 2.4.B

   ○ 65
   ○ 63
   ○ 75

8. Mrs. Garcia has 80 stickers. She buys 18 more stickers. Then she gives 35 stickers to her students. How many stickers does she have now? TEKS 2.4.C

   Great Job!

   ○ 97
   ○ 63
   ○ 77

9. Katie had 46 clips in a box. Then she gave 13 clips to a classmate. How many clips are in the box now? TEKS 2.4.B

   ○ 33
   ○ 53
   ○ 39

Name ______________________

TEKS Number and Operations—2.4.C

MATHEMATICAL PROCESSES 2.1.E, 2.1.F

10.1 Break Apart 3-Digit Addends

Essential Question How do you break apart addends to add hundreds, tens, and then ones?

Explore

Hands On

Write the number. Draw a quick picture for the number. Then write the number in different ways.

______

____ hundreds ____ tens ____ ones

______ + ______ + ______

______

____ hundreds ____ tens ____ ones

______ + ______ + ______

Math Talk Mathematical Processes

What number can be written as 400 + 20 + 9? **Explain.**

FOR THE TEACHER • Have children write 258 on the blank in the left corner of the first box. Have children draw a quick picture for this number and then complete the other two forms for the number. Repeat the activity for 325.

Model and Draw

Break apart the addends into hundreds, tens, and ones.
Add the hundreds, the tens, and the ones.
Then find the total sum.

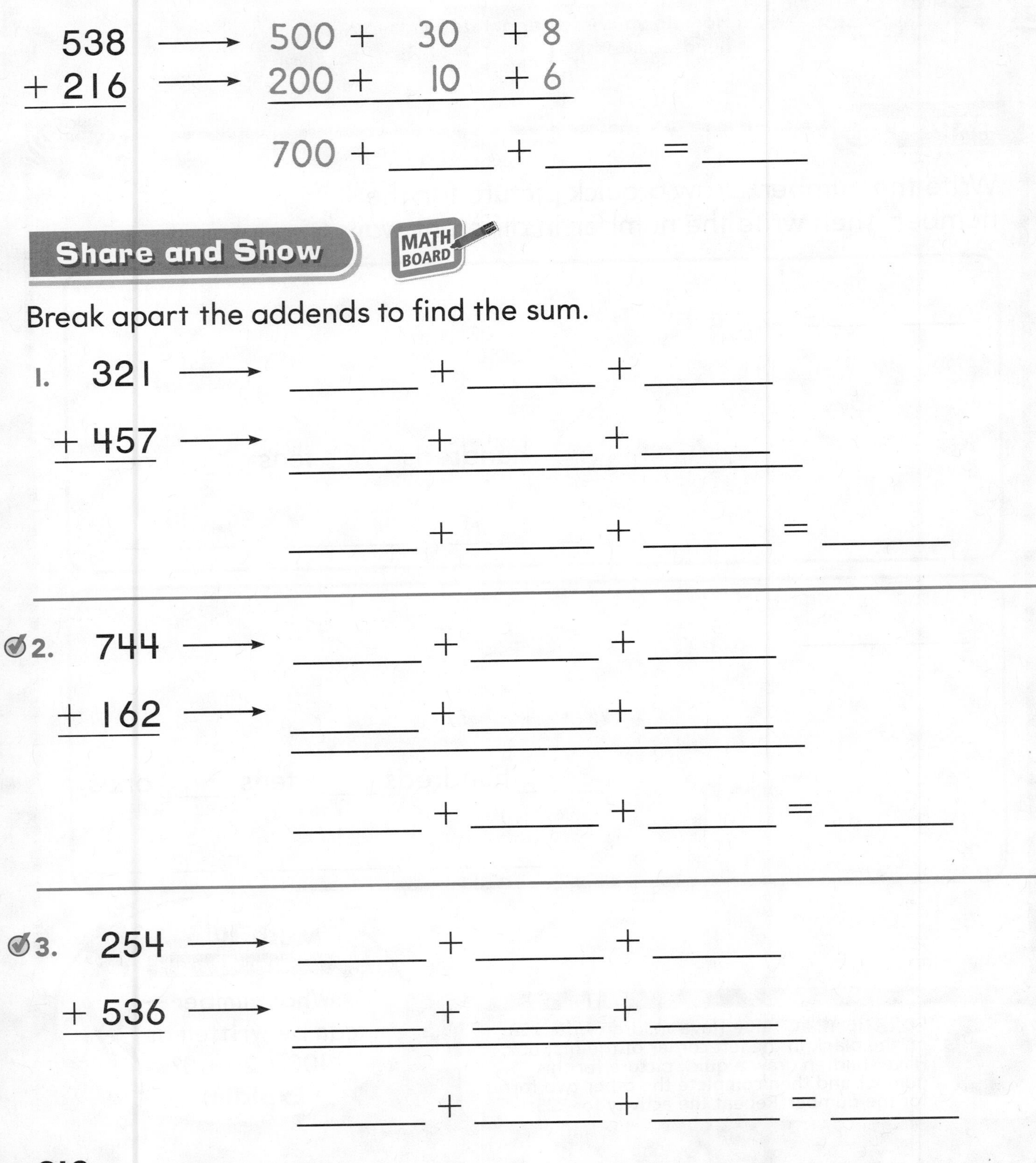

538 ⟶ 500 + 30 + 8
+ 216 ⟶ 200 + 10 + 6

700 + ____ + ____ = ____

Share and Show

MATH BOARD

Break apart the addends to find the sum.

1. 321 ⟶ ____ + ____ + ____
+ 457 ⟶ ____ + ____ + ____

____ + ____ + ____ = ____

2. 744 ⟶ ____ + ____ + ____
+ 162 ⟶ ____ + ____ + ____

____ + ____ + ____ = ____

3. 254 ⟶ ____ + ____ + ____
+ 536 ⟶ ____ + ____ + ____

____ + ____ + ____ = ____

Name ______________________

Problem Solving

Break apart the addends to find the sum.

4. 374 → ______ + ______ + ______

+ 518 → ______ + ______ + ______

______ + ______ + ______ = ______

Solve. Write or draw to explain.

5. **H.O.T.** **Multi-Step** Mr. Jones has 158 sheets of blue paper, 100 sheets of red paper, and 231 sheets of green paper. How many sheets of paper does he have?

Math on the Spot

______ sheets of paper

6. **H.O.T.** Wesley added in a different way.

```
  327
+ 468
  700   7 hundreds
   80   8 tens
+  15   15 ones
  795
```

Use Wesley's way to find the sum.

```
  539
+ 247
```

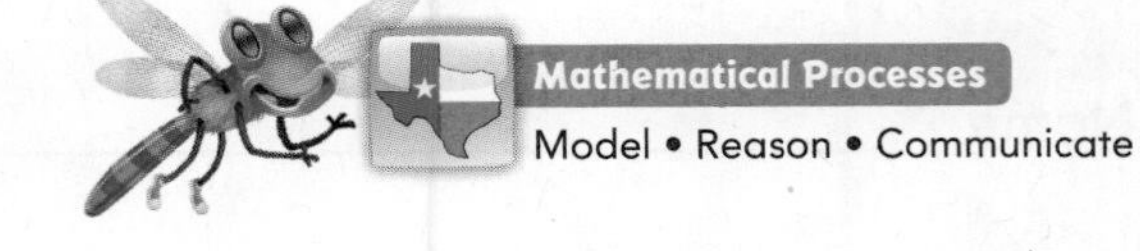

Daily Assessment Task

Choose the correct answer.

7. Jeremy collected 329 acorns on Saturday and 263 acorns on Sunday. How many acorns did he collect?
   - ○ 599
   - ○ 589
   - ○ 592

8. **Analyze** Daryl collects 112 stickers. Millie collects 293 stickers. How many stickers do they collect?
   - ○ 405
   - ○ 395
   - ○ 415

9. There are 452 cars on one side of the mall. There are 348 cars on the other side of the mall. How many cars are there in all?
   - ○ 700
   - ○ 800
   - ○ 788

10. **TEXAS Test Prep** There are 324 children at Theo's school. There are 419 children at Latasha's school. How many children are at the two schools?
   - ○ 743
   - ○ 733
   - ○ 825

TAKE HOME ACTIVITY • Write 347 + 215. Have your child break apart the numbers and then find the sum.

TEKS Number and Operations—2.4.C
MATHEMATICAL PROCESSES 2.1.E, 2.1.F

Name ____________________

10.1 Break Apart 3-Digit Addends

Break apart the addends to find the sum.

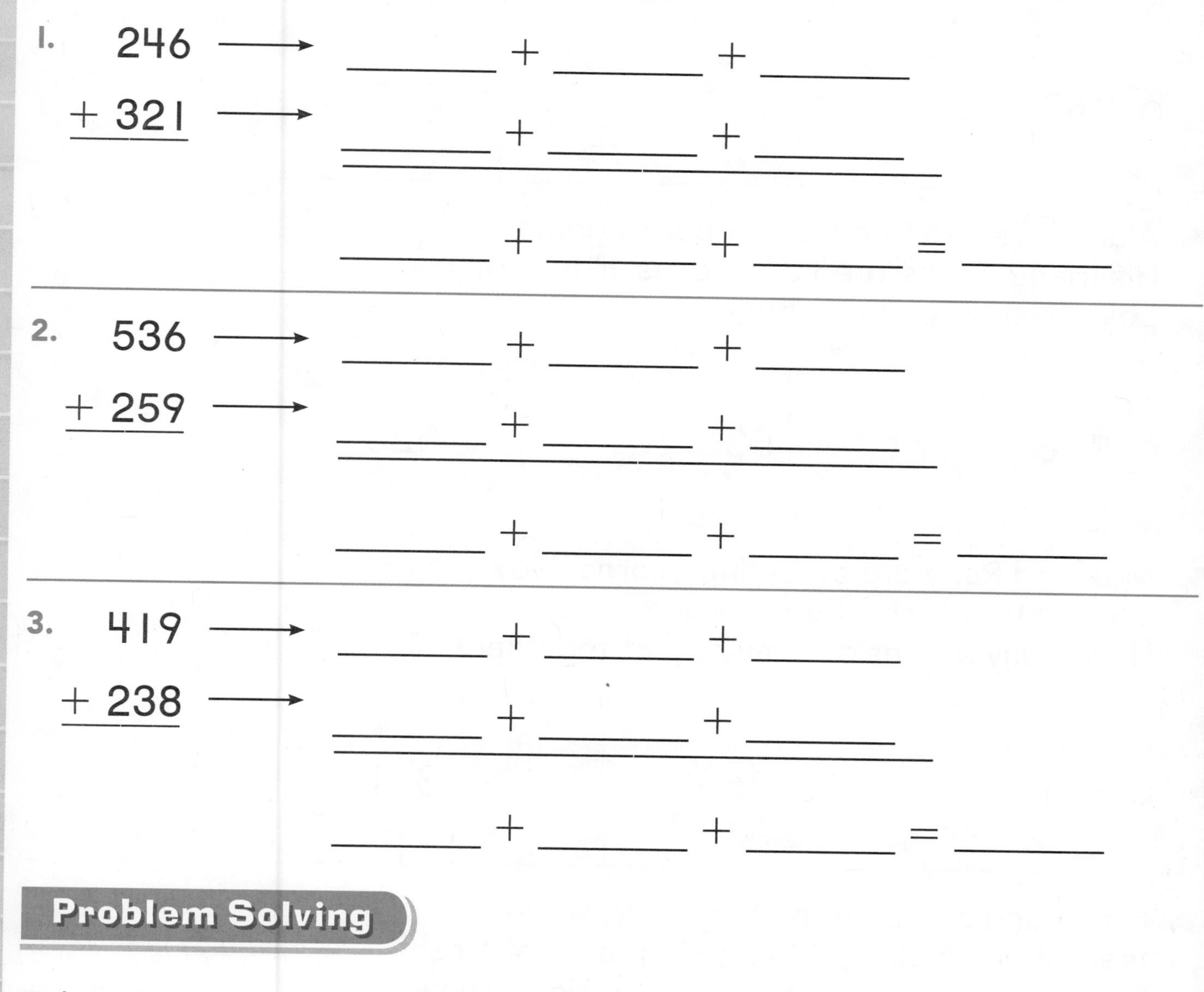

1. 246 → ____ + ____ + ____
   + 321 → ____ + ____ + ____

   ____ + ____ + ____ = ____

2. 536 → ____ + ____ + ____
   + 259 → ____ + ____ + ____

   ____ + ____ + ____ = ____

3. 419 → ____ + ____ + ____
   + 238 → ____ + ____ + ____

   ____ + ____ + ____ = ____

Problem Solving

Solve. Write or draw to explain.

4. There are 108 carrots, 121 beans, and 165 tomatoes. How many vegetables are there?

____ vegetables

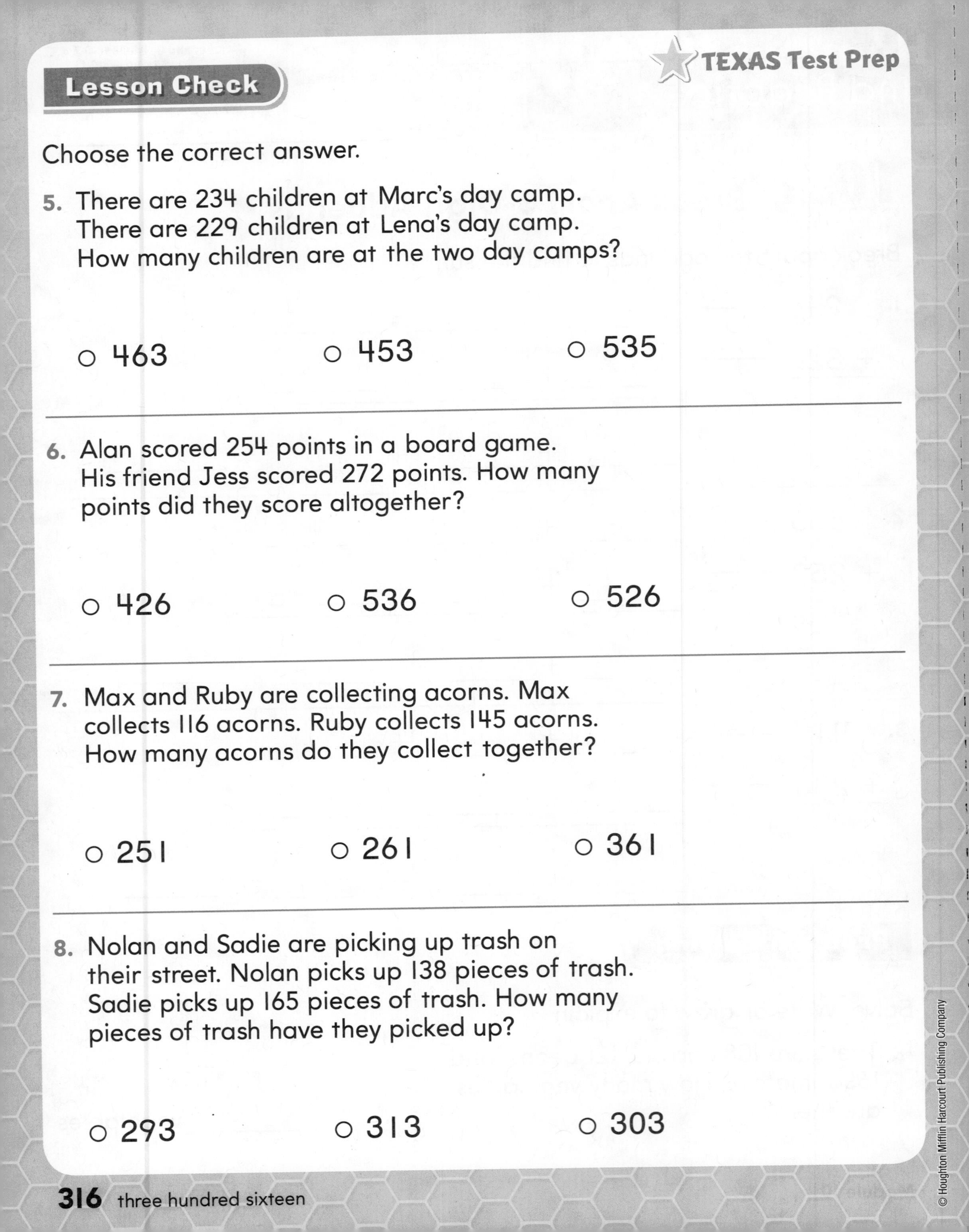

Lesson Check

TEXAS Test Prep

Choose the correct answer.

5. There are 234 children at Marc's day camp. There are 229 children at Lena's day camp. How many children are at the two day camps?

   ○ 463 ○ 453 ○ 535

6. Alan scored 254 points in a board game. His friend Jess scored 272 points. How many points did they score altogether?

   ○ 426 ○ 536 ○ 526

7. Max and Ruby are collecting acorns. Max collects 116 acorns. Ruby collects 145 acorns. How many acorns do they collect together?

   ○ 251 ○ 261 ○ 361

8. Nolan and Sadie are picking up trash on their street. Nolan picks up 138 pieces of trash. Sadie picks up 165 pieces of trash. How many pieces of trash have they picked up?

   ○ 293 ○ 313 ○ 303

Name ___________________________________

TEKS Number and Operations—2.4.C

MATHEMATICAL PROCESSES 2.1.D, 2.1.F

10.2 3-Digit Addition: Regroup Ones

Essential Question When do you regroup ones in addition?

Explore Real World

Hands On

Use [blocks] to model the problem.
Draw quick pictures to show what you did.

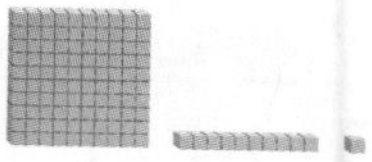

Hundreds	Tens	Ones

FOR THE TEACHER • Read the following problem and have children model it with blocks. There were 213 people at the show on Friday and 156 people at the show on Saturday. How many people were at the show on the two nights? Have children draw quick pictures to show how they solved the problem.

Math Talk Mathematical Processes

Describe how you modeled the problem.

Model and Draw

Add the ones.

6 + 7 = 13

Regroup 13 ones as 1 ten 3 ones.

Hundreds	Tens	Ones
	1	
2	4	6
+ 1	1	7
		3

Add the tens.

1 + 4 + 1 = 6

Hundreds	Tens	Ones
	1	
2	4	6
+ 1	1	7
	6	3

Add the hundreds.

2 + 1 = 3

Hundreds	Tens	Ones
	1	
2	4	6
+ 1	1	7
3	6	3

Write the sum.

1.

Hundreds	Tens	Ones
3	2	8
+ 1	3	4

2.

Hundreds	Tens	Ones
4	4	5
+	2	3

Name ____________________

Problem Solving

Write the sum.

3.

Hundreds	Tens	Ones
	☐	
5	2	6
+ 1	0	3

4.

Hundreds	Tens	Ones
	☐	
3	4	8
+	1	9

5.

Hundreds	Tens	Ones
	☐	
6	2	8
+ 3	4	7

6.

Hundreds	Tens	Ones
	☐	
2	3	5
+ 2	5	7

Solve. Write or draw to explain.

7. H.O.T. **Multi-Step** On Thursday, there were 326 visitors at the zoo. There were 200 more visitors at the zoo on Friday than on Thursday. How many visitors were at the zoo on both days?

_______ visitors

8. H.O.T. The zoo train stop is 235 steps away from the gift shop. Julia walks to the gift shop and back. How many total steps is this?

_______ steps

Mathematical Processes
Model • Reason • Communicate

Daily Assessment Task

Choose the correct answer.

9. On Monday, 328 penguins leave to travel north. On Tuesday, 433 penguins leave. How many penguins leave in these two days?
   - ○ 760
   - ○ 761
   - ○ 751

10. **Communicate** One day 575 seals swim away. The next day, 415 seals swim away. How many seals swim away in the two days?
   - ○ 990
   - ○ 995
   - ○ 980

11. **Reasoning** Fish travel in large groups. One group has 359 fish. Another group has 524 fish. How many fish are in the two groups?
   - ○ 883
   - ○ 873
   - ○ 893

12. **TEXAS Test Prep** On Thursday, 175 drinks were sold at the zoo. On Friday, 219 drinks were sold. How many drinks were sold on both days?
   - ○ 484
   - ○ 394
   - ○ 404

TAKE HOME ACTIVITY • Ask your child to explain why he or she regrouped in only some of the problems in this lesson.

Homework and Practice

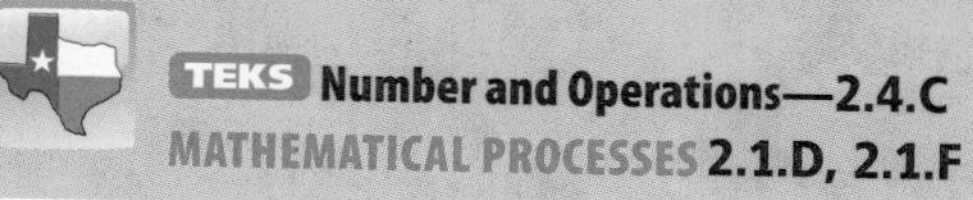

Name ____________________

10.2 3-Digit Addition: Regroup Ones

Write the sum.

1.

	Hundreds	Tens	Ones
		☐	
	3	6	6
+	2	0	8

2.

	Hundreds	Tens	Ones
		☐	
	1	5	3
+	3	3	2

3.

	Hundreds	Tens	Ones
		☐	
	4	2	9
+		1	7

4.

	Hundreds	Tens	Ones
		☐	
	6	6	8
+	2	1	3

Problem Solving

Choose a way to solve. Write or draw to explain.

5. **Multi-Step** On Monday, there were 114 children at the park. There were 150 more children at the park on Tuesday than on Monday. How many children were at the park on both days?

_______ children

Lesson Check

TEXAS Test Prep

Choose the correct answer.

6. On Saturday, 155 pumpkins were sold at the town fair. On Sunday, 138 pumpkins were sold. How many pumpkins were sold on both days?

   ○ 293 ○ 285 ○ 283

7. There were 229 fish in a large fish tank. Another large fish tank has 214 fish. How many fish are there in the two tanks?

   ○ 443 ○ 433 ○ 444

8. On Thursday, 437 workers travel by train to work. On Friday, 353 workers travel by train to work. How many workers traveled by train on these two days?

   ○ 780 ○ 790 ○ 784

9. The bus stop is 227 steps away from Karen's house. One morning she walks to the bus stop. After school, she walks from the bus stop to her house. How many steps does she walk to and from the bus stop?

   ○ 444 ○ 457 ○ 454

Name ______________________________

TEKS Number and Operations—2.4.C

MATHEMATICAL PROCESSES 2.1.E, 2.1.F

10.3 3-Digit Addition: Regroup Tens

Essential Question When do you regroup tens in addition?

Explore Real World

Hands On

Use [hundreds block, tens rod, ones cube] to model the problem.
Draw quick pictures to show what you did.

Hundreds	Tens	Ones

Math Talk Mathematical Processes

Explain how your quick pictures show what happened in the problem.

FOR THE TEACHER • Read the following problem and have children model it with blocks. On Monday, 253 children visited the aquarium. On Tuesday, 324 children visited the aquarium. How many children visited the aquarium those two days? Have children draw quick pictures to show how they solved the problem.

Model and Draw

Add the ones.

$2 + 5 = 7$

Hundreds	Tens	Ones
□	□	
1	4	2
+ 2	8	5
		7

Hundreds	Tens	Ones

Add the tens.

$4 + 8 = 12$

Regroup 12 tens as 1 hundred 2 tens.

Hundreds	Tens	Ones
1	□	
1	4	2
+ 2	8	5
	2	7

Hundreds	Tens	Ones

Add the hundreds.

$1 + 1 + 2 = 4$

Hundreds	Tens	Ones
1	□	
1	4	2
+ 2	8	5
4	2	7

Hundreds	Tens	Ones

Share and Show

Write the sum.

1.

Hundreds	Tens	Ones
□	□	
3	4	7
+ 2	9	1

✓2.

Hundreds	Tens	Ones
□	□	
1	6	5
+ 3	5	4

✓3.

Hundreds	Tens	Ones
□	□	
5	3	8
+ 1	4	0

Name ________________________________

Problem Solving

Write the sum.

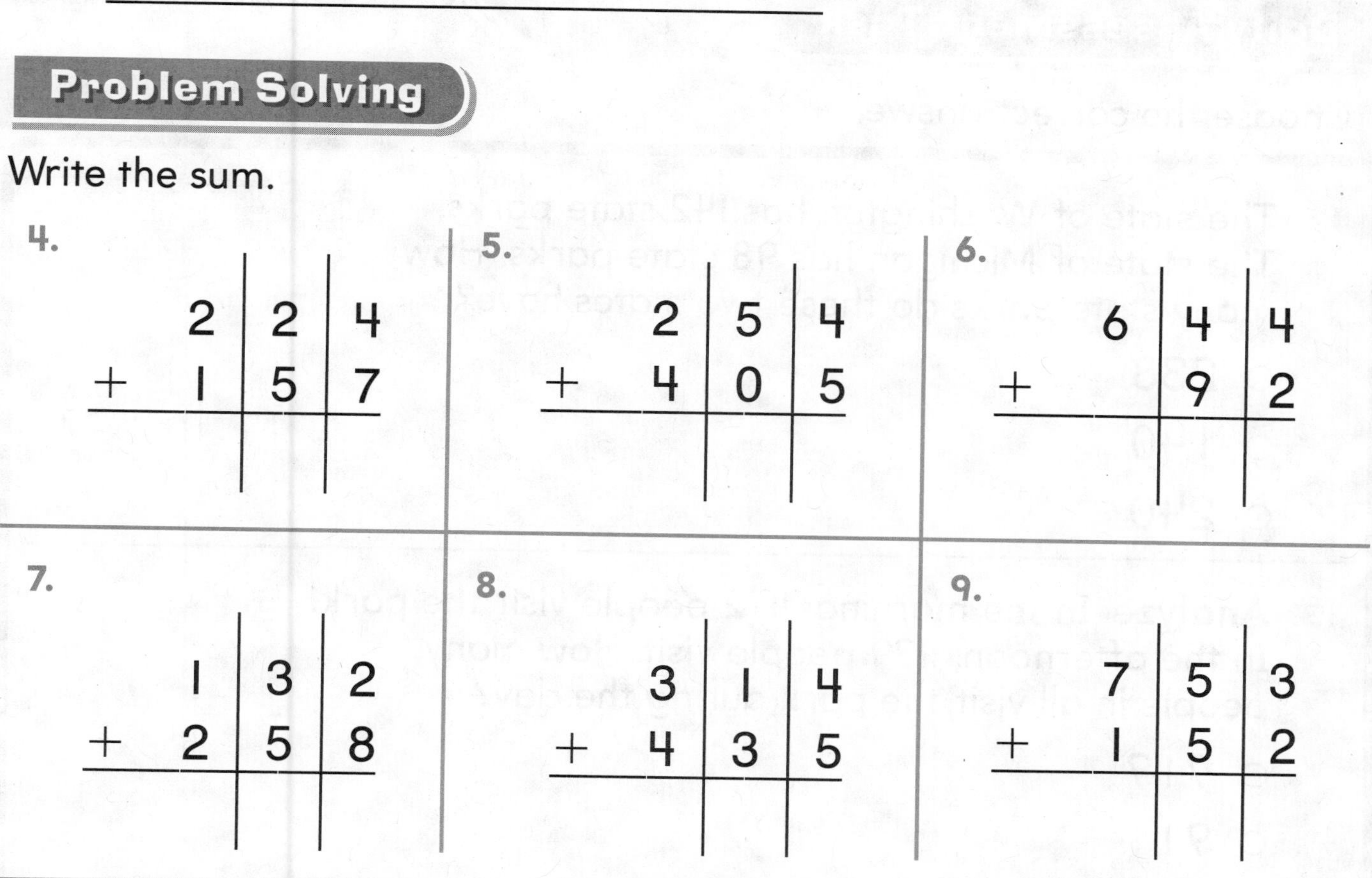

4. $\begin{array}{r} 224 \\ +\ 157 \\ \hline \end{array}$

5. $\begin{array}{r} 254 \\ +\ 405 \\ \hline \end{array}$

6. $\begin{array}{r} 644 \\ +\ 92 \\ \hline \end{array}$

7. $\begin{array}{r} 132 \\ +\ 258 \\ \hline \end{array}$

8. $\begin{array}{r} 314 \\ +\ 435 \\ \hline \end{array}$

9. $\begin{array}{r} 753 \\ +\ 152 \\ \hline \end{array}$

Solve. Write or draw to explain.

10. H.O.T. These lists show the pieces of fruit sold. How many pieces of fruit did Mr. Olson sell?

Mr. Olson	**Mr. Lee**
257 apples	314 pears
281 plums	229 peaches

________ pieces of fruit

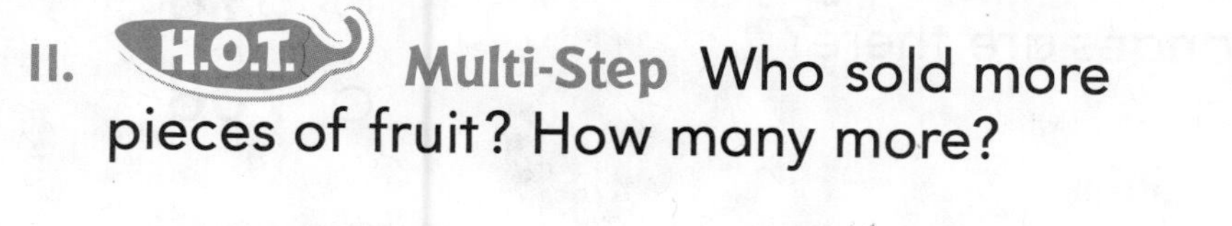

11. H.O.T. **Multi-Step** Who sold more pieces of fruit? How many more?

____

________ more pieces of fruit

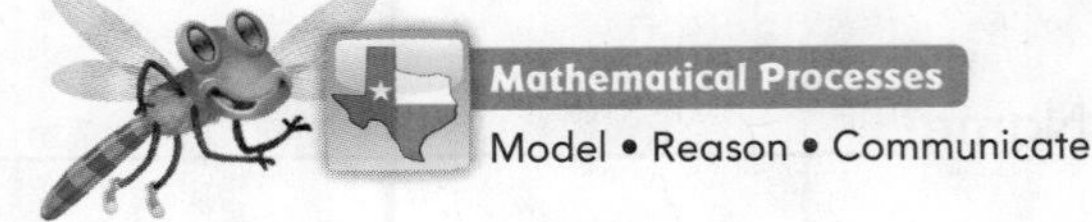

Daily Assessment Task

Choose the correct answer.

12. The state of Washington has 142 state parks. The state of Michigan has 98 state parks. How many state parks do these two states have?

   - ○ 238
   - ○ 140
   - ○ 240

13. **Analyze** In the morning, 472 people visit the park. In the afternoon, 439 people visit. How many people in all visit the park during the day?

   - ○ 919
   - ○ 911
   - ○ 901

14. **Record** On Saturday, 365 children visit a museum. On Sunday, 277 children visit the museum. How many children visit the museum on the two days?

   - ○ 642
   - ○ 547
   - ○ 637

15. **TEXAS Test Prep** There are 465 oranges packed in boxes. There are 253 oranges in baskets. How many oranges are there?

   - ○ 718
   - ○ 698
   - ○ 708

TAKE HOME ACTIVITY • Have your child explain to you how to find the sum for 145 + 173.

Name ________________

10.3 3-Digit Addition: Regroup Tens

Write the sum.

1.

1	5	4
+ 3	1	5

2.

6	6	4
+	7	3

3.

2	7	3
+ 2	3	2

4.

3	4	7
+ 1	9	2

5.

4	3	6
+ 2	5	4

6.

5	7	3
+ 2	1	8

Problem Solving

Solve.

7. **Multi-Step** In a bowling game, Jack scored 116 points and 124 points. Hal scored 128 points and 134 points. Who scored more points? How many more points were scored?

________ ________

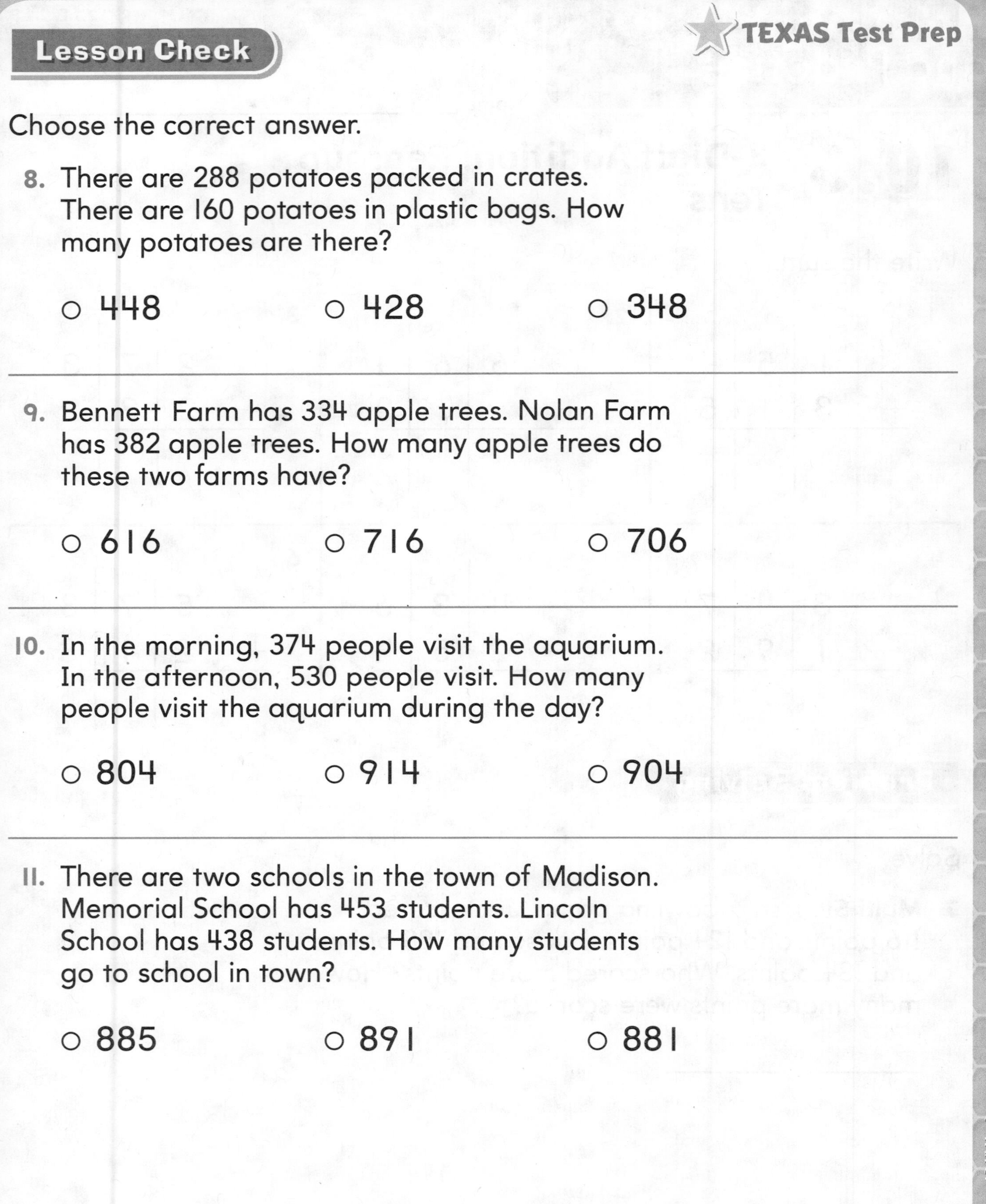

Lesson Check

TEXAS Test Prep

Choose the correct answer.

8. There are 288 potatoes packed in crates. There are 160 potatoes in plastic bags. How many potatoes are there?

○ 448 ○ 428 ○ 348

9. Bennett Farm has 334 apple trees. Nolan Farm has 382 apple trees. How many apple trees do these two farms have?

○ 616 ○ 716 ○ 706

10. In the morning, 374 people visit the aquarium. In the afternoon, 530 people visit. How many people visit the aquarium during the day?

○ 804 ○ 914 ○ 904

11. There are two schools in the town of Madison. Memorial School has 453 students. Lincoln School has 438 students. How many students go to school in town?

○ 885 ○ 891 ○ 881

Name ____________________

10.4 PROBLEM SOLVING • 3-Digit Subtraction

Essential Question How can making a model help when solving subtraction problems?

Unlock the Problem Real World

There were 436 people at the art show. 219 people left the art show early. How many people stayed at the art show?

Read

What information am I given?

________ people were at the art show.

Then, ________ people left the show.

Plan

What is my plan or strategy?

I can ____________________ to solve the problem.

Solve

Show how you solve the problem.

Make a model. Then draw a quick picture of your model.

________ people

HOME CONNECTION • Your child used a model and a quick picture to represent and solve a subtraction problem.

Try Another Problem

- What information am I given?
- What is my plan or strategy?

Make a model to solve. Then draw a quick picture of your model.

1. There are 532 pieces of art at the show. 319 pieces of art are paintings. How many pieces of art are not paintings?

_______ pieces of art

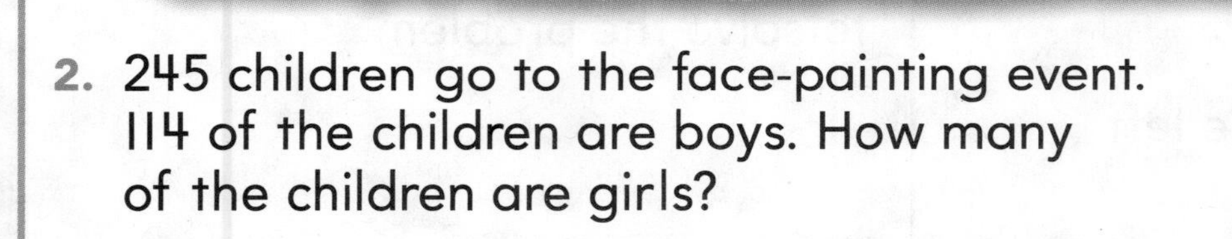

2. 245 children go to the face-painting event. 114 of the children are boys. How many of the children are girls?

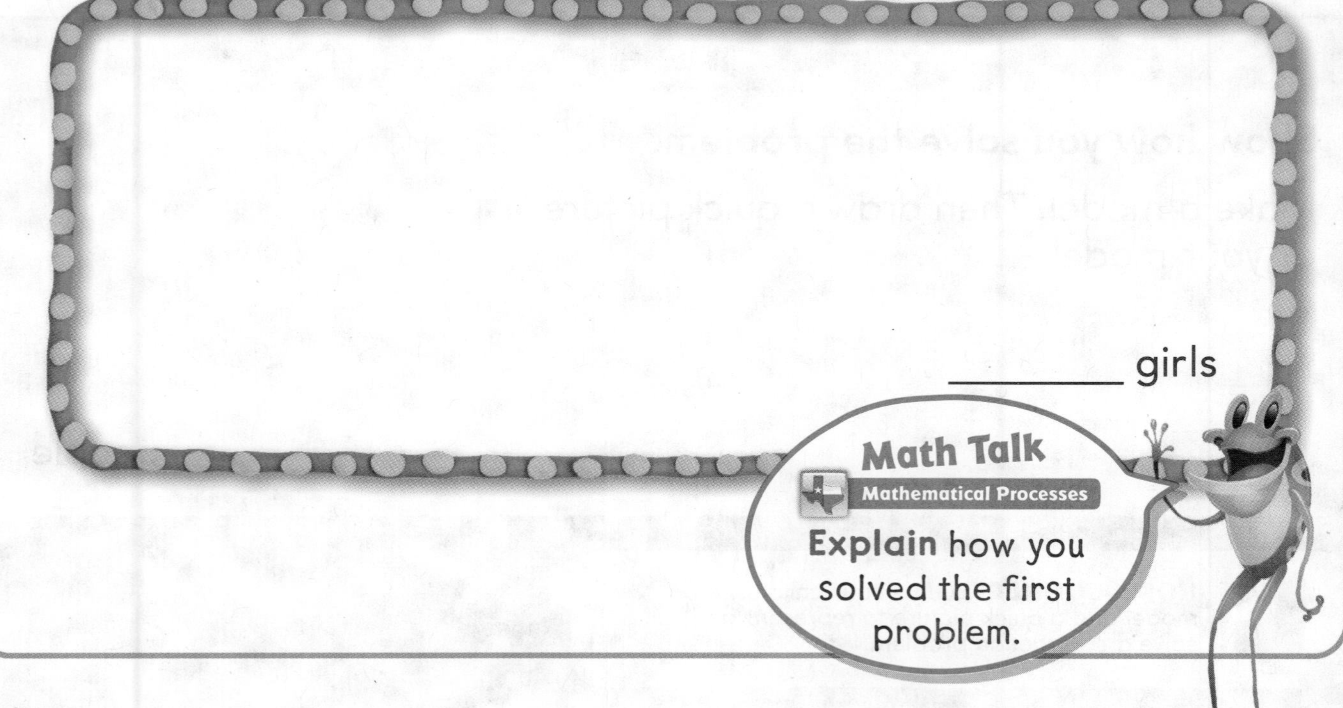

_______ girls

Name ____________________

Share and Show

Make a model to solve. Then draw a quick picture of your model.

3. There were 237 books on the shelves. Miss Lane took 126 books off the shelves. How many books were still on the shelves?

_______ books

Problem Solving

Solve. Write or draw to explain.

4. H.O.T. **Multi-Step** Maria has 127 animal cards. Ellen has twice that number of cards. How many animal cards do the girls have?

_______ animal cards

5. H.O.T. 164 children and 31 adults saw the movie in the morning. 125 children saw the movie in the afternoon. How many fewer children saw the movie in the afternoon than in the morning?

_______ fewer children

Mathematical Processes
Model • Reason • Communicate

Daily Assessment Task

Choose the correct answer.

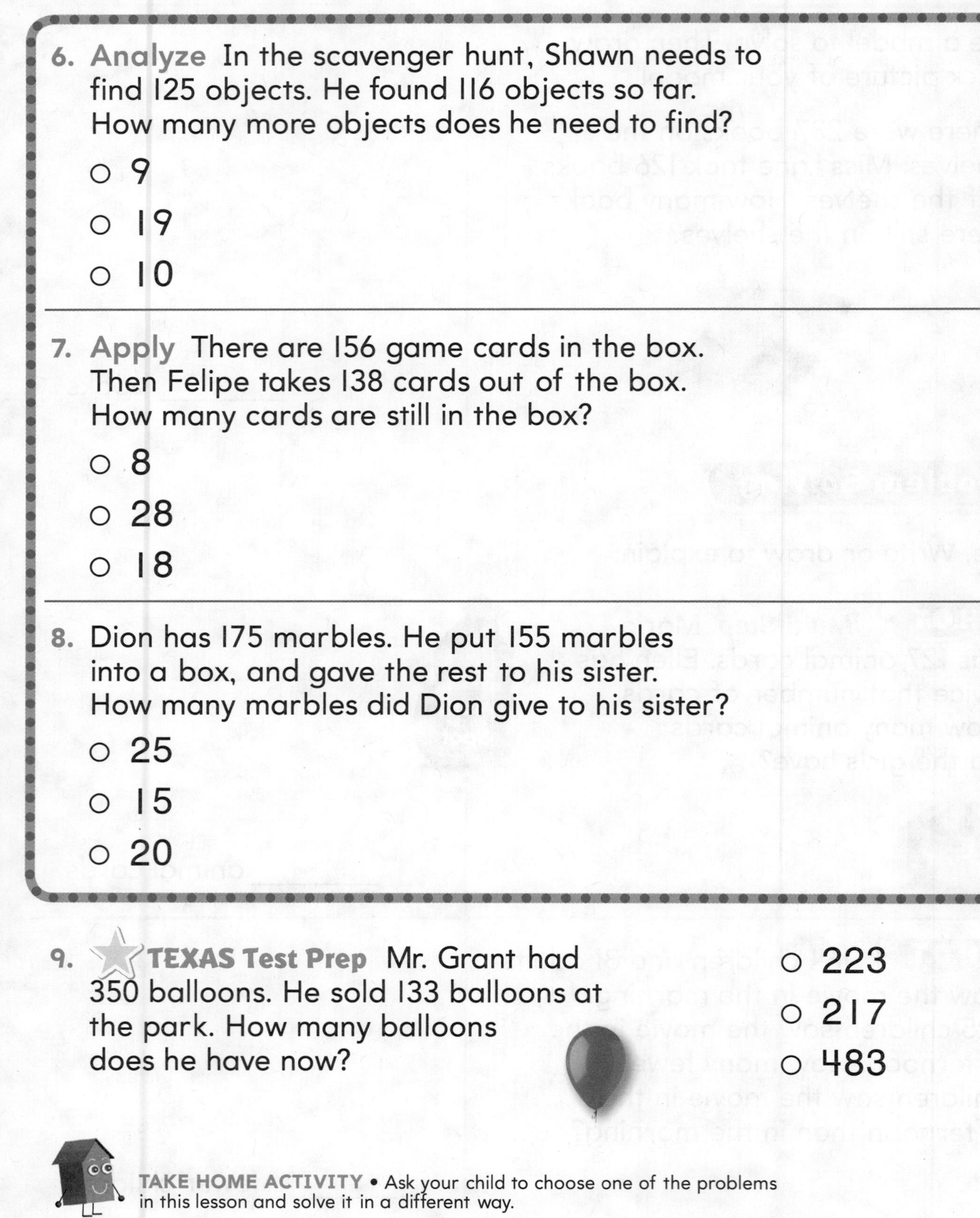

6. **Analyze** In the scavenger hunt, Shawn needs to find 125 objects. He found 116 objects so far. How many more objects does he need to find?

   ○ 9

   ○ 19

   ○ 10

7. **Apply** There are 156 game cards in the box. Then Felipe takes 138 cards out of the box. How many cards are still in the box?

   ○ 8

   ○ 28

   ○ 18

8. Dion has 175 marbles. He put 155 marbles into a box, and gave the rest to his sister. How many marbles did Dion give to his sister?

   ○ 25

   ○ 15

   ○ 20

9. **TEXAS Test Prep** Mr. Grant had 350 balloons. He sold 133 balloons at the park. How many balloons does he have now?

   ○ 223

   ○ 217

   ○ 483

TAKE HOME ACTIVITY • Ask your child to choose one of the problems in this lesson and solve it in a different way.

Name ____________________

10.4 PROBLEM SOLVING • 3-Digit Subtraction

Make a model to solve. Then draw a quick picture of your model.

1. There were 225 rubber ducks in a large box. Angela took 112 rubber ducks out of the box. How many rubber ducks were still in the box?

   ________ rubber ducks

Problem Solving

Solve.

2. There were 142 children and 15 adults at the library on Monday. On Tuesday, 128 children and 15 adults went to the library. How many fewer children were at the library on Tuesday than on Monday?

   ________ fewer children

3. **Multi-Step** Paul has 172 trading cards. Eli has twice that number of cards. Then Paul gave away 24 cards. How many trading cards do the boys have now?

   ________ trading cards

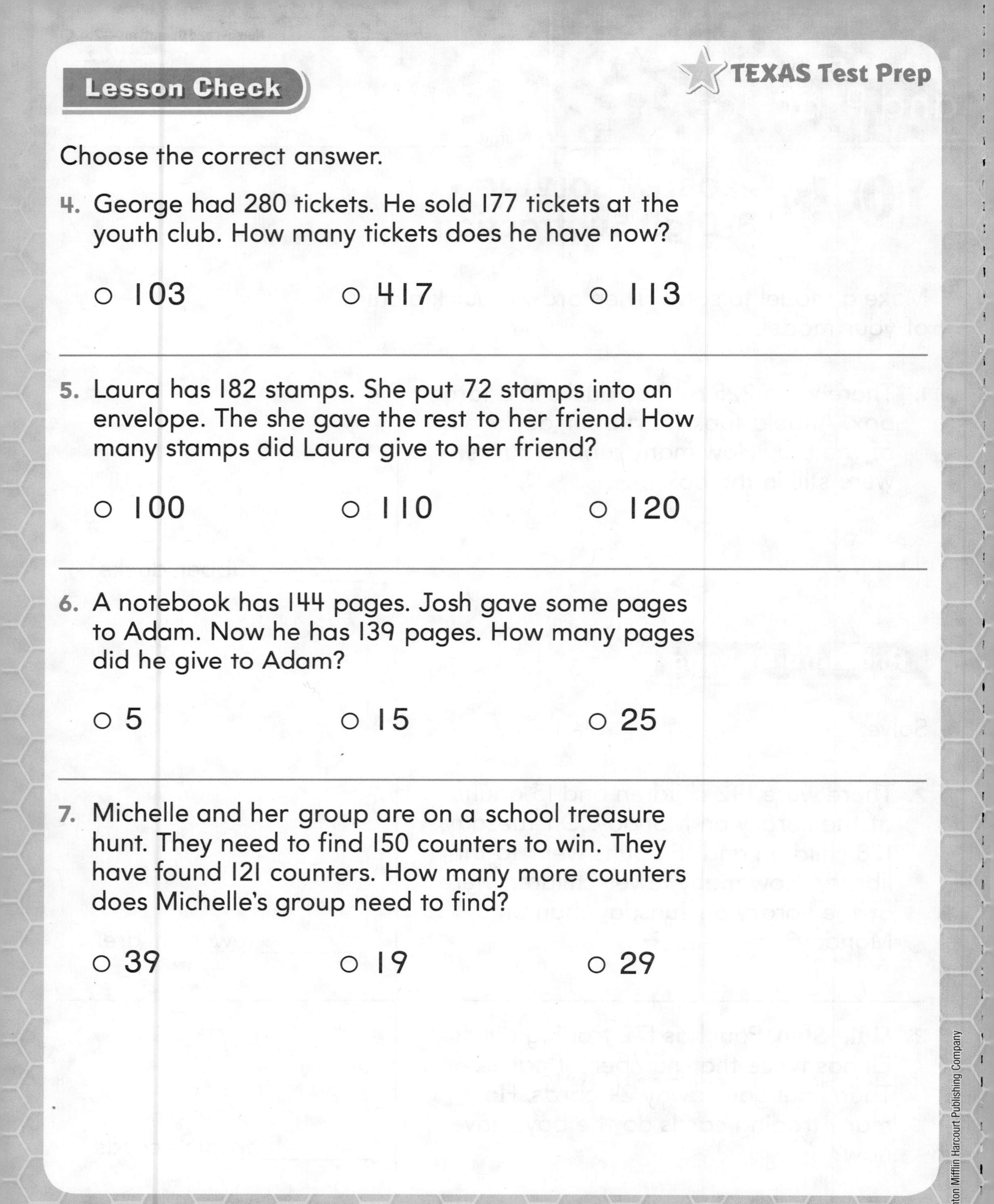

Lesson Check

TEXAS Test Prep

Choose the correct answer.

4. George had 280 tickets. He sold 177 tickets at the youth club. How many tickets does he have now?

   ○ 103 ○ 417 ○ 113

5. Laura has 182 stamps. She put 72 stamps into an envelope. The she gave the rest to her friend. How many stamps did Laura give to her friend?

   ○ 100 ○ 110 ○ 120

6. A notebook has 144 pages. Josh gave some pages to Adam. Now he has 139 pages. How many pages did he give to Adam?

   ○ 5 ○ 15 ○ 25

7. Michelle and her group are on a school treasure hunt. They need to find 150 counters to win. They have found 121 counters. How many more counters does Michelle's group need to find?

   ○ 39 ○ 19 ○ 29

Name ______________________________

MATHEMATICAL PROCESSES 2.1.E, 2.1.F

10.5 3-Digit Subtraction: Regroup Tens

Essential Question When do you regroup tens in subtraction?

Explore Real World

Hands On

Use [hundred block] [ten rod] [one cube] to model the problem.
Draw a quick picture to show what you did.

Hundreds	Tens	Ones

Math Talk Mathematical Processes

Describe what to do when there are not enough ones to subtract from.

FOR THE TEACHER • Read the following problem and have children model it with blocks. 473 people went to the football game. 146 people were still there at the end of the game. How many people left before the end of the game? Have children draw quick pictures of their models.

Model and Draw

354 − 137 = ?

There are not enough ones to subtract 7.

Regroup 1 ten as 10 ones

Hundreds	Tens	Ones
	4	14
3	~~5~~	~~4~~
− 1	3	7

Hundreds	Tens	Ones

Now there are enough ones.

Subtract the ones.

14 − 7 = 7

Hundreds	Tens	Ones
	4	14
3	~~5~~	~~4~~
− 1	3	7
		7

Hundreds	Tens	Ones

Subtract the tens.

4 − 3 = 1

Subtract the hundreds.

3 − 1 = 2

Hundreds	Tens	Ones
	4	14
3	~~5~~	~~4~~
− 1	3	7
2	1	7

Hundreds	Tens	Ones

Share and Show

MATH BOARD

Solve. Write the difference.

1.

Hundreds	Tens	Ones
	☐	☐
4	3	1
− 3	2	6

2.

Hundreds	Tens	Ones
	☐	☐
6	5	8
− 2	3	7

Name ______________________________

Problem Solving

Solve. Write the difference.

3.

	Hundreds	Tens	Ones
		☐	☐
	9	6	5
−	2	3	8

4.

	Hundreds	Tens	Ones
		☐	☐
	4	8	9
−	1	4	9

5.

	Hundreds	Tens	Ones
		☐	☐
	6	4	5
−	2	2	7

6.

	Hundreds	Tens	Ones
		☐	☐
	6	7	0
−	1	3	8

Solve. Write or draw to explain.

7. H.O.T. **Multi-Step** There were 287 music books and 134 science books in the store. After some books were sold, there are 159 books left. How many books were sold?

______ books

8. H.O.T. There are 235 whistles and 42 bells in the store. Ryan counts 128 whistles on the shelf. How many whistles are not on the shelf?

______ whistles

Daily Assessment Task

Choose the correct answer.

9. **Analyze** Harlan has 342 baseball cards. He gives Jack 115 cards. How many cards does Harlan have now?

   ○ 347

   ○ 227

   ○ 237

10. Tywana has 241 soccer cards. She gives her brother 125 cards. How many cards does she have now?

   ○ 115

   ○ 125

   ○ 116

11. Rey wants to collect all 196 cards of a set. So far, he has 157 of the cards. How many more cards does Rey need to complete the set?

   ○ 49

   ○ 39

   ○ 41

12. **TEXAS Test Prep** Ms. Watson has 254 stickers. She gives 123 stickers to her students. How many stickers does she still have?

   ○ 121

   ○ 137

   ○ 131

Great Job!

TAKE HOME ACTIVITY • Ask your child to explain why he or she regrouped in only some of the problems in this lesson.

TEKS Number and Operations—2.4.C
MATHEMATICAL PROCESSES 2.1.E, 2.1.F

Name ________________

10.5 3-Digit Subtraction: Regroup Tens

Solve. Write the difference.

1.

Hundreds	Tens	Ones
	☐	☐
4	6	6
− 2	4	8

2.

Hundreds	Tens	Ones
	☐	☐
5	7	3
− 3	3	7

3.

Hundreds	Tens	Ones
	☐	☐
7	5	9
− 3	1	8

4.

Hundreds	Tens	Ones
	☐	☐
5	4	1
− 3	1	7

Problem Solving

Solve. Write or draw to explain.

5. **Multi-Step** A bookstore has 148 books about people and 136 books about places. Some books were sold. Now there are 137 books left. How many books were sold?

_____ books

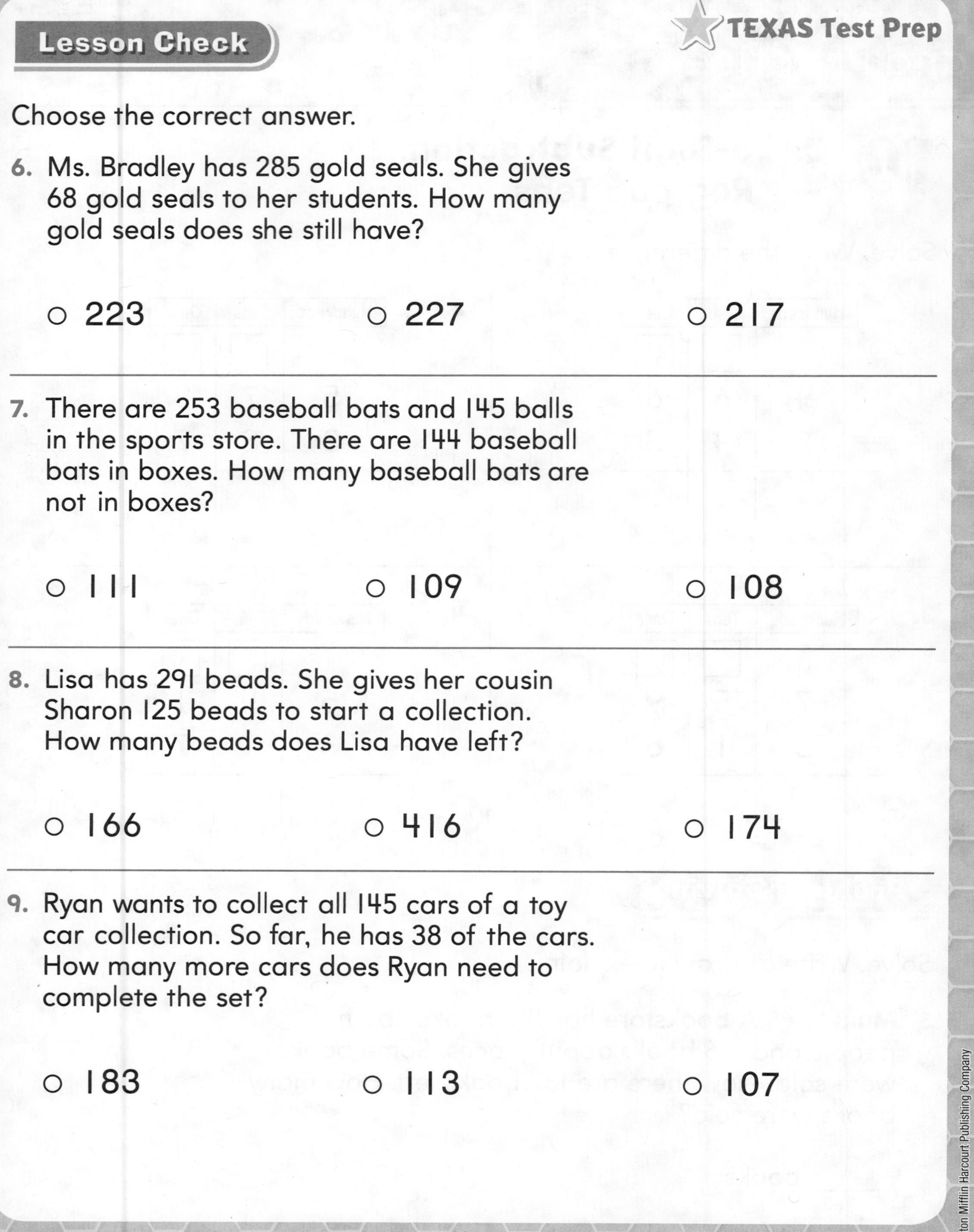

Lesson Check

TEXAS Test Prep

Choose the correct answer.

6. Ms. Bradley has 285 gold seals. She gives 68 gold seals to her students. How many gold seals does she still have?

○ 223 ○ 227 ○ 217

7. There are 253 baseball bats and 145 balls in the sports store. There are 144 baseball bats in boxes. How many baseball bats are not in boxes?

○ 111 ○ 109 ○ 108

8. Lisa has 291 beads. She gives her cousin Sharon 125 beads to start a collection. How many beads does Lisa have left?

○ 166 ○ 416 ○ 174

9. Ryan wants to collect all 145 cars of a toy car collection. So far, he has 38 of the cars. How many more cars does Ryan need to complete the set?

○ 183 ○ 113 ○ 107

Name ________________________________

TEKS Number and Operations—2.4.C
MATHEMATICAL PROCESSES 2.1.D, 2.1.F

10.6 3-Digit Subtraction: Regroup Hundreds

Essential Question When do you regroup hundreds in subtraction?

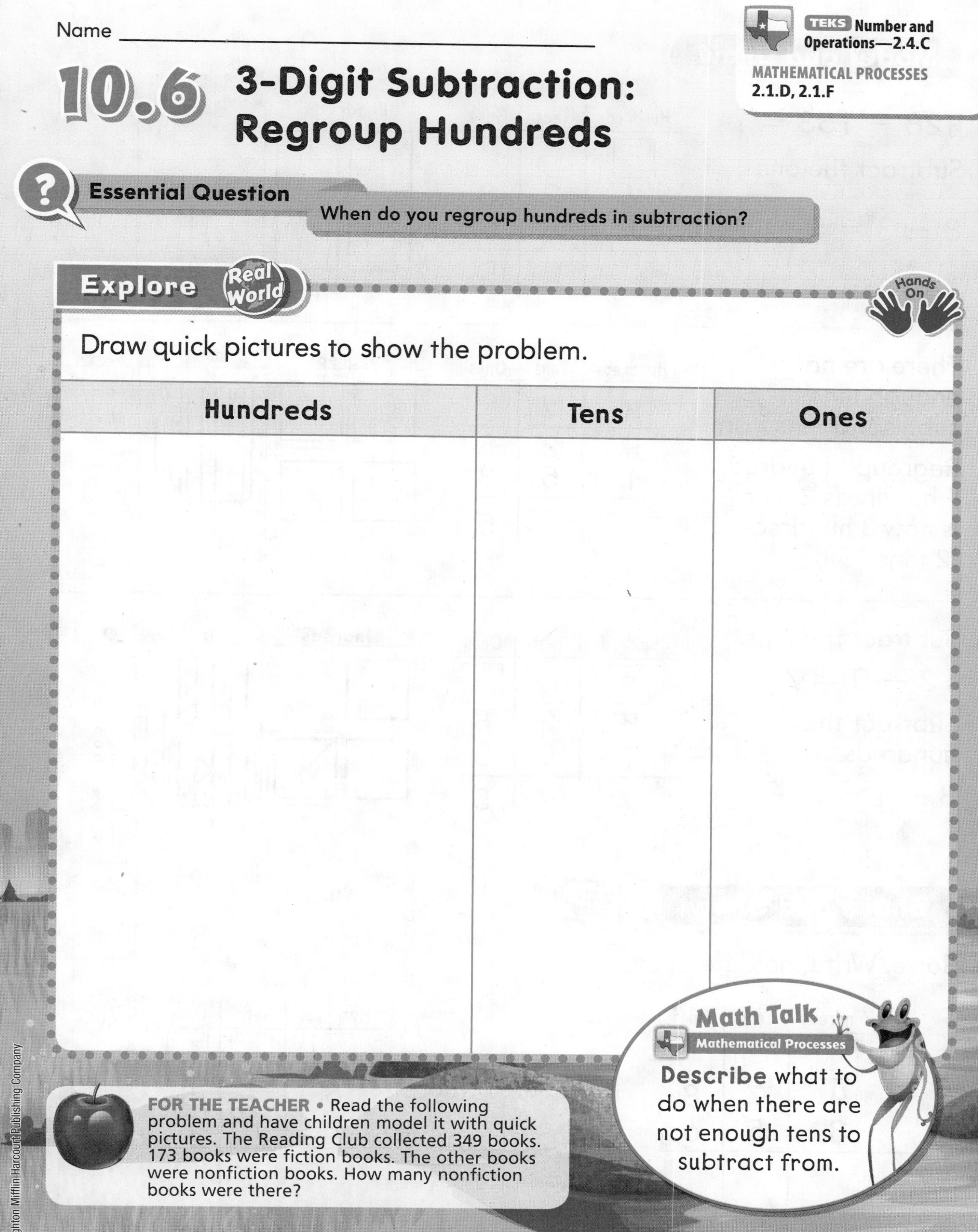

Explore Real World

Hands On

Draw quick pictures to show the problem.

Hundreds	Tens	Ones

FOR THE TEACHER • Read the following problem and have children model it with quick pictures. The Reading Club collected 349 books. 173 books were fiction books. The other books were nonfiction books. How many nonfiction books were there?

Math Talk Mathematical Processes

Describe what to do when there are not enough tens to subtract from.

Model and Draw

428 − 153 = ?

Subtract the ones.

8 − 3 = 5

	Hundreds	Tens	Ones
	☐	☐	☐
	4	2	8
−	1	5	3
			5

Hundreds	Tens	Ones

There are not enough tens to subtract 5 tens from.

Regroup 1 hundred. 4 hundreds 2 tens is now 3 hundreds 12 tens.

	Hundreds	Tens	Ones
	3	12	☐
	~~4~~	~~2~~	8
−	1	5	3
			5

Hundreds	Tens	Ones

Subtract the tens.

12 − 5 = 7

Subtract the hundreds.

3 − 1 = 2

	Hundreds	Tens	Ones
	3	12	☐
	~~4~~	~~2~~	8
−	1	5	3
	2	7	5

Hundreds	Tens	Ones

MATH BOARD

Solve. Write the difference.

1.

	Hundreds	Tens	Ones
	☐	☐	☐
	4	7	8
−	3	5	6

2.

	Hundreds	Tens	Ones
	☐	☐	☐
	8	1	4
−	2	6	3

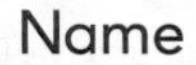

Name ______________________________

Problem Solving

Solve. Write the difference.

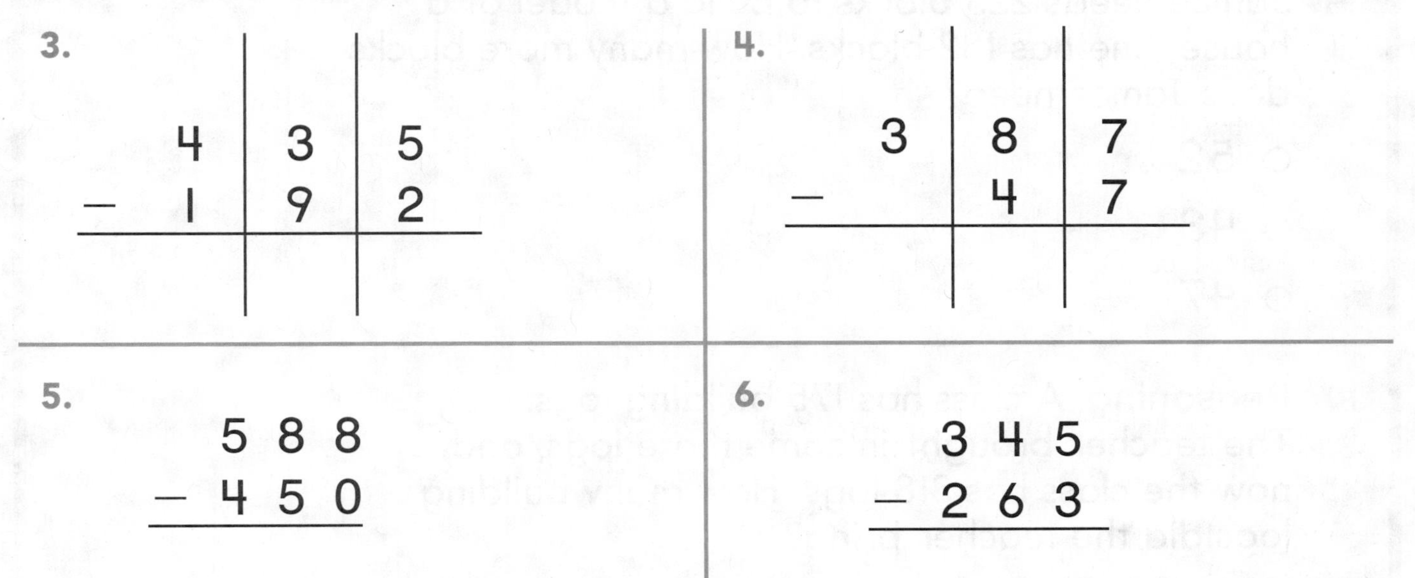

3.

4	3	5
− 1	9	2

4.

3	8	7
−	4	7

5.

$$\begin{array}{r} 588 \\ -\ 450 \\ \hline \end{array}$$

6.

$$\begin{array}{r} 345 \\ -\ 263 \\ \hline \end{array}$$

Solve. Write or draw to explain.

7. **H.O.T.** **Multi-Step** Sam built two towers. He used 139 blocks for the first tower. He used 276 blocks in all. For which tower did he use more blocks? ______________

Explain how you solved the problem.

____

____

8. **H.O.T.** There were 375 puzzle pieces in the box. Liz took 190 pieces out of the box. 95 of those pieces are placed. How many puzzles pieces are still in the box?

________ puzzle pieces

Daily Assessment Task

Choose the correct answer.

9. Janice needs 225 blocks to build a model of a house. She has 182 blocks. How many more blocks does Janice need?

   ○ 52

   ○ 43

   ○ 47

10. **Reasoning** A class has 175 building logs. The teacher brought in some more logs, and now the class has 318 logs. How many building logs did the teacher bring?

   ○ 143

   ○ 233

   ○ 133

11. **Analyze** A model of a ship is made of 445 pieces. Some are metal and some are wooden. There are 375 wooden pieces. How many pieces are metal?

   ○ 75

   ○ 170

   ○ 70

12. **TEXAS Test Prep** Mr. Simms has 315 paper hats. He gives 140 paper hats to students in the parade. How many paper hats does he have now?

   ○ 235

   ○ 255

   ○ 175

TAKE HOME ACTIVITY • Have your child explain how to find the difference for 745 − 341.

Homework and Practice

TEKS Number and Operations—2.4.C
MATHEMATICAL PROCESSES 2.1.D, 2.1.F

Name ____________________

10.6 3-Digit Subtraction: Regroup Hundreds

Solve. Write the difference.

1.

	Hundreds	Tens	Ones
	5	3	5
−	2	7	4

2.

	Hundreds	Tens	Ones
	6	7	6
−	5	8	2

3.

	Hundreds	Tens	Ones
	3	5	9
−	3	4	8

4.

	Hundreds	Tens	Ones
	4	5	2
−	2	7	1

Problem Solving

Solve. Write or draw to explain.

5. **Multi-Step** Greg built a stone wall. He used 374 stones in all. He used 232 stones along the long side. He used the rest for the short side of the wall. On which side of the wall did he use more stones? How can you tell?

____

____

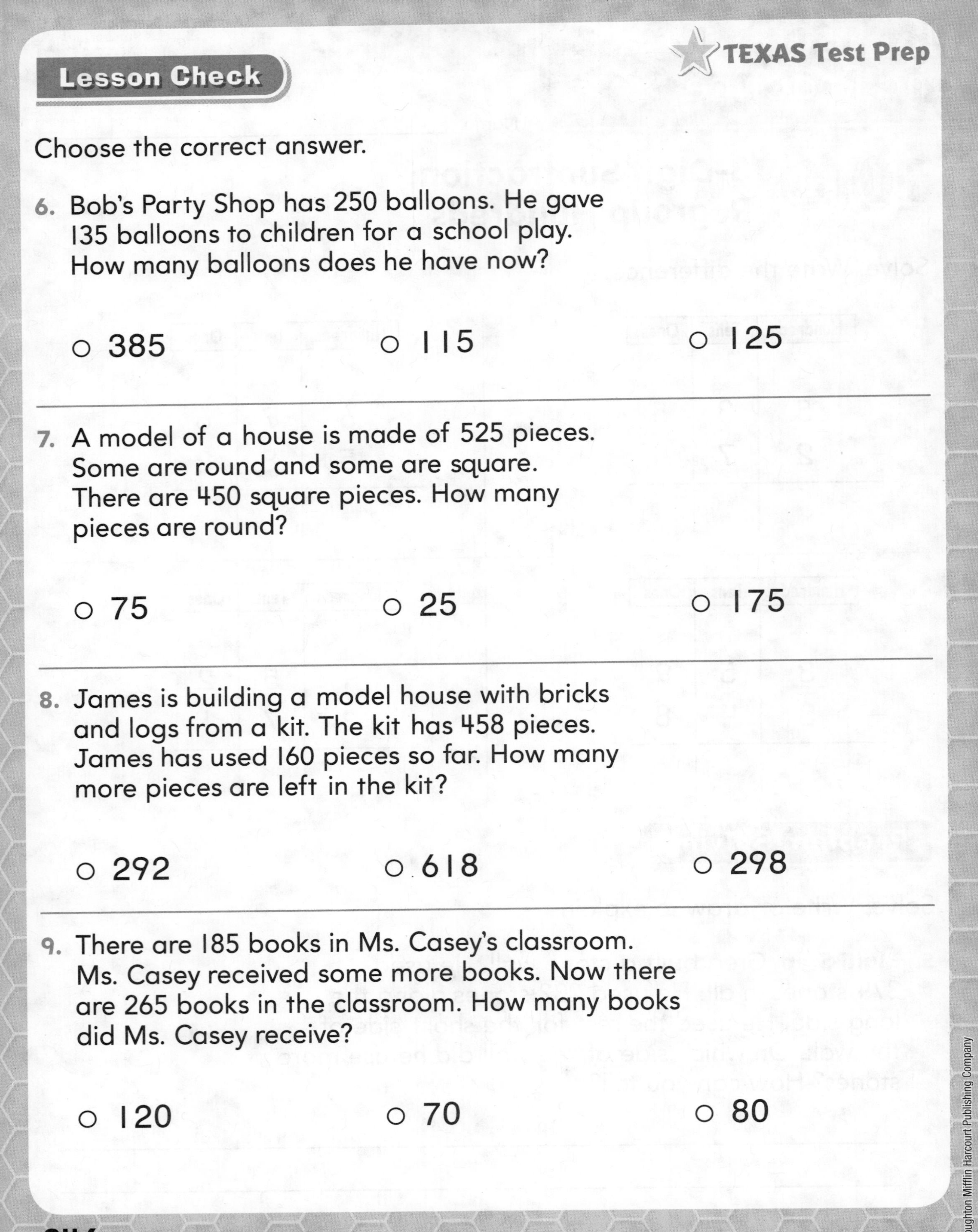

Lesson Check

TEXAS Test Prep

Choose the correct answer.

6. Bob's Party Shop has 250 balloons. He gave 135 balloons to children for a school play. How many balloons does he have now?

○ 385 ○ 115 ○ 125

7. A model of a house is made of 525 pieces. Some are round and some are square. There are 450 square pieces. How many pieces are round?

○ 75 ○ 25 ○ 175

8. James is building a model house with bricks and logs from a kit. The kit has 458 pieces. James has used 160 pieces so far. How many more pieces are left in the kit?

○ 292 ○ 618 ○ 298

9. There are 185 books in Ms. Casey's classroom. Ms. Casey received some more books. Now there are 265 books in the classroom. How many books did Ms. Casey receive?

○ 120 ○ 70 ○ 80

Name ______________________________

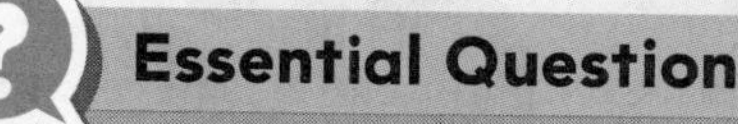

10.7 Solve Mixed Problems

Essential Question How do you decide when to add or subtract to solve problems?

Explore Real World

Hands On

Draw or write to show how you solved the problem.

Math Talk Mathematical Processes

Explain how you solved the problem.

FOR THE TEACHER • Read the following problem and have children solve. There were 687 visitors at a park on Monday. There were 962 visitors at the park on Tuesday. How many more people visited the park on Tuesday than Monday?

Model and Draw

Peter is putting a 500-piece puzzle together. He has placed 216 pieces. 108 pieces fell on the floor, and the rest of the pieces are in the box. How many pieces are in the box?

Step 1 Add the number of pieces that are out of the box.

216 + 108 = ______

Step 2 Subtract that number from the total number of pieces.

500 − ______ = ______

______ pieces are in the box.

Share and Show

Solve. Write or draw to explain.

1. Emma counts flowers at a plant store. She counts 448 daisies, 157 roses, and 347 tulips. How many flowers does she count?

   ______ flowers

2. Mr. Bishop sells drinks at a game. He has 215 waters and 351 lemonades. Then he sells some, and now has 513 drinks. How many drinks did he sell?

   ______ drinks

Name ________________

Problem Solving

Solve. Write or draw to explain.

3. Jenna has 485 stickers. She gives 65 stickers to her sister and 39 stickers to her brother. How many stickers does Jenna have now?

________ stickers

4. H.O.T. **Multi-Step** Joseph has 233 red blocks and 348 green blocks. Amber has 197 red blocks and 471 green blocks. How many more blocks does Amber have than Joseph?

________ more blocks

5. H.O.T. Use the addition and subtraction to complete the story problem.

$$\begin{array}{r} 114 \\ +\ 51 \\ \hline 165 \end{array} \qquad \begin{array}{r} 4\overset{6}{\cancel{7}}\overset{13}{\cancel{3}} \\ -\ 165 \\ \hline 308 \end{array}$$

There are ________ children at Caleb's school.

________ children ride the bus to school.

________ children walk to school. How many children get to school in a different way? ________ children

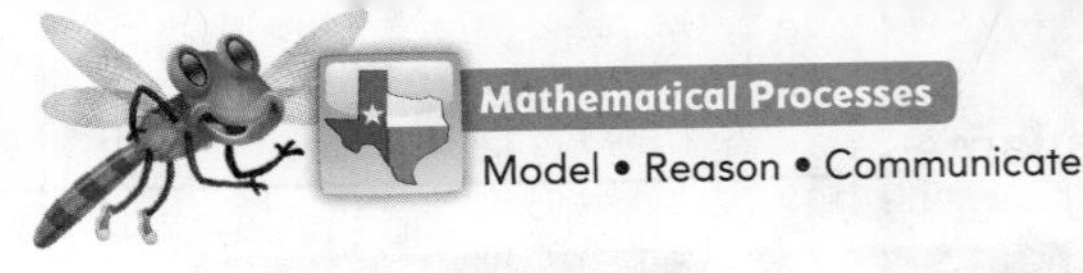

Daily Assessment Task

Choose the correct answer.

6. **Analyze** A pet store has 538 freshwater fish and 270 saltwater fish. After a saltwater fish delivery, the store has 933 fish. How many saltwater fish were delivered?

   ○ 268

   ○ 125

   ○ 663

7. **Multi-Step** There were 370 dog collars in the store. 224 collars were sold in the first week and 127 collars were sold in the second week. How many dog collars are in the store now?

   ○ 10

   ○ 29

   ○ 19

8. **Multi-Step** There were 215 cat toys and 371 dog toys. After some toys were sold, there were 495 toys. How many toys were sold?

   ○ 91

   ○ 191

   ○ 156

9. **TEXAS Test Prep** Levi has 374 yellow marbles, 100 green marbles, and 159 blue marbles. How many marbles does Levi have?

   ○ 474

   ○ 633

   ○ 533

TAKE HOME ACTIVITY • Ask your child to show how he or she solved an exercise in this lesson.

Name ____________________

10.7 Solve Mixed Problems

Solve. Write or draw to explain.

1. Hope counts the coins in her bank. She counts 484 pennies, 175 dimes, and 137 quarters. How many coins does she count?

   ________ coins

2. **Multi-Step** Mr. Oliver sells muffins and bagels outside an office building. He has 125 muffins and 153 bagels. He sells some of each. Now he has 80 muffins and bagels. How many muffins and bagels did he sell?

   ________ muffins and bagels

3. **Multi-Step** There are 150 children at the park. 62 children are riding bikes. 35 children are playing games. The rest of the children are sitting by the pond. How many children are sitting by the pond?

   ________ children

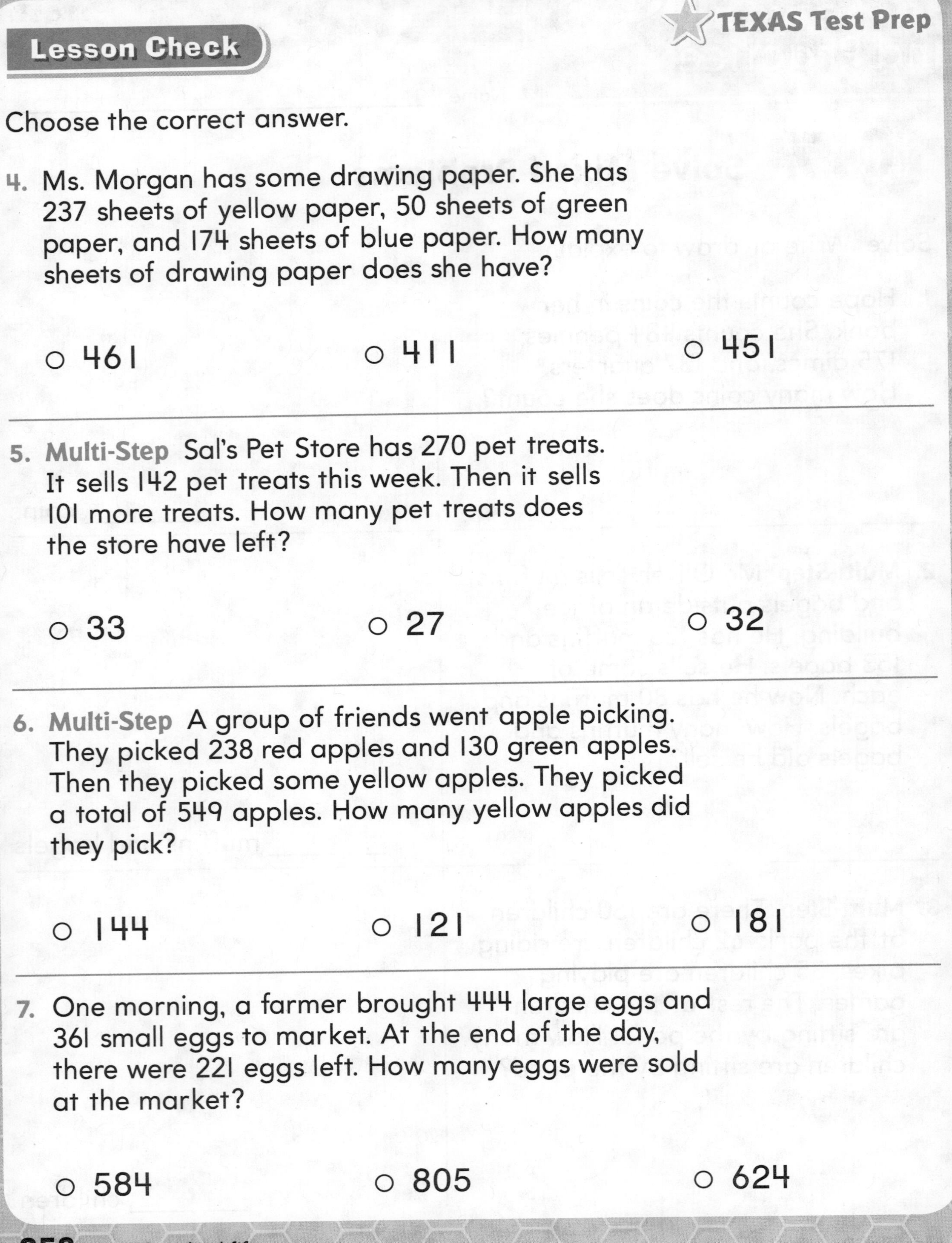

Lesson Check

TEXAS Test Prep

Choose the correct answer.

4. Ms. Morgan has some drawing paper. She has 237 sheets of yellow paper, 50 sheets of green paper, and 174 sheets of blue paper. How many sheets of drawing paper does she have?

○ 461　　○ 411　　○ 451

5. **Multi-Step** Sal's Pet Store has 270 pet treats. It sells 142 pet treats this week. Then it sells 101 more treats. How many pet treats does the store have left?

○ 33　　○ 27　　○ 32

6. **Multi-Step** A group of friends went apple picking. They picked 238 red apples and 130 green apples. Then they picked some yellow apples. They picked a total of 549 apples. How many yellow apples did they pick?

○ 144　　○ 121　　○ 181

7. One morning, a farmer brought 444 large eggs and 361 small eggs to market. At the end of the day, there were 221 eggs left. How many eggs were sold at the market?

○ 584　　○ 805　　○ 624

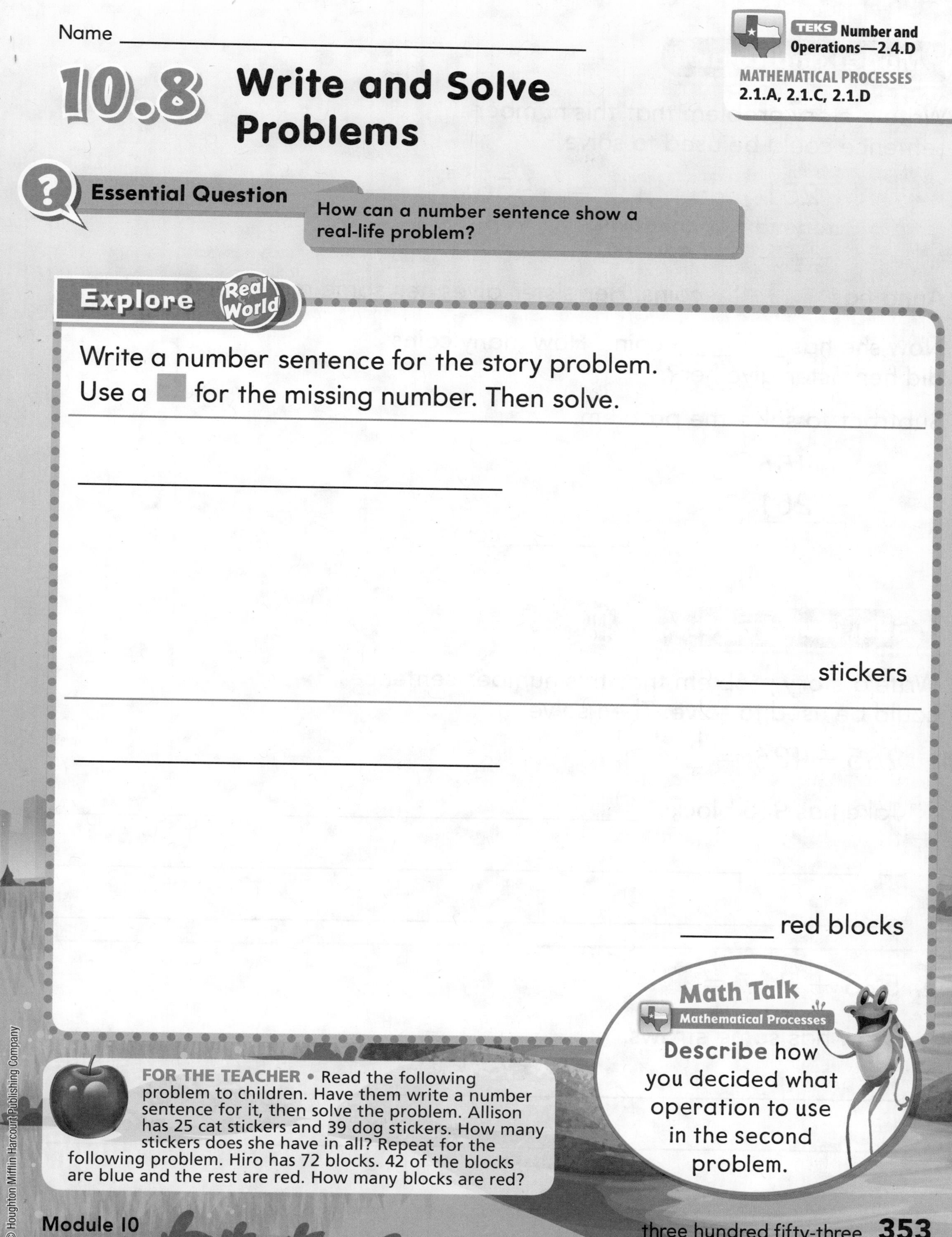

Name ______________________________

TEKS Number and Operations—2.4.D
MATHEMATICAL PROCESSES 2.1.A, 2.1.C, 2.1.D

10.8 Write and Solve Problems

Essential Question How can a number sentence show a real-life problem?

Explore Real World

Write a number sentence for the story problem.
Use a ■ for the missing number. Then solve.

____

______ stickers

____

______ red blocks

FOR THE TEACHER • Read the following problem to children. Have them write a number sentence for it, then solve the problem. Allison has 25 cat stickers and 39 dog stickers. How many stickers does she have in all? Repeat for the following problem. Hiro has 72 blocks. 42 of the blocks are blue and the rest are red. How many blocks are red?

Math Talk Mathematical Processes

Describe how you decided what operation to use in the second problem.

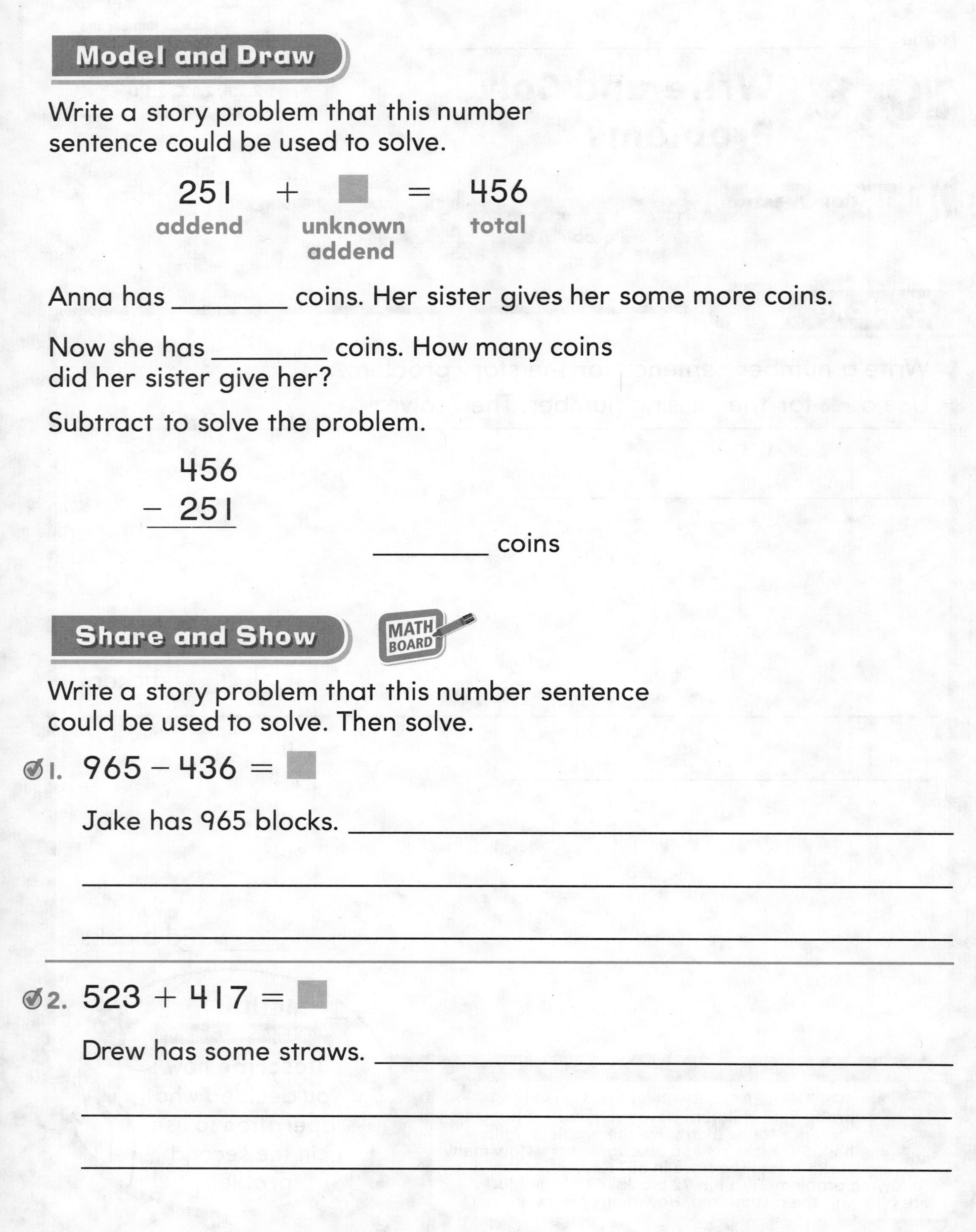

Model and Draw

Write a story problem that this number sentence could be used to solve.

251 + ■ = 456
addend unknown addend total

Anna has ________ coins. Her sister gives her some more coins.

Now she has ________ coins. How many coins did her sister give her?

Subtract to solve the problem.

$$\begin{array}{r} 456 \\ -\ 251 \\ \hline \end{array}$$

________ coins

Share and Show

MATH BOARD

Write a story problem that this number sentence could be used to solve. Then solve.

1. 965 − 436 = ■

Jake has 965 blocks. ____________________

____

____

2. 523 + 417 = ■

Drew has some straws. ____________________

____

____

Name ____________________

Problem Solving

Write a word problem that this number sentence could be used to solve. Then solve.

3. ■ + 345 = 752

Lots of deer live in the state park. ____________________

____

____

4. 384 − 133 = ■

____

____

____

____

Solve. Write or draw to explain.

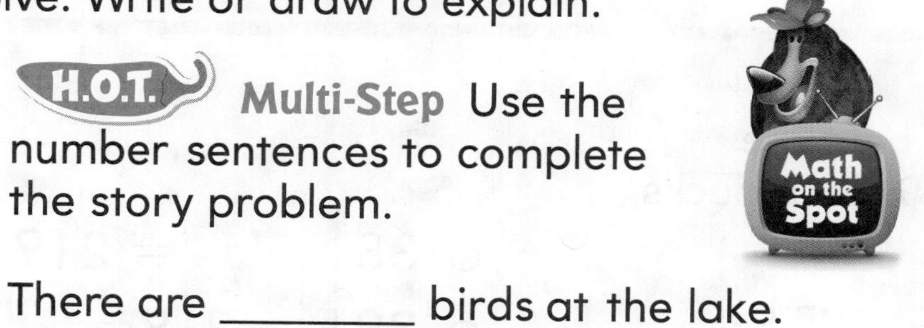

5. **H.O.T.** **Multi-Step** Use the number sentences to complete the story problem.

There are ________ birds at the lake.

________ birds fly away. Then ________ more birds fly to the lake. How many birds are at the lake now?

340 − 214 = ■

■ + 245 = ▲

________ birds

Mathematical Processes
Model • Reason • Communicate

Daily Assessment Task

Choose the correct answer.

6. **Use Symbols** Russell found 101 stones. Becky found 224 stones. Which number sentence can be used to find the total number of stones that they found?

   ○ 224 + 199 = ■
   ○ 224 − 101 = ■
   ○ 224 + 101 = ■

7. Write a story problem that could be shown with the number sentence. Then solve.

   145 + 253 = ■

   ____

   ____

   ____

   ____

8. **TEXAS Test Prep** There are 381 ducks at a lake. 219 more ducks come to the lake.

   Which number sentence can be used to find how many ducks are at the lake now?

   ○ 381 − ■ = 219
   ○ 381 − 219 = ■
   ○ 381 + 219 = ■

TAKE HOME ACTIVITY • Ask your child to explain how he or she solved an exercise in this lesson.

TEKS Number and Operations—2.4.D
MATHEMATICAL PROCESSES 2.1.A, 2.1.C, 2.1.D

Name ______________________

10.8 Write and Solve Problems

Write a story problem that this number sentence could be used to solve. Then solve.

1. $351 + \blacksquare = 465$

Ben has 351 coins. ______________________

____

____

Use the number sentences to complete the story problem.

2. There are ________ pictures to color in Erica's coloring book.

She has ________ pictures left to color. How many pictures has Erica finished?

$325 - \blacksquare = 107$

________ pictures

3. **Multi-Step** There are ________ chickens in a pen.

________ chickens leave the pen.

Then ________ chickens go back into the pen. How many chickens are in the pen now?

$100 - 21 = \blacksquare$

$\blacksquare + 15 = \blacktriangle$

________ chickens

TEXAS Test Prep

Choose the correct answer.

4. There are 183 people at a play. Then 128 more people come to the play. Which number sentence can be used to find how many people are at the play now?

- ○ 183 − ■ = 128
- ○ 183 + 128 = ■
- ○ 183 − 128 = ■

5. On Monday, 346 people went to the movies. On Tuesday, 192 people went to the movies. On Wednesday, 174 people went to the movies. Which number sentence can be used to find how many more people went to the movies on Monday than on Wednesday?

- ○ 192 + 174 = ■
- ○ 346 + 192 = ■
- ○ 346 − 174 = ■

6. Alan and Bret collected 110 canned goods for the town pantry. Sue and Anna collected 242 canned goods for the pantry. Which number sentence can be used to find the total number of canned goods collected?

- ○ 242 − 110 = ■
- ○ 110 + 242 = ■
- ○ 242 − ■ = 110

Name ______________________________

Module 10 Assessment

Concepts and Skills

Break apart the addends to find the sum. TEKS 2.4.C

1. 849 → ______ + ______ + ______

   + 123 → ______ + ______ + ______

   ______ + ______ + ______ = ______

Write the sum or difference. TEKS 2.4.C

2.

	Hundreds	Tens	Ones
		□	
	1	4	7
+	1	2	5

3.

	Hundreds	Tens	Ones
	□	□	
	1	5	6
+		4	2

4.

	Hundreds	Tens	Ones
	□	□	□
	9	8	4
−	7	1	5

5. Write a story problem that could be shown with the number sentence. Then solve. TEKS 2.4.D

276 − 133 = ■

____

____

____

____

Fill in the bubble for the correct answer choice.

TEXAS Test Prep

6. There are 487 people running a race. 215 people have finished the race. How many people are still running in the race? TEKS 2.4.C

- ○ 702
- ○ 272
- ○ 382

7. There are 512 visitors at the zoo on Monday and 437 visitors on Tuesday. Which number sentence could be used to find the total number of visitors on Monday and Tuesday? TEKS 2.4.D

- ○ $512 - 437 = \blacksquare$
- ○ $437 + \blacksquare = 512$
- ○ $512 + 437 = \blacksquare$

8. 258 kites are sold on Saturday and 341 kites are sold on Sunday. How many kites are sold on Saturday and Sunday? TEKS 2.4.C

- ○ 599
- ○ 83
- ○ 609

9. A parking garage has 800 parking spots and has 2 floors. There are 347 cars parked on the first floor and 370 cars parked on the second floor. How many empty spots are in the garage? TEKS 2.4.C

- ○ 453
- ○ 83
- ○ 717

10. Jenny has 564 stickers. She gives 210 stickers to a classmate and then buys 35 more stickers. How many stickers does Jenny have now? TEKS 2.4.C

- ○ 389
- ○ 319
- ○ 739

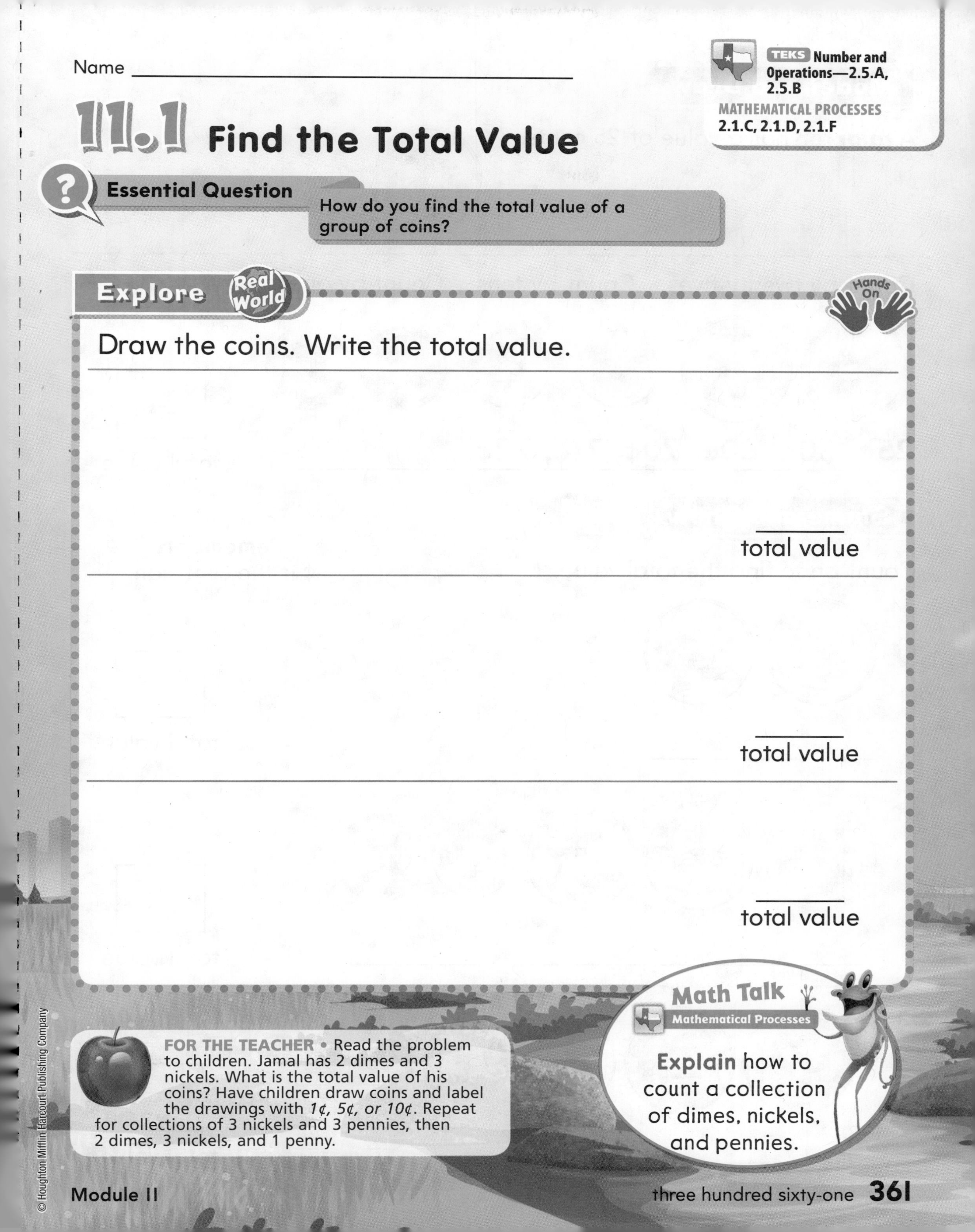

Name ____________________

TEKS Number and Operations—2.5.A, 2.5.B
MATHEMATICAL PROCESSES 2.1.C, 2.1.D, 2.1.F

11.1 Find the Total Value

Essential Question How do you find the total value of a group of coins?

Explore Real World

Hands On

Draw the coins. Write the total value.

______ total value

______ total value

______ total value

FOR THE TEACHER • Read the problem to children. Jamal has 2 dimes and 3 nickels. What is the total value of his coins? Have children draw coins and label the drawings with *1¢, 5¢, or 10¢*. Repeat for collections of 3 nickels and 3 pennies, then 2 dimes, 3 nickels, and 1 penny.

Math Talk Mathematical Processes

Explain how to count a collection of dimes, nickels, and pennies.

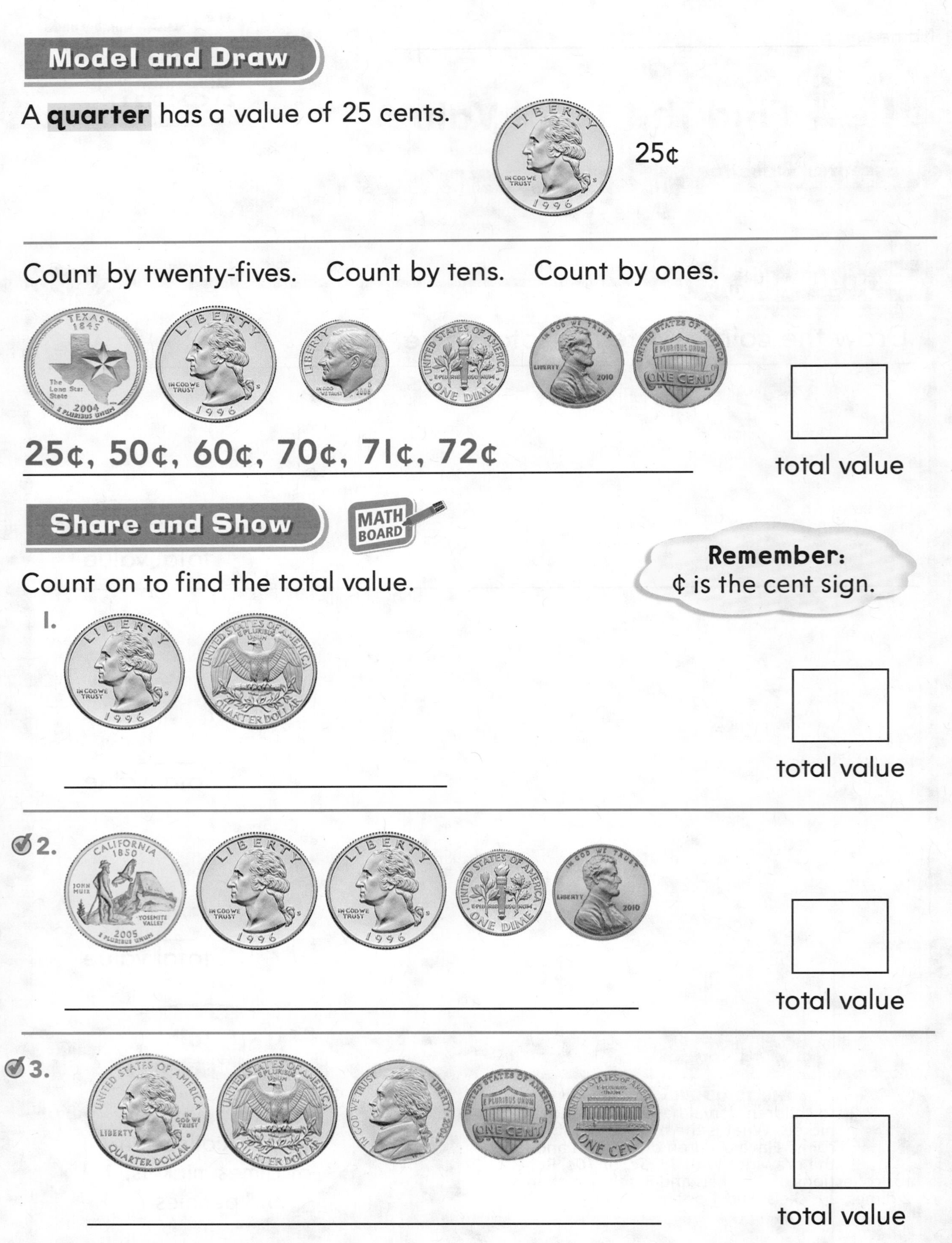

Model and Draw

A **quarter** has a value of 25 cents.

25¢

Count by twenty-fives. Count by tens. Count by ones.

25¢, 50¢, 60¢, 70¢, 71¢, 72¢

total value

Share and Show

MATH BOARD

Count on to find the total value.

Remember:
¢ is the cent sign.

1.

total value

2.

total value

3.

total value

Name ________________________

Problem Solving

Count on to find the total value.

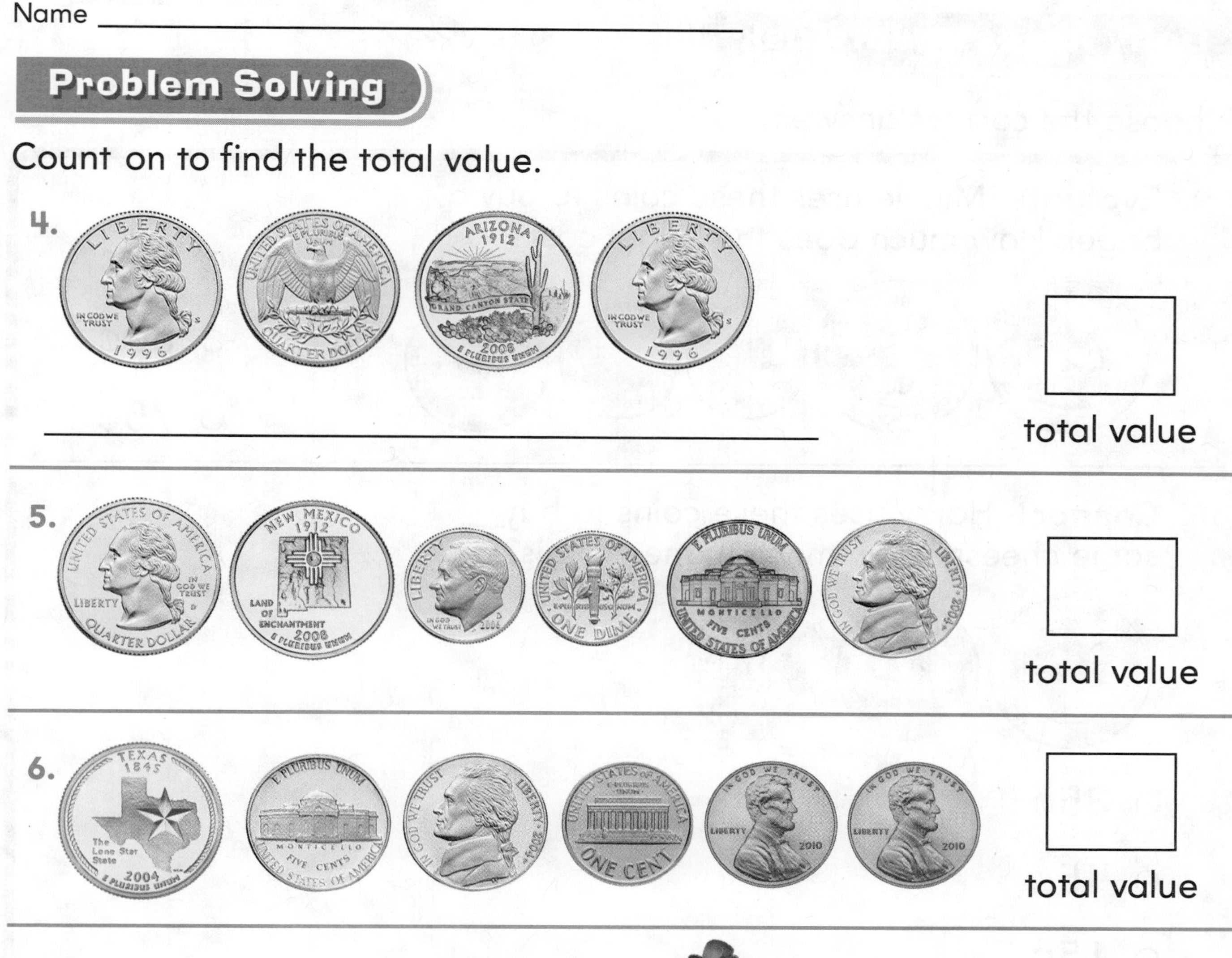

4. ________________________

total value

5.

total value

6.

total value

Draw and label coins to solve.

7. **H.O.T.** Ed's coin has the same value as a group of 5 pennies and 4 nickels. What is his coin?

8. **H.O.T.** **Multi-Step** Ginnie has two groups of coins. Each group has a total value of 51¢. There is at least 1 quarter in each group. What coins could she have?

Daily Assessment Task

Choose the correct answer.

9. **Evaluate** Minnie uses these coins to buy a bagel. How much does the bagel cost?

- ○ 80¢
- ○ 50¢
- ○ 75¢

10. **Connect** Harry uses these coins to buy some cheese. How much money is this?

- ○ 35¢
- ○ 45¢
- ○ 15¢

11. **TEXAS Test Prep** Tom gives these coins to his brother. How much money does Tom give to his brother?

- ○ 50¢
- ○ 25¢
- ○ 65¢

TAKE HOME ACTIVITY • Have your child draw two quarters, two dimes, and two nickels, and then find the total value.

Name ______________________

TEKS Number and Operations—2.5.A, 2.5.B
MATHEMATICAL PROCESSES 2.1.C, 2.1.E, 2.1.F

11.2 One Dollar

Essential Question How can you show the value of one dollar with coins?

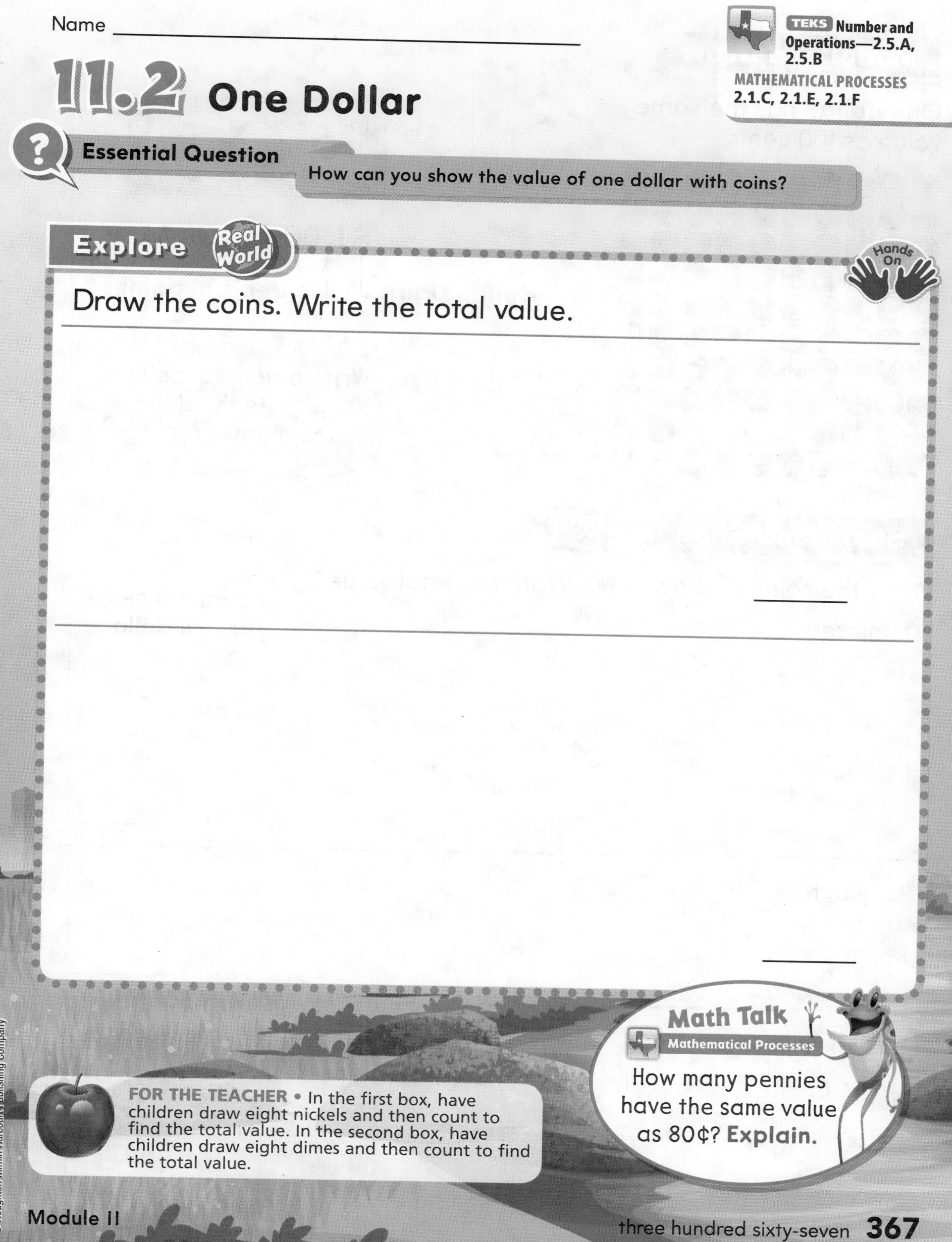

Draw the coins. Write the total value.

______

______

FOR THE TEACHER • In the first box, have children draw eight nickels and then count to find the total value. In the second box, have children draw eight dimes and then count to find the total value.

Model and Draw

One **dollar** has the same value as 100 cents.

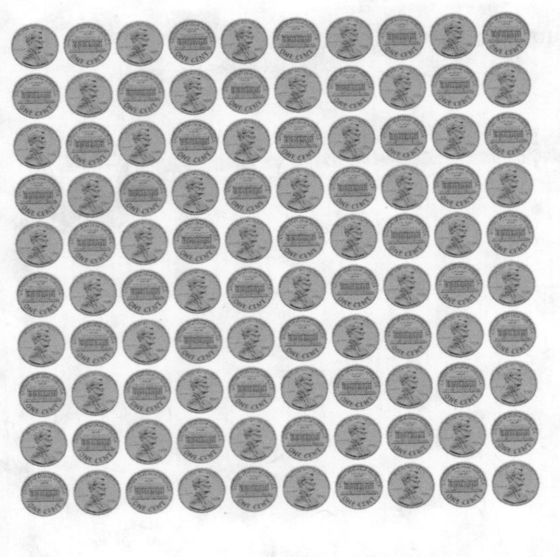

$1.00 = 100¢

dollar sign — decimal point

Write a decimal point to separate the dollars from the cents.

Share and Show

Draw the coins to show $1.00. Write the total value.

Count 100 cents for one dollar.

1. nickels

____

2. quarters

____

3. dimes

____

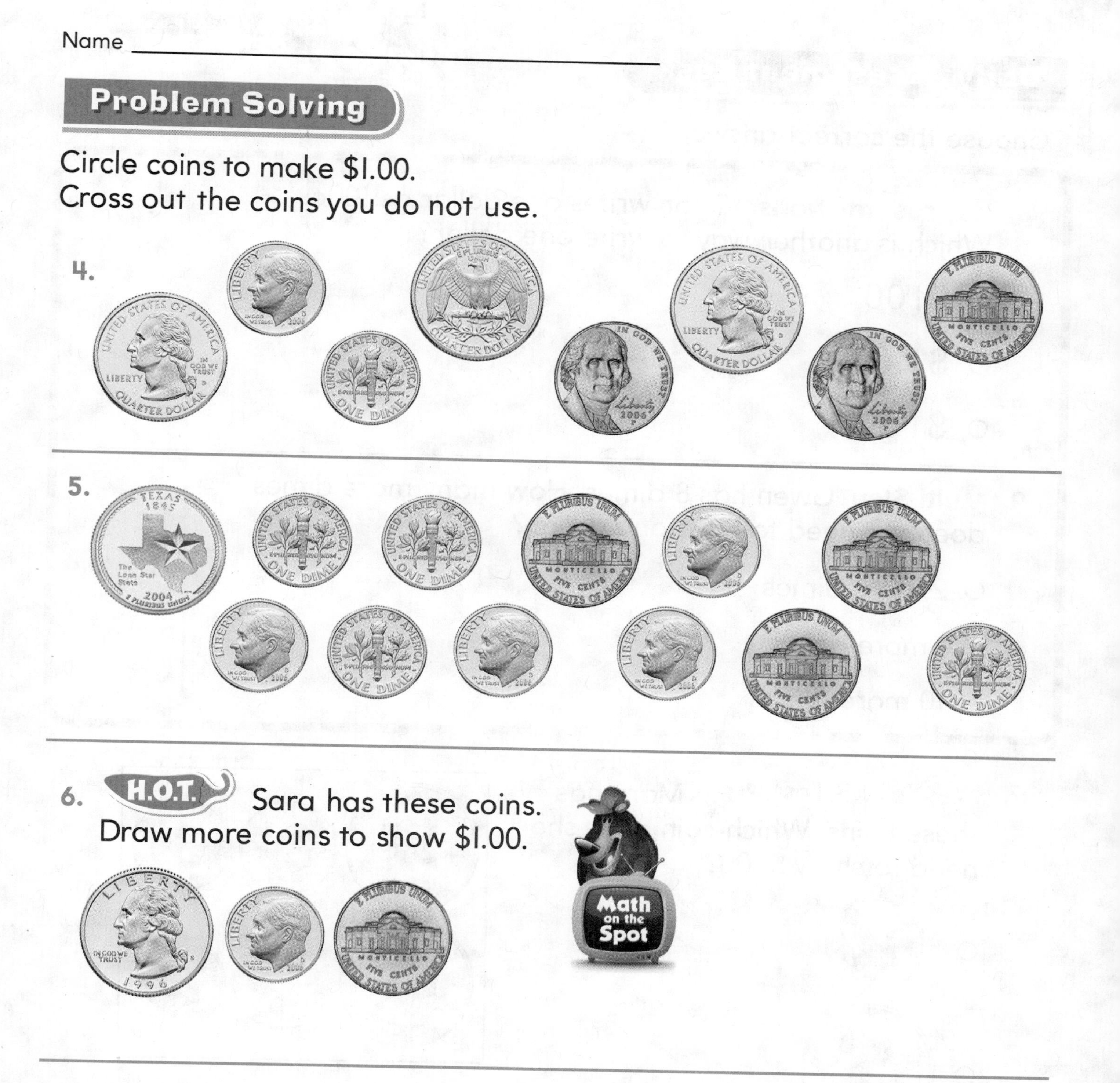

Name ____________________

Problem Solving

Circle coins to make $1.00.
Cross out the coins you do not use.

4.

5.

6. H.O.T. Sara has these coins.
Draw more coins to show $1.00.

7. H.O.T. **Multi-Step** Warren shows $1.00 using only two kinds of coins. Draw and label coins he could use.

Mathematical Processes

Model • Reason • Communicate

Daily Assessment Task

Choose the correct answer.

8. **Representations** Victor writes one dollar as 100¢. Which is another way to write one dollar?

- ○ $100
- ○ $1.00
- ○ $1¢

9. **Multi-Step** Gwen has 8 dimes. How many more dimes does she need to have one dollar?

- ○ 2 more dimes
- ○ 1 more dime
- ○ 10 more dimes

10. **TEXAS Test Prep** Mary has these coins. Which coin does she need to show $1.00?

TAKE HOME ACTIVITY • Have your child draw a group of coins to show $1.00.

TEKS Number and Operations—2.5.A, 2.5.B
MATHEMATICAL PROCESSES 2.1.C, 2.1.E, 2.1.F

Name ______________________

11.2 One Dollar

Circle coins to make $1.00. Cross out the coins you do not use.

1.

2.

Problem Solving

Solve. Write or draw to explain.

3. **Multi-Step** Henry has these coins. Draw more coins to show $1.00.

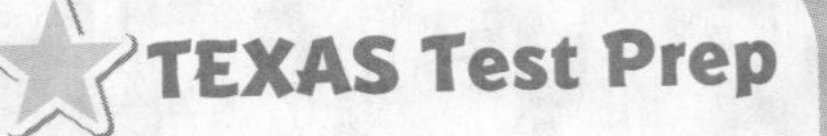

Choose the correct answer.

4. Scott has these coins. Which coin does he need to show $1.00?

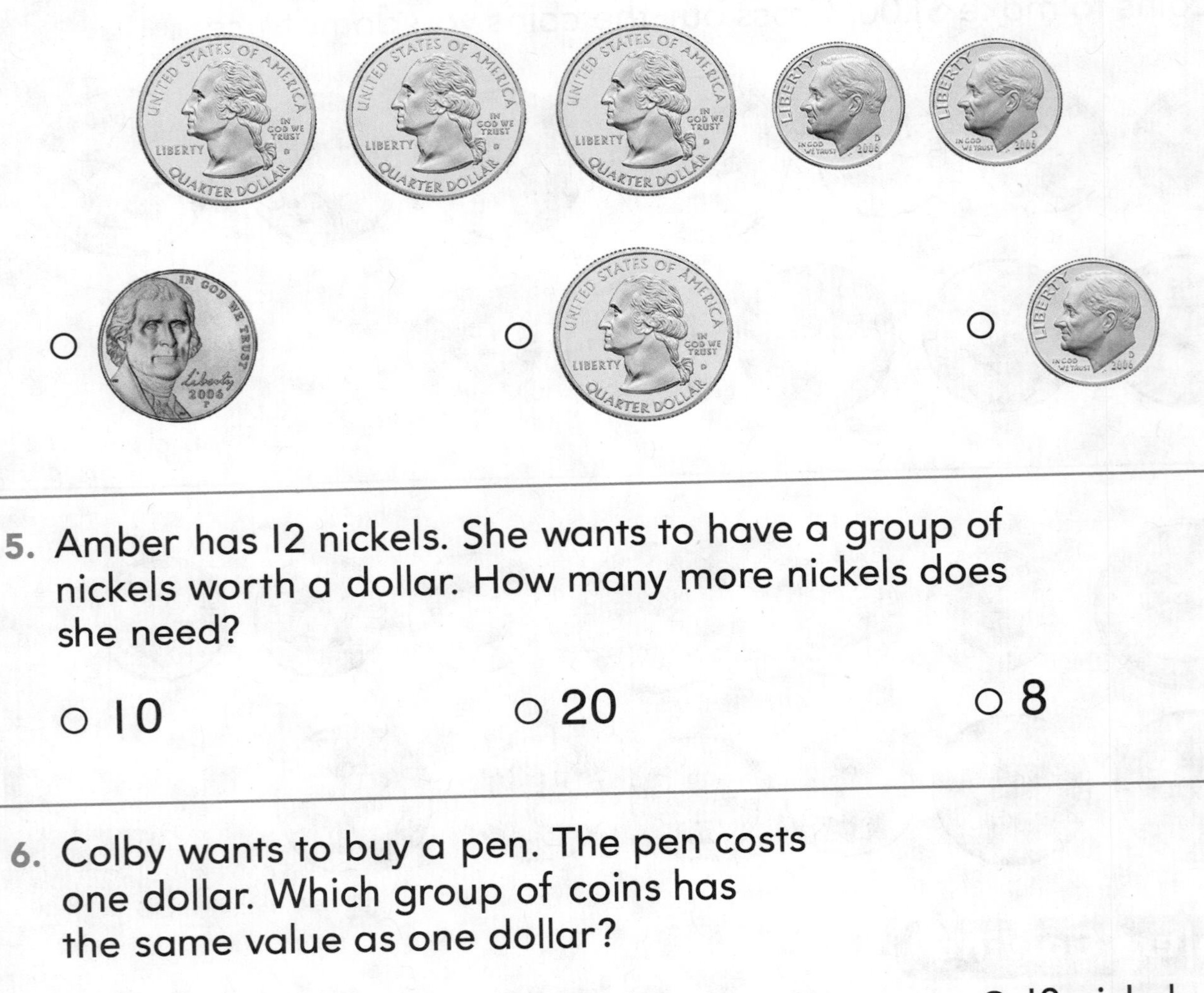

5. Amber has 12 nickels. She wants to have a group of nickels worth a dollar. How many more nickels does she need?

○ 10 ○ 20 ○ 8

6. Colby wants to buy a pen. The pen costs one dollar. Which group of coins has the same value as one dollar?

○ 10 quarters ○ 10 dimes ○ 10 nickels

7. Karen has one dollar. She writes the total value as $1.00. Which is another way to write one dollar?

○ 10¢ ○ 1¢ ○ 100¢

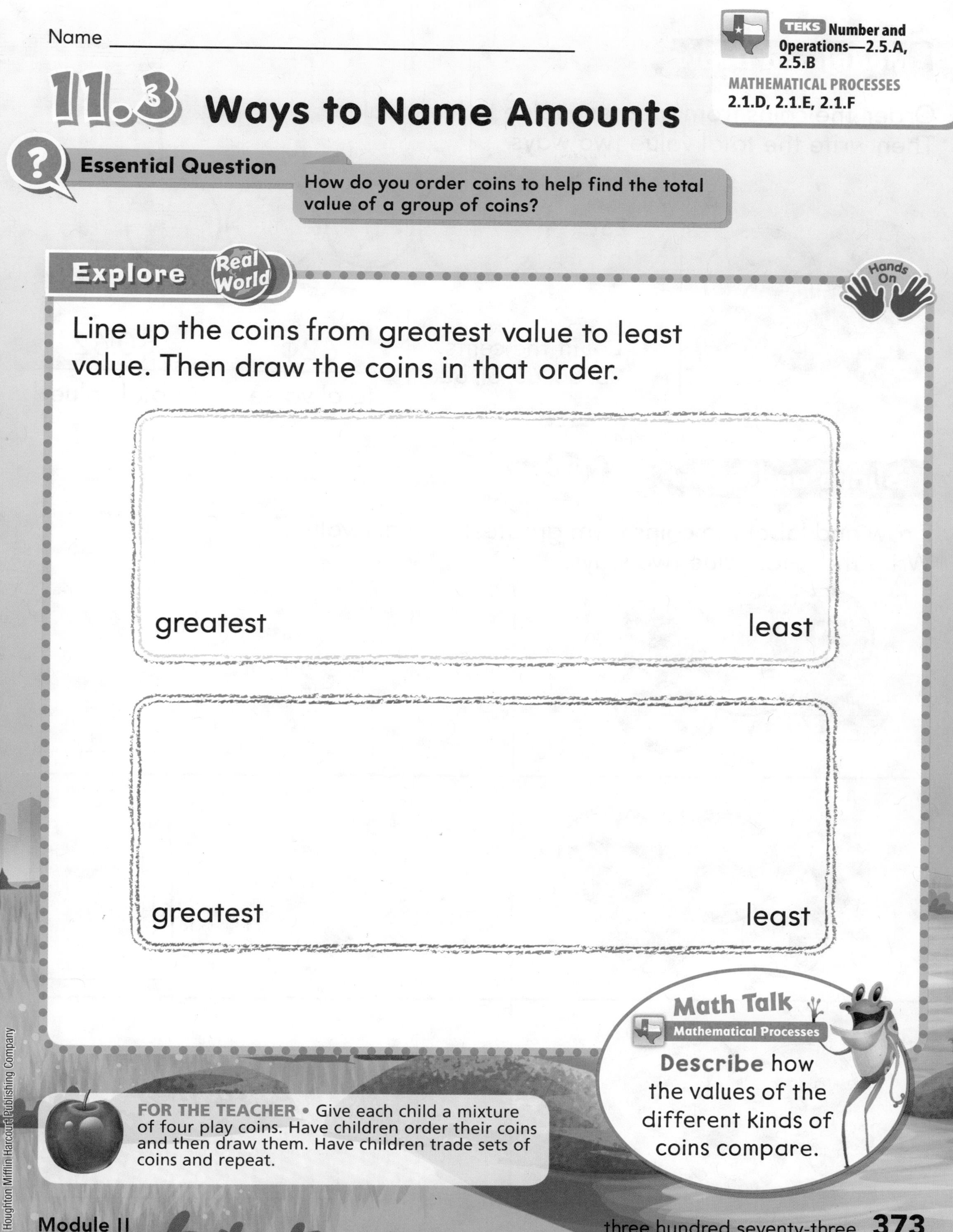

Name ______________________________

TEKS Number and Operations—2.5.A, 2.5.B
MATHEMATICAL PROCESSES 2.1.D, 2.1.E, 2.1.F

11.3 Ways to Name Amounts

Essential Question How do you order coins to help find the total value of a group of coins?

Explore Real World

Hands On

Line up the coins from greatest value to least value. Then draw the coins in that order.

greatest least

greatest least

Math Talk Mathematical Processes

Describe how the values of the different kinds of coins compare.

FOR THE TEACHER • Give each child a mixture of four play coins. Have children order their coins and then draw them. Have children trade sets of coins and repeat.

Model and Draw

Order the coins from greatest value to least value.
Then write the total value two ways.

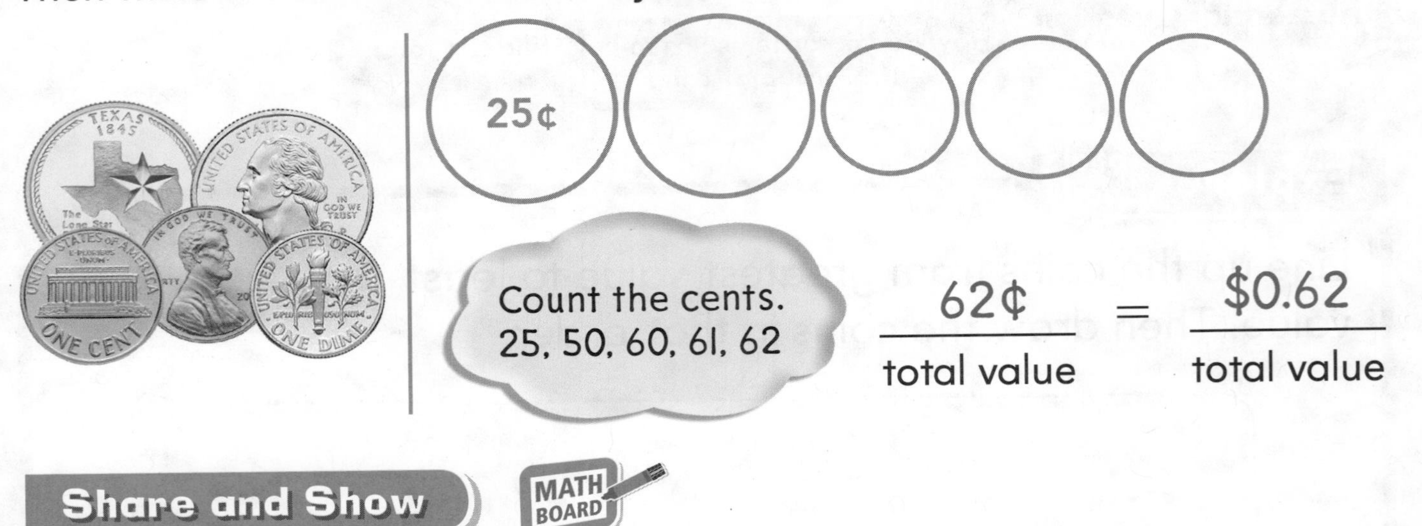

Share and Show

MATH BOARD

Draw and label the coins from greatest to least value.
Write the total value two ways.

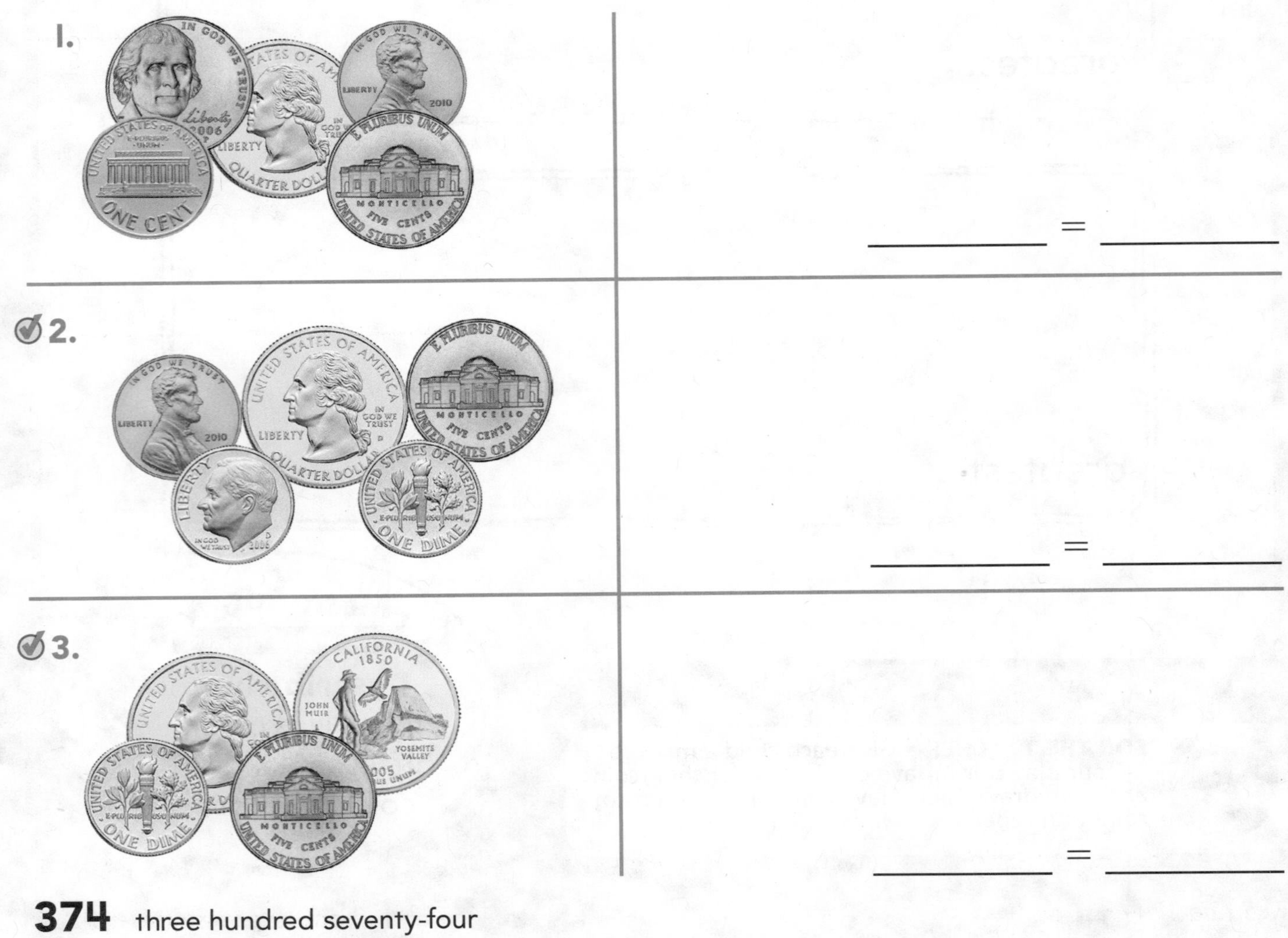

Name ______________________________

Problem Solving

Draw and label the coins from greatest to least value.
Write the total value two ways.

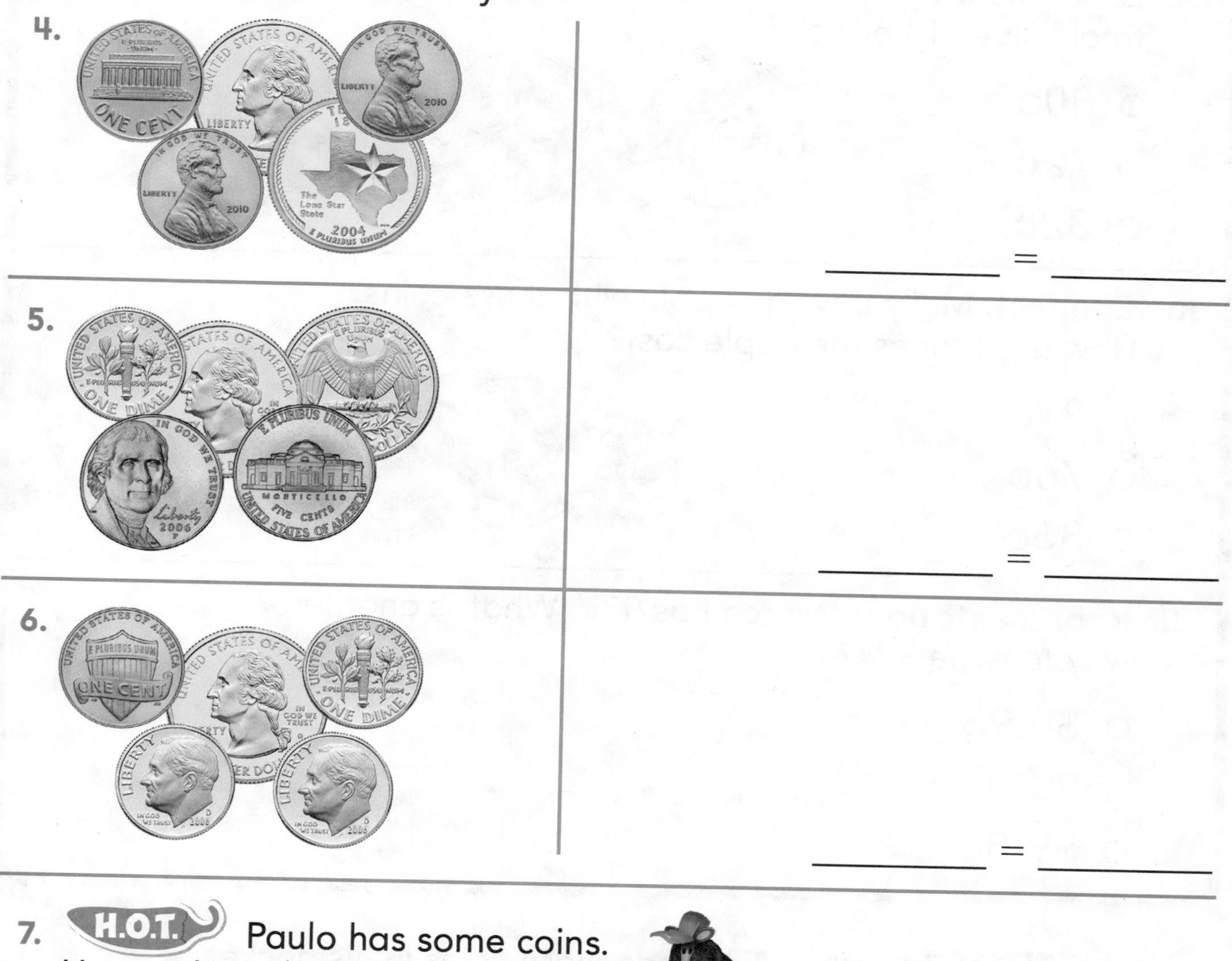

4. ________ = ________

5. ________ = ________

6. ________ = ________

7. H.O.T. Paulo has some coins. He needs 1 nickel to make a dollar. What is the value of his coins?

________ or ________

8. H.O.T. **Multi-Step** Blake has only nickels and dimes. He has twice as many nickels as dimes. The total value of his coins is 60¢. What coins does Blake have?

________ nickels ________ dimes

Mathematical Processes

Model • Reason • Communicate

Daily Assessment Task

Choose the correct answer.

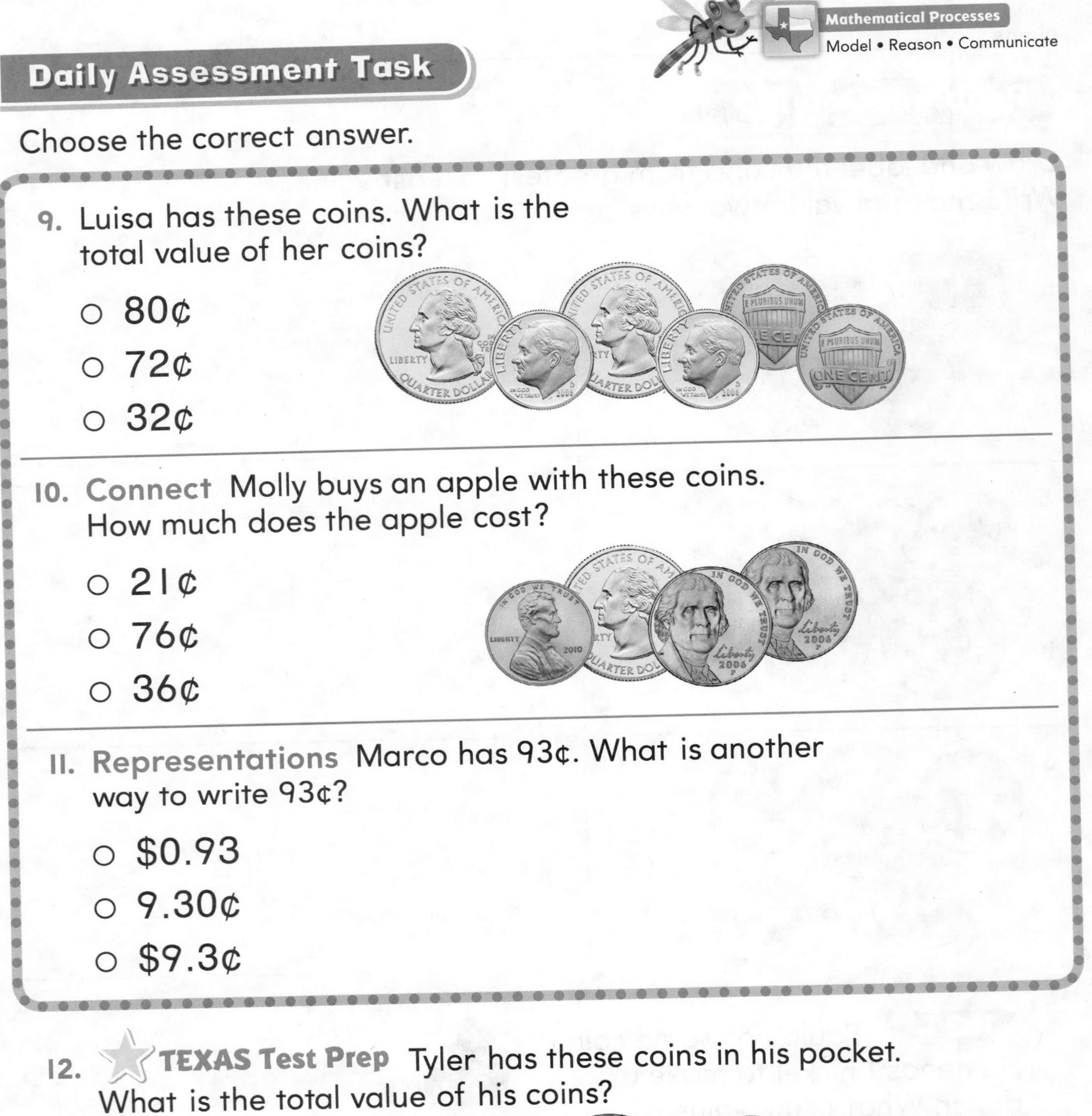

9. Luisa has these coins. What is the total value of her coins?

   ○ 80¢

   ○ 72¢

   ○ 32¢

10. **Connect** Molly buys an apple with these coins. How much does the apple cost?

    ○ 21¢

    ○ 76¢

    ○ 36¢

11. **Representations** Marco has 93¢. What is another way to write 93¢?

    ○ $0.93

    ○ 9.30¢

    ○ $9.3¢

12. **TEXAS Test Prep** Tyler has these coins in his pocket. What is the total value of his coins?

    ○ $0.50

    ○ $0.60

    ○ $0.55

TAKE HOME ACTIVITY • Have your child draw and label coins with a total value of $0.75.

TEKS Number and Operations—2.5.A, 2.5.B
MATHEMATICAL PROCESSES 2.1.D, 2.1.E, 2.1.F

Name ____________________

11.3 Ways to Name Amounts

Draw and label the coins from greatest to least value. Write the total value two ways.

1.

_______ = _______

2.

_______ = _______

Problem Solving

Solve. Write or draw to explain.

3. **Multi-Step** Andy has only quarters and nickels. The total value of his coins is 75¢. What coins could Andy have?

_______ quarters _______ nickels

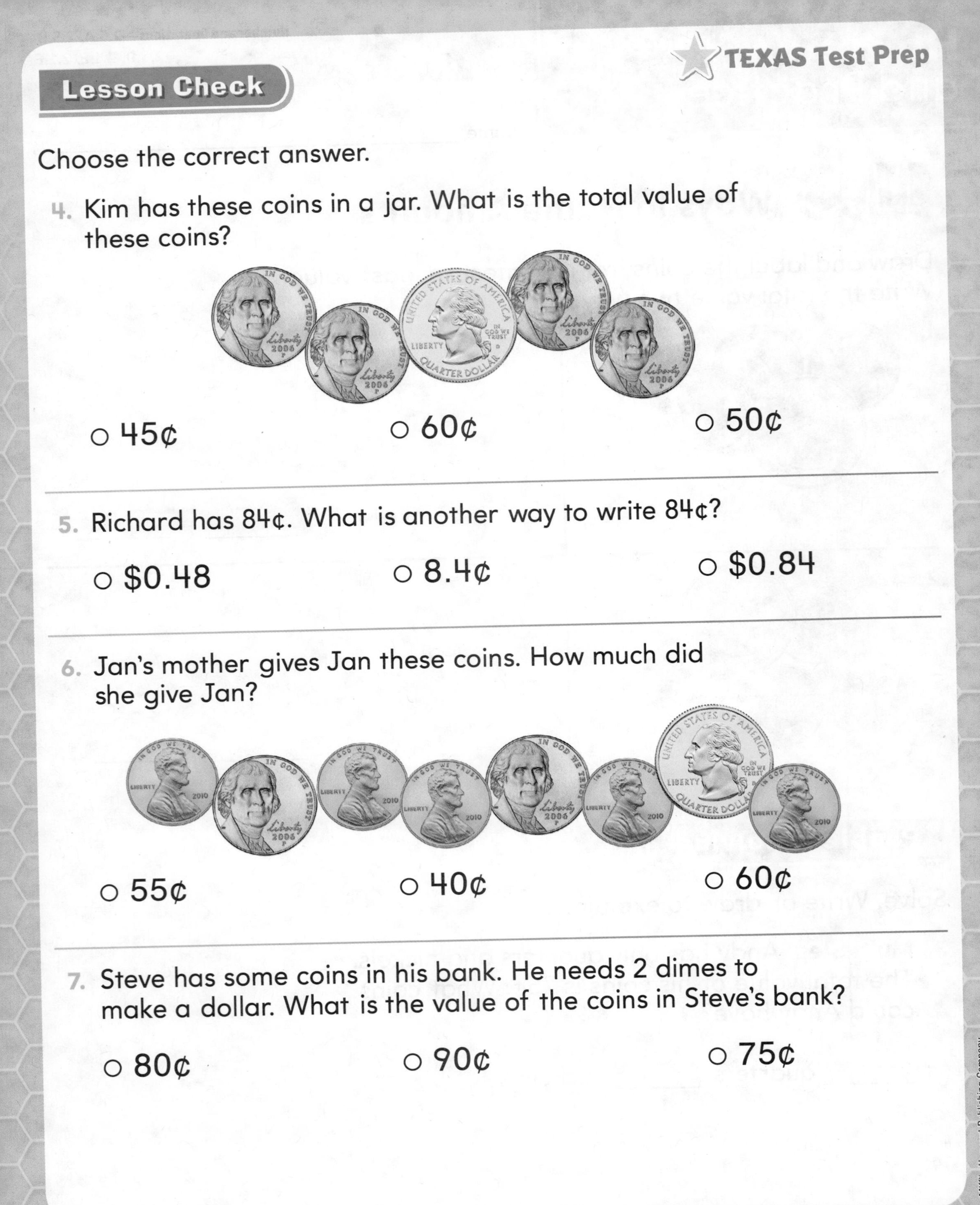

Lesson Check

TEXAS Test Prep

Choose the correct answer.

4. Kim has these coins in a jar. What is the total value of these coins?

○ 45¢ ○ 60¢ ○ 50¢

5. Richard has 84¢. What is another way to write 84¢?

○ $0.48 ○ 8.4¢ ○ $0.84

6. Jan's mother gives Jan these coins. How much did she give Jan?

○ 55¢ ○ 40¢ ○ 60¢

7. Steve has some coins in his bank. He needs 2 dimes to make a dollar. What is the value of the coins in Steve's bank?

○ 80¢ ○ 90¢ ○ 75¢

Name ____________________

TEKS Number and Operations—2.5.A, 2.5.B
MATHEMATICAL PROCESSES 2.1.A, 2.1.B, 2.1.G

11.4 PROBLEM SOLVING • Money

Essential Question

How can acting it out help you solve a problem about money?

Unlock the Problem (Real World)

Meg has 2 quarters, 2 dimes, 1 nickel, and 3 pennies. She wants to buy a whistle for 65¢. How much money will Meg have after she buys the whistle?

Read	Plan
What information am I given?	**What is my plan or strategy?**
The whistle costs ________.	I can ____________________
Meg has these coins:	____________________.
____________________	
____________________	

Solve

Show how you solve the problem.

Draw and label coins to show the problem.

Meg will have ________ after she buys the whistle.

HOME CONNECTION • Your child used play coins to act out the problem. Representing problems with objects can be a useful strategy for children to use to solve problems.

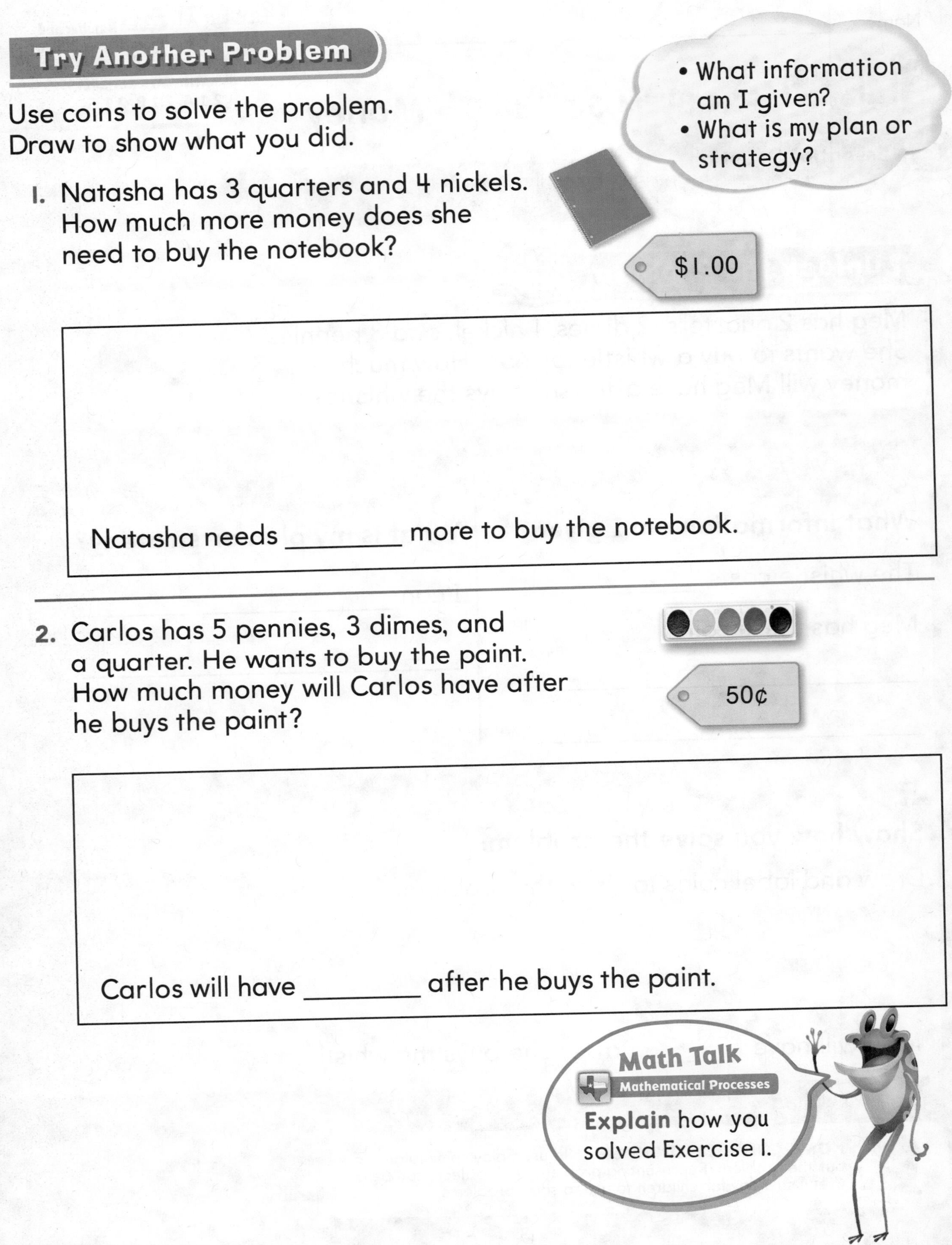

Try Another Problem

Use coins to solve the problem.
Draw to show what you did.

- What information am I given?
- What is my plan or strategy?

1. Natasha has 3 quarters and 4 nickels. How much more money does she need to buy the notebook?

$1.00

Natasha needs ________ more to buy the notebook.

2. Carlos has 5 pennies, 3 dimes, and a quarter. He wants to buy the paint. How much money will Carlos have after he buys the paint?

50¢

Carlos will have ________ after he buys the paint.

Math Talk

Mathematical Processes

Explain how you solved Exercise 1.

Name ______________________________

Share and Show

MATH BOARD

Use coins to solve the problem.
Draw to show what you did.

3. Anna has 3 nickels, 5 pennies, and 1 quarter. Her mom gives her another coin so Anna can buy the balloon. What coin does Anna get from her mom?

Anna gets ______________ from her mom.

Problem Solving

Solve. Write or draw to explain.

4. H.O.T. **Multi-Step** One apple costs 36¢. Chris uses dimes and pennies to buy 2 apples. What coins could Chris use to buy the apples?

_______ dimes

_______ pennies

5. H.O.T. **Multi-Step** James uses 3 quarters and 1 dime to buy a toy. The cashier gives him 1 nickel back. How much did the toy cost?

____

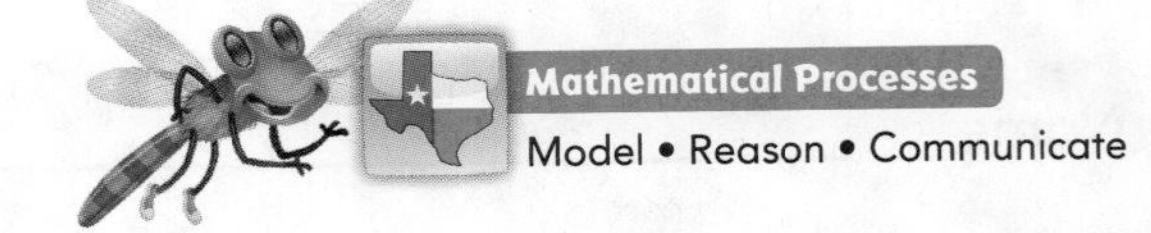

Daily Assessment Task

Choose the correct answer.

6. **Multi-Step** Alex has 3 quarters and 1 dime. He buys a pen for 50¢. How much money does he have now?

   ○ 25¢
   ○ 50¢
   ○ 35¢

7. Todd uses 2 quarters, 2 dimes, and a penny to buy lemonade. How much does the lemonade cost?

   ○ 71¢
   ○ 61¢
   ○ 96¢

8. **Evaluate** Nina has 30¢. Which group of coins have a total value of 30¢?

   ○ 1 quarter, 1 dime
   ○ 2 quarters
   ○ 1 quarter, 1 nickel

9. **TEXAS Test Prep** Jacob has 2 dimes, 2 nickels, and 2 quarters. He uses 65¢ to buy juice. How much money does he have now?

   ○ 25¢
   ○ 10¢
   ○ 15¢

TAKE HOME ACTIVITY • Have your child explain how he or she solved one of the problems in this lesson.

Name ____________________

11.4 PROBLEM SOLVING • Money

Use coins to solve the problem. Draw to show what you did.

1. Trish has 5 pennies, 1 dime, and 3 quarters. She wants to buy a headband that costs 69 cents. How much money will she have after she buys the headband?

Trish has _____ after she buys the headband.

Problem Solving

Solve. Write or draw to explain.

2. **Multi-Step** Jeff uses nickels and pennies to buy a pencil that costs 39¢. What coins could Jeff use to buy the pencil?

_______ nickels

_______ pennies

3. **Multi-Step** Madeline uses 3 quarters and 2 dimes to buy a corn muffin. The cashier gives her 4 pennies back. How much did the corn muffin cost?

____

TEXAS Test Prep

Choose the correct answer.

4. Gary has 3 dimes, 3 nickels, and 2 quarters. He wants to buy a balloon that costs 75¢. How much money will he have after he buys the balloon?

- ○ 15¢
- ○ 25¢
- ○ 20¢

5. Lilly finds three coins at the park. The total value of the coins is 60¢. What three coins does she find?

- ○ 3 quarters
- ○ 2 quarters, 1 dime
- ○ 2 quarters, 1 nickel

6. Tom uses 1 quarter, 2 dimes, and 3 pennies to buy an orange. How much does the orange cost?

- ○ 48¢
- ○ 73¢
- ○ 38¢

7. Ellie wants to buy a juice box. The juice box costs 45¢. Ellie has 3 quarters and 2 dimes. Which coins will Ellie still have after she buys the juice box?

- ○ 2 dimes
- ○ 2 quarters
- ○ 1 quarter, 2 dimes

Name ______________________________

Module 11 Assessment

Concepts and Skills

Write the total value. TEKS 2.5.A, 2.5.B

1.

____

2.

____

Draw and label the coins from greatest to least value.
Write the total value two ways. TEKS 2.5.A, 2.5.B

3.

_______ = _______

Circle coins to make $1.00.
Cross out the coins you do not use. TEKS 2.5.A

4.

Fill in the bubble for the correct answer choice.

TEXAS Test Prep

5. Chandra has these coins. What is the total value of her coins? TEKS 2.5.A

- ○ 47¢
- ○ 27¢
- ○ 32¢

6. Isaac has 83¢. What is another way to write the amount of money Isaac has? TEKS 2.5.B

- ○ ¢0.38
- ○ 0.83¢
- ○ $0.83

7. Dakota wants to buy a book that costs one dollar. Which coins can Dakota use to buy the book? TEKS 2.5.A

- ○ 4 dimes
- ○ 4 quarters
- ○ 4 nickels

8. There are 3 quarters, 1 dime, and 2 nickels in Jan's bank. Jan puts another nickel in the bank. What is the total value of the coins in the bank? TEKS 2.5.A

- ○ $1.00
- ○ 75¢
- ○ 95¢

9. Craig has 3 dimes, 3 nickels, and 1 quarter. He wants to buy a muffin for 45¢. How much money will he have after he buys the muffin? TEKS 2.5.A

- ○ 25¢
- ○ 15¢
- ○ 20¢

Name ____________________

TEKS Number and Operations—2.6.A
MATHEMATICAL PROCESSES 2.1.A, 2.1.C, 2.1.E

12.1 Add Equal Groups

Essential Question How can skip counting help you add equal groups?

Explore

Hands On

Draw to model the problem. Write the skip counting to find the total.

Jim's shoes

____________________ ______ shoes

Ella's flower petals

____________________ ______ flower petals

FOR THE TEACHER • Read this problem to children. Then have them draw a model and skip count to find the answer. Jim has 4 pairs of shoes. How many shoes does he have? Repeat for the following problem. Ella has 5 flowers. Each flower has 5 petals. How many petals are there?

Math Talk Mathematical Processes

Explain how skip counting helped you solve the second problem.

Model and Draw

Chen has 4 pages of postcards. Each page has 5 postcards. How many postcards does Chen have?

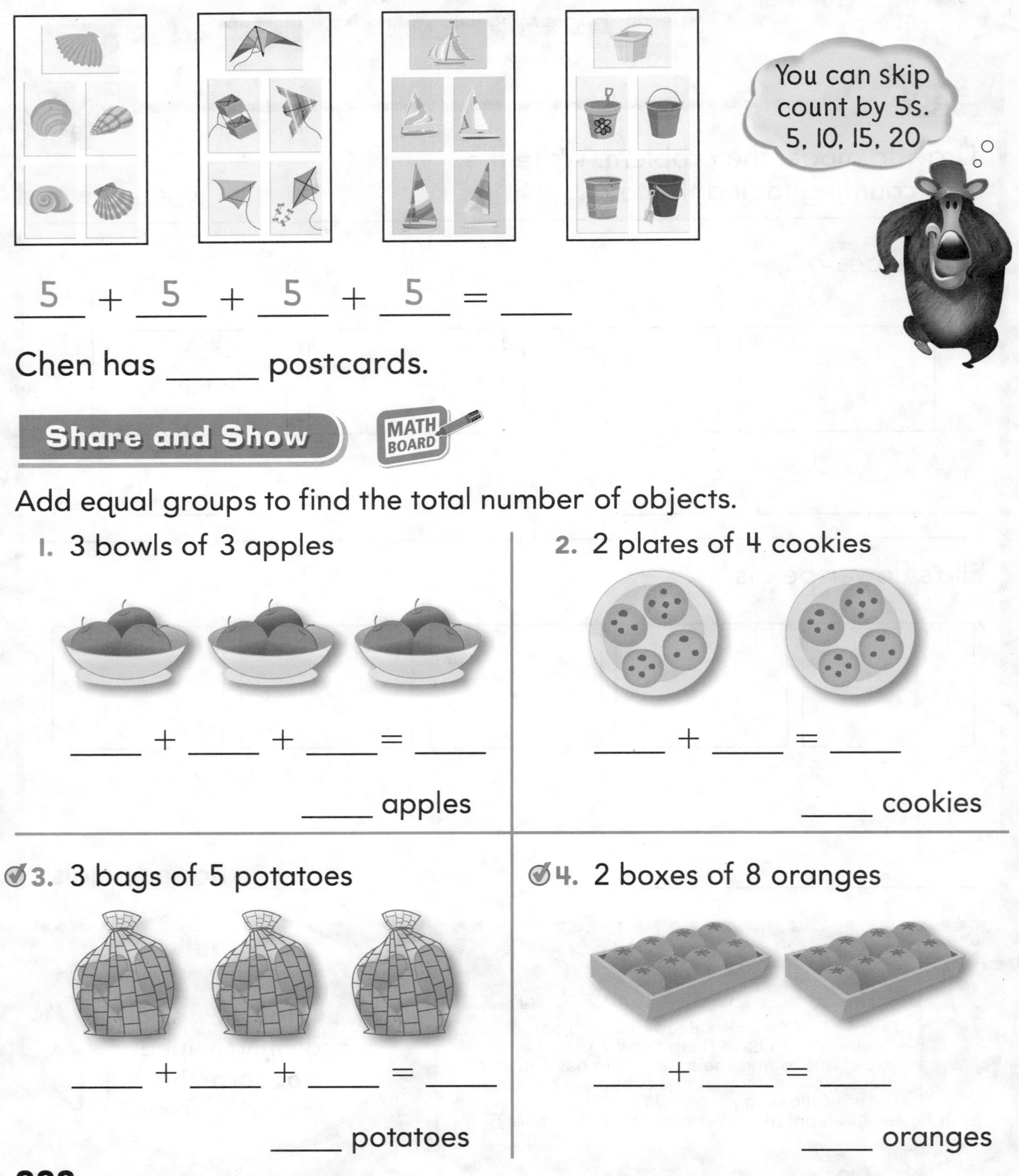

5 + 5 + 5 + 5 = ____

Chen has ____ postcards.

Share and Show

MATH BOARD

Add equal groups to find the total number of objects.

1. 3 bowls of 3 apples

____ + ____ + ____ = ____

____ apples

2. 2 plates of 4 cookies

____ + ____ = ____

____ cookies

✓3. 3 bags of 5 potatoes

____ + ____ + ____ = ____

____ potatoes

✓4. 2 boxes of 8 oranges

____ + ____ = ____

____ oranges

Name ___

Problem Solving

Use counters. Draw and then add equal groups. Find the total.

5. 5 groups of 4 counters

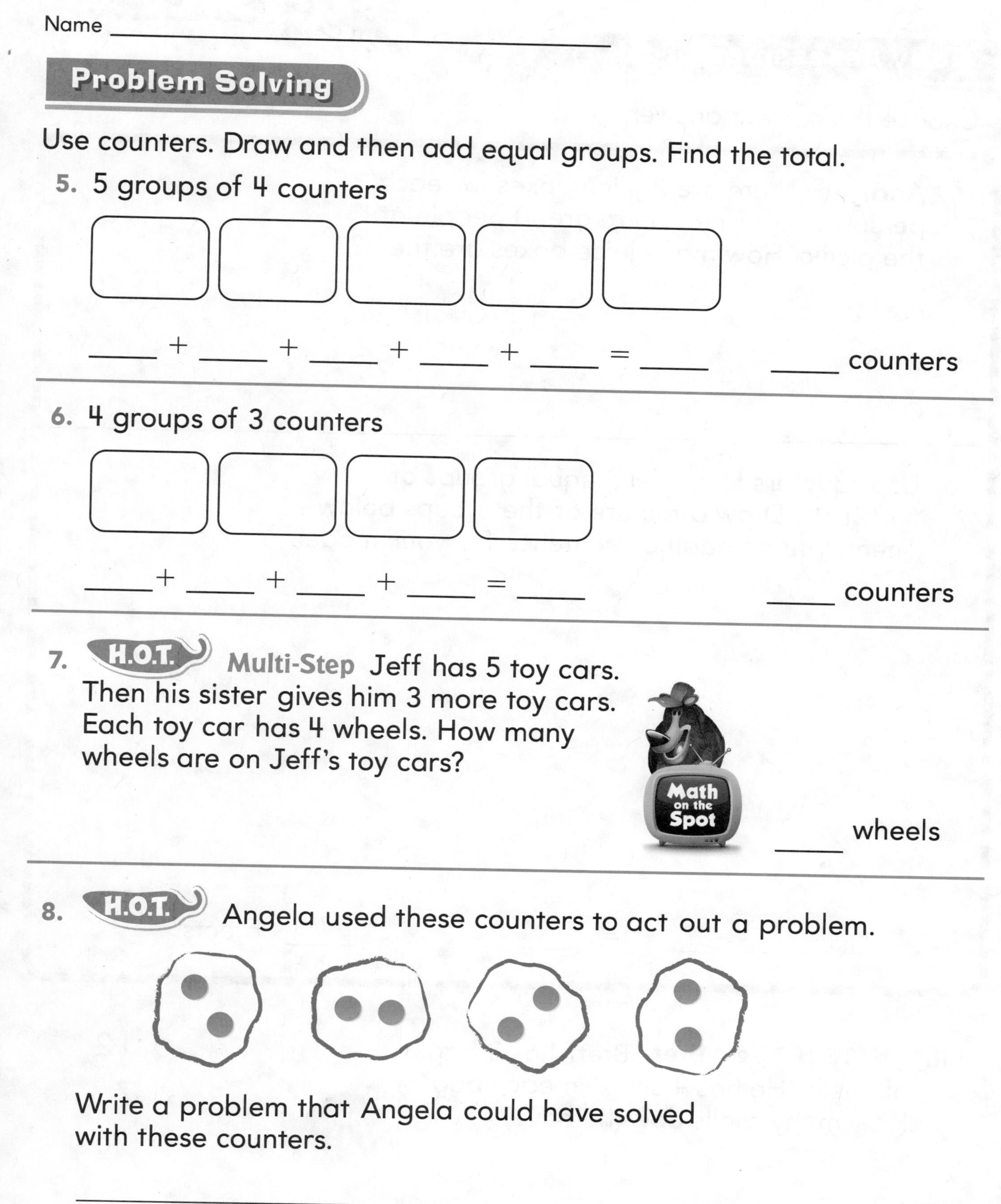

___ + ___ + ___ + ___ + ___ = ___ ___ counters

6. 4 groups of 3 counters

___ + ___ + ___ + ___ = ___ ___ counters

7. H.O.T. **Multi-Step** Jeff has 5 toy cars. Then his sister gives him 3 more toy cars. Each toy car has 4 wheels. How many wheels are on Jeff's toy cars?

___ wheels

8. H.O.T. Angela used these counters to act out a problem.

Write a problem that Angela could have solved with these counters.

___

___

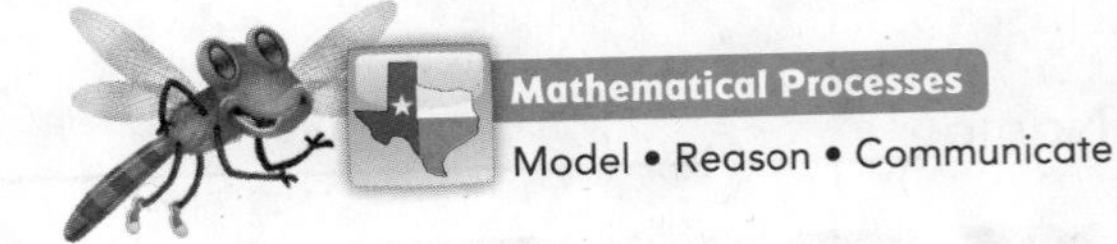

Daily Assessment Task

Choose the correct answer.

9. **Analyze** There are 2 juice boxes for each person at a picnic. There are 10 people at the picnic. How many juice boxes are there?

○ 12
○ 8
○ 20

10. Use counters to model 3 equal groups of 5 objects. Draw a picture of the groups below. Then write an addition sentence for your model.

____ + ____ + ____ = ____   ____ objects

11. **TEXAS Test Prep** Brett has 3 bags of shells. He has 4 shells in each bag. How many shells does he have?

○ 12
○ 7
○ 16

TAKE HOME ACTIVITY • Ask your child to show how he or she solved an exercise in the lesson.

Name ________________

12.1 Add Equal Groups

Add equal groups to find the total number of objects.

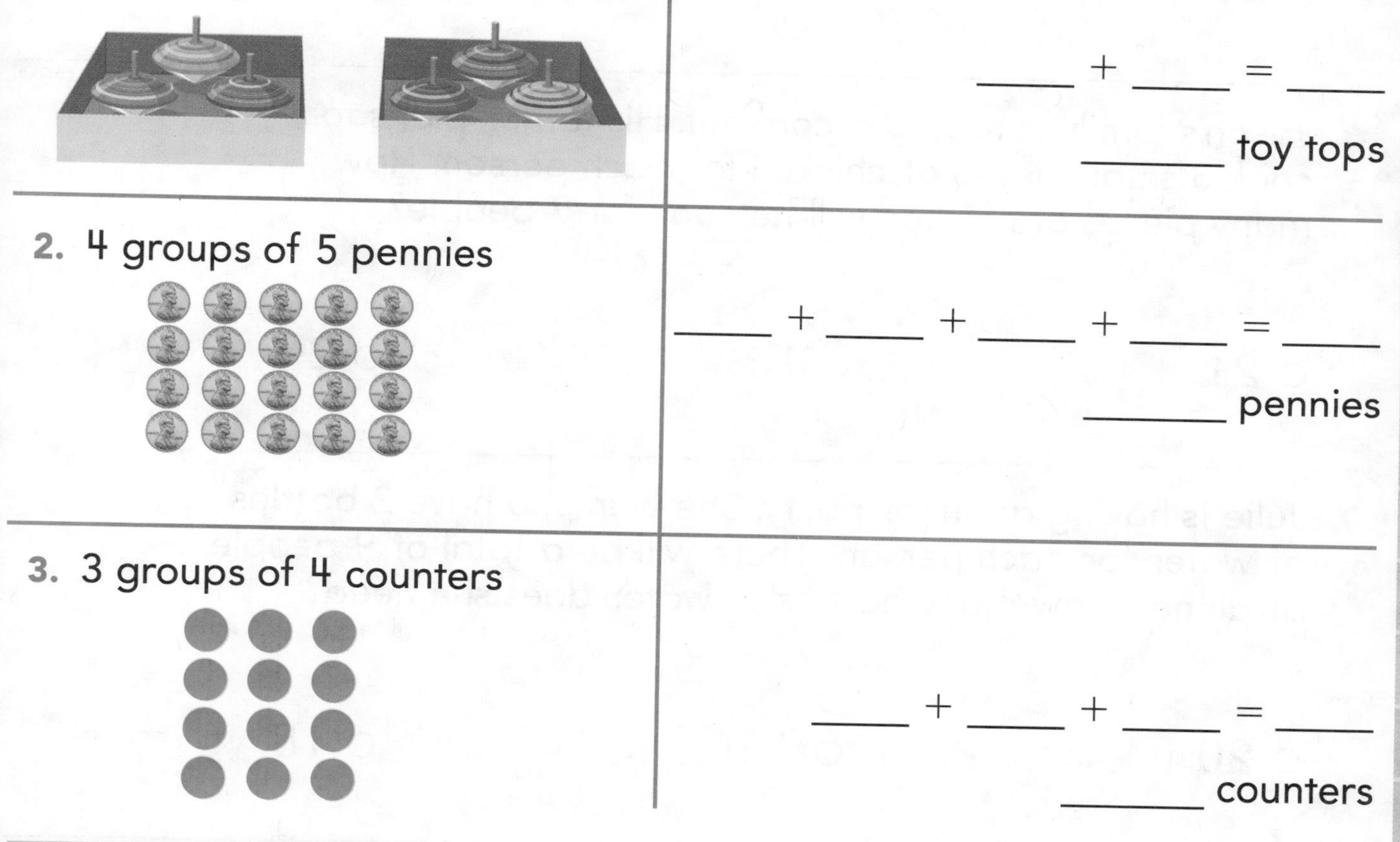

1. 2 boxes of 3 toy tops

____ + ____ = ____

______ toy tops

2. 4 groups of 5 pennies

____ + ____ + ____ + ____ = ____

______ pennies

3. 3 groups of 4 counters

____ + ____ + ____ = ____

______ counters

Problem Solving

Solve. Write or draw to explain.

4. **Multi-Step** Jonathan has 2 toy cars. Then he buys 2 more toy cars. Each toy car has 4 wheels. How many wheels are on Jonathan's toy cars?

______ wheels

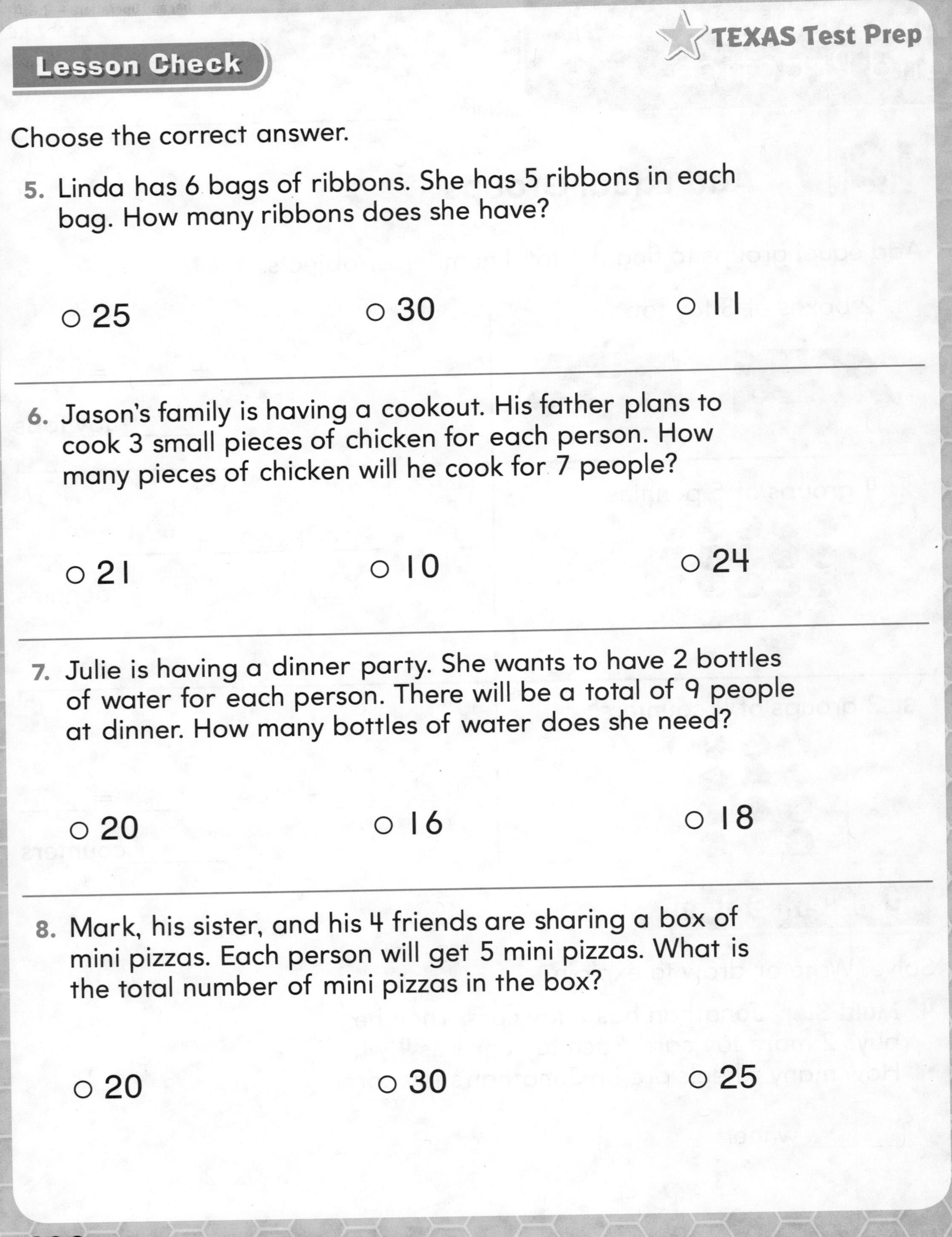

Lesson Check

TEXAS Test Prep

Choose the correct answer.

5. Linda has 6 bags of ribbons. She has 5 ribbons in each bag. How many ribbons does she have?

○ 25 ○ 30 ○ 11

6. Jason's family is having a cookout. His father plans to cook 3 small pieces of chicken for each person. How many pieces of chicken will he cook for 7 people?

○ 21 ○ 10 ○ 24

7. Julie is having a dinner party. She wants to have 2 bottles of water for each person. There will be a total of 9 people at dinner. How many bottles of water does she need?

○ 20 ○ 16 ○ 18

8. Mark, his sister, and his 4 friends are sharing a box of mini pizzas. Each person will get 5 mini pizzas. What is the total number of mini pizzas in the box?

○ 20 ○ 30 ○ 25

Name ________________________________

12.2 Describe Multiplication

Essential Question How can you describe what it means to multiply?

Explore

Use counters to model the problem. Then draw a picture of your model. Write a number sentence for it.

____

Robby has ______ DVDs.

FOR THE TEACHER • Read the problem to children. Then have them model the problem using counters and write a number sentence for it. Robby has 5 boxes of DVDs. Each box holds 7 DVDs. How many DVDs does Robby have?

Math Talk Mathematical Processes

Describe the groups that you drew.

Model and Draw

When you **multiply**, you join equal groups.
Use the pictures to describe equal groups.

There are __4__ cans.

Each can has __3__ tennis balls.

So, there are _____ tennis balls in all.

There are _____ trays.

Each tray has _____ muffins.

So, there are _____ muffins in all.

Share and Show

MATH BOARD

Use the pictures to describe equal groups.

1. There are _____ boxes of crayons.

   Each __________ has

   __________________.

   So, there are __________________ in all.

2. There are _____ bicycles.

   Each __________________ has

   __________________.

   So, there are __________________ in all.

Name ______________________________

Problem Solving

Use the pictures to describe equal groups.

3. There are _____ stacks of books.

Each stack ____________________.

So, ____________________________

____________________________.

4. There are _____ fish bowls.

Each bowl ____________________.

So, ____________________________

____________________________.

5. H.O.T. **Multi-Step** Use the pictures to describe the equal groups. Then write the total number of legs.

Math on the Spot

____

____

____

____

6. H.O.T. Caleb uses 3 toothpicks to make a triangle. He makes 3 triangles. How many toothpicks does he use?

_____ toothpicks

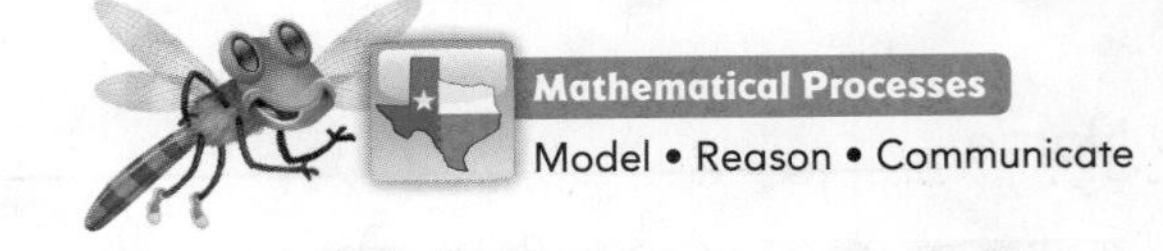

Daily Assessment Task

Choose the correct answer.

7. **Analyze** One egg carton can hold 12 eggs. How many eggs will fit in 2 cartons?

   ○ 24

   ○ 12

   ○ 28

8. Use the pictures to describe equal groups.

   There are _____ bowls of apples.

   Each bowl ____________________.

   So, ____________________

   ____________________.

9. **TEXAS Test Prep** Tim has 5 cards. He puts 3 stickers on each card. How many stickers does he use?

   ○ 8

   ○ 15

   ○ 10

TAKE HOME ACTIVITY • Ask your child to show how he or she solved an exercise in the lesson.

Name ____________________

12.3 Write Multiplication Stories

TEKS Number and Operations—2.6.A
MATHEMATICAL PROCESSES 2.1.E, 2.1.F, 2.1.G

Essential Question What should you include when writing multiplication stories?

Explore

Hands On

Use counters to model the problem. Draw what you modeled. Then write an addition sentence for the problem.

____

Carlos has ______ blocks.

____

Sam has ______ blocks.

FOR THE TEACHER • Read the following two problems. For each problem, have children model with counters and then draw a picture and show the addition. Carlos has 2 blue blocks, 3 red blocks, and 5 green blocks. How many blocks does Carlos have? Sam has 5 blue blocks, 5 red blocks, and 5 green blocks. How many blocks does Sam have?

Math Talk Mathematical Processes

Describe how the two problems are alike and how they are different.

Model and Draw

This story is about equal groups.
The picture shows the story.

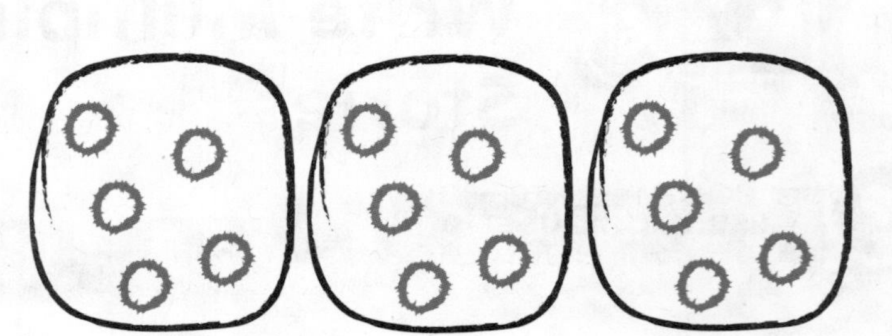

Three children each have 5 marbles. They have 15 marbles in all.

Share and Show

Write stories about equal groups of toys. Use counters to show the groups. Draw a picture for each story.

1. ______________________________

2. ______________________________

Name ______________________

Problem Solving

Write stories about equal groups of marbles. Use counters to show the groups. Draw a picture for each story.

3. ______________________

4. ______________________

Solve.

5. **H.O.T.** **Multi-Step** Drew has 2 bags with 10 marbles in each bag. Tony has 5 bags with 4 marbles in each bag. Use words to compare the number of marbles that Drew and Tony each have.

____

____

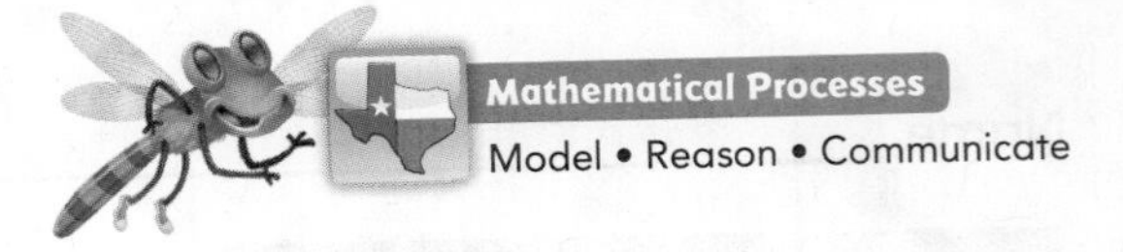

Daily Assessment Task

Choose the correct answer.

6. **Connect** Mary Ann sees 4 starfish like the one shown. Look at the picture of a starfish. Which sentence best describes what she sees?

- ○ She sees 4 starfish with 5 legs each.
- ○ She sees 5 starfish with 4 legs each.
- ○ She sees 4 starfish with 3 legs each.

7. Write a story about equal groups of apples. Use counters to show the groups. Draw a picture for your story.

____

____

____

____

8. **TEXAS Test Prep** Which sentence best matches the picture?

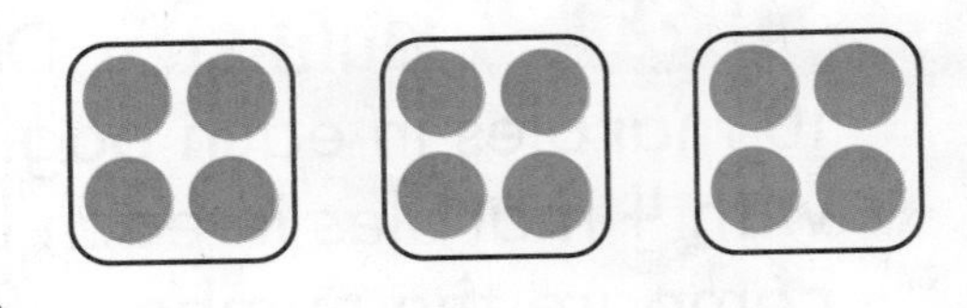

- ○ There are 3 groups of 4 counters each.
- ○ There are 3 groups of 3 counters each.
- ○ There are 7 groups of 2 counters each.

TAKE HOME ACTIVITY • Ask your child to show how he or she solved an exercise in the lesson.

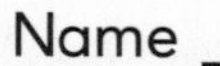
Name ____________________

TEKS Number and Operations—2.6.B

MATHEMATICAL PROCESSES
2.1.A, 2.1.D, 2.1.E

12.4 Separate into Equal Groups

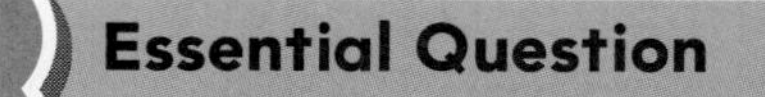
Essential Question

How can you find the number of equal groups or the number in each equal group?

Explore Real World

Hands On

Draw to show the problem. Complete the sentences.

There are ______ groups of marbles.

There are ______ marbles in each group.

There are ______ marbles in all.

FOR THE TEACHER • Read the following problem to children. Then have children model the problem and complete the sentences. Alex has 5 bags. He places 2 marbles in each bag. How many marbles does he have?

Math Talk
Mathematical Processes

Explain how you solved the problem.

Model and Draw

When you **divide**, you separate into equal groups.

Jose has 12 crayons. He puts the same number of crayons in each of 3 boxes. How many crayons does he put in each box?

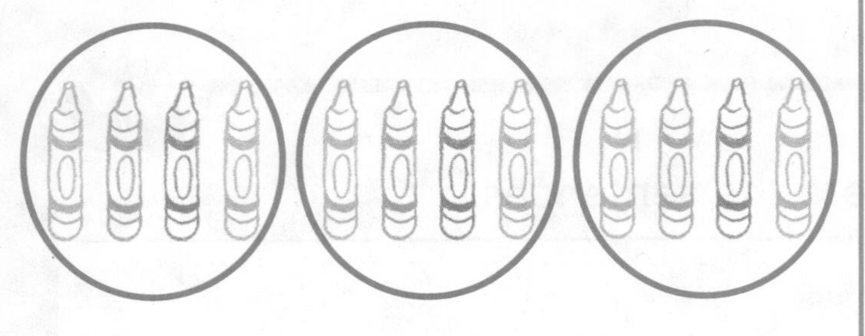

_____ crayons

Anna will place 12 pencils in some boxes. She puts 6 pencils in each box. How many boxes will she use?

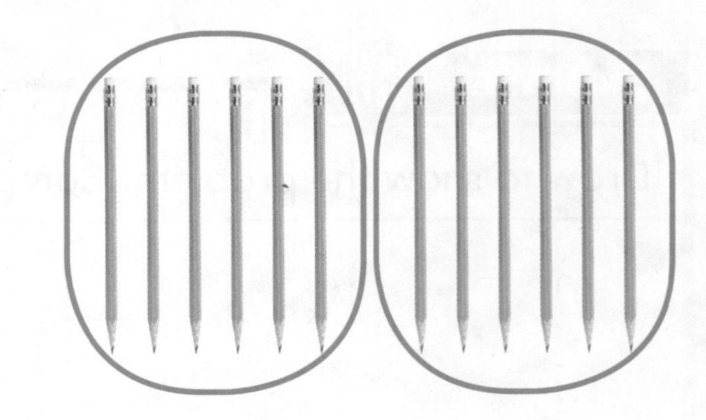

_____ boxes

Share and Show

Use counters. Then draw to show the number in each group.

1. 20 cookies

   5 plates

   _____ cookies on each plate

Draw to find the number of equal groups.

2. 21 buttons

   3 buttons on each shirt

   _____ shirts

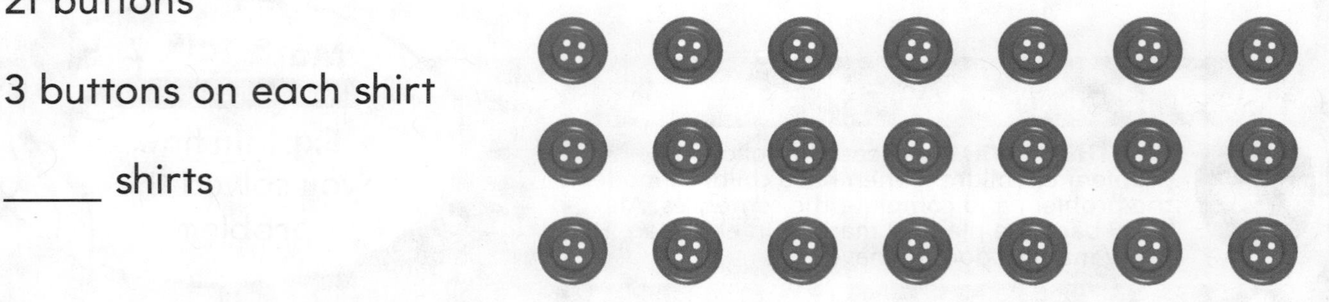

Name ___________________________

Problem Solving

Use counters. Then draw to show the number in each group.

3. 16 birds

4 birdfeeders

_____ birds at each birdfeeder

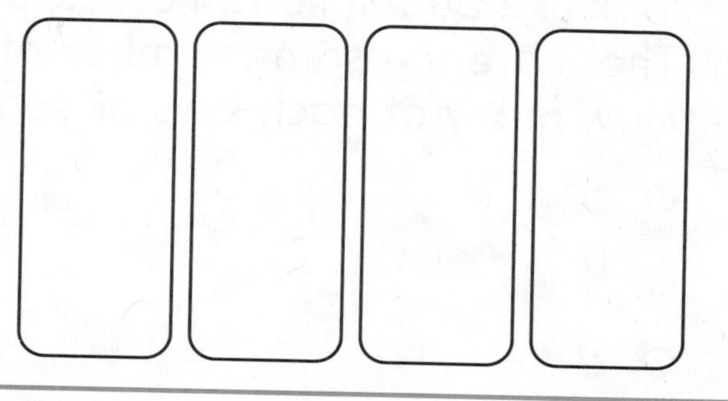

Draw to find the number of equal groups.

4. 15 cupcakes

5 cupcakes on each tray

_____ trays

Solve. Write or draw to explain.

5. H.O.T. **Multi-Step** Amy has 12 stickers. Jen has 9 stickers. They place 7 stickers on each page of a book. How many pages are in the book?

_____ pages

6. H.O.T. Eric has 24 toothpicks. He uses each toothpick as 1 side of a square. How many squares can Eric make?

_____ squares

Daily Assessment Task

Mathematical Processes
Model • Reason • Communicate

Choose the correct answer.

7. **Reasoning** A ride at the fair has 24 seats that look like bears, lions, horses, and zebras. There are the same number of each animal. How many of each kind of seat are there?

- ○ 6
- ○ 4
- ○ 8

8. Use counters to model the problem. Then draw to show the number in each group.

12 oranges

4 baskets

_____ oranges in each basket

9. **TEXAS Test Prep** Oliver has 18 cookies. He places an equal number of cookies on 9 plates. How many cookies are on each plate?

- ○ 8
- ○ 9
- ○ 2

TAKE HOME ACTIVITY • Ask your child to show how he or she solved an exercise in the lesson.

Name ______________________________

TEKS Number and Operations—2.6.B
MATHEMATICAL PROCESSES 2.1.D, 2.1.E, 2.1.G

12.5 Describe Division

Essential Question How can you describe what it means to divide?

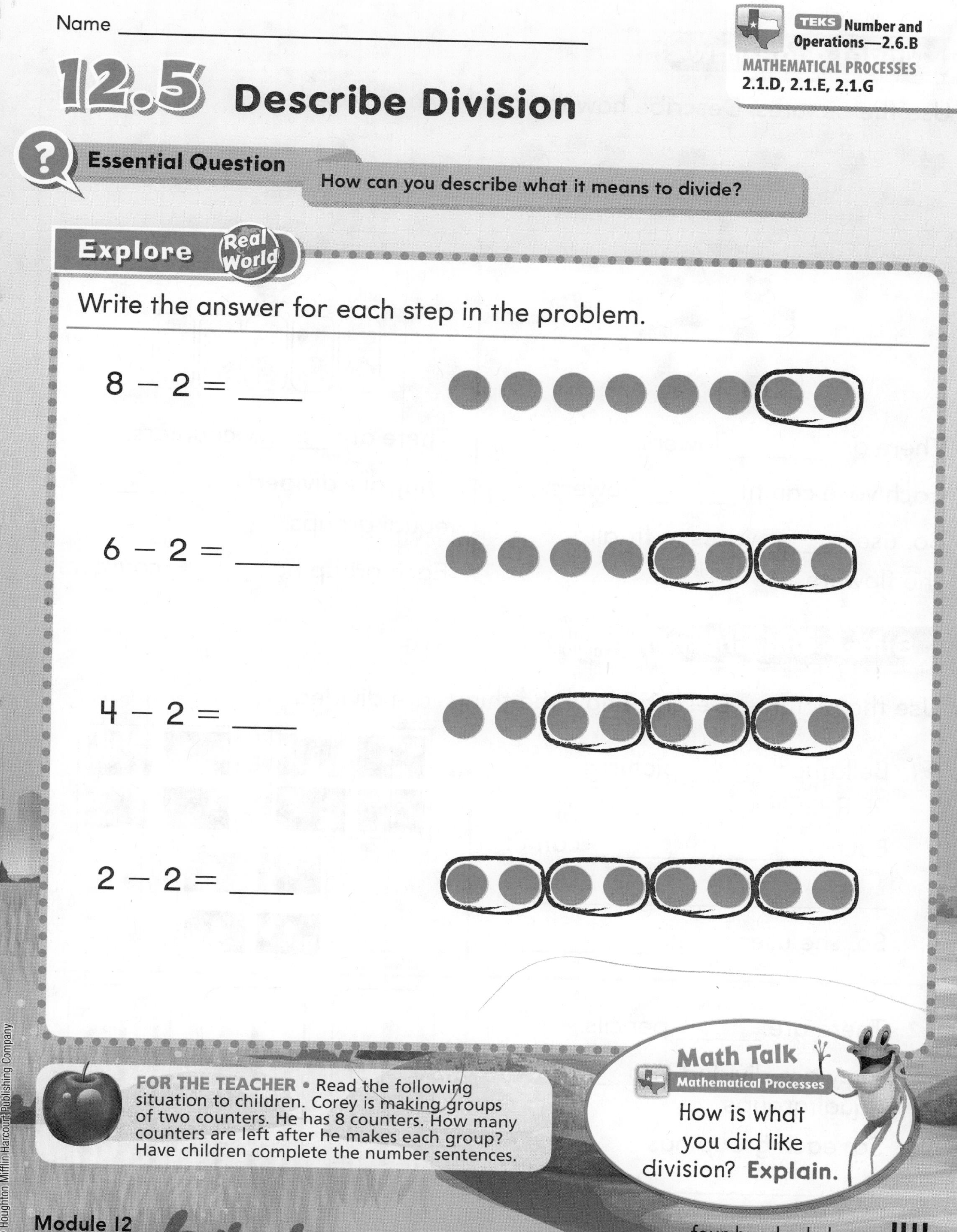

Explore Real World

Write the answer for each step in the problem.

8 − 2 = ____

6 − 2 = ____

4 − 2 = ____

2 − 2 = ____

FOR THE TEACHER • Read the following situation to children. Corey is making groups of two counters. He has 8 counters. How many counters are left after he makes each group? Have children complete the number sentences.

Math Talk Mathematical Processes

How is what you did like division? **Explain.**

Model and Draw

Use the pictures. Describe how the group was divided.

There are ______ flowers.

Each vase can fit ______ flowers.

So, use ______ vases to fit all the flowers.

There are ______ counters.

They are divided into ______ equal groups.

Each group has ______ counters.

Share and Show

MATH BOARD

Use the pictures. Describe how the things are divided.

1. Bella has ______ pictures on pages.

   Each ______________ can fit

   ______________________.

   So, she uses ______________.

2. There are ______ pencils.

   They are divided into ______ equal groups.

   So, each group has

   ______________________.

Name ______________________

Problem Solving

Use the pictures. Describe how the things are divided.

3. Jack has ______ cookies on plates.

   Each ______________________

   ______________________.

   So, he uses ______________________.

4. There are ______ shells. They are

   divided into ______________________.

   So, ______________________

   ______________________.

Solve. Write or draw to explain.

5. **H.O.T.** **Multi-Step** Chase has 20 pebbles and Mia has 7 pebbles. They divide all the pebbles into groups of 3. How many equal groups are there?

   _____ equal groups

6. **H.O.T.** Lily buys 6 bags of dog treats. Each bag has the same number of treats. She buys 24 treats in all. How many treats are in each bag?

   _____ treats

Daily Assessment Task

Choose the correct answer.

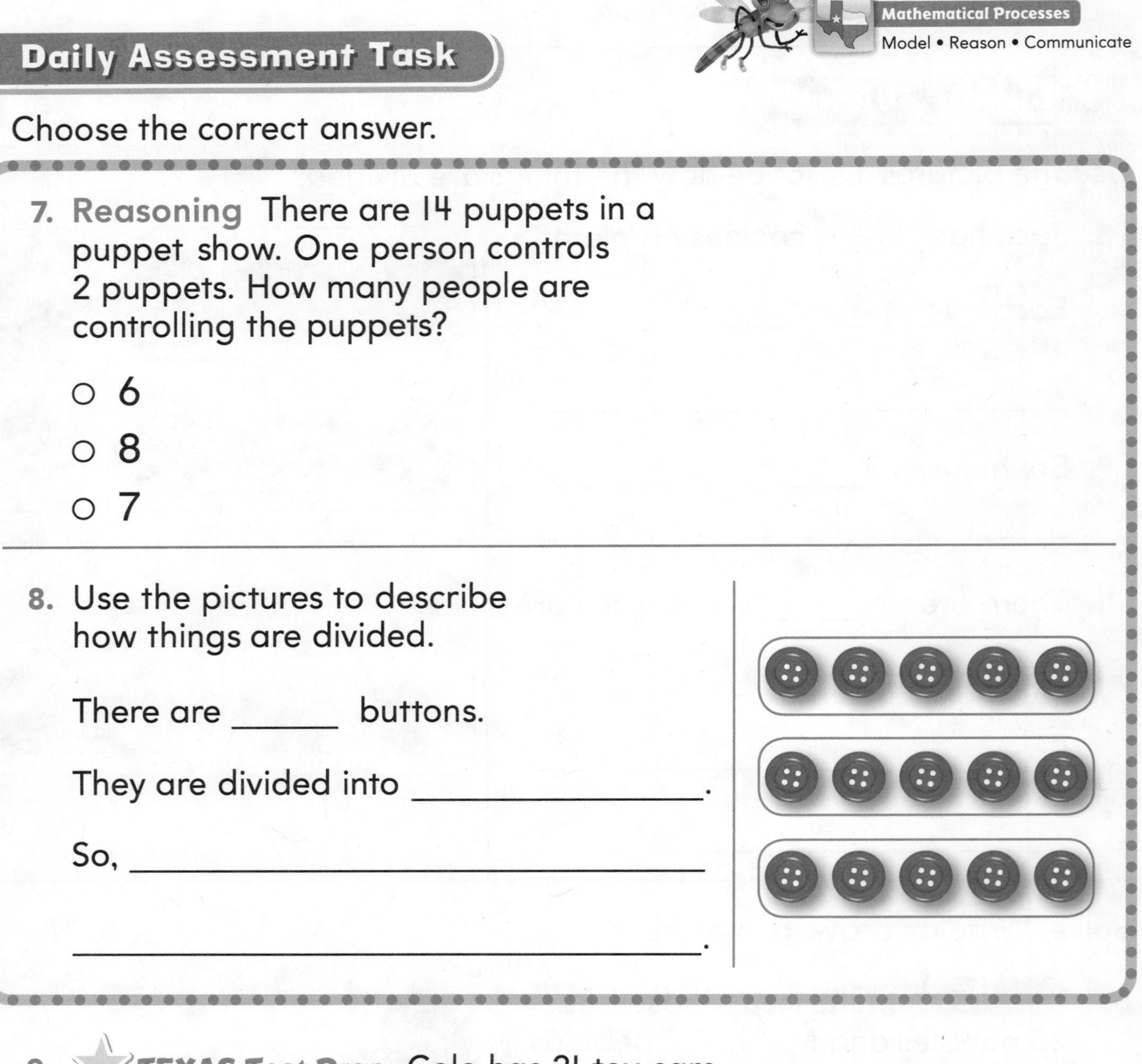

7. **Reasoning** There are 14 puppets in a puppet show. One person controls 2 puppets. How many people are controlling the puppets?

   ○ 6
   ○ 8
   ○ 7

8. Use the pictures to describe how things are divided.

   There are ______ buttons.

   They are divided into ________________.

   So, ______________________________

   ______________________________.

9. **TEXAS Test Prep** Cole has 21 toy cars. He divides them into 3 equal groups. How many toy cars are in each group?

   ○ 18
   ○ 24
   ○ 7

TAKE HOME ACTIVITY • Ask your child to show how he or she solved an exercise in the lesson.

TEKS Number and Operations—2.6.B
MATHEMATICAL PROCESSES 2.1.D, 2.1.E, 2.1.G

Name ______________________

12.5 Describe Division

Use the pictures. Describe how the things are divided.

1. Betty has ______ carrots on plates.

   Each __________________.

   So, she uses __________.

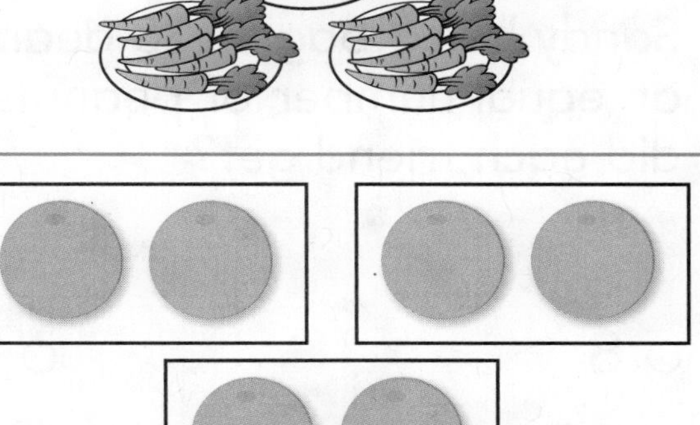

2. There are 6 oranges. They are divided into __________________.

   So, ________________________.

Problem Solving

Solve. Write or draw to explain.

3. Jordan buys 4 boxes of postcards. He buys 28 postcards in all. How many postcards are in each box?

   ______ postcards

4. **Multi-Step** Carla has 12 daisies and 6 roses. She divides the flowers into groups of 3. How many flowers are in each group?

   ______ groups

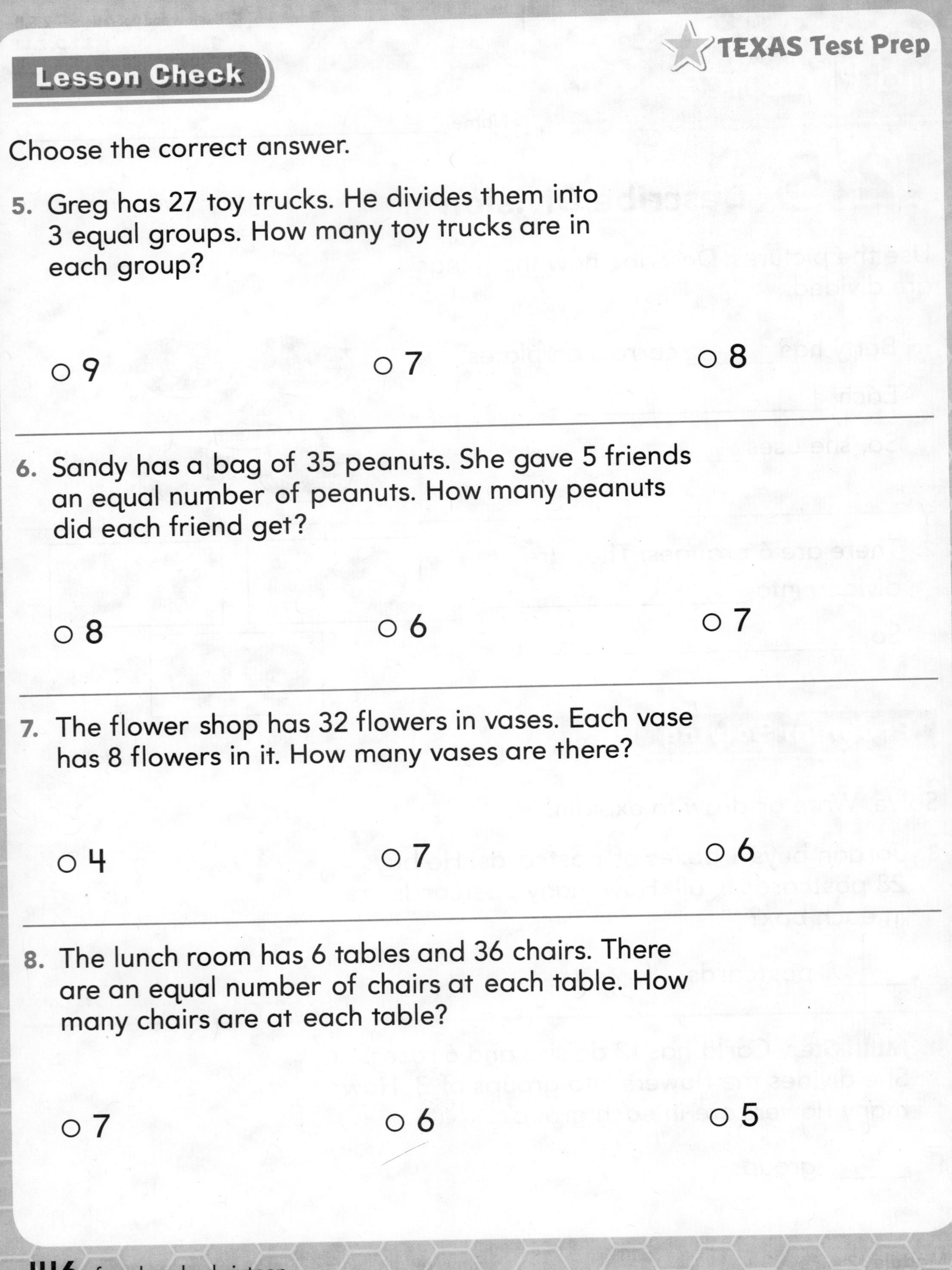

Lesson Check

TEXAS Test Prep

Choose the correct answer.

5. Greg has 27 toy trucks. He divides them into 3 equal groups. How many toy trucks are in each group?

○ 9 ○ 7 ○ 8

6. Sandy has a bag of 35 peanuts. She gave 5 friends an equal number of peanuts. How many peanuts did each friend get?

○ 8 ○ 6 ○ 7

7. The flower shop has 32 flowers in vases. Each vase has 8 flowers in it. How many vases are there?

○ 4 ○ 7 ○ 6

8. The lunch room has 6 tables and 36 chairs. There are an equal number of chairs at each table. How many chairs are at each table?

○ 7 ○ 6 ○ 5

Name ______________________________

TEKS Number and Operations—2.6.B
MATHEMATICAL PROCESSES 2.1.F, 2.1.G

12.6 Write Division Stories

Essential Question What should you include in stories about dividing?

Explore Real World

Hands On

Use counters to model the problem.
Then draw what you modeled.

_____ boxes

_____ cards

FOR THE TEACHER • Read the following problem. Have children use counters to model and then draw the problem. Ian has 18 cupcakes. He places the cupcakes into boxes that can each fit 9 cupcakes. How many boxes will Ian use? Repeat for this problem. Ali has 10 cards. She places them in 2 equal rows. How many cards are in each row?

Math Talk Mathematical Processes

Explain how you found the answer to the first problem.

Model and Draw

This story is about dividing into equal groups.
The picture shows the story.

There are 16 books in 4 equal stacks.

So, there are 4 books in each stack.

Share and Show

Write stories about dividing toys into equal groups. Use counters to show the groups. Draw a picture for each story.

1. ______________________________

2. ______________________________

Name ________________________________

Problem Solving

Write stories about dividing marbles into equal groups.
Use counters to show the groups. Draw a picture for each story.

3. ________________________________
____
____
____
____

4. ________________________________
____
____
____
____

Solve. Write or draw to explain.

5. H.O.T. **Multi-Step** Adam has 29 golf balls. He gives 4 golf balls to his brother. Then he puts an equal amount in each of 5 boxes. How many golf balls are in each box?

_____ golf balls

Math on the Spot

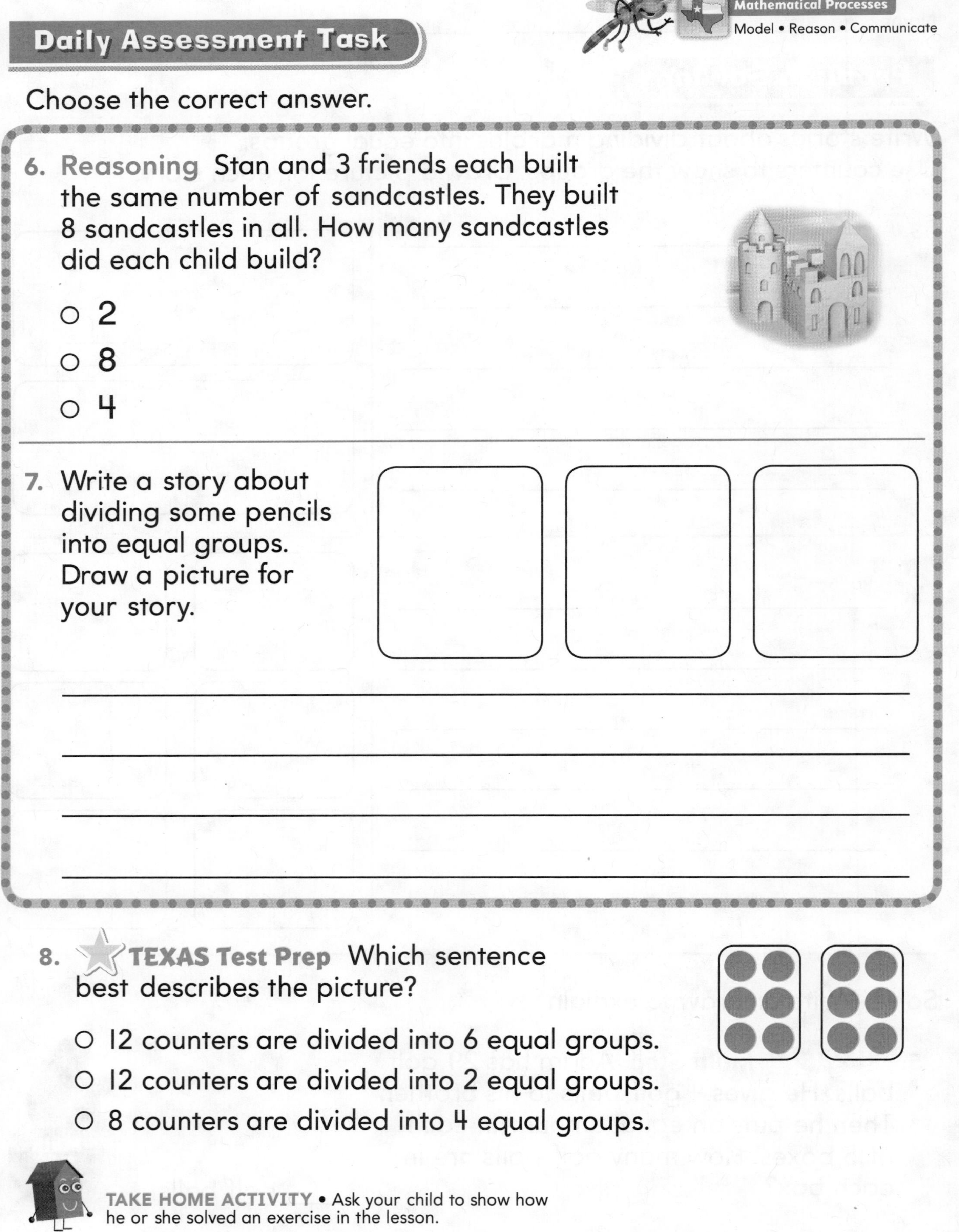

Daily Assessment Task

Mathematical Processes
Model • Reason • Communicate

Choose the correct answer.

6. **Reasoning** Stan and 3 friends each built the same number of sandcastles. They built 8 sandcastles in all. How many sandcastles did each child build?

- ○ 2
- ○ 8
- ○ 4

7. Write a story about dividing some pencils into equal groups. Draw a picture for your story.

____

____

____

____

8. **TEXAS Test Prep** Which sentence best describes the picture?

- ○ 12 counters are divided into 6 equal groups.
- ○ 12 counters are divided into 2 equal groups.
- ○ 8 counters are divided into 4 equal groups.

TAKE HOME ACTIVITY • Ask your child to show how he or she solved an exercise in the lesson.

Name ______________________

12.6 Write Division Stories

Write two stories about equal groups of toy cars. Draw a picture for each story.

1. ______________________________
____
____
____

2. ______________________________
____
____
____

Problem Solving

3. **Multi-Step** Shirley has 30 shells. She gives 9 shells to her sister. Then she puts an equal amount of the remaining shells in each of 3 boxes. How many shells are in each box?

_____ shells

Lesson Check

TEXAS Test Prep

Choose the correct answer.

5. Which sentence best describes the picture?

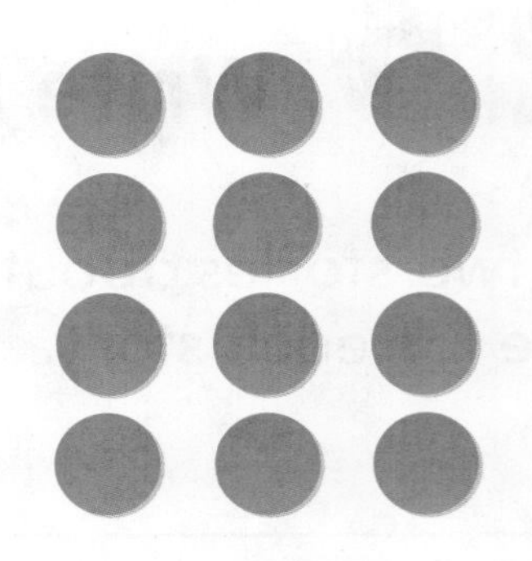

- ○ 12 counters are divided into 6 groups.
- ○ 12 counters are divided into 5 groups.
- ○ 12 counters are divided into 3 groups.

6. There are 6 different colors of shirts at Bell's store. 18 shirts were sold. An equal number of each color was sold. How many of each color shirt was sold?

○ 12 ○ 3 ○ 5

7. There are 35 fish in 5 fish tanks. Each tank has the same number of fish. How many fish are in each tank?

○ 7 ○ 8 ○ 6

8. Tim has 30 golf balls. He divides them equally among 6 friends. Which sentence best describes how many golf balls each friend got?

- ○ 5 friends each get 6 golf balls.
- ○ 7 friends each get 6 golf balls.
- ○ 6 friends each get 5 golf balls.

Name ______________________________

Module 12 Assessment

Concepts and Skills

Use the pictures to describe the equal groups.

1. There are ______ cookies.

   There are ______ plates.

   So, there are ______ cookies on each plate. TEKS 2.6.B

2. There are ______ trays.

   Each tray has ______ muffins.

   So, there are ______ muffins in all. TEKS 2.6.A

3. Write a division story about equal groups of fish. Use counters to show the groups. Draw a picture to show your story. TEKS 2.6.B

____

____

____

____

Fill in the bubble for the correct answer choice.

4. Angie has 20 cookies. She puts an equal number of cookies on each of 5 plates. How many cookies are on each plate? TEKS 2.6.B

- ○ 4
- ○ 25
- ○ 15

5. Peter has 5 pages of pictures. Each page has 5 pictures. How many pictures does Peter have? TEKS 2.6.A

- ○ 15
- ○ 10
- ○ 25

6. Jamie buys 32 crayons. There are 8 crayons in each box. How many boxes does Jamie buy? TEKS 2.6.B

- ○ 24
- ○ 4
- ○ 36

7. Zach buys 3 packs of pencils. Anna buys 3 packs of pencils. Each pack has 5 pencils. How many pencils do they buy? TEKS 2.6.A

- ○ 15
- ○ 11
- ○ 30

Picture Glossary

addend sumando

5 + 8 = 13

(arrows to 5 and 8) **addends**

a.m. a.m.

Times after midnight and before noon are written with **a.m.**

11:00 a.m. is in the morning.

bar graph gráfica de barras

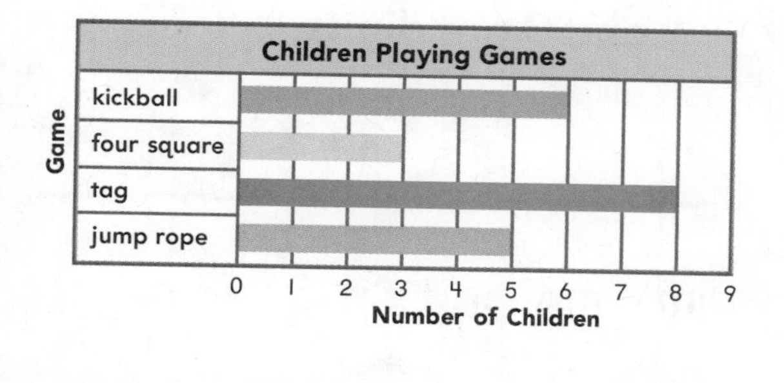

borrow pedir prestado

You **borrow** money when another person gives you money that you will need to pay back.

cent sign signo de centavo

53¢

(arrow to ¢) **cent sign**

centimeter centímetro

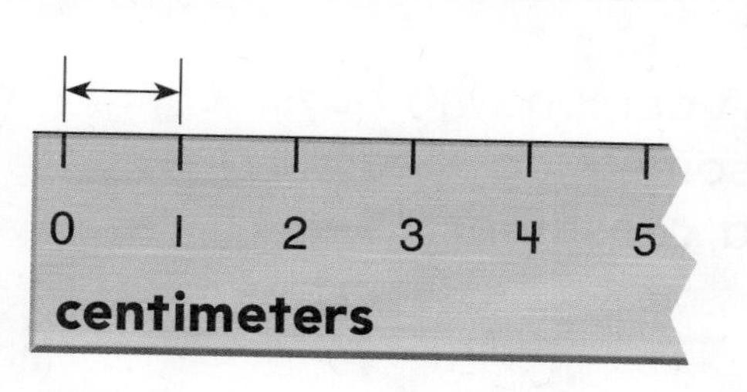

compare comparar

Use these symbols when you **compare**: $>$, $<$, or $=$.

$241 > 234$

$123 < 128$

$247 = 247$

conclusion conclusión

When you look at data and make a judgment about it, this is a **conclusion**.

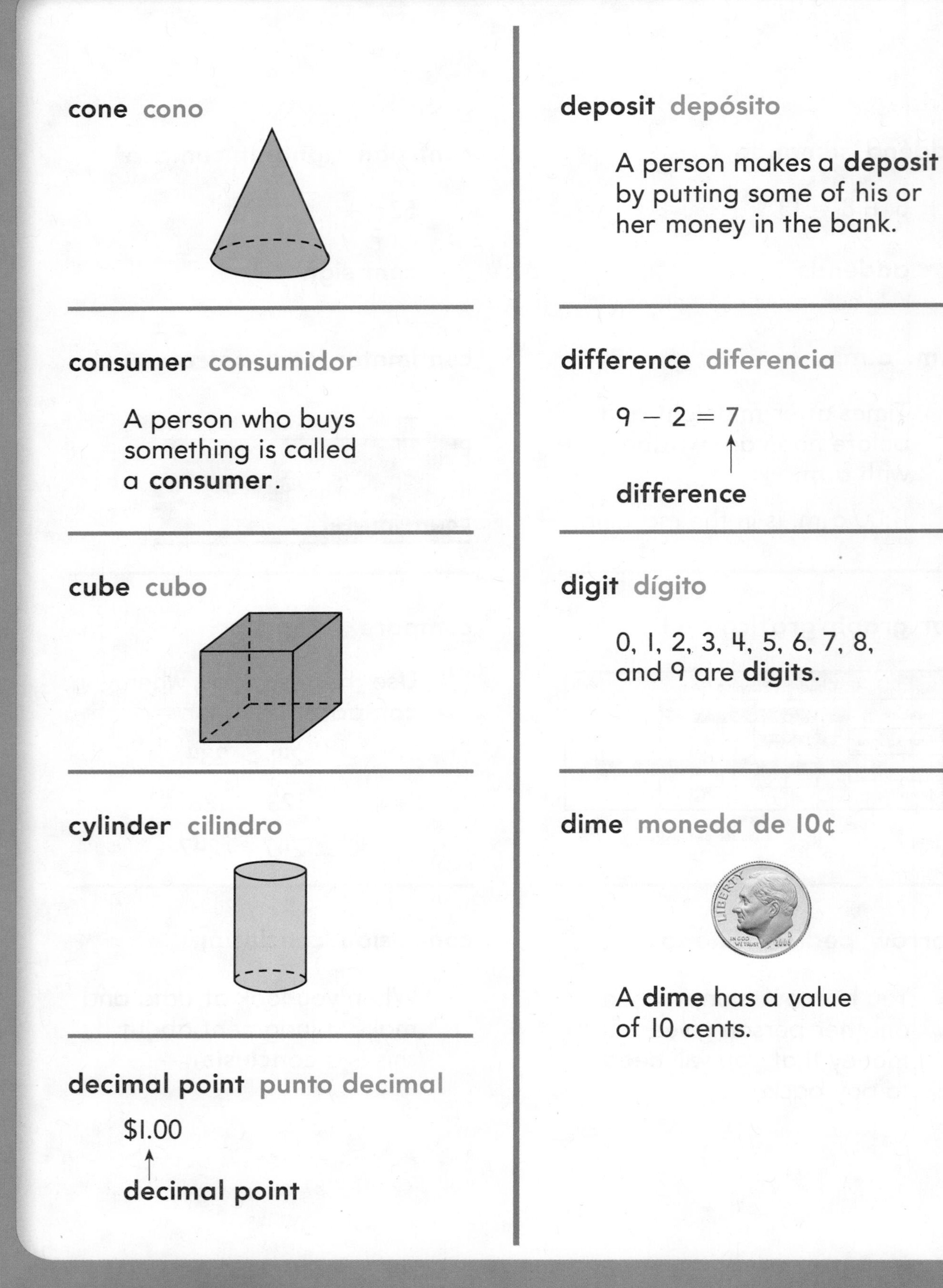

cone cono

consumer consumidor

A person who buys something is called a **consumer**.

cube cubo

cylinder cilindro

decimal point punto decimal

\$1.00

↑

decimal point

deposit depósito

A person makes a **deposit** by putting some of his or her money in the bank.

difference diferencia

9 − 2 = 7

↑

difference

digit dígito

0, 1, 2, 3, 4, 5, 6, 7, 8, and 9 are **digits**.

dime moneda de 10¢

A **dime** has a value of 10 cents.

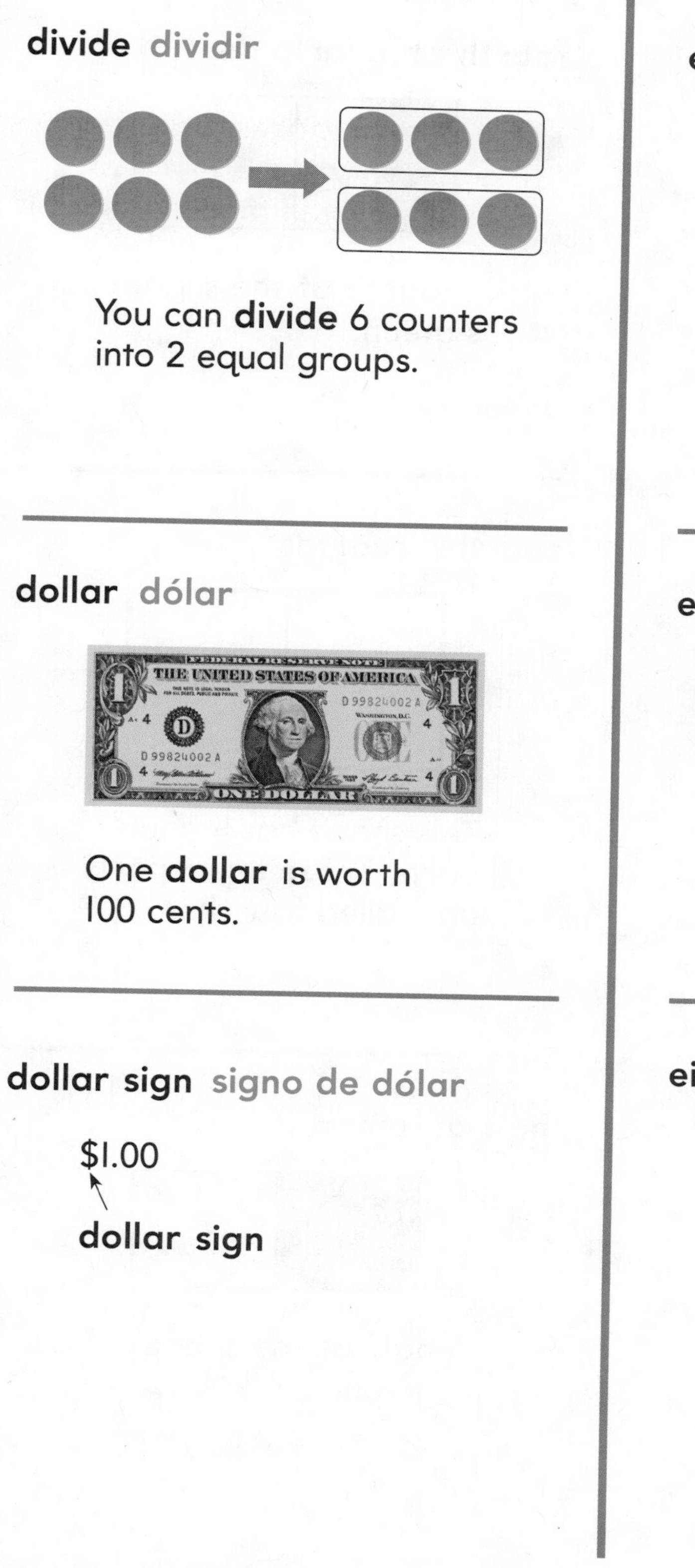

divide dividir

You can **divide** 6 counters into 2 equal groups.

dollar dólar

One **dollar** is worth 100 cents.

dollar sign signo de dólar

$1.00

dollar sign

edge arista

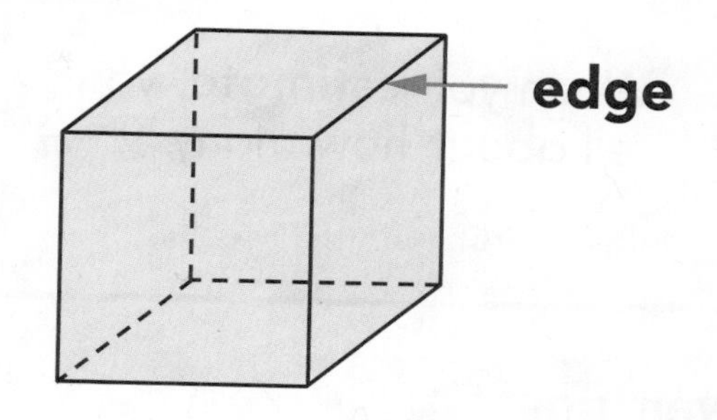

An **edge** is formed where two faces of a three-dimensional solid meet.

eighth of octavo de

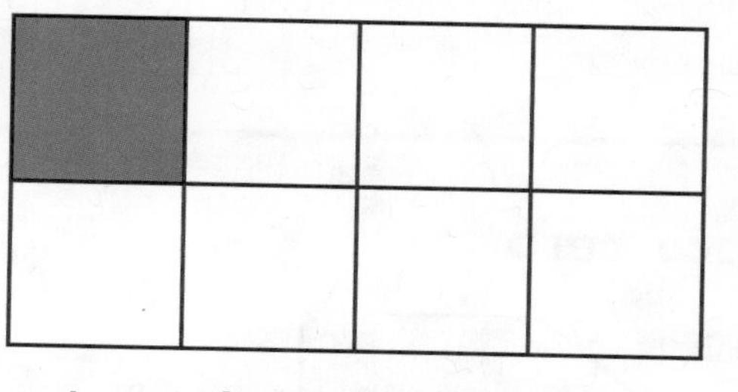

An **eighth of** the shape is blue.

eighths octavos

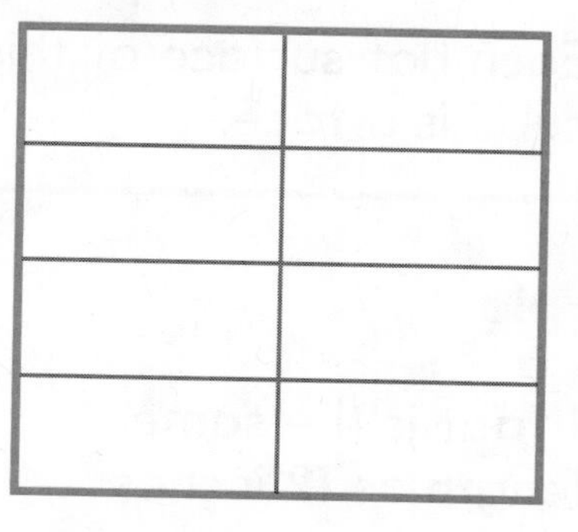

This shape has 8 equal parts. These parts are called **eighths**.

estimate estimar

When you **estimate**, you tell about how many.

even par

2, 4, 6, 8, 10, . . .

even numbers

face cara

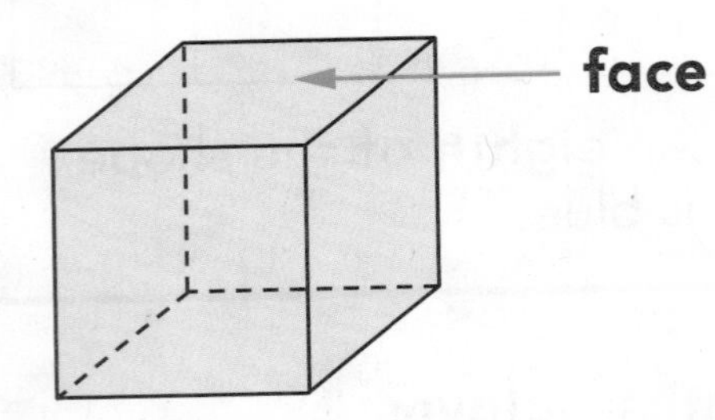

Each flat surface of this cube is a **face**.

foot pie

1 **foot** is the same length as 12 inches.

fourth of cuarto de

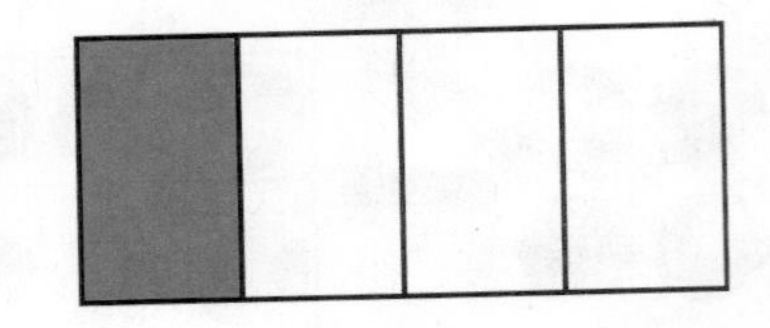

A **fourth of** the shape is green.

fourths cuartos

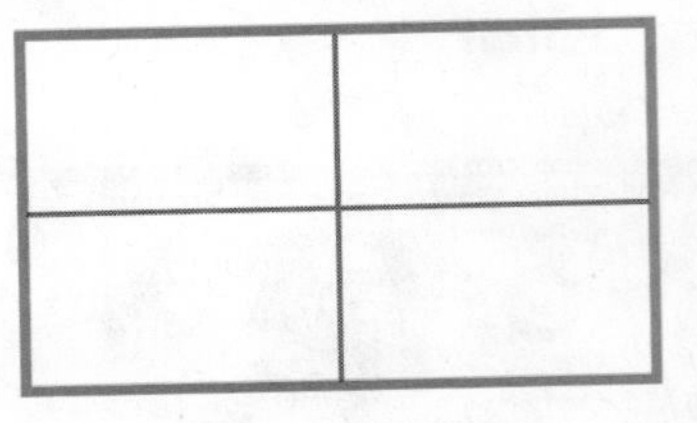

This shape has 4 equal parts. These equal parts are called **fourths**.

half of mitad de

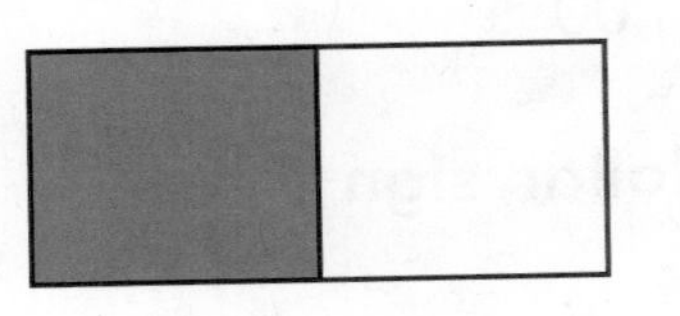

A **half of** the shape is green.

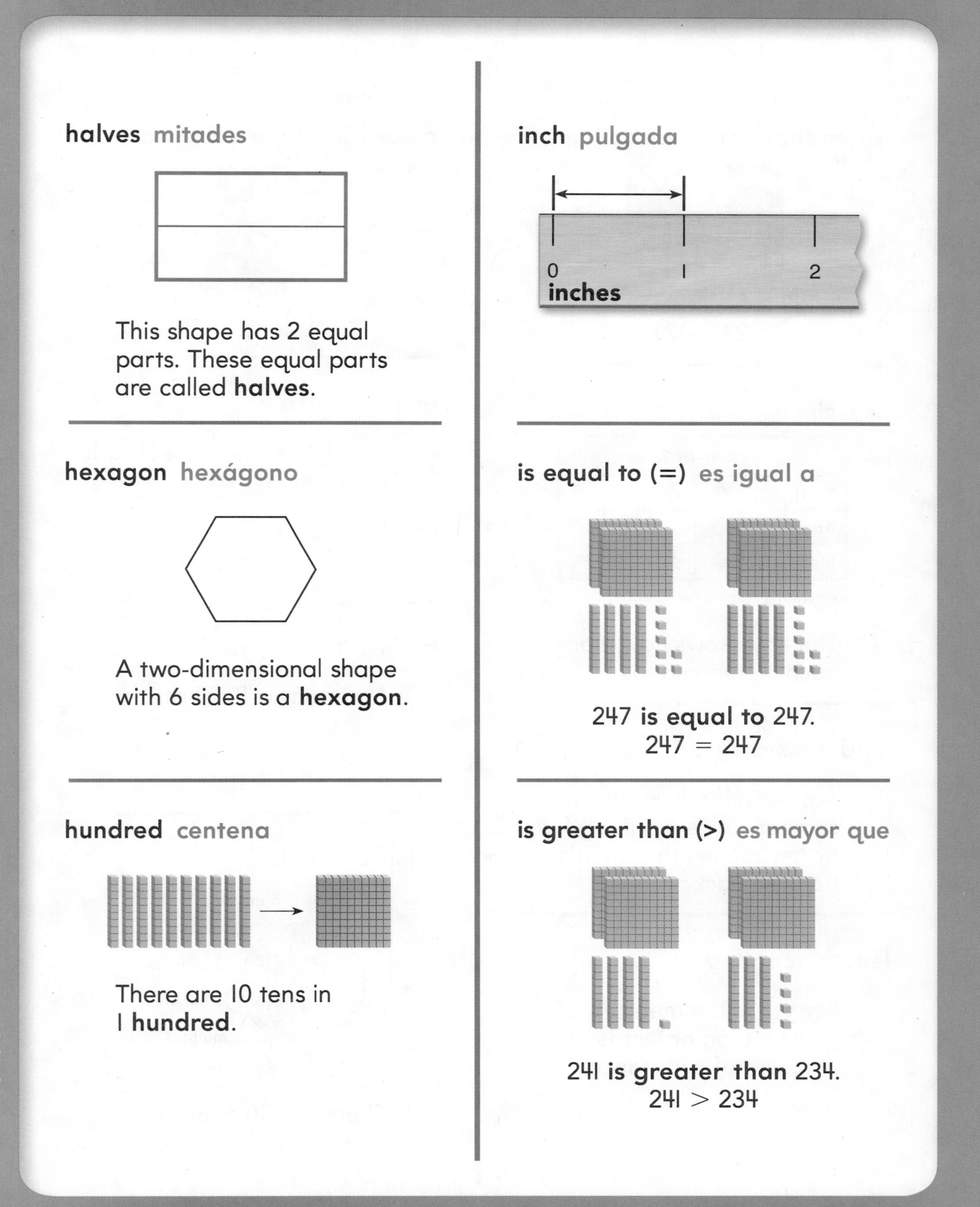

halves mitades

This shape has 2 equal parts. These equal parts are called **halves**.

hexagon hexágono

A two-dimensional shape with 6 sides is a **hexagon**.

hundred centena

There are 10 tens in 1 **hundred**.

inch pulgada

is equal to (=) es igual a

247 **is equal to** 247.
$247 = 247$

is greater than (>) es mayor que

241 **is greater than** 234.
$241 > 234$

is less than (<) es menor que

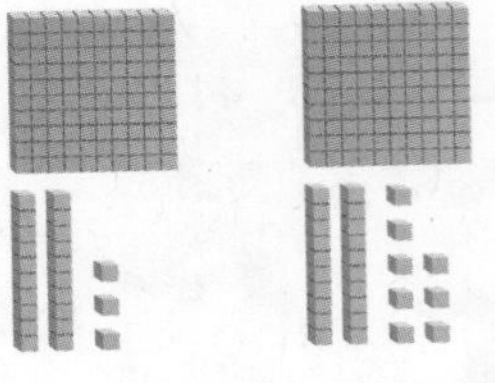

123 **is less than** 128.
$123 < 128$

key clave

Number of Pets				
Scott	◆	◆	◆	
Andre	◆			
Maddie	◆	◆		

Key: Each ◆ stands for 1 pet.

The **key** shows how many each picture stands for.

lend prestar

A person **lends** money to someone else by giving him or her money that needs to be paid back.

length longitud

Length is the measure of how long an object is or the measure of a distance.

measuring tape cinta para medir

meter metro

1 **meter** is the same length as 100 centimeters.

midnight medianoche

Midnight is 12:00 at night.

minute minuto

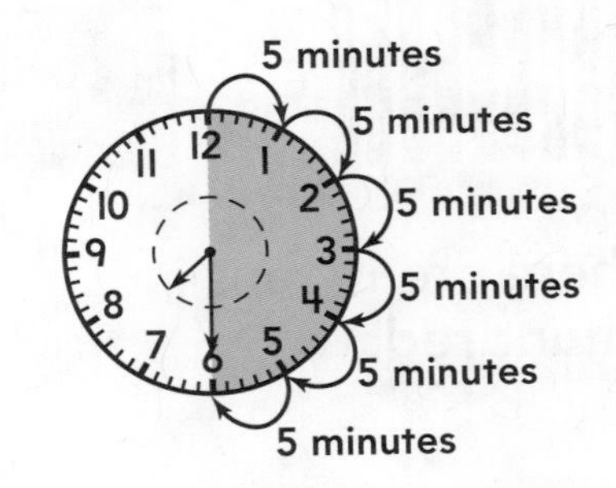

There are 30 **minutes** in a half hour.

multiply multiplicar

6 counters in all

When you **multiply**, you combine equal groups to find how many in all.

nickel moneda de 5¢

A **nickel** has a value of 5 cents.

noon mediodía

Noon is 12:00 in the daytime.

octagon octágono

A two-dimensional shape with 8 sides is an **octagon**.

odd impar

1, 3, 5, 7, 9, 11, . . .

odd numbers

penny moneda de 1¢

A **penny** has a value of 1 cent.

pentagon pentágono

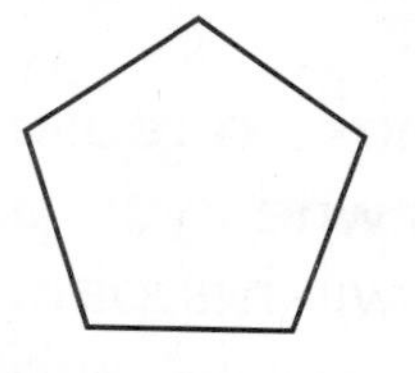

A two-dimensional shape with 5 sides is a **pentagon**.

pictograph pictografía

Number of Soccer Games							
March	⚽	⚽	⚽	⚽			
April	⚽	⚽	⚽				
May	⚽	⚽	⚽	⚽	⚽	⚽	
June	⚽	⚽	⚽	⚽	⚽	⚽	⚽

Key: Each ⚽ stands for 1 game.

polygon polígono

A **polygon** is any closed, two-dimensional shape with only straight sides.

---

p.m. p.m.

Times after noon and before midnight are written with **p.m.**

11:00 p.m. is in the evening.

---

predict predecir

You make a reasonable guess when you **predict** what will happen.

---

producer productor

A person who makes something is called a **producer**.

---

quadrilateral cuadrilátero

A two-dimensional shape with 4 sides is a **quadrilateral**.

---

quarter moneda de 25¢

A **quarter** has a value of 25 cents.

---

rectangular prism prisma rectangular

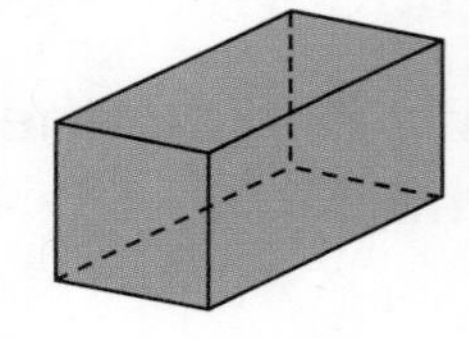

---

regroup reagrupar

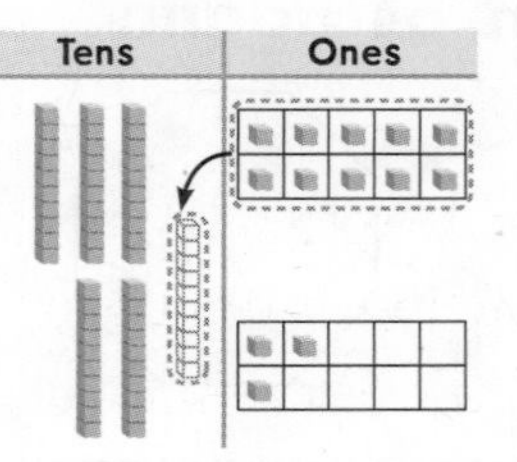

You can trade 10 ones for 1 ten to **regroup**.

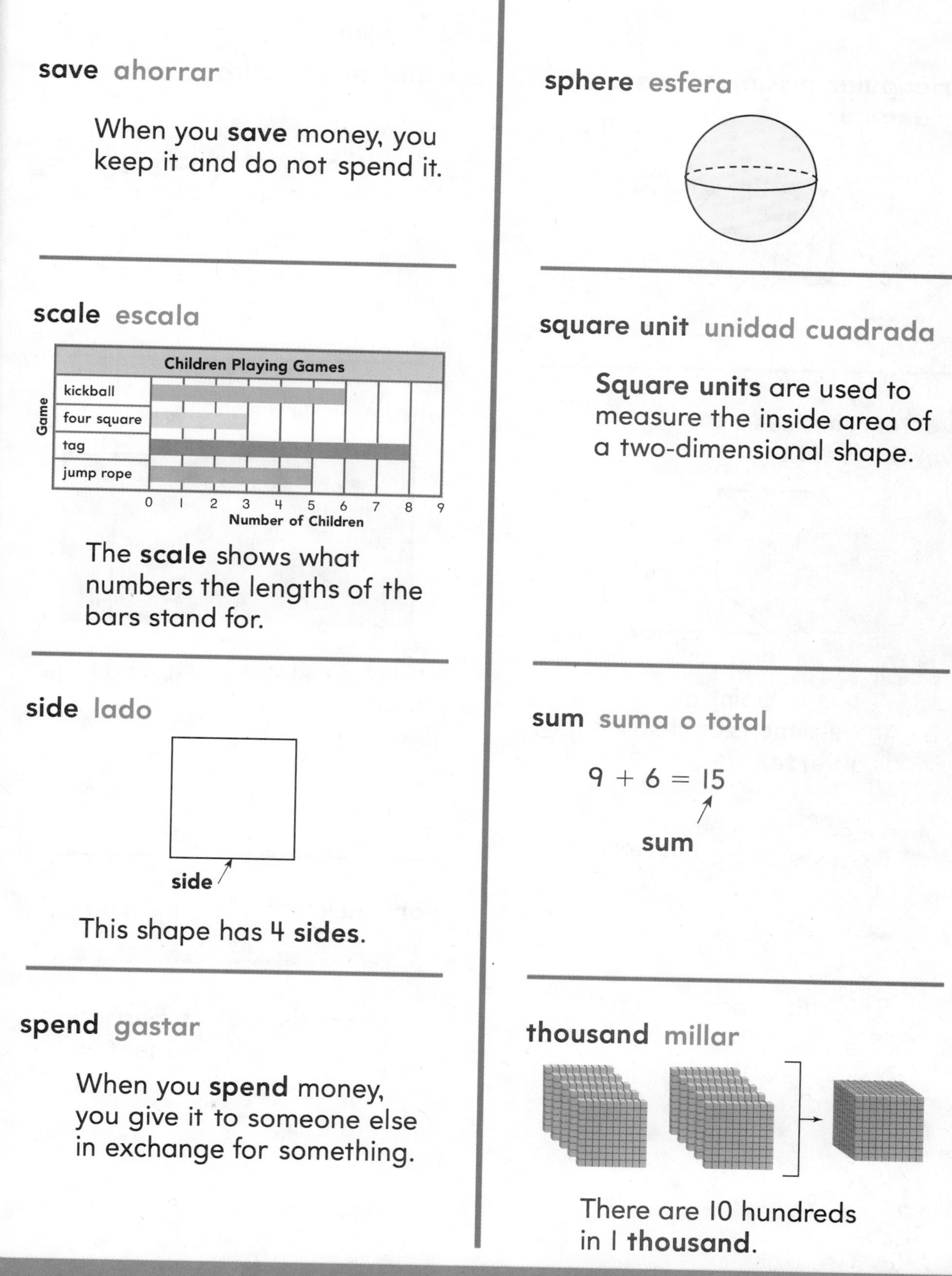

save ahorrar

When you **save** money, you keep it and do not spend it.

scale escala

The **scale** shows what numbers the lengths of the bars stand for.

side lado

This shape has 4 **sides**.

spend gastar

When you **spend** money, you give it to someone else in exchange for something.

sphere esfera

square unit unidad cuadrada

Square units are used to measure the inside area of a two-dimensional shape.

sum suma o total

$9 + 6 = 15$

thousand millar

There are 10 hundreds in 1 **thousand**.

triangular prism prisma triangular

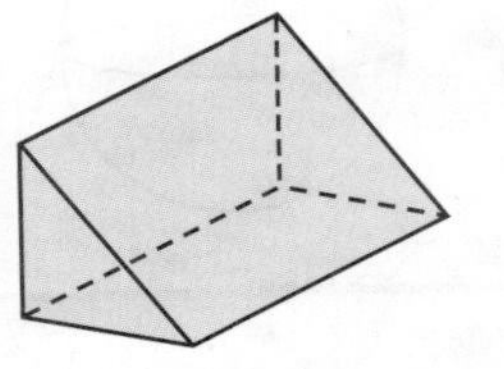

vertex/vertices vértice/vértices

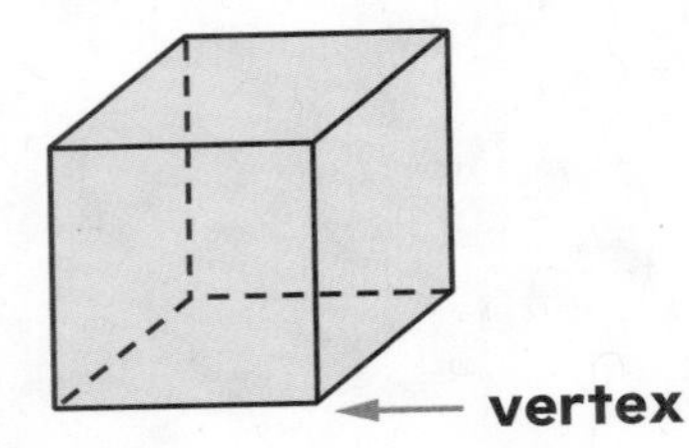

A corner point of a three-dimensional solid is a **vertex**.

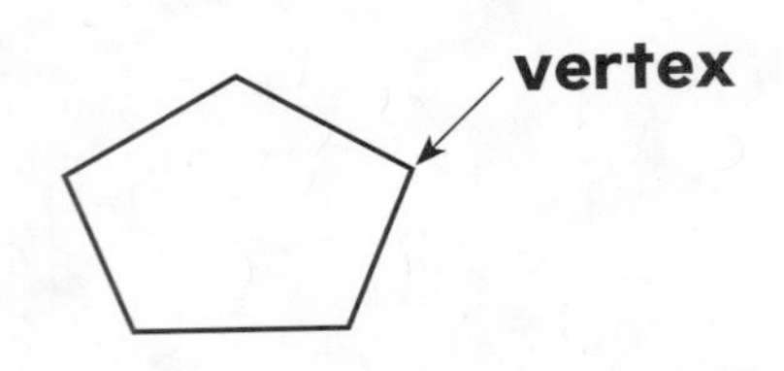

This shape has 5 **vertices**.

withdrawal retiro

A person makes a **withdrawal** by taking some of his or her money out of the bank.

whole entero

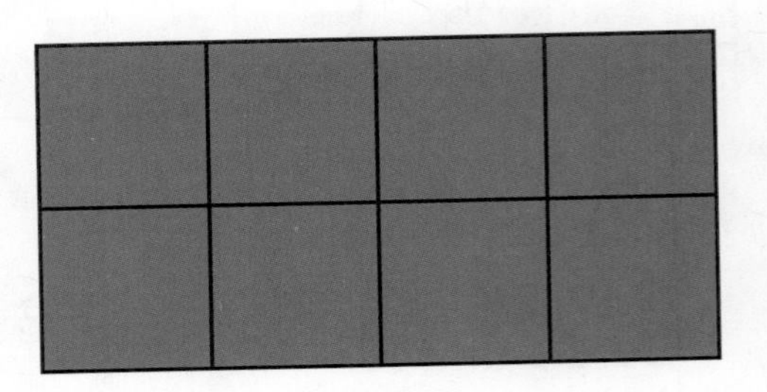

Eight eighths make 1 **whole**.

yardstick regla de 1 yarda

A **yardstick** is a measuring tool that shows 3 feet.